Career accounting fundamentals

Career accounting fundamentals

Douglas J. McQuaig
Wenatchee Valley College

Houghton Mifflin Company   Boston
Atlanta   Dallas   Geneva, Illinois
Hopewell, New Jersey   Palo Alto   London

For Gwen, Bev, Judy, John, and Laurie

Printed in the U.S.A.
Library of Congress Catalog Card Number: 76-15789
ISBN: 0-395-18979-9

Cover design by Roger Sametz.
Chapter opening photographs by James Scherer.

Sources: chapter quotations

1 Robert H. Montgomery, ''Foreword,'' in *Origin and Evolution of Double-Entry Bookkeeping,* Edward Peragallo, American Institute Publishing Co., New York, 1938.

2 Anonymous, in *Accounting in England and Scotland: 1543–1800,* B. S. Yamey, H. C. Edey, and Hugh W. Thomson, Sweet and Maxwell, London, 1963, p. 11.

3 Raymond de Roover, ''The Development of Accounting Prior to Luca Pacioli According to the Account Books of Medieval Merchants,'' in *Studies in the History of Accounting,* ed. A. C. Littleton and B. S. Yamey, Richard D. Irwin, Homewood, Ill., 1956, p. 114.

4 Matthaüs Schwartz, *The Model of Accounting,* 1518, in ''A Little Anthology of Words and Pictures About Accounting and Accountants, from Antiquity to the Present Day,'' Albert Neugarden, *The Arthur Young Journal* (Spring-Summer 1969), 47–62.

5 Anonymous.

6 Raymond de Roover, ''The Development of Accounting Prior to Luca Pacioli According to the Account Books of Medieval Merchants,'' in *Studies in the History of Accounting,* ed. A. C. Littleton and B. S. Yamey, Richard D. Irwin, Homewood, Ill., 1956.

7 Earl Graves, Publisher and Editor, *Black Enterprise,* personal communication, February 1974.

8 Anonymous.

9 Ogden Nash, ''Hymn to the Thing That Makes the Wolf Go,'' *New York American* (January 1934). Reprinted by permission of Curtis Brown, Ltd., and the Estate of Ogden Nash. Copyright © 1934, Ogden Nash; © Copyright renewed 1962 by Ogden Nash.

10 Robert Heller, *The Great Executive Dream,* Delacorte Press, New York, 1972.

11 Norton M. Bedford, *Income Determination Theory,* Addison-Wesley, Reading, Mass., 1965.

12 William Cowper, ''Retirement,'' 1782, line 615.

13 Plutarch, *Of Man's Progress in Virtue.*

14 Anonymous.

15 James M. Fremgen, *Accounting for Managerial Analysis,* rev. ed., Richard D. Irwin, Homewood, Ill., 1972.

Contents

Preface

This book and its ancillary materials are dedicated to the students who will use them. **Career Accounting Fundamentals** provides students with a sound basic knowledge of accounting concepts and procedures, always taking into consideration the widely varying objectives that students have. The book offers:

- Vocational preparation for students entering the job market in the field of accounting.
- A practical background in accounting for students embarking on various other business careers, such as clerical, secretarial, technical, sales, and managerial positions.
- Preparation and background for students planning more advanced studies in accounting.

The writing of **Career Accounting Fundamentals** has been based on my 25 years' experience as a "chalk-in-hand" accounting teacher at the high school, community college, and four-year college levels. From this classroom experience, I feel that I am well acquainted with the nature of the questions students ask, as well as with aspects of the subject that seem to give them trouble. For years I have felt that there is a real need for a teachable book of this nature: an accounting book aimed at students with widely differing goals, and written in language they can understand.

Career Accounting Fundamentals offers a complete package, designed for use primarily in first-year accounting courses and based on the assumption that the reader has had no previous accounting background. It presents the fundamentals of accounting in a logical, easy-to-understand manner, yet uses the most up-to-date accounting terminology. The text starts with simple descriptions and progresses to more complex topics. An appropriate, but not needless amount of repetition is provided to establish fundamental concepts clearly in the minds of the students, as well as to enable them to build up their confidence to handle more complex material. To encourage the transfer of learning, each chapter relates new topics to examples, concepts, and procedures presented previously. The book uses the analysis approach to introduce students to the subject matter and gives concrete examples of business working papers to illustrate each step of the accounting process. In addition, most of the material has been class-tested for instructional soundness.

Special features

Flexibility The instructor who uses this book can achieve a remarkable degree of flexibility by combining chapters in various ways to fit his or her needs. (Various suggestions for combinations of chapters are offered in the foreword to the instructor's manual.) An instructor may establish various modules in order to teach segments of accounting fundamentals. Conveniently, the book may be divided to accommodate either quarter or semester schedules. In terms of topics covered by blocks of chapters, Chapters 1 through 6 cover the accounting cycle for a service enterprise; Chapter 7 covers a professional enterprise; Chapters 8 through 12 cover a merchandising enterprise; and Chapters 13 through 15 cover special accounting systems for bank accounts and payroll.

Latest recognized accounting principles The accounting principles described here are those endorsed by the Financial Accounting Standards Board and its predecessor, the Accounting Principles Board of the American Institute of Certified Public Accountants. All package materials have also undergone numerous professional accuracy checks.

Illustrations Every effort has been made to accompany the introduction of each concept and procedure with an example. Diagrams and exhibits are used widely to portray illustrations of concepts.

Reviews To help the instructor sum up and reiterate important principles, the book presents reviews of ledger account placement and representative transactions in Chapters 6 and 15. In addition, a practical review problem in Chapter 6 enables students to practice what they have learned in those first six chapters.

Appendix An optional appendix on data processing is also included.

Package components

Career Accounting Fundamentals, the text itself, is the principal resource. Each chapter contains the following teaching aids:
- Key points, to accentuate important concepts and principles.
- Chapter contents, to show the order and development of topics covered.
- Specific objectives, to tell students what procedures they can expect to master as they work their way through the chapter.
- A summary, to reinforce new concepts, principles, and procedures covered.
- A glossary, to define terms introduced in the chapter. (For easy reference, these terms are also included in the index, with "defined" subentries.)
- Exercises, based on material contained in the chapter.
- Problems, four regular and four alternate, increasing in difficulty, to require students to use the techniques they have just learned.

Workbook/working papers In addition to working papers on which students may work out and hand in solutions to the text problems, the workbook includes brief objective questions and exercises on the material in each chapter. Special features are a review of business mathematics for everyday accounting use, to help students with a weak mathematics background; and self-check figures from the solutions of most text problems, to allow students to spot-check the accuracy of their work.

Practice set The practice set is a separate booklet with complete business papers for Harmon's Fine Furniture. It offers students the practical task of handling a merchandising firm's accounts for a fiscal period of one month and gives them a chance to put into practice all they have learned in the text.

Instructor's manual This volume includes recommended instructional procedures for each chapter, as well as solutions presented in a form suitable for preparing overhead transparencies. The instructor's manual is available, upon request, to teachers using the text.

Acknowledgments

I would like sincerely to thank the editorial staff of Houghton Mifflin for their continuous support. I also deeply appreciate the constructive suggestions of Professors Hobart W. Adams, of the University of Akron, and Joseph M. Goodman, of Chicago State University, who read and critiqued the entire manuscript; and Bonnie Jack, of Johnson County Community College, who conducted and evaluated readability tests of the text. The cooperation of my colleague Professor Heinz W. Pruss has been most helpful. I am very grateful to the following people for their contributions and suggestions: Professors Barbara Blickensderfer, Community College of Philadelphia; Leroy K. Henry, Los Angeles Trade and Technical College; Jimmie Henslee, El Centro College; Russell W. Johnson, Quinsigamond Community College; Allen H. Katz, Strayer College; Rita Kelly, Houston Community College; Joseph M. McKeon, John Carroll University; and Bertha Metzger, Community College of Philadelphia. I also wish to thank Richard B. Crake, attorney at law; Mary Alice Culp, student, Wenatchee Valley College; Eloise Huckabay, dental office manager; Patricia Wells, student, Central Washington State College; John Whitney, student, Northeastern University; and Margaret Woo, student, Northeastern University.

Finally, I would like to thank my family for their understanding and cooperation during the four years of my writing project. Without their support and patience, this book would never have balanced. Especially, I appreciate the efforts of my daughter and son—Judith L. McQuaig, C.P.A., and John D. McQuaig, C.P.A.—who read significant parts of the manuscript.

Douglas J. McQuaig

Note to the student

The late Hollywood star Clifton Webb once said, ''I am a self-made man. But I think if I had it to do over again, I'd call in an expert.''

You have just called in an expert, by virtue of the fact that you're taking a course in accounting and have obtained this textbook. You're going to need accounting know-how, in some form or another, for the rest of your life. And if you already have a job that involves keeping the books for some small business or a professional office, you're going to need, in the immediate future, every scrap of accounting information you can get your hands on.

So it makes sense for you to keep this book on your desk for at least the first year or two after you have finished taking the course. You won't be able to remember *everything* you learned. Therefore, your textbook will prove to be a ready source of information about techniques of accounting, especially if—as we hope—your job becomes more complex and you are given more responsibility and larger sums of money to deal with.

D. J. M.

Divide

e C)

f capit

edule

hership

F)

t repor

eporte

y if ret

uction—

truct

ets (af

ns and

ates o

Sche

chedu

for yea

see

n pag

1

Analyzing business transactions: asset, liability, and owner's equity accounts

Accounting is the language of finance—a universal language. Robert H. Montgomery, *Origin and Evolution of Double-Entry Bookkeeping*

Key points
- Accounting, because it is the language of business, provides an excellent background for anyone planning to enter the world of business.
- Definition of accounting
- After each transaction has been recorded, the total of one side of the Fundamental Accounting Equation must equal the total of the other side.
- The balance sheet, as a financial statement, is simply a listing of the asset, liability, and owner's equity accounts.

Chapter contents
- Introduction
- Definition of accounting
- Fields in which accounting is needed
- Assets and owner's equity
- The balance sheet
- Summary
- Glossary
- Exercises
- Problems

Specific objectives

After you have completed this chapter, you will be able to:
- Define accounting.
- Record a group of business transactions, in columnar form, involving changes in assets, liabilities, and owner's equity.
- Present a balance sheet.

Introduction

Accounting is often called the *language of business,* because when confronted with events of a business nature, all people in society—owners, managers, creditors, employees, attorneys, engineers, and so forth—must use accounting terms and concepts in order to describe these events. Examples of accounting terms are *net, gross, yield, valuation, accrued, deferred*—the list could go on and on. So it is logical that anyone entering the business world should know enough of the "language" to communicate with others and to understand their communications.

2

Some terms used in accounting have meanings that differ from the meanings of the same words used in a nonbusiness situation. If you have studied a foreign language, you have undoubtedly found that as you became more familiar with the language, you also became better acquainted with the country in which it is spoken, as well as with the customs of the people. Similarly, as you acquire a knowledge of accounting, you will also gain an understanding of the way businesses operate and the reasoning involved in the making of business decisions. Even if you are not involved directly in accounting activities, most assuredly you will need to be sufficiently acquainted with the ''language'' to be able to understand the meaning of accounting information, how it is compiled, how it can be used, and what its limitations are.

Definition of accounting

Accounting is the process of analyzing, classifying, recording, summarizing, and interpreting business transactions in financial or monetary terms. A *business transaction* is an event that has a direct effect on the operation of the economic unit and can be expressed in terms of money. Examples of business transactions are buying or selling goods, renting a building, hiring employees, buying insurance, or any other activity of a business nature.

The accountant is the person who keeps the financial history of an economic unit in written form. The term *economic unit* includes not only business enterprises, but also non-profit-making entities, such as government bodies, churches, clubs, fraternal organizations, etc. All these require some type of accounting records. The primary purpose of accounting is to provide the financial information needed for the efficient operation of the economic unit, and to make the information available in usable forms to the interested parties, such as owners, members, taxpayers, creditors, and so on.

Fields in which accounting is needed

A knowledge of accounting is most valuable in the following three fields:
- **Bookkeeping and accounting** Those who plan to enter the field as a vocation naturally need training in accounting.
- **Business management** Those aspiring to managerial positions must be able to understand financial reports, evaluate operations, and make logical decisions.
- **Personal record keeping** Every person—even one who does not plan to be an accountant or a business manager—benefits from a study of accounting, because such a study enables one to keep better records, understand financial reports, engage in financial planning and budgeting, invest savings, and prepare necessary tax returns.

Bookkeeping and accounting

Considerable confusion exists over the distinction between *bookkeeping* and *accounting*. Actually the two are closely related, and there is no universally accepted line of separation. Generally, bookkeeping involves the systematic recording of business transactions in financial terms. When compared with bookkeeping, accounting is distinguished by level or degree. An accountant sets up the system by which business transactions are to be recorded by a bookkeeper. An accountant may supervise the work of the bookkeeper; the accountant may prepare financial statements and tax reports. Although the work of the bookkeeper is more routine, it is hard to draw a line where the bookkeeper's work ends and the accountant's begins. The bookkeeper must understand the entire accounting system, exercise judgment in recording financial details, and organize and report the appropriate information.

Career opportunities in bookkeeping and accounting

When it comes to career opportunities, accounting is commonly divided into three main fields, in the order of numbers of positions available.

- **Private accounting** Most people who are accountants work for private business firms. The growing importance of accounting often provides opportunities for advancement into managerial positions, such as office managers, data processing supervisors, systems analysts, internal auditors, controllers.
- **Governmental and institutional accounting** Local, state, and federal government bodies employ vast numbers of people in accounting jobs, not only for record keeping but also for auditing tax returns.
- **Public accounting** Certified public accountants (or CPAs) are independent professional persons, comparable to doctors and lawyers, who offer accounting services to clients for a fee. There are approximately 100,000 CPAs and more than 350,000 noncertified public accountants in the U.S. today. Accounting is easily the fastest growing of all the professions; it is expanding, in fact, at twice the rate the economy is expanding. Factors responsible for the growth of professional accounting include the increasing size and complexity of business corporations, the broadening of income taxes and other forms of taxation, and the increase in government regulation of business activities.

The lay person's need for accounting

Anyone who aspires to a position of leadership in business or government needs a knowledge of accounting. Managers, supervisors, and even low-level straw bosses often have to keep financial records, understand accounting data contained in reports and budgets, and express future plans in financial terms. A study of accounting gives a person the necessary background, as well as an understanding of an organization's scope, functions, and policies. People who have managerial jobs must be aware of how accounting information can be developed for use as a tool in the decision-making process, and they should also be acquainted with the record-keeping and management functions of accounting.

Assets and owner's equity

Assets are properties or things owned by the economic unit or business entity, such as cash, equipment, buildings, and land. If there is no money owed against the assets, then the owner's right would be equal to the value of the assets. The owner's right or claim is expressed by the word *equity*, or *investment*. You often see these terms in the classified-advertising section of a newspaper, where a person wants to sell the ownership right to a property. Other terms that may be used include *net worth, capital,* or *proprietorship.*

Assets =	Owner's Equity
Items or property owned by the business	Owner's right or investment in the business

Suppose that the total value of the assets is $10,000, and the owner does not owe any amount against the assets. Then,

Assets =	Owner's Equity
$10,000	$10,000

Or suppose that the asset consists of a truck which cost $8,000; the owner has paid $2,000 down and borrowed the remainder from the bank. This would be shown as follows:

Assets =	Liabilities +	Owner's Equity
Items owned	Amount owed to creditors	Owner's investment
$8,000	$6,000	$2,000

We have now introduced a new classification, *liabilities,* which represents debts and includes the amounts that the owner owes his or her creditors, or the amount by which the owner is liable to the creditors. The debts may originate because the owner bought goods or services on a credit basis, or borrowed money, etc. The creditors' claims to the assets have priority over the interest of the owner.

An equation containing these elements is called the *Fundamental Accounting Equation.* We'll be constantly dealing with this equation from now on. If we know two parts of this equation, we can determine the third. Let us look at some illustrations.

Mr. Smith has $9,000 invested in his advertising agency, and he owes creditors $3,000; that is, he has liabilities of $3,000. Then,

Assets =	Liabilities +	Owner's Equity
?	$3,000	$9,000

We would find the amount of Smith's assets by adding his liabilities and his equity:

$ 3,000	Liabilities
+9,000	Owner's Equity
$12,000	Assets

The completed equation would now read

Assets =	Liabilities +	Owner's Equity
$12,000	$3,000	$9,000

Or take Ms. Jones, who raises geraniums to sell to florists. She has assets of $20,000, and she owes creditors $4,000; that is, she has liabilities of $4,000. Then

Assets =	Liabilities +	Owner's Equity
$20,000	$4,000	?

We find the owner's equity by subtracting Jones's liabilities from her assets:

$20,000	Assets
−4,000	Liabilities
$16,000	Owner's Equity

The completed equation would now read

Assets =	Liabilities +	Owner's Equity
$20,000	$4,000	$16,000

Mr. Anderson, who has an insurance agency, has assets of $18,000, and his investment (his equity) amounts to $12,000. Then

Assets =	Liabilities +	Owner's Equity
$18,000	?	$12,000

In order to find Anderson's total liabilities, we subtract his equity from his assets:

$18,000	Assets
−12,000	Owner's Equity
$ 6,000	Liabilities

The completed equation would now read

Assets =	Liabilities +	Owner's Equity
$18,000	$6,000	$12,000

▶ **Summary of Fundamental Accounting Equation**
Assets = Liabilities + Owner's Equity
Liabilities = Assets − Owner's Equity
Owner's Equity = Assets − Liabilities

Recording business transactions

To reiterate: Business transactions are events that have a direct effect on the operations of an economic unit or enterprise, and are expressed in terms of money. As one records business transactions, one has to change the amounts listed under the headings of Assets, Liabilities, and Owner's Equity. However, the total of one side of the Fundamental Accounting Equation should always equal the total of the other side. The subdivisions under these three main headings, as we shall see, are called *accounts*.

Let us now look at a group of business transactions illustrating a *service* type of business. (Such transactions would pertain to a professional enterprise as well.)

Assume that Dale Armstrong establishes his own business, Dale's Cleaners.

(a) Armstrong invests $16,000 cash in his new business. This means that he deposits $16,000 in the bank in a new, separate account entitled Dale's Cleaners.

	Assets =	Liabilities +	Owner's Equity
	Items owned	Amounts owed to creditors	Owner's investment
	Cash		
(a)	+ $16,000 =		+ $16,000

This separate bank account will help Armstrong keep his business investment separate from his personal funds. The Cash account consists of bank deposits and money on hand. The business now has $16,000 more in cash than before, and Armstrong's investment has also increased. The account, denoted by the owner's name followed by the word *Capital,* records the amount of the owner's investment, or equity in the business.

(b) Dale Armstrong knows that his first task is to get his cleaning shop ready for business. Accordingly he buys, for cash, $9,000 worth of equipment.

	Assets =	Liabilities +	Owner's Equity
	Items owned	Amounts owed to creditors	Owner's investment
	Cash + Equipment =		Dale Armstrong, Capital
Initial investment	$16,000 =		$16,000
(b)	−9,000 + $9,000		
New balances	$ 7,000 + $9,000 =		$16,000

At this point, Armstrong has not invested any new money; he has simply exchanged part of his cash for equipment. Equipment, being a type of property new to the firm, is included under Assets as a new account.

(c) Dale Armstrong buys $2,000 worth of equipment on credit from Johnson Equipment Company.

	Assets =		Liabilities +	Owner's Equity
	Items owned		Amounts owed to creditors	Owner's investment
	Cash +	Equipment =	Accounts Payable +	Dale Armstrong, Capital
Previous balances	$7,000 +	$ 9,000 =		$16,000
(c)		+2,000	+$2,000	
New balances	$7,000 +	$11,000 =	$2,000 +	$16,000

The Equipment account shows an increase because the business owns $2,000 worth of additional equipment, and there is also an increase in liabilities, because the business owes $2,000 more than before. The liabilities account, Accounts Payable, is used for short-term liabilities or charge accounts, due usually within 30 days. There is now a total of $18,000 on both sides of the equals sign.

To continue the idea of equality, observe that the recording of each transaction must result in a balance by itself. For example, transaction **(c)** resulted in a $2,000 increase to both sides of the equation, and transaction **(b)** resulted in a minus $9,000 and a plus $9,000 *on the same side,* with nothing recorded on the other side.

(d) Armstrong pays $500 to Johnson Equipment Company, to be applied against the firm's liability of $2,000.

	Assets =		Liabilities +	Owner's Equity
	Items owned		Amounts owed to creditors	Owner's investment
	Cash +	Equipment =	Accounts Payable +	Dale Armstrong, Capital
Previous balances	$7,000 +	$11,000 =	$2,000 +	$16,000
(d)	−500		−500	
New balances	$6,500 +	$11,000 =	$1,500 +	$16,000

In analyzing this payment, we recognize that cash is involved, and that cash is being reduced. At the same time, the firm *owes* less than before, so it should be recorded as a minus under Liabilities.

(e) Armstrong buys cleaning fluids from Acme Supply Company for $200 on credit. Cleaning fluids are listed under Supplies instead of Equipment because a cleaning business uses up cleaning fluids in a relatively short period of time—as a matter of fact, in one or a few operations. Equipment, on the other hand, normally lasts over a number of operations.

	Assets =			Liabilities +	Owner's Equity
	Items owned			Amounts owed to creditors	Owner's investment
	Cash +	Equipment +	Supplies =	Accounts Payable +	Dale Armstrong, Capital
Previous balances	$6,500 +	$11,000	=	$1,500 +	$16,000
(e)			+ $200	+ 200	
New balances	$6,500 +	$11,000 +	$200 =	$1,700 +	$16,000

Accounting, as we said before, is the process of analyzing, recording, summarizing, and interpreting business transactions. In relating these elements to the transactions of Dale's Cleaners, we made an analysis to decide which accounts were involved, and then determined whether the transaction resulted in an increase or a decrease in the accounts. Then we recorded the transaction. After one records each transaction, the equation should still be in balance, in that the totals of both sides are equal. This represents an introduction to *double-entry accounting*. We have demonstrated that each transaction must be recorded in at least two accounts, and that the equation must always remain in balance, "like any good equation should," as the cigarette commercial would put it.

Summary of illustration

Let us now summarize the business transactions of Dale's Cleaners in columnar form, identifying each transaction by a letter of the alphabet in parentheses. To test your understanding of the recording procedure, describe the nature of the transactions that have taken place.

	Assets =			Liabilities +	Owner's Equity
	Cash +	Equipment +	Supplies	Accounts Payable	Dale Armstrong, Capital
(a)	+16,000				+16,000
(b)	−9,000	+9,000			
Bal.	7,000 +	9,000	=		16,000
(c)		+2,000		+2,000	
Bal.	7,000 +	11,000	=	2,000 +	16,000
(d)	−500			−500	
Bal.	6,500 +	11,000	=	1,500 +	16,000
(e)			+200	+200	
Bal.	6,500 +	11,000 +	200 =	1,700 +	16,000

	Total		Total
Cash	$ 6,500		
Equipment	11,000	Accounts Payable	$ 1,700
Supplies	200	Dale Armstrong, Capital	16,000
	$17,700		$17,700

The following observations apply to *all* types of business transactions.

◆ Every transaction is recorded in terms of increases and/or decreases in two or more accounts.

◆ The equality of the two sides of the accounting equation is always maintained.

The balance sheet

An accountant accomplishes the summarizing element in accounting by means of the financial statements; the *balance sheet* summarizes the balances of the assets, liabilities, and owner's equity accounts on a given date. After Armstrong records his initial transactions, here is how Dale's Cleaners' balance sheet looks on June 15. (Ordinarily the balance sheet is prepared at the end of a month or year.)

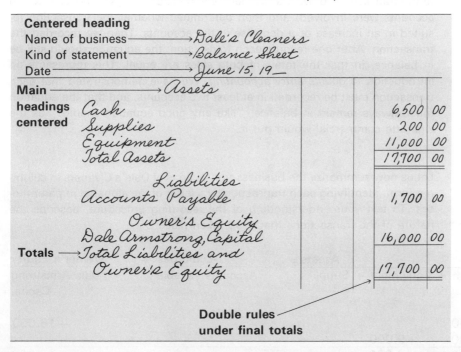

Centered heading
Name of business ——————→ *Dale's Cleaners*
Kind of statement ——————→ *Balance Sheet*
Date ——————→ *June 15, 19__*

Main ——————→ *Assets*
headings   *Cash* .... 6,500 | 00
centered   *Supplies* .... 200 | 00
          Equipment .... 11,000 | 00
          Total Assets .... 17,700 | 00

          Liabilities
          Accounts Payable .... 1,700 | 00

          Owner's Equity
          Dale Armstrong, Capital .... 16,000 | 00
Totals ——→ *Total Liabilities and*
          Owner's Equity .... 17,700 | 00

Double rules under final totals

In the next chapter we shall expand the Fundamental Accounting Equation to include revenue and expense elements. However, with only the three elements—assets, liabilities, and owner's equity—present, we may call it the *Balance Sheet Equation.* Previously it was stated as

Assets = Liabilities + Owner's Equity

Now when one records the same balances in the balance sheet, one shows them as

$$\text{Assets}$$
$$=$$
$$\text{Liabilities}$$
$$+$$
$$\text{Owner's Equity}$$

The balance sheet shows the financial position of the company. Financial position is shown by a list of the values of the assets or property, offset by the liabilities or amounts owed to creditors, and the owner's equity or financial interest. *Financial position,* as used in this accounting concept, means the same thing we would mean if we were to speak of the financial position of a person. It is a listing of what the person owns, as well as a listing of the claims of his or her creditors, and the difference between them is the person's equity or net worth. How quickly could the assets be converted into cash?

Perhaps you might have noticed, in the back pages of a newspaper, the balance sheets of commercial banks and savings and loan associations. The law requires them to publish their balance sheets in daily newspapers at certain times of the year. The purpose of these financial statements is to show the financial position of these institutions; the total of their assets listed must equal the total claims of the depositors plus the owner's equity.

Note some details about the form of the balance sheet.
1 The three-line heading consists of the name of the firm, the title of the financial statement, and the date of the financial statement.

Dale's Cleaners
Balance Sheet
June 15, 19___

2 Use dollar signs on printed or typewritten statements; place them at the head of each column and with each total.
3 Use single lines (drawn with a ruler) to show that figures above are being added or subtracted.
4 Use double lines under the *final* figures in a column.

Summary

Accounting is often called the *language of business,* because record keeping and financial reports use the terms and concepts of accounting. This chapter has presented the definitions of accounting and of business transactions. The Fundamental Accounting Equation, consisting of three elements, is

Assets = Liabilities + Owner's Equity

An accountant analyzes business transactions to determine which accounts are involved, then records them as increases or decreases in the appropriate accounts. After each transaction is recorded, the equation must always remain in balance. The balance sheet—which is a statement showing the balances of asset, liability, and owner's equity accounts—states the financial position of an enterprise.

Glossary

o **Accounting** The process of analyzing, classifying, recording, summarizing, and interpreting business transactions in terms of money.

o **Accounts** Subdivisions under the main heading of assets, liabilities, and owner's equity.
o **Assets** Cash, properties, and other things owned.
o **Balance sheet** A financial statement showing the financial position of a firm or other economic unit at a given point in time, e.g. June 30 or December 31.
o **Business entity** A business enterprise is considered to be separate and distinct from the persons who supply the assets it uses. Property involved in the business is an asset of the business. The owner is separated from the business and occupies the status of a claimant of the enterprise.
o **Capital** The owner's investment or equity in an enterprise.
o **Economic unit** Business enterprises; also non-profit-making entities, such as government bodies, churches, clubs, fraternal organizations, etc.
o **Equity** The value of a right or financial interest in an asset or group of assets.
o **Liabilities** Debts, or amounts owed to creditors.
o **Transaction** An event affecting an economic entity which can be expressed in terms of money and which must be recorded in the accounting records.

Exercises

Exercise 1 Complete the following equations.
a Assets, $18,000 = Liabilities, $6,500 + Owner's Equity, $_____.
b Assets, $27,000 − Owner's Equity, $12,000 = Liabilities, $_____.
c Assets, $_____ = Liabilities, $14,000 + Owner's Equity, $18,000.

Exercise 2 Determine the following values.
a The equity of the owner of a truck, costing $9,000, who owes $6,500 on an installment loan payable to the bank.
b The value of the assets of a business having $5,320 of liabilities, and in which the owner has a $16,124 equity.
c The amount of the liabilities of a business having $27,615 of assets, and in which the owner has a $22,984 equity.

Exercise 3 Rosa Kerenski, a real estate broker, owns office equipment amounting to $6,900, a car, which is used for business purposes only, valued at $3,840, and other property which is used in her business amounting to $2,600; she owes business creditors a total of $1,500. What is the value of Kerenski's equity?

Exercise 4 Describe the transactions that have been recorded in the following equation.

	Assets =		Liabilities +	Owner's Equity
	Cash +	Equipment	Accounts Payable	H. Johnson, Capital
(a)	+6,000			+6,000
(b)	−4,000	+4,000		
Bal.	2,000 +	4,000 =		6,000
(c)		+1,600	+1,600	
Bal.	2,000 +	5,600 =	1,600 +	6,000
(d)	−400	+1,900	+1,500	
Bal.	1,600 +	7,500 =	3,100 +	6,000

Exercise 5 Dr. Sean Largent is a chiropractor. As of June 30 he owned the following property that related to his professional practice: Cash, $620; Professional Equipment, $9,340; Prepaid Insurance, $190; Office Equipment, $2,860. As of the same date he owed business creditors as follows: First State Bank, $2,600; Precision Equipment Company, $410.

Compute the following amounts of the Balance Sheet Equation.

Assets _____ = Liabilities _____ + Owner's Equity _____

Exercise 6 Describe a business transaction that will do the following:
a Increase an asset and increase owner's equity.
b Increase an asset and increase a liability.
c Increase an asset and decrease an asset.
d Decrease an asset and decrease a liability.

Exercise 7 Dr. P. R. Sitton is a dentist. Describe the transactions that have been completed involving the asset, liability, and owner's equity accounts.

	Cash +	Prepaid + Insurance	Dental + Equipment	Assets = Office Furniture & Equipment	Liabilities + Accounts Payable	Owner's Equity P. R. Sitton, Capital
Bal.	1,835 +	310 +	16,725 +	3,716 =	7,790 +	14,796
(a)	−327				−327	
Bal.	1,508 +	310 +	16,725 +	3,716 =	7,463 +	14,796
(b)	−260			+940	+680	
Bal.	1,248 +	310 +	16,725 +	4,656 =	8,143 +	14,796
(c)	+1,200					+1,200
Bal.	2,448 +	310 +	16,725 +	4,656 =	8,143 +	15,996
(d)	+840		−840			
Bal.	3,288 +	310 +	15,885 +	4,656 =	8,143 +	15,996

Exercise 8 From Exercise 7, present a balance sheet, using the ending balances dated as of December 31 of this year.

Problems

Problem 1-1 Ace Dry Cleaners has just been established by the owner, Rita Power, who deposits $9,000 cash in the First National Bank in the name of the business. Record the changes in assets, liabilities, and owner's equity accounts for the following transactions. (Use plus, minus, and equals signs.)
a Power originally invested $9,000 in cash.
b Bought equipment for use in the business, $6,000 in cash.
c Acquired additional equipment for the business, $4,000 on credit.
d Paid $1,500 in cash to creditors as part payment on account.
e Power invested an additional $2,500 in cash.
Instructions
1 Record the transactions in columnar form, using plus and minus signs, and show the balances after each transaction.
2 Prove that the total of one side of the equation equals the total of the other.

Problem 1-2 The Metro Advertising Agency has just been established by the owner, Robert Nathan. Record the following transactions. (Use plus, minus, and equals signs.)

a Nathan deposited $7,500 in cash in the Security State Bank in the name of the business.

b Bought office equipment for use in the business, $3,600 in cash.

c Bought supplies, consisting of stationery and business forms, on account, $300.

d Bought additional equipment for use in the business, $1,700 in cash.

e Paid $90 in cash for postage stamps (supplies) to be used in the business.

f Paid $200 to creditors as part payment on account.

g Nathan invested an additional $900 in cash in the business.

Instructions

1 Record the transactions in columnar form, using plus and minus signs, and show the balances after each transaction.

2 Prove that the total of one side of the equation equals the total of the other.

Problem 1-3 Joseph Marlin owns the Marlin Real Estate Agency. His books show the following balances in assets, liabilities, and owner's equity.

Cash	$ 900
Supplies	260
Office Furniture	3,800
Office Machines	2,400
Building	12,000
Land	4,000
Accounts Payable	6,460
Joseph Marlin, Capital	16,900

Instructions Prepare a balance sheet as of June 30 of this year.

Problem 1-4 The Red Apple Photography Studio is owned by Doris Sturm. The firm's books show the following balances in assets, liabilities, and owner's equity accounts.

Cash	$ 1,900
Film	650
Office Supplies	200
Camera Equipment	6,500
Lighting Equipment	1,400
Office Equipment	2,100
Automobile	2,400
Accounts Payable	950
Doris Sturm, Capital	14,200

Instructions Prepare a balance sheet dated December 31 of this year.

Problem 1-1A The National Shoe Repair Shop has just been established by the owner, Frank Parona, who deposited $12,000 cash in the Northern State Bank in the name of the business. The transactions described below affect the asset, liability, and owner's equity accounts.

a Parona initially invested $12,000 in cash.

b Bought equipment for use in the business, $8,000 in cash.

c Acquired additional equipment for the business, $3,600 on credit.

d Paid $1,200 in cash to creditors as part payment on account.

e Parona invested an additional $1,400 in cash.

Instructions

1 Record the transactions in columnar form, using plus and minus signs, and show the balances after each transaction.

2 Prove that the total of one side of the equation equals the total of the other.

Problem 1-2A The Central Employment Agency has just been established by the owner, Alice Sears. The following transactions affect the asset, liability, and owner's equity accounts.

a Sears deposited $8,200 in cash in the Arizona State Bank in the name of the business.

b Acquired office equipment for use in the business, $3,600 in cash.

c Bought supplies consisting of stationery and business forms on account, $360.

d Bought additional equipment for use in the business on account, $840.

e Bought postage stamps and other supplies for use in the business, $86, paying cash.

f Paid $280 to creditors as part payment on account.

g Sears invested an additional $600 in cash in the business.

Instructions

1 Record the transactions in columnar form, using plus and minus signs, and show the balances after each transaction.

2 Prove that the total of one side of the equation equals the total of the other.

Problem 1-3A Stephen Newell owns the Newell Insurance Agency. His books show the following balances in assets, liabilities, and owner's equity accounts.

Cash	$ 840
Supplies	390
Office Furniture	2,920
Office Machines	3,680
Building	16,000
Land	4,200
Accounts Payable	5,910
Stephen Newell, Capital	22,120

Instructions Prepare a balance sheet as of December 31 of this year.

Problem 1-4A Stay-Brite Cleaners is owned by Marian Marcus. The firm's books show the following balances in assets, liabilities, and owner's equity accounts.

Cash	$ 1,872
Cleaning Supplies	823
Office Supplies	119
Prepaid Insurance	240
Cleaning Equipment	9,378
Delivery Equipment	2,980
Office Furniture and Fixtures	3,816
Accounts Payable	2,985
Marian Marcus, Capital	16,243

Instructions Prepare a balance sheet dated June 30 of this year.

2 Analyzing business transactions: revenue and expense accounts

None can be poor who keep their books correctly. Dutch proverb

Introduction

In Chapter 1, we analyzed and recorded a number of transactions in asset, liability, and owner's equity accounts, and did so in a way that was consistent with the definition of accounting. In this chapter we shall introduce the remaining two classifications of accounts: revenues and expenses. We shall record business transactions involving revenue and expense accounts in the same type of columnar arrangement we used in Chapter 1. Again let us stress that, after each transaction has been recorded, the total of the balances of the accounts on one side of the equals sign should equal the total of the balances of the accounts on the other side of the equals sign. To illustrate, we shall continue to use transactions of Dale's Cleaners.

Revenue and expense accounts

Revenues are the amounts of assets that a business or other economic unit gains as a result of its operations. For example, revenues represent inflows of cash, or other assets, derived from fees earned for the performing of services, sales involving the exchange of goods, rent income for providing the use of property, and interest income for the lending of money. Revenues are *not* only in the form of cash; they may also consist of credit-card receipts or charge accounts maintained for customers.

Expenses are the amounts of assets that a business or other economic unit uses up as a result of its operations. For example, expenses represent outflows of cash, or other assets, for services received, such as wages expense for labor performed, rent expense for the use of property, interest expense for the use of money, and supplies expense for supplies used. When payment is to be made at a later time, an increase in an expense may result in an increase in a liability.

Recording business transactions

Soon after the opening of Dale's Cleaners, the first customers arrive, beginning a flow of revenue for the business. Let us now itemize further transactions of Dale's Cleaners for the first month of operations, including revenue and expenses.

(f) Dale's Cleaners receives cash revenue for the first week, $300.

	Assets =			Liabilities +	Owner's Equity		
	Cash +	Equipment +	Supplies	Accounts Payable	Dale Armstrong, Capital	+	Revenue
*PB	$6,500 +	$11,000 +	$200 =	$1,700 +	$16,000		
(f)	+300						+$300
*NB	$6,800 +	$11,000 +	$200 =	$1,700 +	$16,000	+	$300

Revenue has the effect of increasing the owner's equity. However, it is better to keep the revenue separate from the capital account until you have prepared the financial statements.

(g) Shortly after opening the business, Armstrong pays $200 monthly rent.

	Assets =			Liabilities +	Owner's Equity			
	Cash +	Equipment +	Supplies	Accounts Payable	Dale Armstrong, Capital	+	Revenue –	Expenses
PB	$6,800 +	$11,000 +	$200 =	$1,700 +	$16,000 +		$300	
(g)	−200							+$200 (Rent)
NB	$6,600 +	$11,000 +	$200 =	$1,700 +	$16,000 +		$300 −	$200

*PB stands for Previous Balances. **NB** stands for New Balances.

19 Revenue and expense accounts

Expenses have the effect of decreasing the owner's equity. We shall consider revenues and expenses later as separate elements in the Fundamental Accounting Equation. However, through the medium of the financial statements, they will be connected with owner's equity, and for this reason we are listing them here under the heading of Owner's Equity.

(h) Armstrong pays wages to employees, $120, June 1 through June 10.

	Assets =			Liabilities +	Owner's Equity		
	Cash +	Equipment +	Supplies =	Accounts Payable	Dale Armstrong, Capital +	Revenue –	Expenses
PB	$6,600 +	$11,000 +	$200 =	$1,700 +	$16,000 +	$300 –	$200
(h)	– 120						+ 120 (Wages)
NB	$6,480 +	$11,000 +	$200 =	$1,700 +	$16,000 +	$300 –	$320

We have added the additional expense of $120 to the previous balance of $200, resulting in a total deduction of $320, since the incurring of expense has the result of reducing the owner's equity.

(i) Armstrong pays $160 for a 2-year liability insurance policy. As it expires, the insurance will eventually become an expense. However, since it is paid in advance, it has value, and is accordingly recorded as an asset. At the end of the year or financial period, Armstrong will have to make an adjustment, taking out the expired portion and recording it as an expense. Generally accountants initially record expenses that are paid for more than 1 month in advance as assets.

	Assets =				Liabilities +	Owner's Equity		
	Cash +	Equipment +	Supplies +	Ppd. Ins. =	Accounts Payable	Dale Armstrong, Capital +	Revenue –	Expenses
PB	$6,480 +	$11,000 +	$200	=	$1,700 +	$16,000 +	$300 –	$320
(i)	– 160			+ $160				
NB	$6,320 +	$11,000 +	$200 +	$160 =	$1,700 +	$16,000 +	$300 –	$320

(j) Dale's Cleaners receives cash revenue for the second week, $380.

	Assets =				Liabilities +	Owner's Equity		
	Cash +	Equipment +	Supplies +	Ppd. Ins. =	Accounts Payable	Dale Armstrong, Capital +	Revenue –	Expenses
PB	$6,320 +	$11,000 +	$200 +	$160 =	$1,700 +	$16,000 +	$300 –	$320
(j)	+ 380						+ 380	
NB	$6,700 +	$11,000 +	$200 +	$160 =	$1,700 +	$16,000 +	$680 –	$320

Observe that each time a transaction is recorded, the total amount on one side of the equation *remains equal to* the total amount on the other side. As proof of this, look at the following computation.

	Total		**Total**
		Accounts Payable	$ 1,700
Cash	$ 6,700	Dale Armstrong, Capital	16,000
Equipment	11,000	Revenue	680
Supplies	200		$18,380
Ppd. Ins.	160	Expenses	−320
	$18,060		$18,060

Let us now continue with the transactions.

(k) Dale's Cleaners receives a bill for newspaper advertising, $90, from the *Daily News.*

	Assets =				**Liabilities +**	**Owner's Equity**		
	Cash +	Equipment +	Supplies +	Ppd. Ins. =	Accounts Payable	Dale Armstrong, Capital	+ Revenue −	Expenses
PB	$6,700 +	$11,000 +	$200 +	$160 =	$1,700 +	$16,000 +	$680 −	$320
(k)					+90			+90
								(Advertising)
NB	$6,700 +	$11,000 +	$200 +	$160 =	$1,790 +	$16,000 +	$680 −	$410

Armstrong has simply received the bill for advertising; he has not paid any cash. However, an expense has been incurred, and the firm owes $90 more than it did before, so this transaction must be recorded.

(l) Armstrong pays $900 to Johnson Equipment Company as part payment on account.

	Assets =				**Liabilities +**	**Owner's Equity**		
	Cash +	Equipment +	Supplies +	Ppd. Ins. =	Accounts Payable	Dale Armstrong, Capital	+ Revenue −	Expenses
PB	$6,700 +	$11,000 +	$200 +	$160 =	$ 1,790 +	$16,000 +	$680 −	$410
(l)	−900				−900			
NB	$5,800 +	$11,000 +	$200 +	$160 =	$890 +	$16,000 +	$680 −	$410

(m) Armstrong receives and pays bill for utilities, $110.

	Assets =				Liabilities +	Owner's Equity		
	Cash +	Equipment +	Supplies +	Ppd. Ins.	Accounts Payable	Dale Armstrong, Capital	+ Revenue −	Expenses
PB	$5,800 +	$11,000 +	$200 +	$160 =	$890 +	$16,000 +	$680 −	$410
(m)	− 110							+ 110 (Utilities)
NB	$5,690 +	$11,000 +	$200 +	$160 =	$890 +	$16,000 +	$680 −	$520

Armstrong had not recorded the utility bill previously as a liability.

(n) Now Armstrong pays $90 to the *Daily News* for advertising. Recall that he had previously recorded this bill.

	Assets =				Liabilities +	Owner's Equity		
	Cash +	Equipment +	Supplies +	Ppd. Ins.	Accounts Payable	Dale Armstrong, Capital	+ Revenue −	Expenses
PB	$5,690 +	$11,000 +	$200 +	$160 =	$890 +	$16,000 +	$680 −	$520
(n)	− 90				− 90			
NB	$5,600 +	$11,000 +	$200 +	$160 =	$800 +	$16,000 +	$680 −	$520

(o) Dale's Cleaners receives cash revenue for the third week, $415.

	Assets =				Liabilities +	Owner's Equity		
	Cash +	Equipment +	Supplies +	Ppd. Ins.	Accounts Payable	Dale Armstrong, Capital	+ Revenue −	Expenses
PB	$5,600 +	$11,000 +	$200 +	$160 =	$800 +	$16,000 +	$680 −	$520
(o)	+ 415						+ 415	
NB	$6,015 +	$11,000 +	$200 +	$160 =	$800 +	$16,000 +	$1,095 −	$520

(p) Dale's Cleaners signs a contract with Ace Rental to clean their for-hire formal clothes on a credit basis, and cleans ten dress suits. Accordingly, Dale's bills Ace Rental for services performed, $40.

	Assets =					Liabilities +	Owner's Equity		
	Cash +	Equip. +	Supp. +	Ppd. Ins. +	Accts. Rec.	Accounts Payable	Dale Armstrong, Capital	+ Revenue −	Expenses
PB	$6,015 +	$11,000 +	$200 +	$160		= $800 +	$16,000 +	$1,095 −	$520
(p)					+ $40			+ 40	
NB	$6,015 +	$11,000 +	$200 +	$160 +	$40 =	$800 +	$16,000 +	$1,135 −	$520

A firm uses the *Accounts Receivable account* to record the amounts owed by charge customers. Since Ace Rental owes Dale's Cleaners $40 more than before the transaction took place, it seems logical to add $40 to Accounts Receivable. Revenue is earned when the service has been performed, and hence the corresponding increase in revenue. When Ace pays the $40 bill in cash, Armstrong should record this as an increase in Cash and a decrease in Accounts Receivable. He would not have to make an entry for the Revenue account, as he has previously recorded the amount.

(q) Armstrong pays wages of employees, $195, June 11 through June 24.

	Cash +	Equip. +	Supp. +	Ppd. Ins. +	Accts. Rec.	=	Accounts Payable +	Dale Armstrong, Capital +	Revenue −	Expenses
PB	$6,015 +	$11,000 +	$200 +	$160 +	$40	=	$800 +	$16,000 +	$1,135 −	$520
(q)	− 195									+ 195 (Wages)
NB	$5,820 +	$11,000 +	$200 +	$160 +	$40	=	$800 +	$16,000 +	$1,135 −	$715

(r) Armstrong buys additional equipment on account, $140, from Johnson Equipment Company.

	Cash +	Equip. +	Supp. +	Ppd. Ins. +	Accts. Rec.	=	Accounts Payable +	Dale Armstrong, Capital +	Revenue −	Expenses
PB	$5,820 +	$11,000 +	$200 +	$160 +	$40	=	$800 +	$16,000 +	$1,135 −	$715
(r)		+ 140					+ 140			
NB	$5,820 +	$11,140 +	$200 +	$160 +	$40	=	$940 +	$16,000 +	$1,135 −	$715

Again, because the equipment will last over a number of operations, Armstrong lists this $140 as an increase in the assets.

(s) Dale's Cleaners receives revenue from cash customers for the rest of the month, $480.

	Cash +	Equip. +	Supp. +	Ppd. Ins. +	Accts. Rec.	=	Accounts Payable +	Dale Armstrong, Capital +	Revenue −	Expenses
PB	$5,820 +	$11,140 +	$200 +	$160 +	$40	=	$940 +	$16,000 +	$1,135 −	$715
(s)	+ 480								+ 480	
NB	$6,300 +	$11,140 +	$200 +	$160 +	$40	=	$940 +	$16,000 +	$1,615 −	$715

(t) Dale's Cleaners receives $30 from Ace Rental to apply on the amount previously billed.

	Cash +	Equip. +	Supp. +	Ppd. Ins. +	Accts. Rec. =	Accounts Payable	Dale Armstrong, Capital +	Revenue −	Expenses
Assets =						**Liabilities +**	**Owner's Equity**		
PB	$6,300 +	$11,140 +	$200 +	$160 +	$40 =	$940 +	$16,000 +	$1,615 −	$715
(t)	+30				−30				
NB	$6,330 +	$11,140 +	$200 +	$160 +	$10 =	$940 +	$16,000 +	$1,615 −	$715

Since Ace Rental now owes Dale's Cleaners less than before, Armstrong should deduct the $30 from Accounts Receivable. He previously recorded this amount as revenue.

(u) At the end of the month, Armstrong withdraws $500 in cash from the business for his personal living costs. One may consider this transaction to be the opposite of an investment in cash by the owner.

	Cash +	Equip. +	Supp. +	Ppd. Ins. +	Accts. Rec. =	Accounts Payable	Dale Armstrong, Capital +	Revenue −	Expenses
Assets =						**Liabilities +**	**Owner's Equity**		
PB	$6,330 +	$11,140 +	$200 +	$160 +	$10 =	$940 +	$16,000 +	$1,615 −	$715
(u)	−500						−500 (Drawing)		
NB	$5,830 +	$11,140 +	$200 +	$160 +	$10 =	$940 +	$15,500 +	$1,615 −	$715

Because the owner is taking cash out of the business, there is a decrease in Cash. The withdrawal decreases Capital, because the owner has now decreased his equity. One does not consider a withdrawal as a business expense, since it is not money paid to anyone outside the business for services performed, or for materials received that would benefit the business.

Summary of illustration

On the next page we have summarized the business transactions of Dale's Cleaners in columnar form, identifying the transactions by letter. To test your understanding of the recording procedure, describe the nature of the transactions that have taken place.

The income statement

The *income statement* shows total revenue minus expenses, which yields the net income, or profit. This income statement pictures the results of the business transactions involving revenue and expense accounts over a period of time. In other words, it shows how the business has performed or fared over a period of time, usually a month or year. Other terms that are identical with the name *income statement* are *statement of income and expenses* or

	Cash +	Equipment +	Supplies +	Ppd. Ins. +	Accts. Rec.	=	Accounts Payable	Dale Armstrong, Capital +	Revenue −	Expenses
Bal.	6,500 +	11,000 +	200			=	1,700 +	16,000		
(f)	+300								+300	
Bal.	6,800 +	11,000 +	200			=	1,700 +	16,000 +	300	
(g)	−200									+200 (Rent)
Bal.	6,600 +	11,000 +	200			=	1,700 +	16,000 +	300 −	200
(h)	−120									+120 (Wages)
Bal.	6,480 +	11,000 +	200			=	1,700 +	16,000 +	300 −	320
(i)	−160			+160						
Bal.	6,320 +	11,000 +	200 +	160		=	1,700 +	16,000 +	300 −	320
(j)	+380								+380	
Bal.	6,700 +	11,000 +	200 +	160		=	1,700 +	16,000 +	680 −	320
(k)							+90			+90 (Advertising)
Bal.	6,700 +	11,000 +	200 +	160		=	1,790 +	16,000 +	680 −	410
(l)	−900						−900			
Bal.	5,800 +	11,000 +	200 +	160		=	890 +	16,000 +	680 −	410
(m)	−110									+110 (Utilities)
Bal.	5,690 +	11,000 +	200 +	160		=	890 +	16,000 +	680 −	520
(n)	−90						−90			
Bal.	5,600 +	11,000 +	200 +	160		=	800 +	16,000 +	680 −	520
(o)	+415								+415	
Bal.	6,015 +	11,000 +	200 +	160		=	800 +	16,000 +	1,095 −	520
(p)					+40				+40	
Bal.	6,015 +	11,000 +	200 +	160 +	40 =		800 +	16,000 +	1,135 −	520
(q)	−195									+195 (Wages)
Bal.	5,820 +	11,000 +	200 +	160 +	40 =		800 +	16,000 +	1,135 −	715
(r)		+140					+140			
Bal.	5,820 +	11,140 +	200 +	160 +	40 =		940 +	16,000 +	1,135 −	715
(s)	+480								+480	
Bal.	6,300 +	11,140 +	200 +	160 +	40 =		940 +	16,000 +	1,615 −	715
(t)	+30				−30					
Bal.	6,330 +	11,140 +	200 +	160 +	10 =		940 +	16,000 +	1,615 −	715
(u)	−500							−500 (Drawing)		
Bal.	5,830 +	11,140 +	200 +	160 +	10 =		940 +	15,500 +	1,615 −	715

	Total			Total
Cash	$ 5,830	Accounts Payable	$ 940
Equipment	11,140	Dale Armstrong, Capital	15,500
Supplies	200	Revenue	1,615
Ppd. Ins.	160		$18,055
Accts. Rec.	10	Expenses	−715
	$17,340		$17,340

25 Summary of transactions

profit and loss statement. If the total revenue is less than the expenses, the result is a net loss.

The income statement shown here tabulates the results of the first month of operations of Dale's Cleaners. (This is a tentative income statement, in that adjustments have not been recorded; we shall discuss them in Chapter 5.)

Dale's Cleaners Income Statement For month ended June 30, 19___			
Revenue			
Income from Services			$1,615 00
Expenses			
Wages Expense	$315 00		
Rent Expense	200 00		
Utilities Expense	110 00		
Advertising Expense	90 00		
Total Expenses			715 00
Net Income			$ 900 00

The headings of all financial statements require three lines.

   First line: Name of company (or owner, if there is no company name)

Second line: Title of financial statement

  Third line: Period of time covered by the financial statement, or date

The income statement covers a period of time, whereas the balance sheet has only one date: the end of the financial period. The revenue for June, less the expenses for June, shows the results of operations—a net income of $900. To the accountant, the term *net income* means "clear" income, or profit after all expenses have been deducted.

We said that revenue and expenses are connected with owner's equity through the medium of the financial statements. Let us now demonstrate this by a *statement of owner's equity,* which the accountant prepares after he or she has determined the net income in the income statement.

Dale's Cleaners Statement of Owner's Equity For month ended June 30, 19___		
Dale Armstrong, Capital, June 1, 19___		$16,000 00
Add: Net income for June	$900 00	
Less: Withdrawals for June	500 00	
Increase in Capital		400 00
Dale Armstrong, Capital, June 30, 19___		$16,400 00

Next we prepare a balance sheet, recording the balance of the Capital account as of the date of the balance sheet.

Dale's Cleaners
Balance Sheet
June 30, 19___

Assets		
Cash		$ 5,830|00
Accounts Receivable		10|00
Supplies		200|00
Prepaid Insurance		160|00
Equipment		11,140|00
Total Assets		$17,340|00
Liabilities		
Accounts Payable		$ 940|00
Owner's Equity		
Dale Armstrong, Capital		16,400|00
Total Liabilities and Owner's Equity		$17,340|00

This balance sheet is tentative, due to the fact that adjustments have not been recorded (see Chapter 5).

Statement of owner's equity involving an additional investment and a net loss

Any additional investment by the owner during the period covered by the financial statements should be shown in the statement of owner's equity, since such a statement should show what has affected the Capital account from the *beginning* until the *end* of the period covered by the financial statements. For example, assume the following for the R. T. Jones Company:

Balance of R. T. Jones, Capital, on Oct. 1	$60,000
Additional investment by R. T. Jones on Oct. 20	4,000
Net loss for the month (from income statement)	150
Total withdrawals for the month	760

One can show this information in the statement of owner's equity.

R. T. Jones Company
Statement of Owner's Equity
For month ended October 30, 19___

R. T. Jones, Capital, Oct. 1, 19___		$60,000|00
Additional Investment, Oct. 20, 19___		4,000|00
Total Investment		$64,000|00
Less: Net Loss for October	$150|00	
Withdrawals for October	760|00	
Decrease in Capital		910|00
R. T. Jones, Capital, Oct. 30, 19___		$63,090|00

The importance of financial statements

The owners or managers of a business look on their financial statements as a coach looks on the scoreboard and team statistics, as showing the results of the present game as well as the team's standing. The income statement shows the results of operations for the current month or year. The statement of owner's equity shows why the owner's investment has changed. The balance sheet shows the present standing or financial position. The owner or manager can use the figures on the financial statements to plan future operations. Not only owners or managers are interested in financial statements. Creditors, prospective investors, and government agencies are also interested in the profitability and financial standing of the business. Financial statements are the medium through which one can take the pulse of the business, and consequently they are extremely important.

Summary

We have now defined the final two elements of the Fundamental Accounting Equation: revenues and expenses. Business transactions involving the earning of revenue are recorded as increases in revenue; those involving the incurring of expenses are recorded as increases in expenses. The Fundamental Accounting Equation always remains in balance. With all five elements it now appears as follows in relation to the financial statements we have discussed.

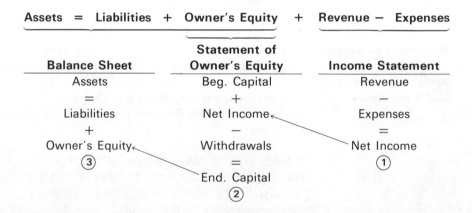

The income statement summarizes the results of operations, condensed into one figure, either *net income* or *net loss.*

Glossary

- **Accounts Receivable** Charge accounts or open-book accounts maintained for customers, representing credit usually extended for 30-day periods.
- **Expenses** Cost of services or goods acquired which have been used up or consumed in the operation of the business or economic unit.
- **Income statement** A financial statement showing the results of business transactions over a period of time: total revenue minus total expenses.
- **Revenue** The total price charged for services rendered or goods sold during a period of time. It may be in the form of cash or receivables.
- **Withdrawal** The taking of cash or goods out of a business by the owner for his or her own personal use. (This is also referred to as a *drawing.*) One

treats a withdrawal as a temporary decrease in the owner's equity, since one anticipates that it will be offset by net income.

Exercise 1 Describe a business transaction that will do the following:

a Increase an asset and increase a revenue.
b Decrease a liability and decrease an asset.
c Increase a liability and increase an expense.
d Decrease an asset and increase an expense.

Exercise 2 Describe the transactions recorded in the following equation.

		Assets =	Liabilities +		Owner's Equity	
	Cash +	Accounts + Equipment Receivable	Accounts Payable	T. C. Moore, + Revenue − Expenses Capital		
(a)	+9,000	+4,500 =		+13,500		
(b)	−2,000	+16,000	+14,000			
Bal.	7,000	+ 20,500 =	14,000 +	13,500		
(c)		+1,600		+1,600		
Bal.	7,000 +	1,600 + 20,500 =	14,000+	13,500 + 1,600		
(d)	−900					+900
Bal.	6,100 +	1,600 + 20,500 =	14,000+	13,500 + 1,600−	900	
(e)	−200			−200 (Drawing)		
Bal.	5,900 +	1,600 + 20,500 =	14,000+	13,300 + 1,600−	900	

Exercise 3 Reliable Shoe Repair has the following account balances. Prepare an income statement for the month ended March 31 of this year.

Cash	$1,400
Supplies	930
Equipment	7,270
Accounts Payable	750
N. C. Howe, Capital, Mar. 1	7,650
Service Sales	2,450
Rent Expense	600
Supplies Expense	540
Utilities Expense	60
Miscellaneous Expense	50

Exercise 4 From Exercise 3, present a statement of owner's equity and a balance sheet.

Exercise 5 From the following balances in the elements of the Fundamental Accounting Equation, determine the amount of the ending owner's equity.

Assets	$29,000
Liabilities	3,000
Owner's Equity (beginning)	14,000
Revenue	20,000
Expense	8,000

Exercise 6 Dr. B. E. Comer is an optometrist. Describe the transactions that have been completed.

	Cash +	Accts. + Rec.	Supp. +	Equip. =	Notes + Payable	Accounts + Payable	B. E. Comer, + Capital	Revenue −	Expenses
Bal.	1,540 +	620 +	215 +	6,426 =	1,000 +	310 +	7,491		
(a)	+300	−300							
Bal.	1,840 +	320 +	215 +	6,426 =	1,000 +	310 +	7,491		
(b)	+215							+215	
Bal.	2,055 +	320 +	215 +	6,426 =	1,000 +	310 +	7,491 +	215	
(c)	−325								+325 (Rent)
Bal.	1,730 +	320 +	215 +	6,426 =	1,000 +	310 +	7,491 +	215 −	325
(d)		+970						+970	
Bal.	1,730 +	1,290 +	215 +	6,426 =	1,000 +	310 +	7,491 +	1,185 −	325
(e)	−200					−200			
Bal.	1,530 +	1,290 +	215 +	6,426 =	1,000 +	110 +	7,491 +	1,185 −	325
(f)	−280								+280 (Wages)
Bal.	1,250 +	1,290 +	215 +	6,426 =	1,000 +	110 +	7,491 +	1,185 −	605
(g)	−560				−500				+60 (Interest)
Bal.	690 +	1,290 +	215 +	6,426 =	500 +	110 +	7,491 +	1,185 −	665
(h)	−500						−500 (Drawing)		
Bal.	190 +	1,290 +	215 +	6,426 =	500 +	110 +	6,991 +	1,185 −	665

Exercise 7 From Exercise 6, present an income statement for the month ending October 31.

Exercise 8 From Exercise 6, present a statement of owner's equity and a balance sheet.

Problems

Problem 2-1 On July 1 of this year, Ralph Baker established a business under the name Baker Realty. Transactions completed during the month were as follows.

a Deposited $2,500 in a bank account entitled Baker Realty.
b Paid office rent for the month, $250.
c Bought supplies consisting of stationery, folders, and stamps for cash, $95.
d Bought office equipment consisting of desks, chairs, filing cabinets, and calculator for $1,900, on account.
e Received bill for newspaper advertising, $110.
f Paid $300 to creditors on amount owed on purchase of equipment recorded previously.
g Earned sales commissions, receiving cash, $1,120.
h Received and paid bill for utilities, $85.
i Paid newspaper for bill previously recorded.
j Paid automobile expense, $90.
k Baker withdrew $415 in cash for his personal use.

Instructions

1 Record the transactions and the balances after each transaction, using the following account headings.

Assets =	Liabilities +		Owner's Equity	
Cash + Supplies + Equipment	Accounts Payable	Ralph Baker, + Revenue − Expenses. Capital		

2 Prepare an income statement and a statement of owner's equity for July, and a balance sheet as of July 31.

Problem 2-2 N. L. Smart, CPA, opened an office for public accounting practice on September 1. Transactions completed during the month were as follows.

a Deposited $9,000 in a bank account in the name of the business, N. L. Smart, CPA.

b Bought office equipment on account, $3,800.

c Invested in a library costing $1,400 (increase the Library account and the account of N. L. Smart, Capital, and include in the statement of owner's equity as Additional Investment).

d Paid $260 as office rent for the month.

e Bought office supplies for cash, $280.

f Paid the premium for a 3-year insurance policy on the equipment and the library, $75.

g Received $680 as professional fees for services rendered.

h Received and paid bill for telephone service, $70.

i Paid salary of part-time receptionist, $250.

j Paid automobile expense, $80.

k Received $720 as professional fees for services rendered.

l Paid $400 to creditor on amount owed on the purchase of office equipment.

m Smart withdrew $640 in cash for personal use.

Instructions

1 Record the transactions and the balances after each transaction, using the following account headings.

Assets =	Liabilities +		Owner's Equity	
Cash + Supplies + Prepaid + Library + Equipment Insurance	Accounts Payable	N. L. Smart, + Revenue − Expenses Capital		

2 Prepare an income statement and a statement of owner's equity for September, and a balance sheet as of September 30.

Problem 2-3 Leonard T. Davis started the Speedy Delivery Service on October 1 of this year. During October, Davis completed the following transactions.

a Invested $6,000 cash in the business.

b Bought delivery equipment for $5,000, paying $600 in cash and giving a note payable for the balance.

c Bought office equipment on account, $1,200.

d Paid rent for the month, $200.

e Paid cash for property and public liability insurance on delivery equipment for the year, $320.

f Cash receipts for the first half of the month from cash customers, $1,600.

g Bought supplies for cash, $120.

h Billed customers for services on account, $165.

i Paid cash for utilities, $55.

j Received bill for gas and oil used during the current month, $140.

k Cash receipts for the remainder of the month from cash customers, $1,860.

l Paid drivers' commissions, $890. (This is an expense.)

m Davis withdrew $640 in cash for personal use.

Instructions

1 Record the transactions and the balance after each transaction, using the following account headings.

Cash	+ Accts. Rec.	+ Supplies	+ Ppd. Ins.	+ Del'y Equip.	+ Office Equip.	Notes Payable	+ Accounts Payable	L. T. Davis, Capital	+ Revenue	− Expenses
				Assets =			**Liabilities +**		**Owner's Equity**	

2 Prepare an income statement and a statement of owner's equity for October, and a balance sheet as of October 31.

Problem 2-4 The Newell Auto Parking Company hires an accountant, who determines the following account balances as of November 30.

Cash	$2,150
Wages Expense	1,600
Advertising Expense	150
Revenue from Parking Fees	4,400
Equipment	3,300
Rent Expense	800
A. T. Newell, Capital, Nov. 1	3,940
A. T. Newell, Drawing	1,100
Accounts Receivable	960
Accounts Payable	1,950
Supplies	120
Miscellaneous Expense	110

Instructions Prepare an income statement and a statement of owner's equity for November, and a balance sheet as of November 30.

Problem 2-1A On March 1 of this year Robert Koski, D.D.S., established an office for the practice of dentistry. Transactions completed during the month were as follows.

a Deposited $6,000 in a bank account entitled Robert Koski, D.D.S.

b Paid office rent for the month, $390.

c Bought dental supplies for cash, $520.

d Bought dental equipment consisting of a chair, electric drills, x-ray equipment, etc., $7,200 on account.

e Bought a desk and furniture for reception room, $1,900, paying $200 down in cash and the remainder on account.

f Earned $710 in professional fees, receiving cash.

g Received and paid bill for utilities, $92.

h Paid $200 to creditors on amount owed on dental equipment recorded previously.

i Paid salary of assistant, $380.

j Earned $1,265 in professional fees, receiving cash.

k Koski withdrew $640 in cash for his own personal use.

Instructions

1 Record the transactions and the balances after each transaction, using the following account headings.

Assets =				Liabilities +	Owner's Equity		
Cash +	Supplies +	Dental + Equipment	Office Equipment	Accounts Payable	Robert Koski, Capital	+ Revenue	− Expenses

2 Prepare an income statement and a statement of owner's equity for March, and a balance sheet as of March 31.

Problem 2-2A Susan J. Adams, a photographer, opened an office for her professional practice on August 1. Transactions completed during the month were as follows.

a Deposited $8,200 in a bank account in the name of the business, Adams Photographic Studio.

b Bought photographic equipment on account, $3,870.

c Invested personal photographic equipment, $2,460. (Increase the Photographic Equipment account and the account of S. J. Adams, Capital, and include in the statement of owner's equity as Additional Investment.)

d Paid $280 as office rent for the month.

e Bought photographic supplies for cash, $415.

f Paid premium for a 3-year insurance policy on photographic equipment, $92.

g Received $421 as professional fees for services rendered.

h Paid salary of part-time assistant, $210.

i Received and paid bill for telephone service, $34.

j Paid $384 to creditor on amount owed on the purchase of photographic equipment.

k Received $919 as professional fees for services rendered.

l Paid $24 for minor repairs to photographic equipment (Repairs Expense).

m Adams withdrew $600 in cash for personal use.

Instructions

1 Record the transactions and the balances after each transaction, using the following account headings.

Assets =				Liabilities +	Owner's Equity		
Cash +	Supplies +	Prepaid Insurance	+ Photographic Equipment	Accounts Payable	S. J. Adams, Capital	+ Revenue	− Expenses

2 Prepare an income statement and a statement of owner's equity for August, and a balance sheet as of August 31.

Problem 2-3A On May 1 of this year L. C. Dawes started the Camden Advertising Agency. During May, Dawes completed these transactions.

a Invested $8,200 cash in the business.
b Bought a car for use in the business for $4,400, paying $800 in cash and giving a note payable for the balance. The Notes Payable account is represented by the issuance of a promissory note.
c Bought office equipment on account, $1,640.
d Paid rent for the month, $280.
e Cash receipts for the first half of the month from cash customers, $1,421.
f Paid cash for property and public liability insurance on car for the year, $194.
g Bought office supplies for cash, $105.
h Paid cash for heating bill, $24.
i Received bill for gas and oil used during the current month for the company car, $42.
j Billed customers for services on account, $246.
k Cash receipts for the remainder of the month from cash customers, $1,683.
l Paid salary of commercial artist, $820.
m Dawes withdrew $1,400 in cash for personal use.

Instructions

1 Record the transactions and the balance after each transaction, using the following headings.

Assets =						Liabilities +		Owner's Equity		
Cash +	Accts. Rec.	+ Supplies	+ Ppd. Ins.	+ Car	+ Office Equipment	Notes Payable	+ Accounts Payable	L. C. Dawes, Capital	+ Revenue	− Expenses

2 Prepare an income statement and a statement of owner's equity for May, and a balance sheet as of May 31.

Problem 2-4A An accountant determines the following account balances for the Stanford Soft-Water Service Company as of October 31 of this year.

Cash	$ 1,757
Advertising Expense	293
Income from Services	4,773
Wages Expense	2,882
Equipment	14,919
Accounts Payable	2,696
Rent Expense	340
Accounts Receivable	3,110
C. T. Stanford, Capital, Oct. 1	17,180
C. T. Stanford, Drawing	700
Miscellaneous Expense	176
Supplies	472

Instructions Prepare an income statement and a statement of owner's equity for October, and a balance sheet as of October 31.

ndα

To

3

civab

To

3 Recording business transactions in ledger account form; the trial balance

There is no double entry without the observance of certain strict rules. All transactions must be recorded twice, once on the debit and once on the credit side. If this requirement is not fulfilled, there is, by definition, no double entry. Raymond de Roover, *Studies in the History of Accounting*

Key points

- The T form of account compared to the columnar arrangement
- The Trial Balance Equation with T accounts and plus and minus signs for each of the five classifications of accounts
- The normal balance of an account is on the plus side.
- The debit side of any T account is the left side.
- The credit side of any T account is the right side.
- For the recording of every transaction, the amount placed on the left, or debit, side of an account or accounts must equal the amount placed on the right, or credit, side of another account or accounts.

Chapter contents

- Introduction
- The T account form
- The Trial Balance Equation
- Recording transactions in T account form
- Left equals right
- Debit side and credit side
- The trial balance
- Summary
- Glossary
- Exercises
- Problems

Specific objectives

After you have completed this chapter, you will be able to:

- Record a group of business transactions for a service business directly in T accounts involving changes in assets, liabilities, owner's equity, revenue, and expense accounts.
- Present the Trial Balance Equation with the T account forms, the plus and minus signs, and the sides labeled as debit and credit.
- Determine balances of T accounts having entries recorded on both sides of the accounts.
- Prepare a trial balance.

<table>
<tr><td>Introduction</td><td>

In Chapters 1 and 2 we discussed the Fundamental Accounting Equation in two installments, as follows:
Chapter 1 Assets = Liabilities + Owner's Equity
Chapter 2 Assets = Liabilities + Owner's Equity + Revenue − Expenses

With the introduction of Revenue and Expenses in Chapter 2, we brought the Fundamental Accounting Equation up to its full size of five classifications of accounts. There are only five; so, as far as you go in accounting—whether you are dealing with a small one-owner business or a large corporation—you can count on the fact that there are only five major classifications of accounts. Let us restate what we have said so far.

</td></tr>
</table>

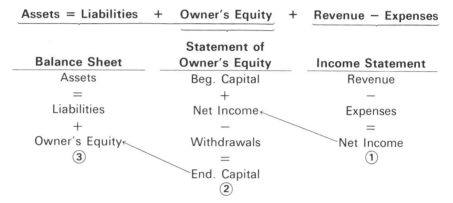

In this chapter, we shall record in T account form the same transactions illustrated in Chapters 1 and 2, and we shall prove the equality of both sides of the Fundamental Accounting Equation. We'll do this by means of a *trial balance,* which we'll talk about soon.

<table>
<tr><td>The T account form</td><td>

In Chapters 1 and 2, we recorded business transactions in a columnar arrangement. For example, in the books for Dale's Cleaners, the Cash account column looked something like this:

</td></tr>
</table>

	Cash			Cash			Cash
(a)	16,000		Bal.	6,480		Bal.	5,600
(b)	−9,000		(i)	−160		(o)	+415
Bal.	7,000		Bal.	6,320		Bal.	6,015
(d)	−500		(j)	+380		(q)	−195
Bal.	6,500		Bal.	6,700		Bal.	5,820
(f)	+300		(l)	−900		(s)	+480
Bal.	6,800		Bal.	5,800		Bal.	6,300
(g)	−200		(m)	−110		(t)	+30
Bal.	6,600		Bal.	5,690		Bal.	6,330
(h)	−120		(n)	−90		(u)	−500
Bal.	6,480		Bal.	5,600		Bal.	5,830

As an introduction to the recording of transactions, this arrangement has two advantages.

1 In the process of analyzing the transaction, you recognize the need to determine *which* account is involved. Next, from the viewpoint of the accounts, you must conclude that the transaction results in either an increase or a decrease in the accounts.

2 You further realize that after each transaction has been recorded, the balance of each account, when combined with the balances of the other accounts, proves the equality of the two sides of the Fundamental Accounting Equation.

The T form of account (shaped like the letter T) is the traditional form. It is also known as a *ledger account* because the records of *all* the accounts are kept in the ledger. The ledger may be as simple as a loose-leaf binder or as complex as a whole filing system.

The T form, developed for convenience as a space-saving device, is subdivided into two sides: one side to record increases in the account, and the other to record decreases. Let us now record those transactions just listed for Dale's Cleaners in the T form.

Cash

	+		−
(a)	16,000	(b)	9,000
(f)	300	(d)	500
(j)	380	(g)	200
(o)	415	(h)	120
(s)	480	(i)	160
(t)	30	(l)	900
	(17,605)	(m)	110
		(n)	90
Balance→5,830		(q)	195
		(u)	500
Footings			(11,775)

After we record a group of transactions in an account, we add both sides and record the totals in small pencil-written figures called *footings*. Next, we subtract the total of the smaller side from the total of the larger side, to determine the balance of the account, as follows:

$$\begin{array}{r} \$17,605 \\ -11,775 \\ \hline \$\ 5,830 \end{array}$$

We now record the balance on the larger side of the account, which, with a few minor exceptions, is always the plus side. Consequently, the plus (+) side of any account is referred to as the *normal balance* of the account. It may, however, be either the left side or the right side of the account.

The Trial Balance Equation

The Trial Balance Equation is simply a restatement of the Fundamental Accounting Equation, rearranged in such form as it would appear in a trial balance. Accordingly, the Fundamental Accounting Equation appears as follows:

▶ **Fundamental Accounting Equation**

Assets = Liabilities + Owner's Equity + Revenue − Expenses

▶ **Trial Balance Equation**

Assets + Expenses = Liabilities + Revenue + Owner's Equity

The trial balance, as we shall see, is a device used to prove the equality of the five classifications of accounts that comprise the Fundamental Accounting Equation.

Plus and minus signs for T accounts

Each of the classifications of accounts consistently has the same placement of the plus and minus signs. For example, we presented the T account for Cash with the plus on the left side and the minus on the right side:

Cash	
+	−
Left	Right

The T accounts for *all* assets are

+	−
Left	Right

and so Cash, being an asset, would have the same arrangement:

Cash	
+	−
Left	Right

Let us now restate the Trial Balance Equation with the T forms and plus and minus signs for each classification of accounts.

Assets +		Expenses =		Liabilities +		Revenue +		Owner's Equity	
+	−	+	−	−	+	−	+	−	+
Left	Right	Left	Right	Left	Right	Left	Right	Left	Right

One observation will help you to remember the placement of the plus and minus signs for each of the classifications: For the classifications on the left side of the equation, the pluses are on the left side of the T accounts; likewise, for the classifications on the right side of the equation, the pluses are on the right side of the T accounts.

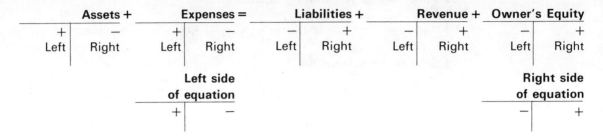

Your accounting background up to this point has taught you to analyze business transactions in order to determine which accounts are involved, and to recognize that the amounts should be recorded as either an increase or a decrease in the accounts. Now, when you are working with the T form, the recording process becomes simply a matter of knowing which side of the accounts should be used to record increases and which side to record decreases. Generally speaking, you will not be using the minus side of the revenue and expense accounts, since transactions involving revenue and expense accounts usually result in increases in these accounts.

Recording transactions in T account form

Our task now is to convert to the recording of business transactions in the T account form. To facilitate this transition, let's use the transactions of Dale's Cleaners again, because we are familiar with them, and we can readily recognize the resultant increases or decreases in the accounts involved.

The setup at the top of the next page represents the *chart of accounts,* or the official list of accounts, for Dale's Cleaners. We have given specific account titles for revenue and expense accounts, as it is necessary to list each account separately in the income statement. The account "Dale Armstrong, Drawing" has been set up to record withdrawals by the owner for his own personal use. As we said in Chapter 2, withdrawals by an owner are made in anticipation that they will be offset by net income, and hence are considered to be a temporary decrease in the owner's equity. Because of this temporary nature, they are recorded in a separate account; only permanent decreases would be recorded in the Capital account. The Drawing account is placed under the heading of owner's equity because it appears in the statement of owner's equity. The Drawing account is an exception, and should be remembered specifically as a deduction from Capital. To accentuate this fact, we have circled the Drawing account. When we want to treat one account as a deduction from another, our way of handling this is to reverse the plus and minus signs.

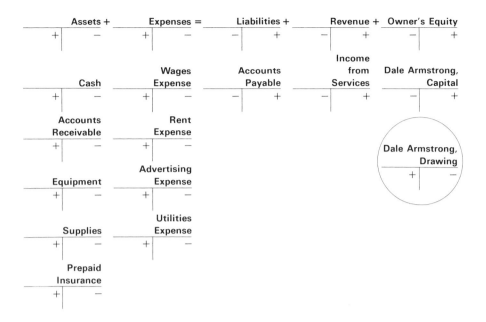

(a) Dale Armstrong invests $16,000 cash in his new business.

Assets +	Expenses =	Liabilities +	Revenue +	Owner's Equity
+ −	+ −	− +	− +	− +

Cash				Dale Armstrong, Capital
+ −				− +
(a) 16,000				(a) 16,000

This transaction results in an increase in Cash and an increase in the Capital account.

(b) Armstrong buys $9,000 worth of equipment, paying cash.

Assets +	Expenses =	Liabilities +	Revenue +	Owner's Equity
+ −	+ −	− +	− +	− +

Cash
+	−
	(b) 9,000

Equipment
+	−
(b) 9,000	

41 Recording transactions in T account form

This transaction results in an increase in the Equipment account and a decrease in the Cash account.

(c) Armstrong buys $2,000 worth of equipment on credit.

Assets +		Expenses =		Liabilities +		Revenue +		Owner's Equity	
+	−	+	−	−	+	−	+	−	+

Equipment			Accounts Payable	
+	−		−	+
(c) 2,000				**(c)** 2,000

This transaction results in an increase in both Equipment and Accounts Payable.

(d) Armstrong pays $500 to be applied against the firm's liability of $2,000.

Assets +		Expenses =		Liabilities +		Revenue +		Owner's Equity	
+	−	+	−	−	+	−	+	−	+

Cash			Accounts Payable	
+	−		−	+
	(d) 500		**(d)** 500	

This transaction results in a decrease in Cash and a decrease in Accounts Payable.

(e) Armstrong buys cleaning fluids for $200, on credit.

Assets +		Expenses =		Liabilities +		Revenue +		Owner's Equity	
+	−	+	−	−	+	−	+	−	+

Supplies			Accounts Payable	
+	−		−	+
(e) 200				**(e)** 200

This transaction results in an increase in Supplies and an increase in Accounts Payable.

Summary of illustration

The transactions were recorded in separate accounts before, but here is a restatement of the accounts in **(a)** through **(e)**. To test your understanding of the recording process, trace through the recording of each transaction and describe the nature of the transaction. Footings, or totals—remember always to write them in pencil—are included as a means of determining the balances of the accounts. The balances are recorded on the large side.

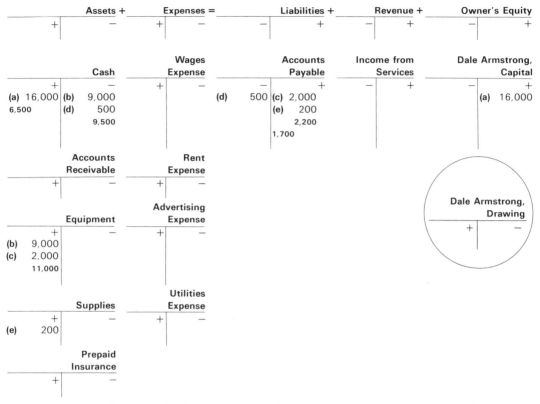

At this point let us pause to determine the equality of the two sides of the equation by listing the balances of the accounts.

	Accounts with the normal balances on the left side	Accounts with the normal balances on the right side
	Assets + Expenses	Liabilities + Revenue + Owner's Equity
Cash	$ 6,500	
Equipment	11,000	
Supplies	200	
Accounts Payable		$ 1,700
Dale Armstrong, Capital		16,000
	$17,700	$17,700

Left equals right

In recording each transaction, we write the same amount that is on the left side of one T account, or accounts, on the right side of another T account, or accounts. This is *double-entry accounting.* The amount of each transaction *must* be recorded at least twice. As an illustration, let us review the recording of the preceding transactions.

(a) Armstrong invests $16,000 cash in his new business.

Cash		Dale Armstrong, Capital	
+	−	−	+
(a) 16,000			**(a)** 16,000

(b) Armstrong buys $9,000 worth of equipment, paying cash.

Cash		Equipment	
+	−	+	−
	(b) 9,000	**(b)** 9,000	

(c) Armstrong buys $2,000 worth of equipment, on credit.

Equipment		Accounts Payable	
+	−	−	+
(c) 2,000			**(c)** 2,000

We observe from the foregoing that transactions are recorded in various combinations of pluses and minuses in the accounts. However, the important element is that:

▶ **The amount recorded on the left side of one T account, or accounts, must equal the amount recorded on the right side of another T account, or accounts.**

(d) Armstrong pays $500 to be applied against the firm's liability of $2,000.

Cash		Accounts Payable	
+	−	−	+
	(d) 500	**(d)** 500	

(Left side of Accounts Payable and right side of Cash.)

(e) Armstrong buys cleaning fluids for $200, on credit.

Supplies		Accounts Payable	
+	−	−	+
(e) 200			**(e)** 200

(Left side of Supplies and right side of Accounts Payable.)

(f) Dale's Cleaners receives $300 cash revenue for the first week.

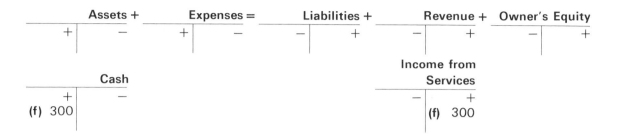

We write $300 on the left, or plus, side of the Cash account, and $300 on the right, or plus, side of the Income from Services account.

(g) Armstrong pays $200 for one month's rent on his shop.

Assets +		Expenses =		Liabilities +		Revenue +		Owner's Equity	
+	−	+	−	−	+	−	+	−	+

	Cash		Rent Expense
+	−	+	−
	(g) 200	(g) 200	

We write $200 on the left, or plus, side of the Rent Expense account. From the point of view of a running record of the Rent Expense account, there is an increase in this account. We also write $200 on the right, or minus, side of the Cash account.

(h) Armstrong pays wages to employees, $120.

Assets +		Expenses =		Liabilities +		Revenue +		Owner's Equity	
+	−	+	−	−	+	−	+	−	+

	Cash		Wages Expense
+	−	+	−
	(h) 120	(h) 120	

We write $120 on the left, or plus, side of the Wages Expense account, and $120 on the right, or minus, side of the Cash account.

Debit side and credit side

In accounting, the *left side* of a T account is called the *debit side;* the *right side* is called the *credit side.* To repeat the Trial Balance Equation with the T's:

Assets +		Expenses =		Liabilities +		Revenue +		Owner's Equity	
+	−	+	−	−	+	−	+	−	+
Left	Right	Left	Right	Left	Right	Left	Right	Left	Right
Debit	Credit	Debit	Credit	Debit	Credit	Debit	Credit	Debit	Credit

Note that the left side is always the debit side, regardless of whether it represents the plus or minus side of an account. One may use the word *debit* as a verb. If we debit Wages Expense for $120, for example, this means that we write $120 on the left side of the Wages Expense account. If the other half of the entry results in a credit to Cash for $120, this means that we write $120 on the right side of the Cash account.

Rules of debit and credit

When we study the Trial Balance Equation with the T's, we can make the following observation.

Debits signify		Credits signify	
Increases in	Assets	Decreases in	Assets
	Expenses		Expenses
Decreases in	Liabilities	Increases in	Liabilities
	Revenues		Revenues
	Owner's Equity		Owner's Equity

Previously we said that when one records each business transaction, the amount placed on the left side of one account (or accounts) must equal the amount placed on the right side of another account (or accounts). Let us now state this rule in terms of debits and credits.

▶ **The amount placed on the debit side of one account, or accounts, must equal the amount placed on the credit side of another account, or accounts.**

The abbreviation for debit is dr, and for credit is cr.

Now let's continue with the illustration of the transactions of Dale's Cleaners.

(i) Armstrong pays $160 for a 2-year insurance policy.

We write $160 on the debit, or plus, side of Prepaid Insurance, and $160 on the credit, or minus, side of Cash.

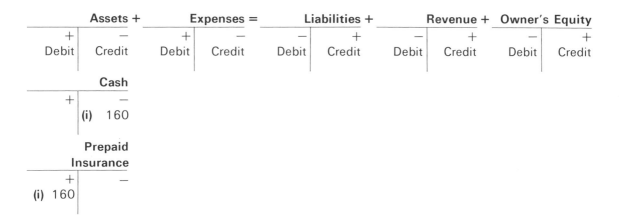

Assets +		Expenses =		Liabilities +		Revenue +		Owner's Equity	
+	−	+	−	−	+	−	+	−	+
Debit	Credit	Debit	Credit	Debit	Credit	Debit	Credit	Debit	Credit

Cash

+	−
	(i) 160

Prepaid Insurance

+	−
(i) 160	

(j) Dale's Cleaners receives cash revenue for the second week, $380.

Assets +		Expenses =		Liabilities +		Revenue +		Owner's Equity	
+	−	+	−	−	+	−	+	−	+
Debit	Credit	Debit	Credit	Debit	Credit	Debit	Credit	Debit	Credit

Cash

+	−
(j) 380	

Income from Services

−	+
	(j) 380

We write $380 on the debit, or plus, side of Cash, and $380 on the credit, or plus, side of Income from Services.

(k) Dale's Cleaners receives a bill for newspaper advertising, $90.

Assets +		Expenses =		Liabilities +		Revenue +		Owner's Equity	
+	−	+	−	−	+	−	+	−	+
Debit	Credit	Debit	Credit	Debit	Credit	Debit	Credit	Debit	Credit

Advertising Expense

+	−
(k) 90	

Accounts Payable

−	+
	(k) 90

We write $90 on the debit, or plus, side of Advertising Expense, and $90 on the credit, or plus, side of Accounts Payable.

(l) Armstrong pays $900 to creditors as part payment on account.

47 Debit side and credit side

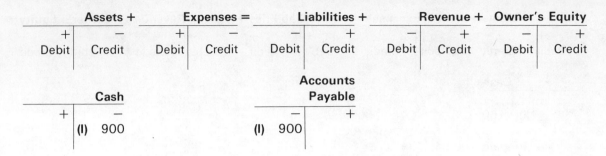

Assets +		Expenses =		Liabilities +		Revenue +		Owner's Equity	
+	−	+	−	−	+	−	+	−	+
Debit	Credit	Debit	Credit	Debit	Credit	Debit	Credit	Debit	Credit

	Cash				Accounts Payable	
+	−				−	+
	(l) 900				(l) 900	

We write $900 on the debit, or minus, side of Accounts Payable, and $900 on the credit, or minus, side of Cash.

In order to help you determine the way to record debits and credits in the foregoing transactions, we have continually repeated the Trial Balance Equation:

Assets +		Expenses =		Liabilities +		Revenue +		Owner's Equity	
+	−	+	−	−	+	−	+	−	+
Debit	Credit	Debit	Credit	Debit	Credit	Debit	Credit	Debit	Credit

Let us again stress the steps you need to follow in the analytical phase of accounting:

1 Ascertain which accounts are involved.
2 Determine whether there is an increase or a decrease in the accounts.
3 Formulate the entry as a debit to one account (or accounts) and a credit to another account (or accounts).

For the last step, you must be able to visualize this last equation. It is so useful that you ought to engrave it in your mind so that it will become automatic to you. For example, in the analysis of transaction (l), when you determine that the Accounts Payable account is involved, then you mentally classify Accounts Payable as a liability account. You should be able to picture in your mind the T account for Liabilities, with the minus (−) sign on the debit side and the plus (+) sign on the credit side. There is a decrease in Accounts Payable, so the entry should be recorded on the debit side. Without a doubt, this is the most important concept that you will ever learn in accounting. Accordingly, we strongly recommend memorizing the Trial Balance Equation with the T's and the plus and minus signs, as well as the accounts which represent exceptions, such as the Drawing account.

Now let's get back to the transactions of Dale's Cleaners.

(m) Armstrong receives and pays bill for utilities, $110.

We write $110 on the debit, or plus, side of Utilities Expense, and $110 on the credit, or minus, side of Cash.

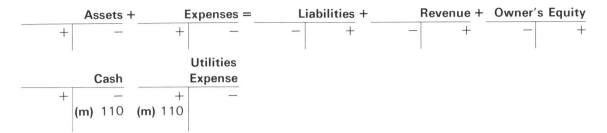

(n) Armstrong pays $90 to a newspaper for advertising. (This bill has previously been recorded.)

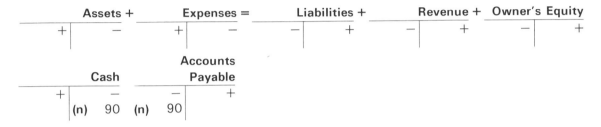

We write $90 on the debit, or minus, side of Accounts Payable, and $90 on the credit, or minus, side of Cash.

(o) Dale's Cleaners receives cash revenue for the third week, $415.

Assets +		Expenses =		Liabilities +		Revenue +		Owner's Equity	
+	−	+	−	−	+	−	+	−	+

Cash			Income from Services	
+	−		−	+
(o) 415				**(o)** 415

We write $415 on the debit, or plus, side of Cash, and $415 on the credit, or plus, side of Income from Services.

(p) Dale's Cleaners signs a contract with Ace Rental to clean their for-hire rental clothes on a credit basis. Accordingly, we bill Ace Rental $40 for services performed.

Assets +		Expenses =		Liabilities +		Revenue +		Owner's Equity	
+	−	┼		−	+	−	+	−	+

Accounts Receivable			Income from Services	
+	−		−	+
(p) 40				**(p)** 40

We write $40 on the debit, or plus, side of Accounts Receivable, and $40 on the credit, or plus, side of Income from Services.

(q) Armstrong pays wages of employees, $195.

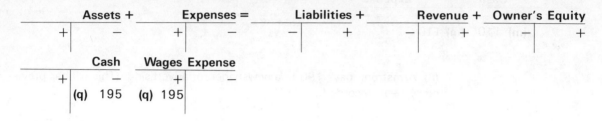

Assets +		Expenses =		Liabilities +		Revenue +		Owner's Equity	
+	−	+	−	−	+	−	+	−	+

Cash		Wages Expense	
+	−	+	−
(q) 195		(q) 195	

We write $195 on the debit, or plus, side of Wages Expense, and $195 on the credit, or minus, side of Cash.

(r) Armstrong buys additional equipment on account, $140.

Assets +		Expenses =		Liabilities +		Revenue +		Owner's Equity	
+	−	+	−	−	+	−	+	−	+

Equipment		Accounts Payable	
+	−	−	+
(r) 140			(r) 140

We write $140 on the debit, or plus, side of Equipment, and $140 on the credit, or plus, side of Accounts Payable.

(s) Dale's Cleaners receives revenue from cash customers for the remainder of the month, $480.

Cash		Income from Services	
+	−	−	+
(s) 480			(s) 480

We write $480 on the debit, or plus, side of Cash, and $480 on the credit, or plus, side of Income from Services.

(t) Dale's Cleaners receives $30 from Ace Rental to apply on the amount previously billed.

Cash		Accounts Receivable	
+	−	+	−
(t) 30			(t) 30

We write $30 on the debit, or plus, side of Cash, and $30 on the credit, or minus, side of Accounts Receivable.

(u) At the end of the month, Armstrong withdraws from the business $500 in cash for his personal use.

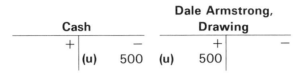

Cash		Dale Armstrong, Drawing	
+	−	+	−
	(u) 500	(u) 500	

We write $500 on the credit, or minus, side of Cash, and $500 on the debit, or plus, side of Dale Armstrong, Drawing. Since the account Dale Armstrong, Drawing, is used to record personal withdrawals by the owner, and since an additional withdrawal has been made, it should be recorded on the debit, or plus, side of the account.

Summary of illustration

Here are the transactions as they are ordinarily recorded in the accounts.

Assets +		Expenses =		Liabilities +		Revenue +		Owner's Equity	
+	−	+	−	−	+	−	+	−	+
Debit	Credit	Debit	Credit	Debit	Credit	Debit	Credit	Debit	Credit

Cash — **Wages Expense** — **Accounts Payable** — **Income from Services** — **Dale Armstrong, Capital**

Cash +		Wages Expense +		Accounts Payable −	+	Income from Services −	+	Dale Armstrong, Capital −	+
(a) 16,000	(b) 9,000	(h) 120		(d) 500	(c) 2,000		(f) 300		(a) 16,000
(f) 300	(d) 500	(q) 195		(l) 900	(e) 200		(j) 380		
(j) 380	(g) 200	315		(n) 90	(k) 90		(o) 415		**Dale Armstrong, Drawing**
(o) 415	(h) 120			1,490	(r) 140		(p) 40		
(s) 480	(i) 160	**Rent Expense**			2,430		(s) 480		
(t) 30	(l) 900						1,615	(u) 500	
17,605	(m) 110	+	−		940				
	(n) 90	(g) 200							
5,830	(q) 195	**Advertising Expense**							
	(u) 500	+	−						
	11,775	(k) 90							

Accounts Receivable

+	−
(p) 40	(t) 30
10	

Utilities Expense

+	−
(m) 110	

Equipment

+	−
(b) 9,000	
(c) 2,000	
(r) 140	
11,140	

Supplies

+	−
(e) 200	

Prepaid Insurance

+	−
(i) 160	

Note that, in the recording of expenses, one places the entries only on the plus, or debit, side. Also, in the recording of revenues, one places the entries on the plus, or credit, side.

Now, for additional practice we recommend that you describe the transactions that have taken place by looking at the listings in the T accounts. For example, Dale Armstrong invested $16,000 in the business.

	Cash			Dale Armstrong, Capital	
	+	−		−	+
(a)	16,000				(a) 16,000

The trial balance

You can now prepare a *trial balance* by simply recording the balances of the T accounts. This is not considered to be a financial statement, but, as the name implies, it is in essence a trial run by the accountant to prove that the debit balances of T accounts equal the credit balances of other T accounts. This represents proof of the equality of both sides of the Fundamental Accounting Equation. The trial balance is a prerequisite to the preparation of financial statements.

Dale's Cleaners
Trial Balance
June 30, 19___

Cash	5,830 00	
Accounts Receivable	10 00	
Supplies	200 00	
Prepaid Insurance	160 00	
Equipment	11,140 00	
Accounts Payable		940 00
Dale Armstrong, Capital		16,000 00
Dale Armstrong, Drawing	500 00	
Income from Services		1,615 00
Wages Expense	315 00	
Rent Expense	200 00	
Advertising Expense	90 00	
Utilities Expense	110 00	
	18,555 00	18,555 00

With the normal balance of each account on its plus side, the five classifications appear as expressed by the Trial Balance Equation. We record the Drawing account in the debit column because it has a debit balance, and we don't deduct it from the Capital account at the time when we prepare the trial balance.

Trial Balance		
Account titles	Left or debit balances	Right or credit balances
	Assets	
		Liabilities
		Owner's Equity
	Drawing	
		Revenue
	Expenses	
Totals	XXXX XX	XXXX XX

The T accounts are kept in a book called the *ledger*. In recording the accounts for the trial balance, we take the balances of the accounts as they appear, one after another, in the ledger. The order in the ledger follows the chart of accounts, in which the balance sheet accounts are listed first, followed by the income statement accounts:

- Assets
- Liabilities
- Owner's Equity
- Revenue
- Expenses

Errors exposed by the trial balance

If the debit and credit columns are not equal, then it is evident that we have made an error. Possible causes of errors include the following.

- Recording only half an entry, such as a debit without a corresponding credit, or vice versa.
- Recording both halves of the entry on the same side, such as two debits, rather than a debit and a credit.
- Recording one or more amounts incorrectly.
- Making errors in arithmetic, such as errors in adding the trial balance columns, or in finding the balances of the ledger accounts.

Procedure for locating errors

Suppose that you are in a business situation in which you have recorded transactions for a month in the account books, and the accounts do not balance. To save yourself time, you need to have a definite procedure for tracking down the errors. The advisable method is to do everything in reverse, as follows.

- Re-add the trial balance columns.
- Check the transferring of the figures from the ledger accounts to the trial balance.
- Verify the footings and balances of the ledger accounts.

As an added precaution, form the habit of verifying all addition and subtraction. You can thus correct many mistakes *before* making a trial balance.

Transpositions and slides

When the trial balance totals do not balance, the difference might indicate that you forgot to post half of an entry in the accounts. Dividing the difference by 2 may provide a clue that you accidentally posted half of an entry twice. If the difference is evenly divisible by 9, the discrepancy may be either a *transposition* or a *slide*. A transposition means that the digits have been transposed, or switched around. For example, one transposition of digits in 916 can be written as 619:

$$
\begin{array}{r}
916 \\
-619 \\
\hline
297
\end{array}
\qquad
\begin{array}{r}
33 \\
9\overline{)297}
\end{array}
$$

A slide refers to an error in recording the decimal point, in other words, a slide in the decimal point. For example, $163 could be inadvertently written as $1.63:

$$
\begin{array}{r}
\$163.00 \\
-1.63 \\
\hline
\$161.37
\end{array}
\qquad
\begin{array}{r}
17.93 \\
9\overline{)161.37}
\end{array}
$$

Or the error may be a combination of transposition and slide, such as when $216 is written as $6.21:

$$
\begin{array}{r}
\$216.00 \\
-6.21 \\
\hline
\$209.79
\end{array}
\qquad
\begin{array}{r}
23.31 \\
9\overline{)209.79}
\end{array}
$$

Again, the difference is evenly divisible by 9.

Summary

There are only five classifications of accounts. These classifications are embodied in the Trial Balance Equation.

Assets +		Expenses =		Liabilities +		Revenue +		Owner's Equity	
+	−	+	−	−	+	−	+	−	+
Left	Right	Left	Right	Left	Right	Left	Right	Left	Right
Debit	Credit	Debit	Credit	Debit	Credit	Debit	Credit	Debit	Credit

To restate for emphasis, let us again stress the most important concept in accounting: When you are recording transactions, the amount you place on the left, or debit, side of an account (or accounts) must equal the amount you place on the right, or credit, side of another account (or accounts).

At the end of the month, to prove the equality of debit and credit balances, prepare a trial balance, as at the top of the next page.

Accounting may be considered as a game of accounts and balances. If you know the rules and make the right moves, you can win the game. The rules

Trial Balance		
Account titles	Left or debit balances	Right or credit balances
	Assets	Liabilities
		Owner's Equity
	Drawing	Revenue
	Expenses	
Totals	XXXX XX	XXXX XX

are the fundamentals, and they are based on logical assumptions. The consequences of a move follow you throughout the game. Take it as a challenge! As a starter, concentrate on mastering the fundamentals.

Glossary

o **Credit** The right side of a ledger T account; to credit is to record an entry on the right side of a ledger T account. Credits represent increases in liability, revenue, and capital accounts, and decreases in asset and expense accounts.

o **Debit** The left side of a ledger T account; to debit is to record an entry on the left side of a ledger T account. Debits represent increases in asset and expense accounts, and decreases in liability, revenue, and capital accounts.

o **Double-entry accounting** Recording the amount of a transaction in at least two accounts, with the total of the amounts recorded as debits equal to the total of the amounts recorded as credits.

o **Footing** The temporary total of one side of a T account, recorded in pencil.

o **Ledger** A book or binder containing all the accounts of an enterprise.

o **Normal balance** The plus side of any T account.

o **Slide** An error in the recording of the decimal point of a number.

o **T account form** A form of ledger account having one side for entries on the debit, or left, side, and one side for entries on the credit, or right, side.

o **Transposition** Interchanging, or switching around, the digits during the recording of a number.

o **Trial Balance Equation** Assets + Expenses = Liabilities + Revenue + Owner's Equity. This is a rearrangement of the Fundamental Accounting Equation, with the normal balances of the accounts as they appear in the trial balance.

Exercises

Exercise 1 The Reliable Telephone Answering Service has the following accounts in its ledger: Cash; Accounts Receivable; Supplies; Equipment; Accounts Payable; Mona Flynn, Capital; Mona Flynn, Drawing; Income from Fees; Rent Expense; Telephone Expense; Utilities Expense; Miscellaneous Expense. On a sheet of ordinary notebook paper, record the Trial Balance Equation with the T's and the plus and minus signs, and record these accounts under the appropriate classification with the T's and the plus and minus signs.

Exercise 2 Using the ledger accounts prepared in Exercise 1 for the Reliable Telephone Answering Service, record the following transactions:

a Paid for supplies, $62.

b Billed customers for services performed, $490.

c Paid rent for the month, $290.

d Collected accounts receivable, $215.

e Purchased a new typewriter, $186, on account.

f Paid $12 for advertising in community brochure.

g Mona Flynn withdrew $30 in cash for personal use.

Exercise 3 Thomas Wills operates the Wills Delivery Service. The company has the following chart of accounts:

| **Assets** |
| Cash |
| Accounts Receivable |
| Prepaid Insurance |
| Delivery Equipment |
| Office Equipment |

| **Liabilities** |
| Notes Payable |
| Accounts Payable |

| **Owner's Equity** |
| Thomas Wills, Capital |
| Thomas Wills, Drawing |

| **Revenue** |
| Fees Earned |

| **Expenses** |
| Wages Expense |
| Truck Expense |
| Telephone Expense |
| Utilities Expense |
| Miscellaneous Expense |

On a sheet of ordinary notebook paper, record the following transactions directly in pairs of T accounts. (*Example:* Paid telephone bill, $38)

Telephone Expense		Cash	
+	−	+	−
38			38

a Paid electric bill, $27.

b Received bill for repairs to truck, $119.

c Paid creditors on account, $260.

d Paid $190 for liability insurance.

e Paid $26 for advertising.

f Received $216 from charge customers to apply on account.

g Thomas Wills withdrew $80 in cash for personal use.

Exercise 4 During the first month of operation, McDonnell's Welding Shop recorded the following transactions. Describe transactions **(a)** through **(k)**.

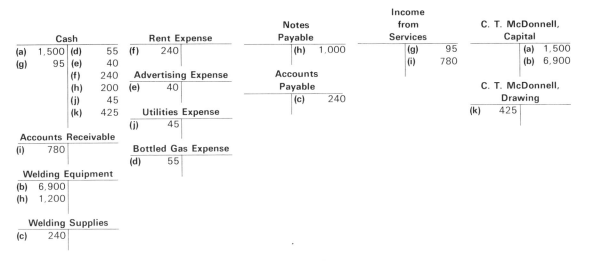

	Cash		
(a)	1,500	(d)	55
(g)	95	(e)	40
		(f)	240
		(h)	200
		(j)	45
		(k)	425

Accounts Receivable	
(i)	780

Welding Equipment	
(b)	6,900
(h)	1,200

Welding Supplies	
(c)	240

Rent Expense	
(f)	240

Advertising Expense	
(e)	40

Utilities Expense	
(j)	45

Bottled Gas Expense	
(d)	55

Notes Payable	
(h)	1,000

Accounts Payable	
(c)	240

Income from Services	
(g)	95
(i)	780

C. T. McDonnell, Capital	
(a)	1,500
(b)	6,900

C. T. McDonnell, Drawing	
(k)	425

Exercise 5 From the accounts in Exercise 4, prepare a trial balance for McDonnell's Welding Shop, dated September 30 of this year.

Exercise 6 The accounts (all normal balances) of the City Taxi Service as of September 30 of this year are listed here in alphabetical order. Prepare a trial balance listing the accounts in proper order.

Accounts Payable	$ 5,500
Accounts Receivable	8,000
Cash	1,000
Equipment	18,000
Fares Earned	20,000
Insurance Expense	400
Miscellaneous Expense	200
Prepaid Insurance	300
Rent Expense	2,000
Supplies	600
Supplies Expense	2,400
Utilities Expense	1,200
Wages Expense	12,000
T. R. Yelland, Capital	21,100
T. R. Yelland, Drawing	500

Exercise 7 From the trial balance prepared in Exercise 6, prepare an income statement for the month of September of this year.

Exercise 8 Assume that a trial balance has been prepared, and that the total of the debit balances is not equal to the total of the credit balances. Note the amount by which the two totals would differ, and label which column is overstated or understated.

Error	Amount of difference	Debit or credit column overstated or understated
A $10 debit to Supplies was not posted.	$10	Debit column under-stated
a A $40 credit to Cash was not posted.		
b A $65 credit to Accounts Payable was posted twice.		
c A $60 debit to Prepaid Insurance was posted twice.		
d A $39 debit to Accounts Receivable was posted as $93.		
e A $41 debit to Equipment was posted as $410.		
f A $16 debit to Supplies was posted as a $16 debit to Miscellaneous Expense.		

Problems

Problem 3-1 During April of this year, Peter R. Adams established the Adams Television Service Company. The following asset, liability, and owner's equity accounts are included in the ledger: Cash; Shop Equipment; Store Equipment; Truck; Accounts Payable; and Peter R. Adams, Capital. During the month the following transactions took place.

a Adams invested $8,000 cash in the business.
b Bought a used cash register for cash, $120 (Store Equipment).
c Bought testing equipment for cash, $450 (Shop Equipment).
d Bought store fixtures for $650; payment is due in 30 days.
e Adams invested his personal tools and testing devices in the business, $185.
f Bought a used service truck for $900, paying $300 down; the balance is due in 30 days.
g Paid $200 on account for the store fixtures in **d** above.

Instructions

1 Record the plus and minus signs under each T account.
2 Record the amounts in the proper positions in the T accounts. Key each entry to the alphabetical symbol identifying each transaction.

Problem 3-2 Robert Sanders established Sanders' Garage during October of this year. The accountant prepared the following chart of accounts.

Assets

Cash
Accounts Receivable
Office Equipment
Shop Equipment
Truck

Liabilities

Accounts Payable

Owner's Equity

Robert Sanders, Capital
Robert Sanders, Drawing

Revenue

Income from Services

Expenses

Rent Expense
Utilities Expense
Wages Expense
Repair Parts Expense

The transactions listed below occurred during the month.
a Sanders invested $6,000 cash to establish an auto repair business.
b Paid $275 rent for the month.
c Bought used truck for $1,200, with $200 as a downpayment; he agreed to pay the balance in 30 days.
d Received $120 in cash for services rendered.
e Bought an office desk and filing cabinet for cash, $105.
f Sanders invested his personal tools in the business, $650.
g Bought an electronic analyzer for $2,900, paying $1,400 down; the balance is due in 30 days.
h Billed customers for repair services, $790.
i Paid wages to employee, $260.
j Received bill for repair parts, $180.
k Paid electric bill, $55.
l Collected $680 from charge customers, billed previously under **h**.
m Paid bill for repair parts, billed previously under **j**.
n Sanders withdrew $200 in cash for personal use.
Instructions
1 Record the plus and minus signs under each T account.

2 Record the transactions in the T accounts. Key each entry to the alphabetical symbol identifying each transaction.

3 Prepare a trial balance, with a three-line heading, dated October 31.

Problem 3-3 Alberta R. Jenkins, an attorney, opens an office for the practice of law. Her accountant recommends the following chart of accounts.

Assets
Cash
Accounts Receivable
Office Equipment
Office Furniture
Law Library

Liabilities
Accounts Payable

Owner's Equity
Alberta R. Jenkins, Capital
Alberta R. Jenkins, Drawing

Revenue
Professional Fees

Expenses
Salary Expense
Rent Expense
Utilities Expense
Travel Expense

The transactions listed below occurred during May of this year.

a Jenkins invested $7,500 cash in her law practice.

b Paid $210 as rent on her office for the month.

c Paid $680 in cash for desks, chairs, and rugs.

d Jenkins invested her personal law books in the firm, $3,200.

e Bought a set of filing cabinets for $120, on account (Office Equipment).

f Bought an electric typewriter for $450, paying $200 down; the balance is due in 30 days.

g Billed clients for legal services performed, $620.

h Paid electric bill for heat and lights, $40.

i Paid $90 on the filing cabinets purchased on credit in **e**.

j Received $400 from clients billed previously in **g**.

k Paid telephone bill, $60.

l Billed clients for $840 for additional legal fees.

m Paid salary of receptionist, $260.

n Paid $90 in expenses for business trip.

o Jenkins withdrew $500 in cash for her personal use.

Instructions

1 Record the plus and minus signs under each T account.
2 Record the transactions in the T accounts. Key each entry to the alphabetical symbol identifying each transaction.
3 Prepare a trial balance as of May 31, 19___.
4 Prepare an income statement for May.
5 Prepare a statement of owner's equity for May.
6 Prepare a balance sheet as of May 31, 19___.

Problem 3-4 On August 1 of this year Delia Fields opened a coin-operated dry cleaning service under the name Fast-Service Dry Cleaners. Her accountant listed the following accounts for the ledger: Cash; Dry Cleaning Supplies; Prepaid Insurance; Dry Cleaning Equipment; Furniture and Fixtures; Notes Payable; Accounts Payable; Delia Fields, Capital; Delia Fields, Drawing; Dry Cleaning Sales; Wages Expense; Rent Expense; Power Expense; Miscellaneous Expense. During August the following transactions were completed.

a Fields deposited $9,500 in a bank account in the name of the business.
b Bought machinery and equipment for $8,000, giving $1,200 cash and a note payable for the balance.
c Paid $120 cash for liability insurance for 12 months.
d Acquired dry cleaning supplies on account, $160.
e Bought used chairs and magazine stands for $125 cash.
f Paid rent for the month, $290.
g Received $700 from cash customers for the first half of the month.
h Paid $100 as an installment on the equipment purchased in **b**.
i Paid wages to employee, $310.
j Paid $110 on account for the dry cleaning supplies acquired in **d**.
k Paid electric bill, $95.
l Paid $20 for license and other miscellaneous expenses.
m Received $940 from cash customers for the second half of the month.
n Fields withdrew $360 in cash for her personal use.

Instructions

1 Label the T accounts and record the plus and minus signs for each T account.
2 Record the amounts directly in the T accounts. Key each entry to the alphabetical symbol identifying each transaction.
3 Prepare a trial balance as of August 31, 19___.
4 Prepare an income statement for the month of August 19___.
5 Prepare a statement of owner's equity for the month of August 19___.
6 Prepare a balance sheet as of August 31, 19___.

Problem 3-1A During March of this year, Robert R. Stewart established the Regal Linen Supply Company. The following asset, liability, and owner's equity accounts are included in the ledger: Cash; Linen Supplies; Laundry Equipment; Office Equipment; Truck; Accounts Payable; and Robert R. Stewart, Capital. During March, the following transactions occurred.

a Stewart invested $3,200 cash in the business.
b Bought used washers and dryers for $1,270, paying cash.

c Bought towels from Dayton Hotel Supply Company, $592, on account.

d Bought a used delivery truck for $1,600, paying $400 as a downpayment, the balance being due in 30 days.

e Bought a typewriter, desk, and filing cabinet for cash, $408.

f Paid $160 on account to Dayton Hotel Supply Company.

g Bought sheets and pillow cases from Scranton Textile Company for cash, $284.

Instructions

1 Record the plus and minus signs under each T account.

2 Record the amounts in the proper positions in the T accounts. Key each entry to the alphabetical symbol identifying each transaction.

Problem 3-2A Donald Sturmer established Sturmer's Garage during November of this year. The accountant prepared the following chart of accounts.

	Assets
	Cash
	Accounts Receivable
	Office Equipment
	Shop Equipment
	Truck

	Liabilities
	Accounts Payable

	Owner's Equity
	Donald Sturmer, Capital
	Donald Sturmer, Drawing

	Revenue
	Income from Services

	Expenses
	Rent Expense
	Utilities Expense
	Wages Expense
	Repair Parts Expense

The transactions listed below occurred during the month.

a Sturmer invested $2,200 cash to establish his auto repair business.

b Paid $320 rent for the month.

c Sturmer invested his personal tools in the business, $910.

d Bought used truck for $1,425, paying $300 as a downpayment; the balance is due in 30 days.

e Received $162 in cash for services rendered.

f Bought an electronic analyzer for $3,150, paying $1,200 down; the balance is due in 30 days.

g Bought an office desk and filing cabinet for cash, $125.

h Billed customers for repair services, $681.

i Received bill for repair parts, $190.

j Paid wages to employee, $316.

k Collected $596 from charge customers, billed previously under **h**.

l Paid electric bill, $61.

m Paid bill for repair parts, billed previously under **i**.

n Sturmer withdrew $210 in cash for personal use.

Instructions

1 Record the plus and minus signs under each T account.

2 Record the transactions in the T accounts. Key each entry to the alphabetical symbol identifying each transaction.

3 Prepare a trial balance with a three-line heading dated November 30, 19___ .

Problem 3-3A Charlotte P. George, an attorney, opens an office for the practice of law. Her accountant recommends the following chart of accounts.

Assets
Cash
Accounts Receivable
Office Equipment
Office Furniture
Law Library

Liabilities
Accounts Payable

Owner's Equity
Charlotte P. George, Capital
Charlotte P. George, Drawing

Revenue
Professional Fees

Expenses
Salary Expense
Rent Expense
Utilities Expense
Travel Expense

The following transactions occurred during June.

a George invested $7,800 cash in her law practice.

b Paid $365 as rent on her office for the month.

c George invested her personal law books in the firm, $4,160.

d Bought desks, chairs, and rugs, $924, paying cash.

e Bought a set of filing cabinets for $160, on account.

f Bought an electric typewriter for $390, paying $190 down; the balance is due in 30 days.

g Billed clients for legal services performed, $716.

h Paid telephone bill, $52.

i Paid $60 on the filing cabinets purchased on credit in **e**.

j Paid electric bill for heat and lights, $41.

k Billed clients for $920 for additional legal fees.

l Paid expenses for business trip, $72.

m Paid salary of receptionist, $325.

n Bought bookcases for $210, on account (Office Furniture).

o George withdrew $560 in cash for her personal use.

Instructions

1 Record the plus and minus signs under each T account.

2 Record the transactions in the T accounts. Key each entry to the alphabetical symbol identifying each transaction.

3 Prepare a trial balance as of June 30, 19___.

4 Prepare an income statement for June.

5 Prepare a statement of owner's equity for June.

6 Prepare a balance sheet as of June 30, 19___.

Problem 3-4A On July 1 of this year, Lee Meyer opened a coin-operated dry cleaning service called Fast-Service Dry Cleaners. His accountant listed the following accounts for the ledger: Cash; Dry Cleaning Supplies; Prepaid Insurance; Dry Cleaning Equipment; Furniture and Fixtures; Notes Payable; Accounts Payable; Lee Meyer, Capital; Lee Meyer, Drawing; Dry Cleaning Sales; Wages Expense; Rent Expense; Power Expense; Miscellaneous Expense. During July the following transactions were completed.

a Meyer deposited $11,200 in a bank account in the name of the business.

b Bought machinery and equipment for $9,600, giving $1,600 cash, and a note payable for the balance.

c Acquired dry cleaning supplies on account, $216.

d Bought used chairs and magazine stand for $156 in cash.

e Paid $96 cash for liability insurance for 12 months.

f Paid rent for the month, $415.

g Received $860 from cash customers for the first half of the month.

h Paid wages to employee, $326.

i Paid $200 as an installment on the equipment purchased in **b**.

j Paid electric bill, $103.

k Paid $120 on account for the dry cleaning supplies acquired in **c**.

l Received $980 from cash customers for the second half of the month.

m Paid $25 for license and other miscellaneous expenses.

n Meyer withdrew $375 in cash for personal use.

Instructions

1 Label the T accounts and record the plus and minus signs for each.

2 Record the amounts directly in the T accounts. Key each entry to the alphabetical symbol identifying each transaction.

3 Prepare a trial balance as of July 31, 19___.

4 Prepare an income statement for July 19___.

5 Prepare a statement of owner's equity for the month of July.

6 Prepare a balance sheet as of July 31, 19___.

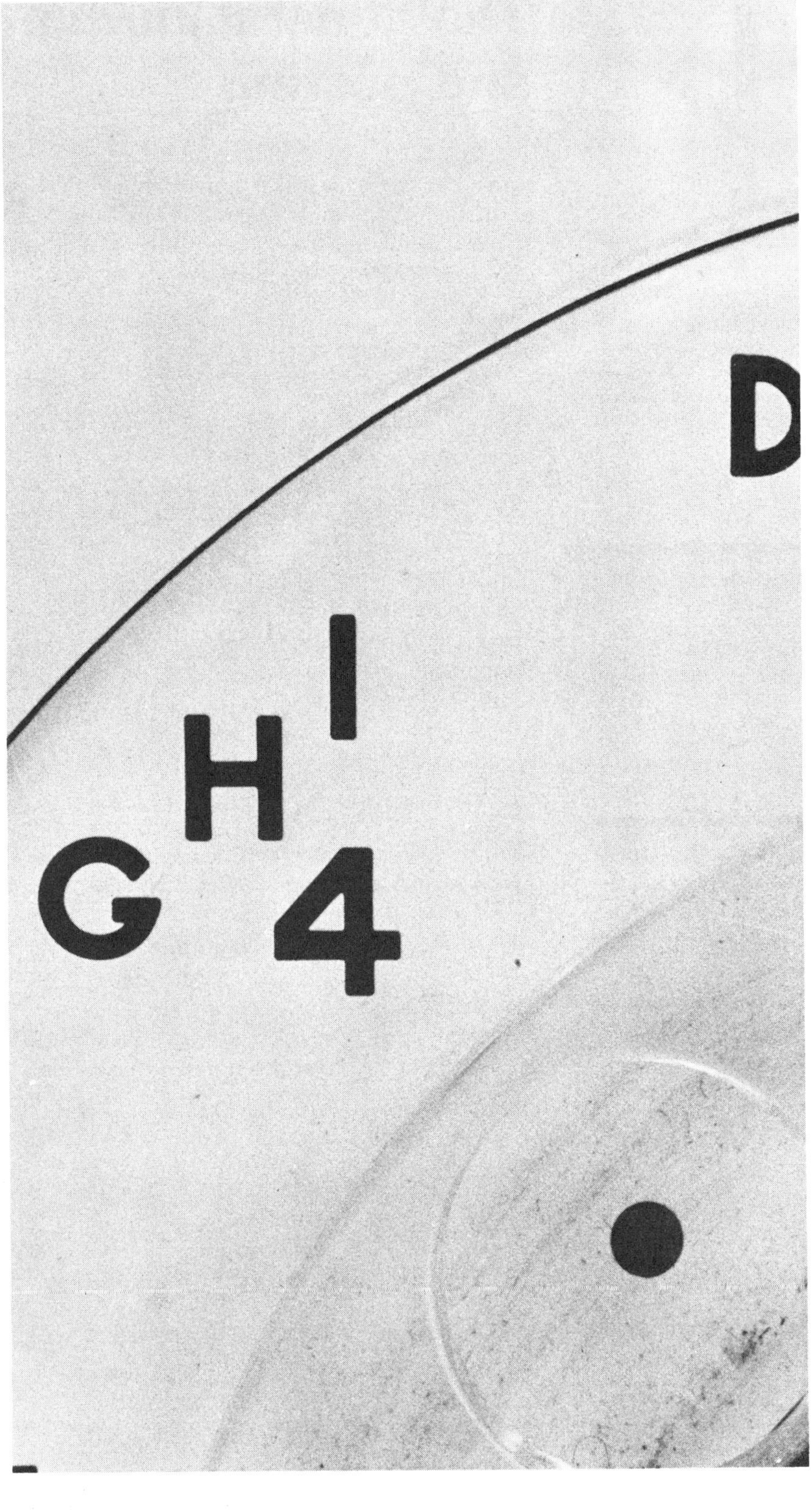
D
I
H
G
4

4

The general journal and posting

When the book lies in front of you, and you look at the book (not the book at you), then the side where you have your heart is the left or Debit side. The side away from your heart is the right side and is called Credit. Matthäus Schwartz, *The Model of Accounting,* 1518

Key points
- Transactions recorded in a journal first
- Cross-reference in the posting process
- Numbering system in the chart of accounts

Chapter contents
- Introduction
- The general journal
- Posting to the general ledger
- Summary
- Glossary
- Exercises
- Problems

Specific objectives

After you have completed this chapter, you will be able to:
- Record a group of transactions pertaining to a service-type enterprise in a two-column general journal.
- Post entries from a two-column general journal to general ledger accounts.

Introduction

In Chapter 3 we recorded business transactions directly as debits and credits to T accounts. This enabled you to visualize the accounts and tell which should be debited and which should be credited.

The initial steps in the accounting process are:
1 Recording business transactions in a journal
2 Posting to T accounts in the ledger
3 Footing the T accounts and determining the balances
4 Preparing a trial balance

Up to this time we have covered steps 2, 3, and 4. In our previous presentation, we introduced T accounts because, in the process of formulating debits and credits for business transactions, one has to think in terms of T accounts. Now we need to backtrack slightly in order to take up step 1, recording business transactions in a journal. Accordingly, in this chapter we shall present the general journal and the posting procedure.

The general journal

We have seen that an accountant must keep a written record of *each* transaction. One *could* record the transactions directly in T accounts; however, one would list only part of the transaction in each T account. A *journal* serves the function of recording both the debits and credits of the entire transaction. This journal is like a diary for the business, in which one records all the events involving financial affairs. A journal is called a *book of original entry*. In other words, always record a transaction in the journal first, and from there record it in the T accounts. The process of recording in the journal is called *journalizing*. One obtains information about transactions from business papers, such as checks, invoices, receipts, letters, memos, etc. These documents furnish proof that a transaction has taken place, so we should identify them in the journal entry whenever possible. Later on we shall introduce a variety of special journals. However, the basic form of journal is the two-column *general journal*. The term *two-column* refers to the two money columns which are used for debit and credit amounts.

Journalizing business transactions

As an illustration, let's use the transactions for Dale's Cleaners, covering the transactions listed in Chapter 3. Each page of the journal is numbered in consecutive order. This is the first page, so we write a 1 in the space for the page number. And of course we must always remember to put the date of each transaction. Now let's get on with the first entry.

a June 1: Dale Armstrong deposited $16,000 in a bank account in the name of Dale's Cleaners.

We write the year and month in the left part of the date column. We don't have to repeat the year and month until we start a new page, or until the year or month changes. (The illustrations we show, however, may repeat the month simply to eliminate confusion.) We write the day in the right part of the date column, and repeat it for each journal entry.

General Journal					Page 1
Date	Description	Post. Ref.	Debit		Credit
19__ June	1				

Since we are familiar with the chart of accounts, the next step is to decide which accounts should be debited and which credited. We do this by first figuring out which accounts are involved, and whether they are increased or decreased. We then visualize the accounts mentally, with their respective plus and minus sides, and thus we can make the debit and credit entries. Here is an example.

Cash is involved. Cash is considered to be an asset because it falls within the definition of ''things owned,'' and assets are

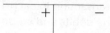

Cash is increased, so we debit Cash. Dale Armstrong, Capital is involved; Dale Armstrong, Capital is an owner's equity account because it represents the owner's investment, and Owner's Equity is

Dale Armstrong, Capital is increased, so credit Dale Armstrong, Capital.

As we said earlier, you perform this process mentally. Or, if the transaction is more complicated, then use scratch paper, drawing the T accounts. Using T accounts is the accountant's way of drawing a picture of the transaction. This is why we stressed the Trial Balance Equation, with the T accounts and plus and minus signs, so heavily in Chapter 3. You are urged to *get in the T account habit.*

Record the *debit* part of the entry first. Enter the account title—in this case, Cash—in the description column. Record the amount—$16,000—in the debit money column.

Next, record the *credit* part of the entry. Enter the account title—in this case, Dale Armstrong, Capital—on the line below the debit, in the Description column, indented about ½ inch. Do not abbreviate account titles, and do not extend them into the Posting Reference column.

General Journal					Page 1	
Date		Description	Post. Ref.	Debit		Credit
19__ June	1	Cash		16,000 00		
		Dale Armstrong, Capital			16,000	00

You should now give a brief explanation, in which you may refer to business papers, such as check numbers or invoice numbers; you may also list names of charge customers or creditors, or terms of payment. Indent the explanation an additional ½ inch, below the credit entry.

General Journal   **Page 1**

Date		Description	Post. Ref.	Debit	Credit
19___					
June	1	Cash		16,000 00	
		Dale Armstrong, Capital			16,000 00
		Original investment by			
		Armstrong in Dale's			
		Cleaners			

In order for an entry in the general journal to be complete, it must contain a *debit entry*, a *credit entry*, and an *explanation.* To anyone thoroughly familiar with the accounts, the explanation may seem to be quite obvious or redundant. This will take care of itself later; but in the meantime, let us record the explanation as a required, integral part of the entry. The next transaction is as follows:

b June 2: Armstrong buys $9,000 worth of equipment, for cash.

Mentally select the accounts that are involved. Next classify them under the five possible classifications. Visualize the plus and minus signs under the classifications. Now decide whether the accounts are increased or decreased. When you use T accounts to analyze the transaction, the results are:

Equipment		Cash	
+	−	+	−
Dr	Cr	Dr	Cr
9,000			9,000

Now journalize this analysis below the first transaction. For the sake of appearance, leave one blank line between transactions. Record the day of the month in the date column; remember that it is necessary to list only the day, because you don't have to record the month and year again until the month or year changes, or you use a new journal page.

General Journal   **Page 1**

Date		Description	Post. Ref.	Debit	Credit
	2	Equipment		9,000 00	
		Cash			9,000 00
		Bought equipment for			
		cash			

c June 2: Armstrong buys $2,000 worth of equipment on credit from Johnson Equipment Company. In order to get organized, think of the T accounts first.

Equipment		Accounts Payable	
+	−	−	+
Dr	Cr	Dr	Cr
2,000			2,000

Skip one more line and record the day of the month.

General Journal					Page 1
Date	**Description**	**Post. Ref.**	**Debit**		**Credit**
2	Equipment		2,000 00		
	Accounts Payable				2,000 00
	Bought equipment on				
	account from Johnson				
	Equipment Company				

d June 4: Armstrong pays $500 to be applied against the firm's liability of $2,000. Mentally picture the T accounts like this.

Cash		Accounts Payable	
+	−	−	+
Dr	Cr	Dr	Cr
	500	500	

Cash is an easy one to recognize. So, in every transaction, ask yourself, "Is Cash involved?" If Cash *is* involved, determine whether it is coming in or going out. In this case we see that cash is going out, so we record it on the minus side. We now have a credit to Cash and half of the entry. Next, we recognize that Accounts Payable is involved. We ask ourselves, "Do we owe more or less as a result of this transaction?" The answer is "less," so we record it on the minus, or debit, side of the account.

General Journal					Page 1
Date	**Description**	**Post. Ref.**	**Debit**		**Credit**
4	Accounts Payable		500 00		
	Cash				500 00
	Paid Johnson Equipment				
	Company on account				

Now let's list the transactions for June for Dale's Cleaners, with the date of each transaction. The journal entries are illustrated on the following pages.

June	1	Armstrong invests $16,000 cash in his new business.
	2	Buys $9,000 worth of equipment in cash.
	2	Buys $2,000 worth of equipment on credit from Johnson Equipment Company.
	4	Pays $500 to Johnson Equipment Company, to be applied against the firm's liability of $2,000.
	4	Buys cleaning fluids for $200 on credit from Acme Supply Company.
	7	Cash revenue received for first week, $300.
	8	Pays $200 rent for the month.
	10	Pays wages to employees, $120, June 1 through June 10.
	10	Pays $160 for a 2-year liability insurance policy.
	14	Cash revenue received for second week, $380.
	14	Receives bill for newspaper advertising, $90, from the *Daily News*.
	15	Pays $900 to Johnson Equipment Company as part payment on account.
	15	Receives and pays bill for utilities, $110.
	15	Pays $90 to the *Daily News* for advertising. (This bill has previously been recorded.)
	21	Cash revenue received for third week, $415.
	23	Armstrong enters into a contract with Ace Rental to clean their for-hire formal garments on a credit basis. Bills Ace Rental $40 for services performed.
	24	Pays wages of employees, $195, June 11 through June 24.
	26	Buys additional equipment on account, $140, from Johnson Equipment Company.
	30	Cash revenue received for the remainder of the month, $480.
	30	Receives $30 from Ace Rental to apply on amount previously billed.
	30	Armstrong withdraws $500 in cash for own personal use.

General Journal   **Page 1**

Date		Description	Post. Ref.	Debit	Credit
19__					
June	1	Cash		16,000 00	
		Dale Armstrong, Capital			16,000 00
		Original investment by Armstrong in Dale's Cleaners			
	2	Equipment		9,000 00	
		Cash			9,000 00
		Bought equipment for cash			

General Journal

Date		Description	Post. Ref.	Debit	Credit
June	2	Equipment		2,000 00	
		Accounts Payable			2,000 00
		Bought equipment on			
		account from Johnson			
		Equipment Company			
	4	Accounts Payable		500 00	
		Cash			500 00
		Paid Johnson Equipment			
		Company on account			
	4	Supplies		200 00	
		Accounts Payable			200 00
		Bought cleaning fluids			
		on account from Acme			
		Supply Company			
	7	Cash		300 00	
		Income from Services			300 00
		For week ended June 7			
	8	Rent Expense		200 00	
		Cash			200 00
		For month ended			
		June 30			

General Journal

Date		Description	Post. Ref.	Debit	Credit
19__					
June	10	Wages Expense		120 00	
		Cash			120 00
		Paid wages, June 1 to			
		June 10			
	10	Prepaid Insurance		160 00	
		Cash			160 00
		Premium for 2-year			
		liability insurance			
	14	Cash		380 00	
		Income from Services			380 00
		For week ended June 14			

General Journal

Date		Description	Post. Ref.	Debit	Credit
June	14	Advertising Expense		90 00	
		Accounts Payable			90 00
		Received bill for adv.			
		from *Daily News*			
	15	Accounts Payable		900 00	
		Cash			900 00
		Paid Johnson Equipment			
		Company on account			
	15	Utilities Expense		110 00	
		Cash			110 00
		Paid bill for utilities			
	15	Accounts Payable		90 00	
		Cash			90 00
		Paid *Daily News* for			
		advertising			
	21	Cash		415 00	
		Income from Services			415 00
		For week ended June 21			

General Journal

Date		Description	Post. Ref.	Debit	Credit
19__					
June	23	Accounts Receivable		40 00	
		Income from Services			40 00
		Ace Rental, for services			
		rendered			
	24	Wages Expense		195 00	
		Cash			195 00
		Paid wages, June 11 to			
		June 24			
	26	Equipment		140 00	
		Accounts Payable			140 00
		Bought equipment on			
		account from Johnson			
		Equipment Company			

General Journal

Date		Description	Post. Ref.	Debit		Credit	
June	30	Cash		480	00		
		Income from Services				480	00
		For remainder of June,					
		ended June 30					
	30	Cash		30	00		
		Accounts Receivable				30	00
		Ace Rental, to apply on					
		account					
	30	Dale Armstrong, Drawing		500	00		
		Cash				500	00
		Withdrawal for personal					
		use					

Posting to the general ledger

From this illustration, you can see that the journal is the *book of original entry,* meaning that each transaction must first be recorded in the journal in its entirety. Ledger accounts give us a cumulative record of the transactions recorded in each individual account. The general ledger is simply a book which contains all the accounts. The book used for the ledger is usually a loose-leaf binder, so that one can add or remove leaves. The process of transferring figures from the journal to the ledger accounts is called *posting.*

The chart of accounts

As we have said, one arranges the accounts in the ledger according to the chart of accounts: Assets are first, liabilities second, owner's equity third, revenue fourth, and expenses fifth. The chart of accounts for Dale's Cleaners is as follows.

Chart of Accounts

	Assets		Revenue
111	Cash	411	Income from Services
112	Accounts Receivable		
113	Supplies		**Expenses**
114	Prepaid Insurance	511	Wages Expense
121	Equipment	512	Rent Expense
		513	Advertising Expense
	Liabilities	514	Utilities Expense
211	Accounts Payable		
	Owner's Equity		
311	Dale Armstrong, Capital		
312	Dale Armstrong, Drawing		

The arrangement consists of the balance sheet accounts followed by the income statement accounts. The numbers preceding the account titles are the *account numbers*. Accounts in the ledger are kept by numbers rather than by pages because it's hard to tell in advance how many pages to reserve for a particular account. When you use the number system, you can add sheets quite readily. The digits in the account numbers also indicate *classifications* of accounts: Assets start with 1, liabilities with 2, owner's equity with 3, revenue with 4, and expenses with 5. The second and third digits indicate the positions of the individual accounts within their respective classifications. (We'll get around to explaining this in greater detail in Chapter 12.)

The ledger account form

We have been looking at accounts in the simple T form primarily because T accounts illustrate situations so well. The two sides, the debit side and the credit side, are readily apparent. As we have said, accountants trying to solve problems usually use the T form, because it's such a good way to visualize accounts. However, the T form is awkward when you are trying to determine the balance of an account, since it necessitates adding both columns and subtracting the smaller total from the larger. To overcome this disadvantage, accountants generally use the four-column account form, with a *running balance*. As a comparison, let's look at the Cash account of Dale's Cleaners in four-column form and in T form.

General Ledger

Cash — Account No. 111

Date		Item	Post. Ref.	Debit	Credit	Balance Debit	Balance Credit
19__							
June	1			16,000 00		16,000 00	
	2				9,000 00	7,000 00	
	4				500 00	6,500 00	
	7			300 00		6,800 00	
	8				200 00	6,600 00	
	10				120 00	6,480 00	
	10				160 00	6,320 00	
	14			380 00		6,700 00	
	15				900 00	5,800 00	
	15				110 00	5,690 00	
	15				90 00	5,600 00	
	21			415 00		6,015 00	
	24				195 00	5,820 00	
	30			480 00		6,300 00	
	30			30 00		6,330 00	
	30				500 00	5,830 00	

```
                    Cash
              +            −
(a) 16,000   (b)  9,000
(f)    300   (d)    500
(j)    380   (g)    200
(o)    415   (h)    120
(s)    480   (i)    160
(t)     30   (l)    900
    17,605   (m)    110
             (n)     90
    5,830    (q)    195
             (u)    500
                  11,775
```

The posting process

In the posting process, you must transfer the following information from the journal to the ledger accounts: the *date of the transaction,* the *debit and credit amounts,* and the *page number* of the journal. Post each account separately, using the following steps.

Steps in the posting process (Post the debit part of the entry first.)
1 Write the date of transaction.
2 Write the amount of transaction.
3 Write the page number of the journal in the Posting Reference column of the ledger account.
4 Record the ledger account number in the Posting Reference column of the journal. (This is a cross reference.)

The transactions for Dale's Cleaners are illustrated below. Let's look first at the debit part of the entry.

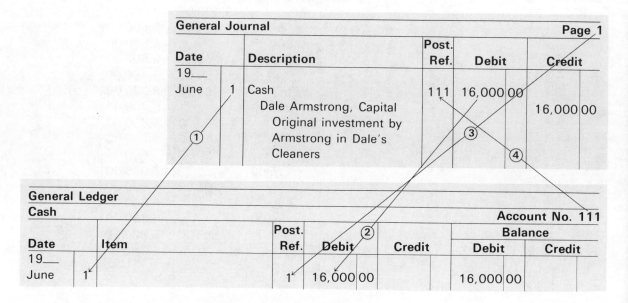

General Journal   Page 1

Date		Description	Post. Ref.	Debit	Credit
19__					
June	1	Cash	111	16,000 00	
		Dale Armstrong, Capital			16,000 00
		Original investment by			
		Armstrong in Dale's			
		Cleaners			

General Ledger

Cash   Account No. 111

Date		Item	Post. Ref.	Debit	Credit	Balance Debit	Credit
19__							
June	1		1	16,000 00		16,000 00	

And now we post the credit part of the entry.

General Journal   Page 1

Date			Description	Post. Ref.	Debit	Credit
19__						
June	1		Cash	111	16,000 00	
			Dale Armstrong, Capital	311		16,000 00
			Original investment by		③	②
			Armstrong in Dale's			
	①		Cleaners			④

General Ledger

Dale Armstrong, Capital   **Account No. 311**

Date		Item	Post. Ref.	Debit	Credit	Balance Debit	Balance Credit
19__							
June	1		1		16,000 00		16,000 00

Entering the account number in the Posting Reference column of the journal should be the last step. It acts as a verification of the three preceding steps.

The accountant usually uses the Item column only at the end of a financial period. The words that may appear in this column are *balance, closing, adjusting,* and *reversing.* We'll introduce all these terms later.

Follow the four steps in the recording of the second transaction.

General Journal   Page 1

Date			Description	Post. Ref.	Debit	Credit
June	2		Equipment	121	9,000 00	
			Cash	111		9,000 00
			Bought equipment for			
			cash			

General Ledger

Cash   **Account No. 111**

Date		Item	Post. Ref.	Debit	Credit	Balance Debit	Balance Credit
19__							
June	1		1	16,000 00		16,000 00	
	2		1		9,000 00	7,000 00	

Equipment								Account No. 121	
			Post.				Balance		
Date	Item		Ref.	Debit	Credit		Debit	Credit	
19__									
June	2		1	9,000 00			9,000 00		

Now we are ready to look at the journal entries for the first month of operation for Dale's Cleaners. As you can see from the general journal and general ledger on the following pages, the Posting Reference column has been filled in, since the posting has been completed.

General Journal				Page 1	
Date	Description	Post. Ref.	Debit	Credit	
19__					
June	1	Cash	111	16,000 00	
		Dale Armstrong, Capital	311		16,000 00
		Original investment by Armstrong in Dale's Cleaners			
	2	Equipment	121	9,000 00	
		Cash	111		9,000 00
		Bought equipment for cash			
	2	Equipment	121	2,000 00	
		Accounts Payable	211		2,000 00
		Bought equipment on account from Johnson Equipment Company			
	4	Accounts Payable	211	500 00	
		Cash	111		500 00
		Paid Johnson Equipment Company on account			
	4	Supplies	113	200 00	
		Accounts Payable	211		200 00
		Bought cleaning fluids on account from Acme Supply Company			
	7	Cash	111	300 00	
		Income from Services	411		300 00
		For week ended June 7			

General Journal   Page 1 (cont.)

Date		Description	Post. Ref.	Debit		Credit	
June	8	Rent Expense	512	200	00		
		Cash	111			200	00
		For month ended					
		June 30					

General Journal   Page 2

Date		Description	Post. Ref.	Debit		Credit	
19__							
June	10	Wages Expense	511	120	00		
		Cash	111			120	00
		Paid wages, June 1 to					
		June 10					
	10	Prepaid Insurance	114	160	00		
		Cash	111			160	00
		Premium for 2-year					
		liability insurance					
	14	Cash	111	380	00		
		Income from Services	411			380	00
		For week ended June 14					
	14	Advertising Expense	513	90	00		
		Accounts Payable	211			90	00
		Received bill for adv.					
		from *Daily News*					
	15	Accounts Payable	211	900	00		
		Cash	111			900	00
		Paid Johnson Equipment					
		Company on account					
	15	Utilities Expense	514	110	00		
		Cash	111			110	00
		Paid bill for utilities					
	15	Accounts Payable	211	90	00		
		Cash	111			90	00
		Paid *Daily News* for					
		advertising					

General Journal   Page 2 (cont.)

Date		Description	Post. Ref.	Debit	Credit
June	21	Cash	111	415 00	
		Income from Services	411		415 00
		For week ended June 21			

General Journal   Page 3

Date		Description	Post. Ref.	Debit	Credit
19__					
June	23	Accounts Receivable	112	40 00	
		Income from Services	411		40 00
		Ace Rental, for services rendered			
	24	Wages Expense	511	195 00	
		Cash	111		195 00
		Paid wages, June 11 to June 24			
	26	Equipment	121	140 00	
		Accounts Payable	211		140 00
		Bought equipment on account from Johnson Equipment Company			
	30	Cash	111	480 00	
		Income from Services	411		480 00
		For remainder of June, ended June 30			
	30	Cash	111	30 00	
		Accounts Receivable	112		30 00
		Ace Rental, to apply on account			
	30	Dale Armstrong, Drawing	312	500 00	
		Cash	111		500 00
		Withdrawal for personal use			

General Ledger

Cash
Account No. 111

Date		Item	Post. Ref.	Debit		Credit		Balance Debit		Balance Credit	
19__											
June	1		1	16,000	00			16,000	00		
	2		1			9,000	00	7,000	00		
	4		1			500	00	6,500	00		
	7		1	300	00			6,800	00		
	8		1			200	00	6,600	00		
	10		2			120	00	6,480	00		
	10		2			160	00	6,320	00		
	14		2	380	00			6,700	00		
	15		2			900	00	5,800	00		
	15		2			110	00	5,690	00		
	15		2			90	00	5,600	00		
	21		2	415	00			6,015	00		
	24		3			195	00	5,820	00		
	30		3	480	00			6,300	00		
	30		3	30	00			6,330	00		
	30		3			500	00	5,830	00		

Accounts Receivable
Account No. 112

Date		Item	Post. Ref.	Debit		Credit		Balance Debit		Balance Credit	
19__											
June	23		3	40	00			40	00		
	30		3			30	00	10	00		

Supplies
Account No. 113

Date		Item	Post. Ref.	Debit		Credit		Balance Debit		Balance Credit	
19__											
June	4		1	200	00			200	00		

Prepaid Insurance
Account No. 114

Date		Item	Post. Ref.	Debit		Credit		Balance Debit		Balance Credit	
19__											
June	10		2	160	00			160	00		

Equipment   Account No. 121

Date		Item	Post. Ref.	Debit		Credit		Balance Debit		Credit	
19__											
June	2		1	9,000	00			9,000	00		
	2		1	2,000	00			11,000	00		
	26		3	140	00			11,140	00		

Accounts Payable   Account No. 211

Date		Item	Post. Ref.	Debit		Credit		Balance Debit		Credit	
19__											
June	2		1			2,000	00			2,000	00
	4		1	500	00					1,500	00
	4		1			200	00			1,700	00
	14		2			90	00			1,790	00
	15		2	900	00					890	00
	15		2	90	00					800	00
	26		3			140	00			940	00

Dale Armstrong, Capital   Account No. 311

Date		Item	Post. Ref.	Debit		Credit		Balance Debit		Credit	
19__											
June	1		1			16,000	00			16,000	00

Dale Armstrong, Drawing   Account No. 312

Date		Item	Post. Ref.	Debit		Credit		Balance Debit		Credit	
19__											
June	30		3	500	00			500	00		

Income from Services   Account No. 411

Date		Item	Post. Ref.	Debit		Credit		Balance Debit		Credit	
19__											
June	7		1			300	00			300	00
	14		2			380	00			680	00
	21		2			415	00			1,095	00
	23		3			40	00			1,135	00
	30		3			480	00			1,615	00

Wages Expense   Account No. 511

Date		Item	Post. Ref.	Debit	Credit	Balance Debit	Balance Credit
19__							
June	10		2	120 00		120 00	
	24		3	195 00		315 00	

Rent Expense   Account No. 512

Date		Item	Post. Ref.	Debit	Credit	Balance Debit	Balance Credit
19__							
June	8		1	200 00		200 00	

Advertising Expense   Account No. 513

Date		Item	Post. Ref.	Debit	Credit	Balance Debit	Balance Credit
19__							
June	14		2	90 00		90 00	

Utilities Expense   Account No. 514

Date		Item	Post. Ref.	Debit	Credit	Balance Debit	Balance Credit
19__							
June	15		2	110 00		110 00	

All right, now let's strike a trial balance.

Dale's Cleaners
Trial Balance
June 30, 19__

	Debit	Credit
Cash	5,830 00	
Accounts Receivable	10 00	
Supplies	200 00	
Prepaid Insurance	160 00	
Equipment	11,140 00	
Accounts Payable		940 00
Dale Armstrong, Capital		16,000 00
Dale Armstrong, Drawing	500 00	
Income from Services		1,615 00
Wages Expense	315 00	
Rent Expense	200 00	
Advertising Expense	90 00	
Utilities Expense	110 00	
	18,555 00	18,555 00

Summary

The journal is a chronological record of the business transactions of a firm. The first step in the accounting process is recording the transactions in the journal. Each journal entry should be based on some material evidence that a transaction has occurred, such as a sales invoice, a receipt, a check, etc. The second step in the accounting process is posting to the T accounts in the ledger. This step consists of transferring the amounts to the debit or credit columns of the specified accounts in the ledger, using a cross-reference system. The *ledger* is the book in which all accounts are kept. Accounts are placed in the ledger according to the account numbers in the chart of accounts. After one has journalized and posted a group of transactions for a period of time, one prepares a trial balance to prove that the totals of the debit balances and of the credit balances of the ledger accounts are equal.

Glossary

o **Account numbers** The numbers assigned to accounts according to the chart of accounts.

o **Chart of accounts** The official list of the ledger accounts in which the transactions of a business are to be recorded.

o **Journal** The book in which a person originally records business transactions; commonly referred to as a *book of original entry*.

o **Journalizing** The process of recording a business transaction in a journal.

o **Posting** The process of recording accounting entries in ledger accounts, the source of information being a journal.

o **Running balance** The balance of an account after the recording of each transaction.

Exercises

Exercise 1 In the two-column general journal below, the capital letters represent parts of a journal entry. In the blanks provided, record the letter which indicates where in the journal the items are recorded.

General Journal		Post. Ref.	Debit	Credit	Page ___
Date	Description				
L M	N O	R S	T	U	
	P				
	Q				

___ Title of account credited
___ Year
___ Amount of debit
___ Explanation
___ Ledger account number of account debited
___ Month
___ Title of account debited
___ Day of the month

Exercise 2 The accounts of Groening Realty on December 31 of this year are listed below in alphabetical order. Prepare a trial balance, with a three-line heading, and list the accounts in the proper sequence.

Accounts Payable	$ 2,400
Accounts Receivable	16,200
Automobile	4,000
Building	30,000
Cash	7,600
G. C. Groening, Capital	68,600
Land	8,000
Office Equipment	5,200

Exercise 3 Record the balance of the following ledger account, inserting the appropriate footings.

Accounts Payable

1,300	6,200
2,700	4,800
900	2,300
1,800	

Exercise 4 How would the following entry be posted?

General Journal Page 1

Date	Description	Post. Ref.	Debit	Credit
19__				
Sept. 1	Cash		3,662 00	
	Shop Equipment		2,184 00	
	R. E. Stanfield, Capital			5,846 00
	Original investment in			
	Stanfield Auto Repair			

General Ledger

Cash Account No. 111

Date	Item	Post. Ref.	Debit	Credit	Balance Debit	Balance Credit

Shop Equipment Account No. 121

Date	Item	Post. Ref.	Debit	Credit	Balance Debit	Balance Credit

R. E. Stanfield, Capital Account No. 411

Date	Item	Post. Ref.	Debit	Credit	Balance Debit	Balance Credit

Exercise 5 The following transactions of Miller Office Supply occurred during this year. Journalize the transactions in general journal form, including brief explanations.

May	5	Bought equipment for $6,000 from Denton Equipment Company, paying $1,500 down; balance due in 30 days.
	9	Paid wages for the period May 1 through 7, $620.
	11	Billed Randolph Motor Inn for services performed, $162.

Exercise 6 Enter the following transactions of the Langdon Soft-Water Service in a general journal. Include a brief explanation of the transaction as part of each journal entry.

June	3	Collected $632 from William Rae, a charge customer.
	8	Issued a check for $324 in full payment of an Accounts Payable to Fouch and Stevens.
	9	The owner, C. T. Langdon, withdrew $416 in cash for personal use.

Exercise 7 For the Spic 'n' Span Cleaning Service, the accountant has recommended the following accounts to be used in recording transactions on the firm's books. Arrange the accounts in a chart of accounts.

311	B. R. Snow, Capital
112	Accounts Receivable
511	Wages Expense
113	Cleaning Supplies
212	Accounts Payable
516	Telephone Expense
411	Cleaning Service Income
121	Truck
111	Cash
122	Cleaning Equipment
514	Truck Repair Expense
211	Notes Payable
512	Payroll Tax Expense
515	Advertising Expense
513	Truck Operating Expense
412	Window Washing Income
517	Miscellaneous Expense
312	B. R. Snow, Drawing

Exercise 8 Which of the following errors would cause unequal totals in a trial balance? Explain why.

a An accountant recorded a payment of $165 to a creditor by a debit to Accounts Payable of $65 and a credit to Cash of $165.

b An accountant recorded a withdrawal of $60 in cash by the owner as a debit to Accounts Payable of $60 and a credit to Cash of $60.

c An accountant recorded a $20 payment for Supplies as a debit to Supplies of $22 and a credit to Cash of $22.

Problem 4-1 The chart of accounts of the Model Launderette is given below, after which is a list of the transactions that took place during July.

	Assets
111	Cash
112	Accounts Receivable
121	Equipment
131	Supplies

	Liabilities
211	Accounts Payable

	Owner's Equity
311	A. K. Rogers, Capital
312	A. K. Rogers, Drawing

	Revenue
411	Income from Services

	Expenses
511	Wages Expense
512	Rent Expense
513	Utilities Expense
514	Repair Expense

July	1	Paid rent for July, $180.
	2	Sold services for cash, $90.
	3	Bought laundry soap on account, $36, from Argus Supply Company.
	5	Billed Tempe Athletic Club for services performed, $120.
	9	Paid electric bill, $72.
	15	Paid wages to employees, $160, for 2 weeks.
	16	Sold services for cash, $110.
	17	Bought equipment on account, $450, from Ambrose and Son.
	21	Received $105 from Tempe Athletic Club on account.
	25	Paid $36 to Argus Supply Company on account.
	28	Received bill for repairs to equipment, $32, Nowell Repair Shop.
	30	Sold services for cash, $216.
	31	Billed Edwards Hotel for services performed, $226.
	31	Paid wages to employees, $180, for 2 weeks.
	31	A. K. Rogers withdrew $120 in cash for personal use.

Instructions Record the transactions in a general journal, with a brief explanation for each entry. Start numbering the journal with page 26.

Problem 4-2 or 4-2A The journal entries in the Workbook relate to Dale's Cleaners for Dale Armstrong's second month of operation. The balances of the accounts as of July 1 have been recorded in the accounts in the ledger.

Instructions

1 Post the journal entries to ledger accounts.
2 Prepare a trial balance as of July 31.

Problem 4-3 Valley Telephone Answering Service had the following transactions during March of this year. The chart of accounts is as follows.

	Assets
111	Cash
112	Accounts Receivable
121	Office Equipment
131	Supplies

	Liabilities
211	Accounts Payable

	Owner's Equity
311	Joan Canfield, Capital
312	Joan Canfield, Drawing

	Revenue
411	Income from Fees

	Expenses
511	Rent Expense
512	Equipment Rental Expense
513	Advertising Expense
514	Telephone Expense
515	Utilities Expense
516	Miscellaneous Expense

March	2	Canfield transferred cash from a personal bank account to an account to be used for the business, $920.
	2	Paid rent for the month, $150.
	3	Paid $70 as rental for telephone equipment.
	3	Bought desk and chair on account, $115, from Roberts Supply Company.
	4	Paid cash for stationery and other supplies, $75.
	5	Billed charge customers for services rendered, $90.
	7	Bought filing cabinet for cash, $18.
	7	Received and paid bill for newspaper advertising, $26.
	9	Bought typewriter from Hendrick Equipment Company for $150. Paid $30 as a downpayment; balance due in 30 days.
	11	Billed charge customers for services rendered, $120.
	16	Paid Roberts Supply Company $65 to apply on account.

March 21	Collected $80 from charge customers to apply on account.
28	Paid electric bill for the month, $16.
28	Paid telephone bill, $33.
29	Paid $6 for delivery charges (Miscellaneous Expense).
30	Billed charge customers on account, $360.
31	Canfield withdrew $205 in cash for personal use.

Instructions

1 Record the transactions in the general journal, with a brief explanation for each entry. Start numbering the journal with page 1.

2 Post the entries to the ledger accounts.

3 Prepare a trial balance dated March 31.

Problem 4-4 The chart of accounts of S. A. Walsh, M.D., is as follows.

	Assets
111	Cash
112	Accounts Receivable
113	Supplies
114	Prepaid Insurance
121	Equipment

	Liabilities
211	Accounts Payable

	Owner's Equity
311	S. A. Walsh, Capital
312	S. A. Walsh, Drawing

	Revenue
411	Professional Fees

	Expenses
511	Salary Expense
512	Laboratory Expense
513	Rent Expense
514	Utilities Expense

Dr. Walsh completed the following transactions during September.

Sept. 2	Bought laboratory equipment on account, $620.
2	Paid office rent for the month, $400.
3	Bought bandages and other supplies on account, $55.
5	Received cash on account from patients, $2,600.
7	Paid cash to creditors on account, $840.
9	Received and paid bill for laboratory analyses, $175.
11	Billed patients on account for professional services rendered, $1,420.
13	Paid cash for property insurance policy for the year, $40.

Sept. 15	Part of the laboratory equipment purchased on Sept. 2 was defective. Returned the equipment and received a reduction in bill, $40.
16	Received cash for professional services, $260.
29	Paid salary of nurse, $620.
30	Received and paid telephone bill for the month, $26.
30	Received and paid electric bill, $85.
30	Billed patients on account for professional services rendered, $940.
30	Dr. Walsh withdrew $975 in cash for personal use.

Instructions

1 Journalize the transactions for September.
2 Post the entries to the ledger accounts.
3 Prepare a trial balance as of September 30.

Problem 4-1A Here is the chart of accounts of the Moderne Laundry, followed by the transactions that took place during June.

	Assets
111	Cash
112	Accounts Receivable
121	Equipment
131	Supplies

	Liabilities
211	Accounts Payable

	Owner's Equity
311	A. D. Boyd, Capital
312	A. D. Boyd, Drawing

	Revenue
411	Income from Services

	Expenses
511	Wages Expense
512	Rent Expense
513	Utilities Expense
514	Repair Expense

June	1	Paid rent for June, $220.
	3	Sold services for cash, $123.
	5	Billed Orlando Bright Spot for services performed, $181.
	6	Bought laundry soap on account, $42, from Model Supply Company.
	9	Paid electric bill, $76.
	16	Paid wages to employees, $175, for 2 weeks.
	19	Received $156 from Orlando Bright Spot on account.

June 20	Bought equipment on account, $460, from Niebauer Equipment Company.
22	Sold services for cash, $162.
24	Paid $42 to Model Supply Company, paying account in full.
29	Sold services for cash, $318.
30	Billed NuWay Motel for services performed, $302.
30	Paid wages to employees, $185, for 2 weeks.
30	Received bill for repairs to equipment, $39, Holman Repair Shop.
30	A. D. Boyd withdrew $315 in cash for personal use.

Instructions Record the transactions in a general journal, explaining each entry briefly. Number the journal page 29.

Problem 4-3A Valley Telephone Answering Service had the following transactions during March of this year. The chart of accounts is as follows.

	Assets
111	Cash
112	Accounts Receivable
121	Office Equipment
131	Supplies

	Liabilities
211	Accounts Payable

	Owner's Equity
311	Joan Canfield, Capital
312	Joan Canfield, Drawing

	Revenue
411	Income from Fees

	Expenses
511	Rent Expense
512	Equipment Rental Expense
513	Advertising Expense
514	Telephone Expense
515	Utilities Expense
516	Miscellaneous Expense

March 2	Canfield transferred cash from a personal bank account to an account to be used for the business, $760.
2	Paid rent for the month, $165.
3	Bought desk and chair on account, $135, from Roberts Supply Company.
3	Paid $76 as rental for telephone equipment.
4	Bought filing cabinet for cash, $29.
5	Paid cash for stationery and other supplies, $78.

March	7	Billed charge customers for services rendered, $106.
	10	Bought typewriter for $180; paid $35 as downpayment; balance due to Hendrick Equipment Company in 30 days.
	14	Billed charge customers for services rendered, $162.
	17	Paid Roberts Supply Company, $135, in full payment of account.
	22	Collected $94 from charge customers to apply on account.
	27	Paid telephone bill, $47.
	29	Paid electric bill for the month, $16.
	29	Paid $7 for delivery charges (Miscellaneous Expense).
	31	Billed charge customers on account, $416.
	31	Canfield withdrew $200 in cash for personal use.
	31	Received bill for advertising, $57.

Instructions

1 Record the transactions in the general journal, giving a brief explanation for each entry. Number the journal page 1.

2 Post to the ledger accounts.

3 Prepare a trial balance dated March 31.

Problem 4-4A The chart of accounts of S. A. Walsh, M.D., is as follows.

	Assets
111	Cash
112	Accounts Receivable
113	Supplies
114	Prepaid Insurance
121	Equipment

	Liabilities
211	Accounts Payable

	Owner's Equity
311	S. A. Walsh, Capital
312	S. A. Walsh, Drawing

	Revenue
411	Professional Fees

	Expenses
511	Salary Expense
512	Laboratory Expense
513	Rent Expense
514	Utilities Expense

Dr. Walsh completed the following transactions during September.

Sept.	2	Bought laboratory equipment on account, $717, from Aston Surgical Supply Company.
	2	Paid office rent for the month, $465.
	3	Received cash on account from patients, $2,720.
	6	Bought bandages and other supplies on account, $59.
	10	Received and paid bill for laboratory analyses, $183.
	12	Paid cash for property insurance policy, $46.
	13	Billed patients on account for professional services rendered, $1,518.
	16	Received cash for professional services, $281 (patients not billed previously).
	17	Part of the laboratory equipment purchased on Sept. 2 was defective; returned equipment and received a reduction in bill, $49.
	23	Received cash for professional services, $285.
	30	Paid salary of nurse, $640.
	30	Received and paid telephone bill for the month, $32.
	30	Billed patients on account for professional services rendered, $1,015.
	30	Dr. Walsh withdrew $1,010 in cash for personal use.

Instructions

1 Journalize the transactions for September.
2 Post the entries to the ledger accounts.
3 Prepare a trial balance as of September 30.

5 Adjustments and the work sheet

I hear, and I forget. I see, and I remember. I do, and I understand. Chinese proverb

Specific objectives

After you have completed this chapter, you will be able to:
- Complete a work sheet for a service-type enterprise, involving adjustments for supplies consumed, expired insurance, depreciation, and accrued wages.
- Prepare an income statement and a balance sheet for a service-type business directly from the work sheet.
- Journalize the adjusting entries.

Introduction

Now that you have become familiar with the classifying and recording phase of accounting for a service-type enterprise, let's look at the remaining steps in the accounting procedure, to give you a feel for the scope of accounting operations, as embodied in the accounting cycle.

Fiscal period

The *fiscal period* or *year* is 12 consecutive months. It does not necessarily have to coincide with the calendar year. If a business has seasonal peaks, it's a good idea to complete the accounting operations at the end of the most active season. At that time the management wants to know the results of the year and how they stand financially. As an example, the fiscal period of a resort that is operated during the summer months may be from October 1 of one year to September 30 of the next year. Government, at all levels, has a fiscal period from July 1 of one year to June 30 of the following year. Department stores often use a fiscal period extending from February 1 of one year to January 31 of the next year. For income tax purposes, any period of 12 consecutive months may be selected. However, you have to be consistent and continue to use the same fiscal period, as a change can be made only with permission from the Internal Revenue Service.

The accounting cycle

The *accounting cycle* represents the entire accounting process that takes place between the beginning and the end of a fiscal period. In Chapter 4 we summarized the first four steps in the accounting cycle. Here are the remaining steps and their placement in this text: Chapters 5 and 6 cover a service-type enterprise; Chapters 11 and 12 cover a merchandising-type enterprise.

The steps in the accounting cycle are as follows:

1 Record business transactions in a journal.	
2 Post to the accounts in the ledger.	Chapter 4
3 Prepare a trial balance.	
4 Compile adjustment data and record the adjusting entries in the work sheet.	Chapters 5 and 11
5 Complete the work sheet.	
6 Complete the financial statements.	Chapters 1, 2, and 12
7 Journalize and post adjusting entries.	Chapters 5 and 11
8 Journalize and post closing entries.	Chapters 6 and 12
9 Prepare a post-closing trial balance.	Chapters 6 and 12
10 Journalize and post reversing entries.	Chapter 12

First we shall complete the entire accounting cycle for a service type of business and for a professional enterprise, because the accounting involved in these types of economic units is fairly elementary. That is why we have talked about Dale's Cleaners (representing a service type of business). To show you the accounts for a professional enterprise, Chapter 7 will present the transactions of Dr. John A. Tanner. We'll go through the entire accounting cycle for each of these illustrations. Our next project will be merchandising enterprises, and this will involve introducing special journals, as well as an array of additional adjustments.

This summary has brought you up to date on what we have accomplished thus far, and what we hope to do in the future. The chapters that are not listed above cover additional topics about the steps in the accounting cycle.

The work sheet

At the moment we are concerned with the *work sheet.* As we said in listing the steps of the accounting cycle, the work sheet is a prelude to the preparation of financial statements. Thus the work sheet serves as a medium for recording necessary adjustments and for furnishing the account balances for making up the income statement and balance sheet. We described the income statement and balance sheet that we looked at in Chapter 2 as being tentative, in that adjustments had not been recorded at that time. Often accountants refer to the work sheet as *working papers,* in the sense that the work sheet is a tool accountants use to bring all the accounts up to date. Accountants use pencil to make entries in the work sheet, since it is a working document.

The columns of the work sheet

When you use a work sheet, you do not have to write the trial balance on a separate sheet of paper, since you record it in the first two columns of the work sheet.

Let's continue with the illustration of Dale's Cleaners. First we fill in the heading, consisting of three lines: the name of the company, the title of the statement, and the period of time covered by the statement.

Dale's Cleaners
Work Sheet
For month ended June 30, 19___

Account Name	Trial Balance		Adjustments		Adjusted Trial Balance	
	Debit	Credit	Debit	Credit	Debit	Credit
Cash	5,830 00					
Accounts Receivable	10 00					
Equipment	11,140 00					
Supplies	200 00					
Prepaid Insurance	160 00					
Accounts Payable		940 00				
Dale Armstrong, Capital		16,000 00				
Dale Armstrong, Drawing	500 00					
Income from Services		1,615 00				
Wages Expense	315 00					
Rent Expense	200 00					
Advertising Expense	90 00					
Utilities Expense	110 00					
	18,555 00	18,555 00				

We have seen that the trial balance is merely a statement of the Trial Balance Equation. The normal balance of every account is on the plus side. To accentuate this fact, we have written the word *balance* on the plus side of each account classification.

Assets +		Expenses =		Liabilities +		Revenue +		Owner's Equity	
+	−	+	−	−	+	−	+	−	+
Balance		Balance			Balance		Balance		Balance

In making up the trial balance, we list the accounts as they appear according to the chart of accounts in the ledger. This gives us the following order.

100s	Assets
200s	Liabilities
300s	Owner's Equity
400s	Revenue
500s	Expenses

Trial Balance

Debit	Credit
100s ⟶ Assets	
	Liabilities ⟵ 200s
	Owner's Equity ⟵ 300s
	Revenue ⟵ 400s
500s ⟶ Expenses	

We have seen that the income statement, in abbreviated form, is:

Revenue
–
Expenses
=
Net Income
or
Net Loss

Income Statement

Debit	Credit
	Revenue
Expenses	

The balance sheet, in abbreviated form, is:

Assets
=
Liabilities
+
Owner's Equity

Balance Sheet

Debit	Credit
Assets	
	Liabilities
	Owner's Equity

Now we combine all these in the work sheet. It is vitally important that you know the placement of the classifications of accounts in the various columns. Observe that all five classifications are placed in the Trial Balance and Adjusted Trial Balance columns. The up-to-date balances are taken directly from the Adjusted Trial Balance columns, with the revenue and expense accounts in the Income Statement columns, and the assets, liabilities, and owner's equity accounts in the Balance Sheet columns.

Account Name	Trial Balance		Adjustments		Adjusted Trial Balance		Income Statement		Balance Sheet	
	Debit	Credit	Debit	Credit	Debit	Credit	Debit	Credit	Debit	Credit
	A				A				→A	
		L				L				→L
		OE				OE				→ OE
		R				R		→R		
	E				E	→E				

99 The work sheet

Adjustments

We can best describe the use of the Adjustments and Adjusted Trial Balance columns by drawing an analogy with a television set. Adjustments are an effort to "fine-tune" the account balances that appear in the trial balance. One may compare this to fine-tuning a television set in order to get the best possible picture. In the accounting sense, we want to get the best possible picture of the income statement and the balance sheet.

Adjustments may be considered internal transactions. They have not been recorded in the accounts up to this time because no outside party has been involved. In the steps of the accounting cycle, as stipulated in Chapter 4, one determines the adjustments after the trial balance has been prepared.

The accounts that require adjusting are few in number, and after a limited exposure one can readily recognize them. They are applicable to service as well as merchandising businesses. To describe the reasons for—and techniques of handling—adjustments, let's return to the illustration of Dale's Cleaners. First, let's select the accounts that require adjustments. For the moment, we'll show the adjusting entries by T accounts; later on we'll record them in the work sheet and journalize them.

Supplies In the trial balance, the Supplies account has a balance of $200. Each time Dale's Cleaners bought supplies, Armstrong wrote the entry as a debit to Supplies and a credit to either Cash or Accounts Payable. So he recorded each purchase of supplies as an increase in the Supplies account.

But we haven't taken into consideration the fact that any business is continually consuming supplies in the process of carrying on business operations. For Dale's Cleaners, the items recorded under Supplies consist of cleaning fluids. At the end of the month, obviously some of these supplies have been used. It would be very time-consuming to keep a continual record of the exact amount of supplies on hand; so at the end of the month someone takes a physical count of the amount on hand.

Accordingly, Armstrong takes an inventory on June 30, and he finds that there are $160 worth of supplies left. The situation looks like this:

Had	$200	(Recorded under Supplies)
−Have left	−160	(Determined by taking an inventory)
=Used	$ 40	(The amount used is an expense of doing business. This is Supplies Expense.)

To correct the books, Armstrong has to make an *adjusting entry*. Let's look at this in the form of T accounts.

Supplies		Supplies Expense	
+	−	+	−
Balance 200	Adjusting 40	Adjusting 40	

Drawing T accounts on scratch paper is an excellent way of organizing the adjusting entry. By making this entry, Armstrong has merely taken the amount used out of Supplies and put it into Supplies Expense. The new balance of Supplies, $160, represents the true figure for the asset section of the balance sheet, and the $40 figure in Supplies Expense represents the true figure for the expense section of the income statement.

Prepaid Insurance The $160 balance in Prepaid Insurance stands for the premium paid in advance for a 2-year liability insurance policy. One month of the premium has now expired, which amounts to

$$24 \text{ months} \overline{)\$160.00} \quad \$ \ 6.67 \text{ per month}$$

In the adjustment, Armstrong deducts the expired or used portion from Prepaid Insurance and transfers it to Insurance Expense.

Prepaid Insurance		Insurance Expense	
+	−	+	−
Balance 160	Adjusting 6.67	Adjusting 6.67	

Now he records Prepaid Insurance in the asset section of the balance sheet at its true amount, $153.33 ($160 minus $6.67). Then he writes Insurance Expense in the expense section of the income statement.

Depreciation of equipment We have followed the policy of recording durable items such as appliances and fixtures under Equipment, because they will last longer than 1 year. However, since these assets will eventually have to be replaced, we should systematically apportion their costs over the period of their useful lives. In other words, we write off the cost of the assets as an expense, and call it *depreciation,* because such equipment depreciates, or loses usefulness. In the case of Dale's Cleaners, the Equipment account has a balance of $11,140. Suppose that we estimate that Armstrong's dry cleaning equipment will have a useful life of 10 years, and will have *no* value at the end of the tenth year. The depreciation for 1 month is

$$10 \text{ years} \overline{)\$11,400 \text{ cost}} \quad \$ \ 1,140 \text{ per year}$$

$$12 \text{ months} \overline{)\$1,140 \text{ per year}} \quad \$ \ 95 \text{ per month}$$

One always records this as a debit to Depreciation Expense and a credit to Accumulated Depreciation. On the balance sheet, the balance of Accumulated Depreciation is a deduction from the balance of the Assets account; Accumulated Depreciation is contrary to Assets, so we call it a *contra* account.

To show the accounts under their proper headings, let's look at the Trial Balance Equation.

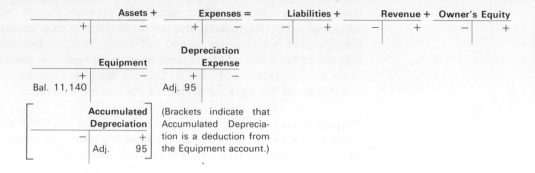

Assets +		Expenses =		Liabilities +		Revenue +		Owner's Equity	
+	−	+	−	−	+	−	+	−	+

Equipment		Depreciation Expense	
+	−	+	−
Bal. 11,140		Adj. 95	

Accumulated Depreciation		(Brackets indicate that Accumulated Depreciation is a deduction from the Equipment account.)
−	+	
	Adj. 95	

Incidentally, there are a number of legally recognized ways of computing depreciation. The method illustrated here is the *straight-line method,* in which one apportions the cost of the asset, less any trade-in value, on an average basis over the useful life of the asset. Regardless of the method used, however, the accounts that are debited and credited are always the same. Accumulated Depreciation, as the title implies, is the total depreciation that the owner has taken since the original purchase of the asset. Rather than crediting the Equipment account, Armstrong uses a separate account to keep track of the total depreciation that he has taken since he first acquired the asset. The maximum depreciation that he could take would be the cost of the equipment, which in this case is $11,140. So, month after month, the Accumulated Depreciation will increase at the rate of $95 per month, assuming that he hasn't bought any additional equipment. The *book value* of an asset is the cost of the asset minus the accumulated depreciation.

Wages expense Usually the end of the fiscal period and the end of the employees' payroll period do not fall on the same day. By diagram it looks like this.

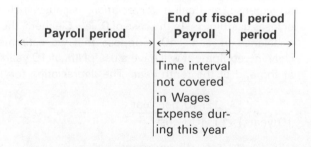

As an illustration, assume that a firm pays its employees a total of $100 per day, and that payday falls on Friday throughout the year. When the employees pick up their paychecks on Friday, at the end of the work day, the amount of the checks includes their wages for that day as well as for the preceding 4 days. The employees work a 5-day week. And suppose that the last day of the fiscal period falls on Wednesday, December 31. We can diagram this as shown on the next page.

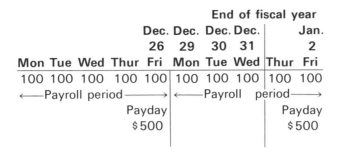

End of fiscal year

									Jan.
Dec. 26	Dec. 29	Dec. 30	Dec. 31						2
Mon	Tue	Wed	Thur	Fri	Mon	Tue	Wed	Thur	Fri
100	100	100	100	100	100	100	100	100	100

←——Payroll period——→ ←——Payroll period——→

Payday $500   Payday $500

December

S	M	T	W	T	F	S
	1	2	3	4	⑤	6
7	8	9	10	11	⑫	13
14	15	16	17	18	⑲	20	→Paydays
21	22	23	24	25	㉖	27
28	29	30	31			

In order to show the true amount of the Wages Expense, you should add an extra $300 for the amount incurred between the last payday, December 26, and the end of the year, December 31. You should also add the $300 to Wages Payable, a liability account, to show that the firm owes the additional $300.

Wages Expense		Wages Payable	
+	−	−	+
Adjusting 300			Adjusting 300

Returning to our illustration of Dale's Cleaners: The last payday was June 24. Dale's Cleaners owes an additional $50 in wages at the end of the month. Accountants refer to this extra amount that has not been recorded at the end of the month as being *accrued*.

Wages Expense		Wages Payable	
+	−	−	+
Balance 315			Adjusting 50
Adjusting 50			

First we have to record the adjustments in the work sheet.

Before doing so, however, let's digress briefly to recapitulate the work sheet, with the addition of the Drawing and Accumulated Depreciation accounts, as well as the net income. The Drawing account looks like this:

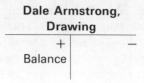

Dale Armstrong, Drawing

+	−
Balance	

Drawing is a deduction from owner's equity, and is shown in the column opposite the normal balance of the Owner's Equity (Capital) account. The Accumulated Depreciation account looks like this:

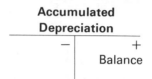

Accumulated Depreciation

−	+
	Balance

Accumulated Depreciation is a deduction from the respective Asset account, and, as we have said, it is shown in the column opposite the normal balance of the Asset account. *Net income* is the difference between revenue and expenses. It is used to balance off the Income Statement columns, and, since revenue is larger than expenses, it must be added to the expense side. Net income (or net loss) is also used to balance off the Balance Sheet columns. And, as in the statement of owner's equity itself, one adds net income to the owner's equity; similarly, one deducts net loss from owner's equity.

Account Name	Trial Balance		Adjustments		Adjusted Trial Balance		Income Statement		Balance Sheet	
	Debit	Credit	Debit	Credit	Debit	Credit	Debit	Credit	Debit	Credit
	A	L			A	L			A	L
	+	+			+	+			+	+
	E	R			E	R	E	R	Draw.	OE
	+	+			+	+				+
	Draw.	OE			Draw.	OE				Accum.
		+				+				Depr.
		Accum.				Accum.				
		Depr.				Depr.				
Net Income							NI			NI

On the other hand, if expenses are larger than revenue, the result is a net loss. One must add net loss to the revenue side to balance off the Income Statement columns. Also, because one deducts a net loss from the owner's equity, one includes net loss in the debit side of the Balance Sheet columns, thereby balancing off these columns. To show this, let's look at the Income Statement and Balance Sheet columns diagramed on the next page.

	Income Statement		Balance Sheet	
	Debit	Credit	Debit	Credit
			A	L
			+	+
			Draw.	OE
	E	R		+
				Accum.
				Depr.
Net Loss		NL	NL	

Adjustments columns of the work sheet

When we record adjustments, we identify them as **(a)**, **(b)**, **(c)**, and **(d)** to indicate the relationships between the debits and the credits.

Dale's Cleaners
Work Sheet
For month ended June 30, 19___

	Trial Balance		Adjustments	
	A + E + Draw.	L + R + OE + Accum. Depr.		
Account Name	Debit	Credit	Debit	Credit
Cash	5,830 00			
Accounts Receivable	10 00			
Supplies	200 00			(a) 40 00
Prepaid Insurance	160 00			(b) 6 67
Equipment	11,140 00			
Accounts Payable		940 00		
Dale Armstrong, Capital		16,000 00		
Dale Armstrong, Drawing	500 00			
Income from Services		1,615 00		
Wages Expense	315 00		(d) 50 00	
Rent Expense	200 00			
Advertising Expense	90 00			
Utilities Expense	110 00			
	18,555 00	18,555 00		
Supplies Expense			(a) 40 00	
Insurance Expense			(b) 6 67	
Depreciation Expense			(c) 95 00	
Accumulated Depreciation				(c) 95 00
Wages Payable				(d) 50 00
			191 67	191 67

Note that Supplies Expense, Insurance Expense, Depreciation Expense, and Wages Payable did not appear in the trial balance because there were no balances in the accounts to record. So we wrote them below the Trial Balance totals. Some people consider them to be new accounts, because they were never used during the fiscal period. But observe that they all have one thing in common: *They are all increased.* In other words, one brings a new account into existence in order to increase it; definitely not to decrease it. This hint can help you when it comes to formulating any adjusting entry. After the first fiscal period, Accumulated Depreciation will always have a balance, and consequently will be included in the trial balance.

Dale's Cleaners
Work Sheet
For month ended June 30, 19___

Account Name	Trial Balance	
	A + E + Draw.	L + R + OE + Accum. Depr.
	Debit	Credit
Cash	5,830 00	
Accounts Receivable	10 00	
Supplies	200 00	
Prepaid Insurance	160 00	
Equipment	11,140 00	
Accounts Payable		940 00
Dale Armstrong, Capital		16,000 00
Dale Armstrong, Drawing	500 00	
Income from Services		1,615 00
Wages Expense	315 00	
Rent Expense	200 00	
Advertising Expense	90 00	
Utilities Expense	110 00	
	18,555 00	18,555 00
Supplies Expense		
Insurance Expense		
Depreciation Expense		
Accumulated Depreciation		
Wages Payable		

Now we include the Adjusted Trial Balance columns, as shown below, bringing the balances of the accounts that were adjusted up to date.

After we get to the stage at which the Adjusted Trial Balance columns are completed, then we go through the mental process of classifying the accounts so that we know where to place the classifications in the various columns, and we record each account balance in the appropriate column. We now carry forward the amounts in the Adjusted Trial Balance columns to the remaining four columns, recording each amount in only one column. The completed work sheet is shown on pages 108–109.

Adjustments				Adjusted Trial Balance	
				A + E + Draw.	L + R + OE + Accum. Depr.
Debit		Credit		Debit	Credit
				5,830 00	
				10 00	
		(a)	40 00	160 00	
		(b)	6 67	153 33	
				11,140 00	
					940 00
					16,000 00
				500 00	
					1,615 00
(d)	50 00			365 00	
				200 00	
				90 00	
				110 00	
(a)	40 00			40 00	
(b)	6 67			6 67	
(c)	95 00			95 00	
		(c)	95 00		95 00
		(d)	50 00		50 00
	191 67		191 67	18,700 00	18,700 00

Dale's Cleaners
Work Sheet
For month ended June 30, 19___

Account Name	Trial Balance A + E + Draw. Debit	Trial Balance L + R + OE + Accum. Depr. Credit	Adjustments Debit		Adjustments Credit	
Cash	5,830 00					
Accounts Receivable	10 00					
Supplies	200 00				(a)	40 00
Prepaid Insurance	160 00				(b)	6 67
Equipment	11,140 00					
Accounts Payable		940 00				
Dale Armstrong, Capital		16,000 00				
Dale Armstrong, Drawing	500 00					
Income from Services		1,615 00				
Wages Expense	315 00		(d)	50 00		
Rent Expense	200 00					
Advertising Expense	90 00					
Utilities Expense	110 00					
	18,555 00	18,555 00				
Supplies Expense			(a)	40 00		
Insurance Expense			(b)	6 67		
Depreciation Expense			(c)	95 00		
Accumulated Depreciation					(c)	95 00
Wages Payable					(d)	50 00
				191 67		191 67
Net Income						

Accountants refer to accounts such as Supplies and Prepaid Insurance, as they appear in the trial balance, as being *mixed accounts*—accounts with balances that are partly income statement amounts and partly balance sheet amounts. For example, Supplies is recorded as $200 in the Trial Balance, but after adjustment this is apportioned as $40 in Supplies Expense in the Income Statement columns and $160 in Supplies in the Balance Sheet columns. Similarly, Prepaid Insurance is recorded as $160 in the trial bal-

Adjusted Trial Balance		Income Statement		Balance Sheet	
A + E + Draw.	L + R + OE + Accum. Depr.	E	R	A + Draw.	L + OE + Accum. Depr.
Debit	Credit	Debit	Credit	Debit	Credit
5,830 00				5,830 00	
10 00				10 00	
160 00				160 00	
153 33				153 33	
11,140 00				11,140 00	
	940 00				940 00
	16,000 00				16,000 00
500 00				500 00	
	1,615 00		1,615 00		
365 00		365 00			
200 00		200 00			
90 00		90 00			
110 00		110 00			
40 00		40 00			
6 67		6 67			
95 00		95 00			
	95 00				95 00
	50 00				50 00
18,700 00	18,700 00	906 67	1,615 00	17,793 33	17,085 00
		708 33			708 33
		1,615 00	1,615 00	17,793 33	17,793 33

ance, but is apportioned as $6.67 in Insurance Expense in the Income Statement columns and as $153.33 in Prepaid Insurance in the Balance Sheet columns.

Completion of the financial statements

We now prepare the income statement, the statement of owner's equity, and the balance sheet, taking the figures directly from the work sheet.

Dale's Cleaners
Income Statement
For month ended June 30, 19___

Revenue			
Income from Services			$1,615 00
Expenses			
Wages Expense	$365 00		
Rent Expense	200 00		
Utilities Expense	110 00		
Depreciation Expense	95 00		
Advertising Expense	90 00		
Supplies Expense	40 00		
Insurance Expense	6 67		
Total Expenses			906 67
Net Income			$708 33

Dale's Cleaners
Statement of Owner's Equity
For month ended June 30, 19___

Dale Armstrong, Capital, June 1, 19___			$16,000 00
Add: Net Income for month of June	$708 33		
Less: Withdrawals for month of June	500 00		
Increase in Capital			208 33
Dale Armstrong, Capital, June 30, 19___			$16,208 33

Dale's Cleaners
Balance Sheet
June 30, 19___

Assets			
Cash			$ 5,830 00
Accounts Receivable			10 00
Supplies			160 00
Prepaid Insurance			153 33
Equipment	$11,140 00		
Less Accumulated Depreciation	95 00		11,045 00
Total Assets			$17,198 33
Liabilities			
Accounts Payable	$ 940 00		
Wages Payable	50 00		
Total Liabilities			$ 990 00
Owner's Equity			
Dale Armstrong, Capital			16,208 33
Total Liabilities and Owner's Equity			$17,198 33

Note that one records Accumulated Depreciation in the asset section of the balance sheet as a direct deduction from Equipment. As we have said, accountants refer to it as a *contra account,* because it is contrary to its companion account. The difference, $11,045, is called the *book value,* because it represents the cost of the assets after the Accumulated Depreciation has been deducted.

Adjusting entries

In order to change the balance of an account, you need a journal entry as evidence of the change. Up to this time, we have been listing adjustments in the Adjustments columns of the work sheet only. Since this does not constitute a journal, you must journalize the entries. You can take the information of these entries directly from the Adjustments columns of the work sheet, debiting and crediting exactly the same accounts.

In the Description column of the general journal, write "Adjusting Entries," and this does away with the need to write explanations for each entry. The adjusting entries for Dale's Cleaners are as follows.

General Journal					Page 4
Date		Description	Post. Ref.	Debit	Credit
19__		**Adjusting Entries**			
June	30	Supplies Expense		40 00	
		Supplies			40 00
	30	Insurance Expense		6 67	
		Prepaid Insurance			6 67
	30	Depreciation Expense		95 00	
		Accumulated Depreciation			95 00
	30	Wages Expense		50 00	
		Wages Payable			50 00

When you post the adjusting entries to the ledger accounts, write the word "Adjusting" in the Item column of the ledger account. For example, the adjusting entry for Supplies is posted as shown here and on the next page.

Supplies								Account No. 113
			Post. Ref.	Debit	Credit	Balance		
Date		Item				Debit	Credit	
19__								
June	4		1	200 00		200 00		
	30	Adjusting	4		40 00	160 00		

Supplies Expense						Account No. 515	
		Post.			Balance		
Date	Item	Ref.	Debit	Credit	Debit	Credit	
19__							
June	30	Adjusting	4	40 00		40 00	

Summary

The steps in the accounting cycle that we have talked about up to now are as follows.

1 Record business transactions in a journal, from source documents.
2 Post to the accounts in the ledger.
3 Record the trial balance in the first two columns of the work sheet.
4 Record any adjustments in the work sheet.
5 Complete the work sheet.
6 Prepare the financial statements.
7 Record adjusting entries in the journal and post to the ledger accounts.

Adjustments are internal transactions, and are necessary to bring the accounts up to date. One records adjustments first in the work sheet.

We discussed four adjustments, illustrated by T accounts.

To record the supplies used:

Supplies			Supplies Expense	
+	−		+	−
Bal. 200	Adj. 40		Adj. 40	

To record the amount of insurance expired:

Prepaid Insurance			Insurance Expense	
+	−		+	−
Bal. 160	Adj. 6.67		Adj. 6.67	

To record additional depreciation:

Depreciation Expense			Accumulated Depreciation	
+	−		−	+
Adj. 95				Balance (after 1 yr.) Adj. 95

To record accrued wages owed between last payday and end of year:

Wages Expense		Wages Payable	
+	−	−	+
Bal. 315			Adj. 50
Adj. 50			

It is extremely important to know the *classification* of accounts that occupy the various columns of the work sheet.

Trial Balance		Adjustments		Adjusted Trial Balance		Income Statement		Balance Sheet	
Debit	Credit	Debit	Credit	Debit	Credit	Debit	Credit	Debit	Credit
A	L			A	L			A	L
+	+			+	+			+	+
E	R			E	R	E	R	Draw.	OE
+	+			+	+				+
Draw.	OE			Draw.	OE				Accum.
	+				+				Depr.
	Accum.				Accum.				
	Depr.				Depr.				

The adjusting entries are taken directly from the Adjustments columns of the work sheet.

Glossary

o **Accounting cycle** The steps in the accounting process that are completed during the fiscal period.

o **Accrued wages** The amount of wages owed to employees for the time between the last payday and the end of the fiscal period.

o **Adjustments** Internal transactions that bring ledger accounts up to date, as a planned part of the accounting procedure. They are first recorded in the Adjustments columns of the work sheet.

o **Book value** The cost of an asset minus the accumulated depreciation.

o **Contra account** An account that is contrary to, or a deduction from, another account; for example, Accumulated Depreciation entered as a deduction from Equipment.

o **Depreciation** An expense, based on the expectation that an asset will gradually decline in usefulness due to time, wear and tear, or obsolescence; the cost of the asset is therefore prorated over its estimated useful life. A portion of depreciation expense is apportioned to each fiscal period.

o **Fiscal period** The period of time covered by the entire accounting cycle, generally consisting of 12 consecutive months.

o **Mixed accounts** The balances of certain accounts that appear in the trial balance that are partly income statement accounts and partly balance sheet accounts—for example, Prepaid Insurance and Supplies.

o **Straight-line method** A means of calculating depreciation by taking the cost of an asset, less any trade-in value, and allocating this amount, on an average basis, over the useful life of the asset.

Exercises

Exercise 1 From the following ledger accounts, journalize the adjusting entries.

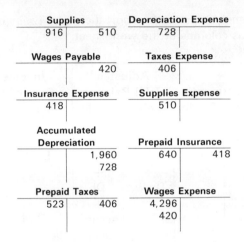

Supplies		Depreciation Expense	
916	510	728	

Wages Payable		Taxes Expense	
	420	406	

Insurance Expense		Supplies Expense	
418		510	

Accumulated Depreciation		Prepaid Insurance	
	1,960	640	418
	728		

Prepaid Taxes		Wages Expense	
523	406	4,296	
		420	

Exercise 2 Record the adjusting entry in each of the following situations.

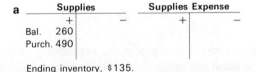

a

Supplies		Supplies Expense	
+	−	+	−
Bal. 260			
Purch. 490			

Ending inventory, $135.

b

Supplies		Supplies Expense	
+	−	+	−
Bal. 400			
Purch. 920			

Supplies used, $840.

Exercise 3 Journalize the necessary adjusting entries at June 30, the close of the current fiscal year, based on the following data.

a The Prepaid Insurance account before adjustments on June 30 has a balance of $1,260. You now figure out that $820 worth of the insurance has expired during the year.

b The Supplies account before adjustments on June 30 has a balance of $872. By taking a physical inventory, you now determine that the amount of supplies on hand is worth $260.

c The last payday was June 27. From June 28 to 30, $590 of wages accrue.

Exercise 4 From the ledger accounts for Supplies, determine the missing figures on the next page.

a Supplies

Balance	310	Used	728
Bought	916		
End. Inv.	( )		

c Supplies

Balance	148	Used	( )
Bought	480		
End. Inv.	160		

b Supplies

Balance	( )	Used	114
Bought	260		
End. Inv.	210		

d Supplies

Balance	670	Used	820
Bought	( )		
End. Inv.	711		

Exercise 5 List the following in all the columns in which they appear in the work sheet, with the exception of the Adjustments columns: Liabilities, Drawing, Owner's Equity, Expenses, Accumulated Depreciation, Revenue, Net Income. (*Example:* Assets)

	Trial Balance		Adjustments		Adjusted Trial Balance		Income Statement		Balance Sheet	
	Debit	Credit	Debit	Credit	Debit	Credit	Debit	Credit	Debit	Credit
	Assets				Assets				Assets	

Exercise 6 Complete each horizontal line in the following work sheet. (*Examples:* Prepaid Taxes; Accounts Receivable) Consider each as a separate line, rather than trying to complete the entire adjustment.

Account Name	Trial Balance Debit	Trial Balance Credit	Adjustments Debit	Adjustments Credit	Adjusted Trial Balance Debit	Adjusted Trial Balance Credit	Income Statement Debit	Income Statement Credit	Balance Sheet Debit	Balance Sheet Credit
Prepaid Taxes	324			124	200				200	
Accounts Receivable	3,690				3,690				3,690	
Accounts Payable		2,927								
C. T. Andrews, Cap.		10,764								
Utilities Expense	878									
Equipment	6,420									
Wages Expense	11,624		360							
Taxes Expense			124							
Depr. Exp.			476							
Sales		46,718								
Wages Payable				360						
C. T. Andrews, Draw.	1,460									

Exercise 7 Journalize the year-end adjusting entry for each of the following.
a Depreciation on equipment was estimated at $3,460 for the year.
b The payment of the $360 insurance premium for 3 years in advance was originally recorded as Prepaid Insurance. One year of the policy has now expired.
c The Supplies account had a $116 balance on January 1, the beginning of

the year; $340 worth of supplies were bought during the year; a year-end inventory shows that $180 worth are still on hand.

d Six employees earn a total of $200 per day for a 5-day week beginning on Monday and ending on Friday. They were all paid for the work week ending December 28. They all worked on Monday, December 31.

Exercise 8 If the required adjusting entries for Exercise 7 were not made at the end of the year, what would be the effect of the omissions on the net income?

Problems

Problem 5-1 The trial balance of the N. B. Ryan Company, as of November 30, after the company has completed the first month of operations, is:

N. B. Ryan Company
Trial Balance
November 30, 19___

Cash	4,116 00	
Accounts Receivable	5,621 00	
Office Equipment	3,110 00	
Accounts Payable		654 00
N. B. Ryan, Capital		11,308 00
N. B. Ryan, Drawing	1,200 00	
Commissions Earned		3,072 00
Salary Expense	650 00	
Rent Expense	210 00	
Advertising Expense	85 00	
Utilities Expense	25 00	
Miscellaneous Expense	17 00	
	15,034 00	15,034 00

Instructions
1 Record the trial balance in the Trial Balance columns of the work sheet.
2 Record the letters standing for the account classifications at the top of each column of the work sheet.
3 Complete the work sheet. (Data for the adjustments: Depreciation expense of office equipment, $96; accrued salaries, $108.)

Problem 5-2 or 5-2A The Workbook presents the completed work sheet for R. L. Hinds, Attorney at Law, for Hinds' law practice for August.
Instructions
1 Prepare an income statement.
2 Prepare a statement of owner's equity.
3 Prepare a balance sheet.
4 Journalize the adjusting entries.

Problem 5-3 The trial balance of the Fashion Beauty Shop as of December 31, the end of the current fiscal year, and data needed for year-end adjustments are as shown on the next page.

Fashion Beauty Shop
Trial Balance
December 31, 19___

Cash	1,460 00	
Beauty Supplies	2,980 00	
Prepaid Insurance	484 00	
Shop Equipment	26,922 00	
Accumulated Depreciation, Shop Equipment		17,616 00
Accounts Payable		492 00
D. Hoover, Capital		3,040 00
D. Hoover, Drawing	10,800 00	
Income from Services		32,620 00
Wages Expense	8,400 00	
Rent Expense	1,800 00	
Utilities Expense	486 00	
Telephone Expense	120 00	
Miscellaneous Expense	316 00	
	53,768 00	53,768 00

Data for the adjustments:

a Inventory of beauty supplies at December 31, $826.

b Insurance expired during year, $289.

c Depreciation of shop equipment during year, $1,810.

d Wages accrued at December 31, $104.

Instructions

1 Complete the work sheet.

2 Journalize the adjusting entries.

Problem 5-4 Here is the trial balance of Holiday Lanes, a bowling alley, as of June 30, the end of the current fiscal year. Data for the year-end adjustments are given on the next page.

Holiday Lanes
Trial Balance
June 30, 19___

Cash	2,984 00	
Supplies	862 00	
Prepaid Insurance	620 00	
Bowling Equipment	90,460 00	
Accumulated Depreciation, Bowling Equipment		47,200 00
Furniture and Fixtures	8,400 00	
Accumulated Depreciation, Furniture and Fixtures		4,160 00
Building	70,500 00	
Accumulated Depreciation, Building		20,000 00
Land	8,000 00	
Accounts Payable		3,820 00
Mortgage Payable		42,000 00
Thomas Bowen, Capital		42,338 00
Thomas Bowen, Drawing	12,500 00	
Bowling Fees Income		47,664 00
Concession Income		5,820 00
Wages Expense	10,600 00	
Advertising Expense	3,820 00	
Repair Expense	2,170 00	
Utilities Expense	1,570 00	
Miscellaneous Expense	516 00	
	213,002 00	213,002 00

Data for the adjustments:

a Inventory of supplies at June 30, $272.
b Insurance expired during the year, $418.
c Depreciation of bowling equipment during the year, $14,000.
d Depreciation of furniture and fixtures during the year, $1,610.
e Depreciation of building during the year, $2,700.
f Wages accrued at June 30, $384.

Instructions

1 Complete the work sheet.
2 Journalize the adjusting entries.

Problem 5-1A Here is the trial balance for the R. L. James Insurance Agency as of March 31, after it has completed its first month of operations.

R. L. James Insurance Agency		
Trial Balance		
March 31, 19___		
Cash	2,732 00	
Accounts Receivable	1,087 00	
Prepaid Insurance	286 00	
Office Equipment	2,964 00	
Automobile	3,200 00	
R. L. James, Capital		9,922 00
R. L. James, Drawing	420 00	
Commissions Earned		1,335 00
Rent Expense	260 00	
Advertising Expense	144 00	
Travel Expense	98 00	
Utility Expense	16 00	
Telephone Expense	32 00	
Miscellaneous Expense	18 00	
	11,257 00	11,257 00

Instructions

1 Record the trial balance in the Trial Balance columns of the work sheet.
2 Record the letters standing for the account classifications at the top of each column of the work sheet.
3 Complete the work sheet. (Data for the adjustments: Depreciation expense of office equipment, $26; Depreciation expense of automobile, $63; Expired insurance, $21.)

Problem 5-3A The trial balance of the Caldwell Washerama at December 31, the end of the current fiscal year, is shown on the next page. Data needed for year-end adjustments are as follows.

a Inventory of laundry supplies at December 31, $916.
b Insurance expired during the year, $213.
c Depreciation of furniture and equipment, $1,620.
d Wages accrued at December 31, $104.

Instructions

1 Complete the work sheet.
2 Journalize the adjusting entries.

Caldwell Washerama
Trial Balance
December 31, 19___

Cash	2,392 00	
Laundry Supplies	2,841 00	
Prepaid Insurance	626 00	
Furniture and Equipment	29,768 00	
Accumulated Depreciation, Furniture and Equipment		17,160 00
Accounts Payable		419 00
Noel Caldwell, Capital		15,276 00
Noel Caldwell, Drawing	8,640 00	
Income from Services		27,716 00
Wages Expense	10,640 00	
Rent Expense	3,600 00	
Utilities Expense	1,271 00	
Advertising Expense	418 00	
Miscellaneous Expense	375 00	
	60,571 00	60,571 00

Problem 5-4A The trial balance for Leisure Miniature Golf at September 30, the end of the current fiscal year, is as follows.

Leisure Miniature Golf
Trial Balance
September 30, 19___

Cash	1,962 00	
Supplies	519 00	
Prepaid Insurance	476 00	
Golf Clubs	515 00	
Field Equipment	19,760 00	
Accumulated Depreciation, Field Equipment		6,466 00
Lighting Fixtures	1,878 00	
Accumulated Depreciation, Lighting Fixtures		420 00
Accounts Payable		321 00
Contracts Payable		960 00
Jason Cody, Capital		10,181 00
Jason Cody, Drawing	4,878 00	
Golf Fees Income		20,667 00
Concession Income		923 00
Wages Expense	6,820 00	
Repair Expense	1,986 00	
Advertising Expense	489 00	
Utilities Expense	364 00	
Miscellaneous Expense	291 00	
	39,938 00	39,938 00

Data for year-end adjustments are as follows:

a Inventory of supplies at September 30, $146.

b Insurance expired during the year, $184.

c Depreciation of field equipment during the year, $3,860.

d Depreciation of lighting fixtures during the year, $416.

e Wages accrued at September 30, $288.

Instructions

1 Complete the work sheet.

2 Journalize the adjusting entries.

6

Closing entries and the post-closing trial balance

In Genoa, in 1421, the Bank of St. George kept its books in double entry. To check the books, the bank employed auditors who were paid 10 percent of the amount of each error which they discovered. Raymond de Roover, *Studies in the History of Accounting*

Key points

- In closing or clearing an account, one makes its balance equal to zero.
- There are four steps in the closing procedure.

Chapter contents

- Introduction
- Interim statements
- Closing entries
- The post-closing trial balance
- Summary
- Glossary
- Review of T account placement
- Review of representative transactions
- Exercises
- Problems
- Practical review problem

Specific objectives

After you have completed this chapter, you will be able to:

- Journalize and post closing entries for a service-type enterprise.
- Prepare a post-closing trial balance for any type of enterprise.

Introduction

In the accounting cycle, after you have prepared the financial statements from the work sheet and journalized and posted the adjusting entries, the remaining steps consist of (1) journalizing and posting the closing entries, and (2) preparing a post-closing trial balance.

In this chapter we shall explain the functions and procedures for accomplishing these final steps in the accounting cycle.

Interim statements

Interim statements consist of the financial statements that are prepared during the fiscal year for periods of *less* than 12 months. For example, a business may prepare the income statement, the statement of owner's equity, and the balance sheet *monthly*. These statements provide up-to-date information about the results and status of operations. Suppose a company has a fiscal period extending from January 1 of one year through December 31 of the same year; it might have the following interim statements.

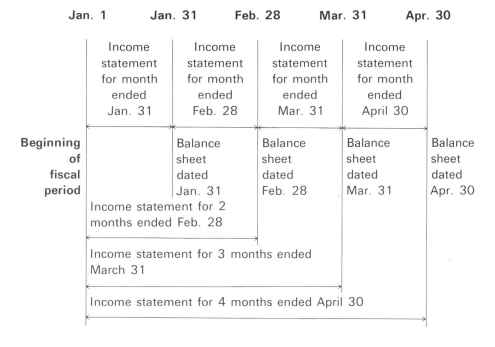

| Jan. 1 | Jan. 31 | Feb. 28 | Mar. 31 | Apr. 30 |

In this case, the company would prepare statements of owner's equity for the same periods as the income statements.

With respect to the accounting cycle, the work sheet and the financial statements would be completed. However, the accountant would perform the remaining steps—consisting of the journalizing of adjusting and closing entries and the preparation of the post-closing trial balance—only at the end of the fiscal period. Just for the sake of illustration and practice in the text, however, let's take a fiscal period, with the closing entries and post-closing trial balance, which consists of 1 month. We need to do this for practical purposes, so that we can thoroughly cover the material. Let us now proceed with these latter steps.

Closing entries

So that you will understand the reason for the closing entries, let us first repeat the Trial Balance Equation.

Assets + Expenses = Liabilities + Revenue + Owner's Equity

We know that the income statement, as stated in the third line of its heading, is for a definite period of time. It consists of revenue minus expenses, for this period of time only. So, when this period is over, we should start from zero for the next period. In other words, we wipe the slate clean, so that we can start all over again next period.

Purposes of closing entries

This brings us to the *purpose* of the closing entries, which is to close off the revenue and expense accounts. We do this because their balances apply to only one fiscal period. As stated before, with the coming of the next fiscal period, we want to start from scratch, recording brand-new revenue and expenses. Accountants also refer to this as *clearing the accounts*. For income tax purposes, this is certainly understandable. No one wants to pay income tax more than once on the same income, and the Internal Revenue Service frowns on counting an expense more than once. So now we have

(closed)   (closed)

Assets + ~~Expenses~~ = Liabilities + ~~Revenue~~ + Owner's Equity

The assets, liabilities, and owner's equity accounts remain open. The balance sheet, with its one date in the heading, merely gives the present balances of these accounts, and the accountant will carry them over to the next fiscal period.

Procedure for closing

The procedure for closing is to simply balance off the account, in other words, to make the balance *equal to zero.* This meets our objective, which is to be able to start from zero in the next fiscal period. Let's illustrate this first with T accounts. For example, suppose an account happens to have a debit balance; then, to make the balance equal to zero, we *credit* the account.

Balance	960	Closing	960

We put the label *closing* in the Item column of the ledger account.

For another example, suppose an account happens to have a credit balance; then, to make the balance equal to zero, we *debit* the account.

Closing	1,200	Balance	1,200

Four steps in the closing procedure:
1 Close the revenue accounts into Revenue and Expense Summary.
2 Close the expense accounts into Revenue and Expense Summary.
3 Close the Revenue and Expense Summary account into the Capital account.
4 Close the Drawing account into the Capital account.

Every entry should, of course, have both a debit and a credit. So, in order to give us the other half of the entry, we bring into existence the Revenue and Expense Summary account. To illustrate the entries directly in T accounts, we again fall back on the accounts of our friendly neighborhood business, Dale's Cleaners. For the purpose of the illustration, assume that Dale's Cleaners' fiscal period consists of 1 month. We now have the following revenue and expense accounts.

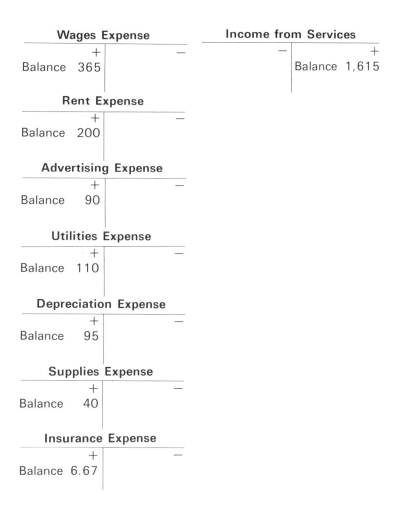

Wages Expense				Income from Services	
+		−		−	+
Balance 365					Balance 1,615

Rent Expense	
+	−
Balance 200	

Advertising Expense	
+	−
Balance 90	

Utilities Expense	
+	−
Balance 110	

Depreciation Expense	
+	−
Balance 95	

Supplies Expense	
+	−
Balance 40	

Insurance Expense	
+	−
Balance 6.67	

Step 1 Close the revenue account, or accounts, into Revenue and Expense Summary. In order to make the balance of Income from Services equal to zero, we *balance it off,* or debit it, in the amount of $1,615. Because we need an offsetting credit, we now credit the Revenue and Expense Summary account for the same figure.

Income from Services		Revenue and Expense Summary	
−	+		
Closing 1,615	Balance 1,615		1,615

In essence, the balance of Income from Services is transferred to Revenue and Expense Summary. To learn how to formulate the journal entry, let's look at the journal entry for this step.

General Journal				Page 4	
Date		Description	Debit	Credit	

		Closing Entries			
June	30	Income from Services	1,615 00		
		Revenue and Expense Summary		1,615	00

Writing *Closing Entries* in the Description column makes it possible to elimi-nate explanations for all the closing entries.

Step 2 Close the expense accounts into Revenue and Expense Summary. In order to make the balances of the expense accounts equal to zero, we need to balance them off, or credit them. Again the T accounts are a basis for formulating the journal entry. In essence, the balances of the expense accounts are transferred to Revenue and Expense Summary.

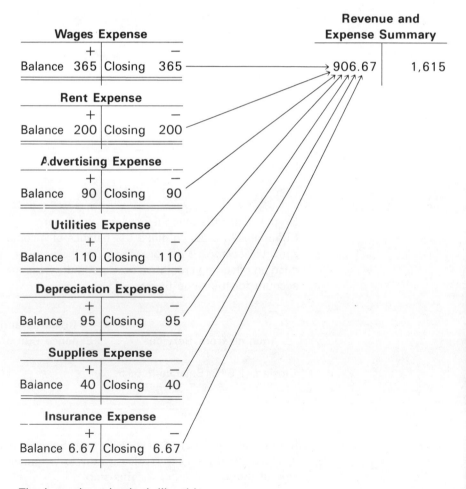

The journal entries look like this.

General Journal Page 4

Date		Description	Debit	Credit
		Closing Entries		
June	30	Income from Services	1,615 00	
		Revenue and Expense Summary		1,615 00
	30	Revenue and Expense Summary	906 67	
		Wages Expense		365 00
		Rent Expense		200 00
		Advertising Expense		90 00
		Utilities Expense		110 00
		Depreciation Expense		95 00
		Supplies Expense		40 00
		Insurance Expense		6 67

Step 3 Recall that we instigated the Revenue and Expense Summary account only in order to have a debit and credit with each closing entry. So now that it has done its job, we close it out. We use the same procedure as before, in that we make the balance equal to zero, or balance off the account. In essence, we transfer, or close, the balance of the Revenue and Expense Summary account into the Capital account.

Revenue and Expense Summary		Dale Armstrong, Capital	
		−	+
906.67	1,615	Balance 16,000	
Closing 708.33		(Net Inc.) 708.33	

General Journal Page 4

Date		Description	Debit	Credit
		Closing Entries		
June	30	Income from Services	1,615 00	
		Revenue and Expense Summary		1,615 00
	30	Revenue and Expense Summary	906 67	
		Wages Expense		365 00
		Rent Expense		200 00
		Advertising Expense		90 00
		Utilities Expense		110 00
		Depreciation Expense		95 00
		Supplies Expense		40 00
		Insurance Expense		6 67

General Journal				Page 4 (cont.)	
Date		Description	Debit	Credit	
June	30	Revenue and Expense Summary	708 33		
		Dale Armstrong, Capital		708	33

"Revenue and Expense Summary" is well named, as it does summarize the total revenue and the total expenses of a business. The difference between the totals is the net income or the net loss. So Revenue and Expense Summary is always closed into the Capital account by the amount of the net income or the net loss. This can act as a check point or verification.

At the same time, it seems logical that net income should be added or credited to the Capital account, because in the statement of owner's equity, as we have seen, net income is treated as an addition. Conversely, any net loss should be subtracted or debited to the Capital account, because in the statement of owner's equity net loss is treated as a deduction.

Step 4 The Drawing account, since it also applies to one fiscal period only, must also be closed. Because it appears in the statement of owner's equity as a deduction from the Capital account, it is closed directly into the Capital account. So we balance off the Drawing account, or make the balance of it equal to zero. The balance of Drawing is transferred to the Capital account.

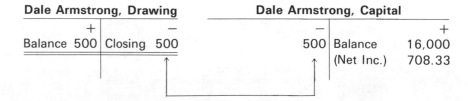

Dale Armstrong, Drawing

+	−
Balance 500	Closing 500

Dale Armstrong, Capital

−	+
500	Balance 16,000
	(Net Inc.) 708.33

General Journal				Page 4	
Date		Description	Debit	Credit	
		Closing Entries			
June	30	Income from Services	1,615 00		
		Revenue and Expense Summary		1,615	00
	30	Revenue and Expense Summary	906 67		
		Wages Expense		365	00
		Rent Expense		200	00
		Advertising Expense		90	00
		Utilities Expense		110	00
		Depreciation Expense		95	00
		Supplies Expense		40	00
		Insurance Expense		6	67

General Journal				Page 4 (cont.)	
Date		Description	Debit	Credit	
June	30	Revenue and Expense Summary	708 33		
		Dale Armstrong, Capital		708 33	
	30	Dale Armstrong, Capital	500 00		
		Dale Armstrong, Drawing		500 00	

These closing entries show that the owner has had a net income of $708.33, has withdrawn $500 for personal expenses, and has retained or plowed back $208.33 into the business, thereby increasing the capital investment.

Closing entries taken directly from the work sheet

One can gather the information for the closing entries either directly from the ledger accounts, or from the work sheet. Since the Income Statement columns of the work sheet consist entirely of revenues and expenses, one can pick up the figures for the closing entries from these columns. Here we see a partial work sheet for Dale's Cleaners.

Account Name	Trial Balance		Income Statement	
	Debit	Credit	Debit	Credit
Cash	5,830 00			
Accounts Receivable	10 00			
Supplies	200 00			
Prepaid Insurance	160 00			
Equipment	11,140 00			
Accounts Payable		940 00		
Dale Armstrong, Capital		16,000 00		
Dale Armstrong, Drawing	500 00			
Income from Services		1,615 00		1,615 00
Wages Expense	315 00		365 00	
Rent Expense	200 00		200 00	
Advertising Expense	90 00		90 00	
Utilities Expense	110 00		110 00	
	18,555 00	18,555 00		
Supplies Expense			40 00	
Insurance Expense			6 67	
Depreciation Expense			95 00	
Accumulated Depreciation				
Wages Payable				
			906 67	1,615 00
Net Income			708 33	
			1,615 00	1,615 00

One student observed a direct way of making closing entries by merely balancing off all the figures that appear in the Income Statement columns. Here there is a credit for $1,615; so we debit that account for the same amount, and we credit Revenue and Expense Summary.

There are debits for $365, $200, $90, $110, $40, $6.67, and $95. So now we *credit* these accounts for the same amounts, and we credit Revenue and Expense Summary for their total.

Next, as usual, we close the Revenue and Expense Summary account into Capital, by using the net-income figure already shown on the work sheet.

We would of course have to pick up the last entry from the Balance Sheet columns to close Drawing.

Collectively, we call these accounts that are closed *temporary-equity accounts.* In this context they are temporary in that the balances apply to one fiscal period only, and in the last analysis they are closed into the Capital account.

We indicate that the accounts are closed by writing in the ledger, in the Item column, the word *Closing,* and by extending a line through both the debit and credit balance columns.

Posting the closing entries

After we have posted the closing entries, the Capital, Drawing, Revenue and Expense Summary, revenue, and expense accounts of Dale's Cleaners appear as follows.

Dale Armstrong, Capital   Account No. 311

Date		Item	Post. Ref.	Debit	Credit	Balance Debit	Balance Credit
19__							
June	1		1		16,000 00		16,000 00
	30		4		708 33		16,708 33
	30		4	500 00			16,208 33

Dale Armstrong, Drawing   Account No. 312

Date		Item	Post. Ref.	Debit	Credit	Balance Debit	Balance Credit
19__							
June	30		4	500 00		500 00	
	30	Closing	4		500 00	———	———

Revenue and Expense Summary   Account No. 313

Date		Item	Post. Ref.	Debit	Credit	Balance Debit	Balance Credit
19__							
June	30		4		1,615 00		1,615 00
	30		4	906 67			708 33
	30	Closing	4	708 33	708 33	———	———

Income from Services   Account No. 411

Date		Item	Post. Ref.	Debit	Credit	Balance Debit	Balance Credit
19__							
June	7		1		300 00		300 00
	14		2		380 00		680 00
	21		2		415 00		1,095 00
	23		3		40 00		1,135 00
	30		3		480 00		1,615 00
	30	Closing	4	1,615 00		———	———

Wages Expense   Account No. 511

Date		Item	Post. Ref.	Debit	Credit	Balance Debit	Balance Credit
19__							
June	10		2	120 00		120 00	
	24		3	195 00		315 00	
	30	Adjusting	4	50 00		365 00	
	30	Closing	4		365 00	———	———

Rent Expense   Account No. 512

Date		Item	Post. Ref.	Debit	Credit	Balance Debit	Balance Credit
19__							
June	8		1	200 00		200 00	
	30	Closing	4		200 00	———	———

Advertising Expense   Account No. 513

Date		Item	Post. Ref.	Debit	Credit	Balance Debit	Balance Credit
19__							
June	14		2	90 00		90 00	
	30	Closing	4		90 00	———	———

Utilities Expense — Account No. 514

Date		Item	Post. Ref.	Debit	Credit	Balance Debit	Balance Credit
19__ June	15		2	110 00		110 00	
	30	Closing	4		110 00	——	——

Depreciation Expense — Account No. 515

Date		Item	Post. Ref.	Debit	Credit	Balance Debit	Balance Credit
19__ June	30	Adjusting	4	500 00		500 00	
	30	Closing	4		500 00	——	——

Supplies Expense — Account No. 516

Date		Item	Post. Ref.	Debit	Credit	Balance Debit	Balance Credit
19__ June	30	Adjusting	4	40 00		40 00	
	30	Closing	4		40 00	——	——

Insurance Expense — Account No. 517

Date		Item	Post. Ref.	Debit	Credit	Balance Debit	Balance Credit
19__ June	30	Adjusting	4	6 67		6 67	
	30	Closing	4		6 67	——	——

The post-closing trial balance

After one has posted the closing entries, and before one goes on to the next year, it is wise to verify the balances of the accounts that remain open. Therefore, one makes up a *post-closing trial balance,* using the final-balance figures from the ledger accounts. This represents a last-ditch effort to make absolutely sure that the debit balances equal the credit balances.

The accounts listed in the post-closing trial balance are called *real accounts* (assets, liabilities, owner's equity, balance sheet accounts). The accountant carries forward the balances of real accounts from one fiscal period to another. This is in contrast to temporary-equity accounts, which, as you have seen, are closed at the end of each fiscal period.

Dale's Cleaners
Post-closing Trial Balance
June 30, 19___

Cash	5,830 00	
Accounts Receivable	10 00	
Supplies	160 00	
Prepaid Insurance	153 33	
Equipment	11,140 00	
Accumulated Depreciation		95 00
Accounts Payable		940 00
Wages Payable		50 00
Dale Armstrong, Capital		16,208 33
	17,293 33	17,293 33

Summary

The purpose of closing entries is to close off temporary-equity accounts. These accounts consist of revenues, expenses, Revenue and Expense Summary, and the Drawing account. In the closing process we balance off the account, or make the balance equal to zero. The four steps for closing are:

1 Close the revenue accounts into Revenue and Expense Summary.
2 Close the expense accounts into Revenue and Expense Summary.
3 Close the Revenue and Expense Summary account into the Capital account by the amount of the net income or net loss.
4 Close the Drawing account into the Capital account.

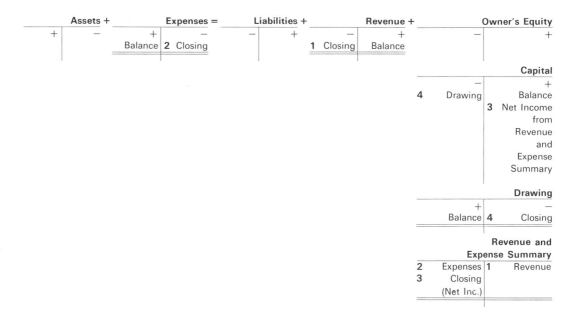

One writes the word *Closing* in the Item column of the ledger accounts, and extends lines through the balance columns, indicating that the balance of each account closed is zero.

A post-closing trial balance consists of the final balances of the accounts remaining open. It is the final proof that the debit balances equal the credit balances.

Glossary

o **Closing entry** An entry made at the end of a fiscal period to intentionally make the balance of a temporary-equity account equal to zero. This is also referred to as *clearing the accounts*.

o **Interim statements** Financial statements prepared during the fiscal period, and covering a period of time less than the fiscal period.

o **Post-closing trial balance** The listing of the final balances of the real accounts at the end of the fiscal period.

o **Real accounts** Assets, liabilities, and the Capital account in owner's equity, having balances which are carried forward from one fiscal period to another.

o **Temporary-equity accounts** Revenue, expense, Revenue and Expense Summary, and Drawing accounts. This category may also be described as being all accounts except assets, liabilities, and the Capital account.

Review of T account placement

The following sums up the placement of T accounts covered in Chapters 1 through 6 in relation to the Trial Balance Equation.

Assets +		Expenses =		Liabilities +		Revenue +		Owner's Equity	
+	−	+	−	−	+	−	+	−	+
Dr	Cr	Dr	Cr	Dr	Cr	Dr	Cr	Dr	Cr

Cash		Rent Expense		Accounts Payable		Income from Services		J. R. Doe, Capital	
+	−	+	−	−	+	−	+	−	+

Accounts Receivable		Wages Expense				Professional Fees		J. R. Doe, Drawing	
+	−	+	−			−	+	+	−

Supplies		Advertising Expense				Commissions Earned		Revenue and Expense Summary	
+	−	+	−			−	+	Expenses	Revenue
									Net Inc.

Prepaid Insurance		Utilities Expense	
+	−	+	−

Equipment		Supplies Expense	
+	−	+	−

Accumulated Depreciation		Insurance Expense	
−	+	+	−

Depreciation Expense	
+	−

The following summarizes the recording of transactions covered in Chapters 1 through 6, along with a classification of the accounts involved.

Transaction	Accounts involved	Class.	Increase or decrease	Therefore debit or credit
Owner invested cash in business	Cash	A	I	Dr
	J. R. Doe, Capital	OE	I	Cr
Bought equipment for cash	Equipment	A	I	Dr
	Cash	A	D	Cr
Bought supplies on account	Supplies	A	I	Dr
	Accounts Payable	L	I	Cr
Paid premium for insurance policy	Prepaid Insurance	A	I	Dr
	Cash	A	D	Cr
Paid creditor on account	Accounts Payable	L	D	Dr
	Cash	A	D	Cr
Sold services for cash	Cash	A	I	Dr
	Income from Services	R	I	Cr
Paid rent for month	Rent Expense	E	I	Dr
	Cash	A	D	Cr
Billed customers for services performed	Accounts Receivable	A	I	Dr
	Income from Services	R	I	Cr
Owner withdrew cash for personal use	J. R. Doe, Drawing	OE	I	Dr
	Cash	A	D	Cr
Received cash from charge customers to apply on account	Cash	A	I	Dr
	Accounts Receivable	A	D	Cr
Paid wages to employees	Wages Expense	E	I	Dr
	Cash	A	D	Cr
Adjusting entry for supplies used	Supplies Expense	E	I	Dr
	Supplies	A	D	Cr
Adjusting entry for insurance expired	Insurance Expense	E	I	Dr
	Prepaid Insurance	A	D	Cr
Adjusting entry for depreciation of assets	Depreciation Expense	E	I	Dr
	Accumulated Depreciation	A	I	Cr
Adjusting entry for accrued wages	Wages Expense	E	I	Dr
	Wages Payable	L	I	Cr
Closing entry for revenue accounts	Revenue accounts	R	—	Dr
	Revenue and Expense Summary	OE	—	Cr
Closing entry for expense accounts	Revenue and Expense Summary	OE	—	Dr
	Expense accounts	E	D	Cr
Closing entry for Revenue and Expense Summary account (Net Income)	Revenue and Expense Summary	OE	—	Dr
	J. R. Doe, Capital	OE	I	Cr
Closing entry for Drawing account	J. R. Doe, Capital	OE	D	Dr
	J. R. Doe, Drawing	OE	D	Cr

Exercise 1 From the following ledger accounts, prepare the closing entries in proper order.

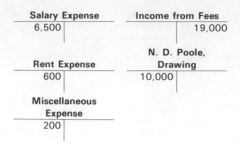

Salary Expense	Income from Fees
6,500	19,000

Rent Expense	N. D. Poole, Drawing
600	10,000

Miscellaneous Expense
200

Exercise 2 Complete the posting of the closing entry for the Professional Fees account.

Professional Fees   Account No. 411

Date		Item	Post. Ref.	Debit	Credit	Balance Debit	Balance Credit
19—							
Mar.	31		64		11,600 00		11,600 00
June	30		72		12,920 00		24,520 00
Sept.	30		83		15,680 00		40,200 00
Dec.	31		94		10,410 00		50,610 00
	31		95	50,610 00			

Exercise 3 The Revenue and Expense Summary ledger account is as follows.

Revenue and Expense Summary	
5,500	6,000

Total revenue is _____ .

Total expenses are _____ .

Net income is _____ .

Exercise 4 After all revenues and expenses have been closed at the end of the fiscal period, Revenue and Expense Summary has a credit of $27,000 and a debit of $16,000. On the same date, T. C. Turner, Drawing, has a debit balance of $9,500 and T. C. Turner, Capital, has a credit balance of $34,000. Record the journal entries necessary to complete the closing of the accounts. What is the new balance of T. C. Turner, Capital?

Exercise 5 On the next page are the ledger accounts of T. L. Moore Company. Prepare a statement of owner's equity.

Revenue and Expense Summary			
Dec. 31	18,000	Dec. 31	38,000
Dec. 31 Clos.	20,000		

T. L. Moore, Capital			
Dec. 31	15,000	Jan. 1 Bal.	22,000
		Dec. 31	20,000

T. L. Moore, Drawing			
Mar. 31	5,000	Dec. 31 Clos.	15,000
Aug. 31	5,000		
Nov. 30	5,000		

Exercise 6 The Income Statement columns of the work sheet of N. B. Jackson Company for the fiscal year ended April 30 contain the following.

	Debit	Credit
Income from Services		$36,000
Salary Expense	$12,000	
Rent Expense	2,000	
Supplies Expense	1,500	
Miscellaneous Expense	500	

The Balance Sheet columns of the work sheet contain the following.

	Debit	Credit
N. B. Jackson, Capital		$60,000
N. B. Jackson, Drawing	$18,000	

Record the four closing entries.

Exercise 7 From the following ledger accounts, journalize the adjusting entries and closing entries that have been posted to the accounts.

Accumulated Depreciation			Prepaid Insurance		Depreciation Expense	
	1,600		480	240	400	400
	400		80			

Insurance Expense		Income from Services		Wages Expense	
240	240	2,400	200	600	1,290
			1,800	600	
			400	90	

Wages Payable		Miscellaneous Expense		Revenue and Expense Summary	
	90	120	120	2,050	2,400

Exercise 8 With reference to a statement of owner's equity, determine the missing figures.

a
Net income for year	$30,000
Owner's equity at beginning of year	70,000
Owner's equity at end of year	
Owner's drawings during year	$20,000

b Owner's drawings during year $25,000
Owner's equity at beginning of year   42,000
Net income for year

| Owner's equity at end of year | $36,000 |

Problems

Problem 6-1 The revenue, expense, Revenue and Expense Summary, Drawing, and Capital accounts of the S. L. Miller Advertising Agency are as follows.

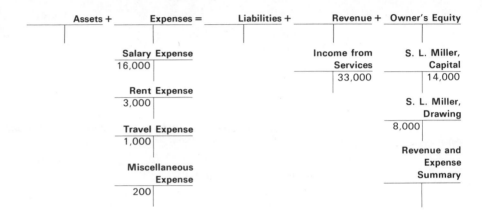

Assets +	Expenses =	Liabilities +	Revenue +	Owner's Equity
	Salary Expense 16,000		**Income from Services** 33,000	**S. L. Miller, Capital** 14,000
	Rent Expense 3,000			**S. L. Miller, Drawing** 8,000
	Travel Expense 1,000			**Revenue and Expense Summary**
	Miscellaneous Expense 200			

Instructions Record in the Workbook the closing entries as of December 31, 19___, with the four steps in order.

Problem 6-2 At the top of the next page is a partial work sheet for Tip Top Sign Painting for the fiscal year ending December 31 of this year.
Instructions Record the closing entries, with the four steps in order.

Problem 6-3 After the adjusting entries have been posted, the ledger of T. S. Wheeler, architect, contains the following account balances.

Cash	$3,637
Office Supplies	190
Furniture and Fixtures	1,586
Accumulated Depreciation, Furniture and Fixtures	1,084
Accounts Payable	853
Salaries Payable	164
T. S. Wheeler, Capital	3,249
T. S. Wheeler, Drawing	1,200
Revenue and Expense Summary	0
Income from Professional Fees	3,820
Salary Expense	1,688
Rent Expense	208
Telephone Expense	24

Account Name	Trial Balance		Income Statement		Problem 6-2
	Debit	Credit	Debit	Credit	
Cash	3,400 00				
Accounts Receivable	1,800 00				
Supplies	910 00				
Equipment	4,220 00				
Accumulated Depreciation, Equipment		2,600 00			
Truck	3,190 00				
Accumulated Depreciation, Truck		1,472 00			
Accounts Payable		640 00			
S. Austin, Capital		7,598 00			
S. Austin, Drawing	9,600 00				
Service Income		23,670 00		23,670 00	
Wages Expense	8,420 00		8,420 00		
Rent Expense	2,400 00		2,400 00		
Truck Operating Expense	1,860 00		1,860 00		
Telephone Expense	180 00		180 00		
	35,980 00	35,980 00			
Supplies Expense			227 00		
Depreciation Expense, Equipment			326 00		
Depreciation Expense, Truck			482 00		
			13,895 00	23,670 00	
Net Income			9,775 00		
			23,670 00	23,670 00	

Office Supplies Expense	$421
Depreciation Expense, Furniture and Fixtures	216

Instructions Record the closing entries, with the four steps in order.

Problem 6-4 The trial balance section of the work sheet for the Dan-Dee Window Washing Service as of December 31, the end of the current fiscal year, is as shown on the next page. Data for the adjustments are as follows.

a Accrued wages, $128.
b Inventory of cleaning supplies, $120.
c Depreciation of cleaning equipment, $225.
d Depreciation of truck, $340.
   Instructions
1 Complete the work sheet.
2 Prepare an income statement.
3 Prepare a statement of owner's equity.
4 Prepare a balance sheet.
5 Journalize the closing entries with the four steps in order.

Account Name	Trial Balance Debit	Trial Balance Credit
Cash	1,683 00	
Accounts Receivable	1,790 00	
Cleaning Supplies	243 00	
Cleaning Equipment	2,970 00	
Accumulated Depreciation, Cleaning Equipment		1,860 00
Truck	3,175 00	
Accumulated Depreciation, Truck		1,425 00
Accounts Payable		627 00
T. L. Mellon, Capital		3,332 00
T. L. Mellon, Drawing	9,600 00	
Service Income		19,641 00
Wages Expense	6,420 00	
Advertising Expense	264 00	
Truck Operating Expense	415 00	
Utilities Expense	325 00	
	26,885 00	26,885 00

Problem 6-1A The revenue, expense, Revenue and Expense Summary, Drawing, and Capital accounts of T. C. Purdy Insurance Agency are as follows.

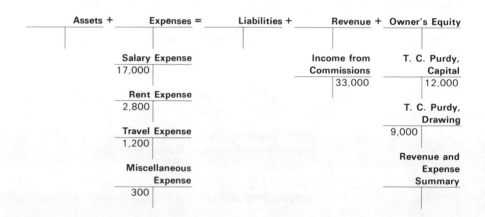

Instructions Record the closing entries as of December 31, 19___, with the four steps in order.

Problem 6-2A The partial work sheet for Norris Rug Cleaning Service for the fiscal year ending December 31 of this year is as shown at the top of the next page.

Instructions Record the closing entries, with the four steps in order.

Problem 6-3A After the adjusting entries have been posted, the ledger of B. E. Elliott, architect, contains the following account balances.

Account Name	Trial Balance Debit	Trial Balance Credit	Income Statement Debit	Income Statement Credit
				Problem 6-2A
Cash	2,963 00			
Accounts Receivable	1,781 00			
Supplies	887 00			
Equipment	4,914 00			
Accumulated Depreciation, Equipment		3,298 00		
Truck	3,584 00			
Accumulated Depreciation, Truck		2,780 00		
Accounts Payable		826 00		
R. T. Norris, Capital		3,899 00		
R. T. Norris, Drawing	10,400 00			
Service Income		25,716 00		25,716 00
Wages Expense	7,420 00		7,420 00	
Rent Expense	2,400 00		2,400 00	
Truck Operating Expense	1,930 00		1,930 00	
Telephone Expense	240 00		240 00	
	36,519 00	36,519 00		
Supplies Expense			232 00	
Depreciation Expense, Equipment			312 00	
Depreciation Expense, Truck			440 00	
			12,974 00	25,716 00
Net Income			12,742 00	
			25,716 00	25,716 00

Cash	$4,722
Office Supplies	471
Furniture and Fixtures	2,879
Accumulated Depreciation, Furniture and Fixtures	1,841
Accounts Payable	941
Salaries Payable	40
B. E. Elliott, Capital	4,400
B. E. Elliott, Drawing	1,080
Revenue and Expense Summary	0
Income from Professional Fees	5,063
Salary Expense	2,260
Rent Expense	350
Telephone Expense	52
Office Supplies Expense	120
Depreciation Expense, Furniture and Fixtures	76
Miscellaneous Expense	275

Instructions Record the closing entries, with the four steps in order.

Problem 6-4A The trial balance section of the work sheet for Clean-Rite Janitorial Service as of December 31, the end of the current fiscal year, is as follows.

Account Name	Trial Balance Debit	Trial Balance Credit
Cash	1,298 00	
Accounts Receivable	2,110 00	
Cleaning Supplies	426 00	
Cleaning Equipment	3,864 00	
Accumulated Depreciation, Cleaning Equipment		1,932 00
Truck	2,980 00	
Accumulated Depreciation, Truck		2,120 00
Accounts Payable		872 00
C. F. Sager, Capital		1,839 00
C. F. Sager, Drawing	10,800 00	
Service Income		24,840 00
Wages Expense	8,640 00	
Advertising Expense	262 00	
Truck Operating Expense	424 00	
Utilities Expense	319 00	
Miscellaneous Expense	480 00	
	31,603 00	31,603 00

Data for the adjustments are as follows.
a Accrued wages, $116.
b Inventory of cleaning supplies, $304.
c Depreciation of cleaning equipment, $120.
d Depreciation of truck, $296.

Instructions
1 Complete the work sheet.
2 Prepare an income statement.
3 Prepare a statement of owner's equity.
4 Prepare a balance sheet.
5 Journalize the closing entries, with the four steps in order.

Practical review problem	The purpose of this problem is to get you to review and apply the knowledge that you have acquired in the preceding chapters. In accounting, the ultimate test is to be able to handle data in real life situations; the following will give you valuable experience.

You have been given the job of keeping the books for the Grandview Drive-In Theater. The owner, Roosevelt Owens, has formulated a chart of accounts. |

Chart of Accounts

	Assets
111	Cash
112	Accounts Receivable
113	Supplies
114	Prepaid Insurance
121	Projection Equipment

Chart of Accounts (cont.)

Assets (cont.)

122	Accumulated Depreciation, Projection Equipment
123	Screen and Speakers
124	Accumulated Depreciation, Screen and Speakers
125	Office Equipment
126	Accumulated Depreciation, Office Equipment
127	Buildings
128	Accumulated Depreciation, Buildings
129	Land

Liabilities

211	Accounts Payable
212	Wages Payable
221	Mortgage Payable

Owner's Equity

311	Roosevelt Owens, Capital
312	Roosevelt Owens, Drawing
313	Revenue and Expense Summary

Revenue

411	Admissions Income
412	Concessions Income

Expenses

511	Film Rental Expense
512	Wages Expense
513	Advertising Expense
514	Utilities Expense
515	Interest Expense
516	Supplies Expense
517	Insurance Expense
518	Depreciation Expense, Projection Equipment
519	Depreciation Expense, Screen and Speakers
520	Depreciation Expense, Office Equipment
521	Depreciation Expense, Buildings
522	Miscellaneous Expense

You are to record transactions in a two-column general journal. To get in a little more practice, assume that the fiscal period is 1 month, so that you will be able to complete all the steps in the accounting cycle.

When you are analyzing the transactions, think them through by mentally visualizing the T accounts or by writing them down on scratch paper. In the case of unfamiliar types of transactions, the book gives specific instructions for recording them. However, go ahead and reason them out for yourself as well.

The following transactions were completed during July of this year.

July	1	Owens deposited $28,000 in a bank account for the purpose of buying the Grandview Drive-In Theater.
	2	Bought the Grandview Drive-In Theater in its entirety for a total price of $52,500. The assets include: projection equipment, $6,000; screen and speakers, $3,500; office equipment, $2,000; buildings, $16,000; land, $25,000. Paid cash as a downpayment, $18,000, and signed a mortgage note for the remainder. (Debit the assets, and credit Cash and the liability.)
	2	Paid cash for newspaper advertising, $190.
	2	Paid cash for insurance on property and liability insurance, $480.
	2	Paid for billboard advertising for month, $90.
	2	Received bill for film rental, $610, from Intermountain, Inc.
	2	Bought supplies on account, $110, from L. D. Wonich Company.
	2	Made a contract for leasing a refreshment stand. The rental is to be 12% of sales, payable in advance. Accordingly, received $200 in cash as advance payment for month. (Debit Cash and credit Concession Income.)
	3	Paid cash for miscellaneous expenses, $27.
	8	Received $1,600 in cash from admissions for week.
	9	Bought office equipment on account, $88, from Jones Office Supply Company.
	15	Paid wages expense for period ending July 14, $1,640.
	16	Paid the bill for film rental previously recorded on July 2.
	16	Owens withdrew $270 in cash for personal use.
	16	Received $1,940 in cash from admissions for week.
	17	Bought additional speakers on account, $525, from Ronald Electronics.
	19	Paid for advertising brochures, $98.
	20	Paid cash to L. D. Wonich Company in full payment of account, $110.
	22	Bought stationery and other supplies on account, $87, from Jones Supply Company.
	22	Received $2,060 in cash from admissions for week.
	23	Returned some of the speakers purchased on July 17 and received full credit, or a reduction in bill, $180.
	24	Received bill for film rental, $960, from Intermountain, Inc.
	26	Paid cash for bill for electricity, $110.
	29	Paid wages for period July 15 through 28, $1,780.
	29	Paid bill for film rental previously recorded on July 24.
	29	Paid cash to Ronald Electronics to apply on account, $240.
	30	Paid cash for telephone bill, $22.
	31	Paid cash as an installment payment on the mortgage, $240. Of this amount, $175 is a payment on the principal; the remainder is interest. (Debit Mortgage Payable, debit Interest Expense, and credit Cash.)
	31	Paid cash for water bill, $20.

July 31	Sales for concession stand for month amounted to $2,200, and 12% of $2,200 equals $264. Since you have already recorded $200 as rent received in advance, list the additional $64 owed the Grandview Drive-In Theater by the concessionaire for July.
31	Owens received $2,110 in cash from admissions for week.
31	Owens withdrew $320 in cash for personal use.
31	Received bill for film rental, $730, from Intermountain, Inc.

Instructions

1 Journalize the transactions beginning with page 1 of the general journal.
2 Post the transactions to the ledger accounts.
3 Prepare a trial balance in the first two columns of the work sheet.
4 Complete the work sheet. Data for the adjustments are as follows.
    a Inventory of supplies at July 31, $147.
    b Insurance expired during the month, $40.
    c Depreciation of projection equipment for the month, $100.
    d Depreciation of screen and speakers for the month, $110.
    e Depreciation of office equipment for the month, $34.
    f Depreciation of building for the month, $65.
    g Wages accrued at July 31, $162.
5 Prepare the income statement.
6 Prepare the statement of owner's equity.
7 Prepare the balance sheet.
8 Journalize the adjusting entries.
9 Journalize the closing entries.
10 Prepare a post-closing trial balance.

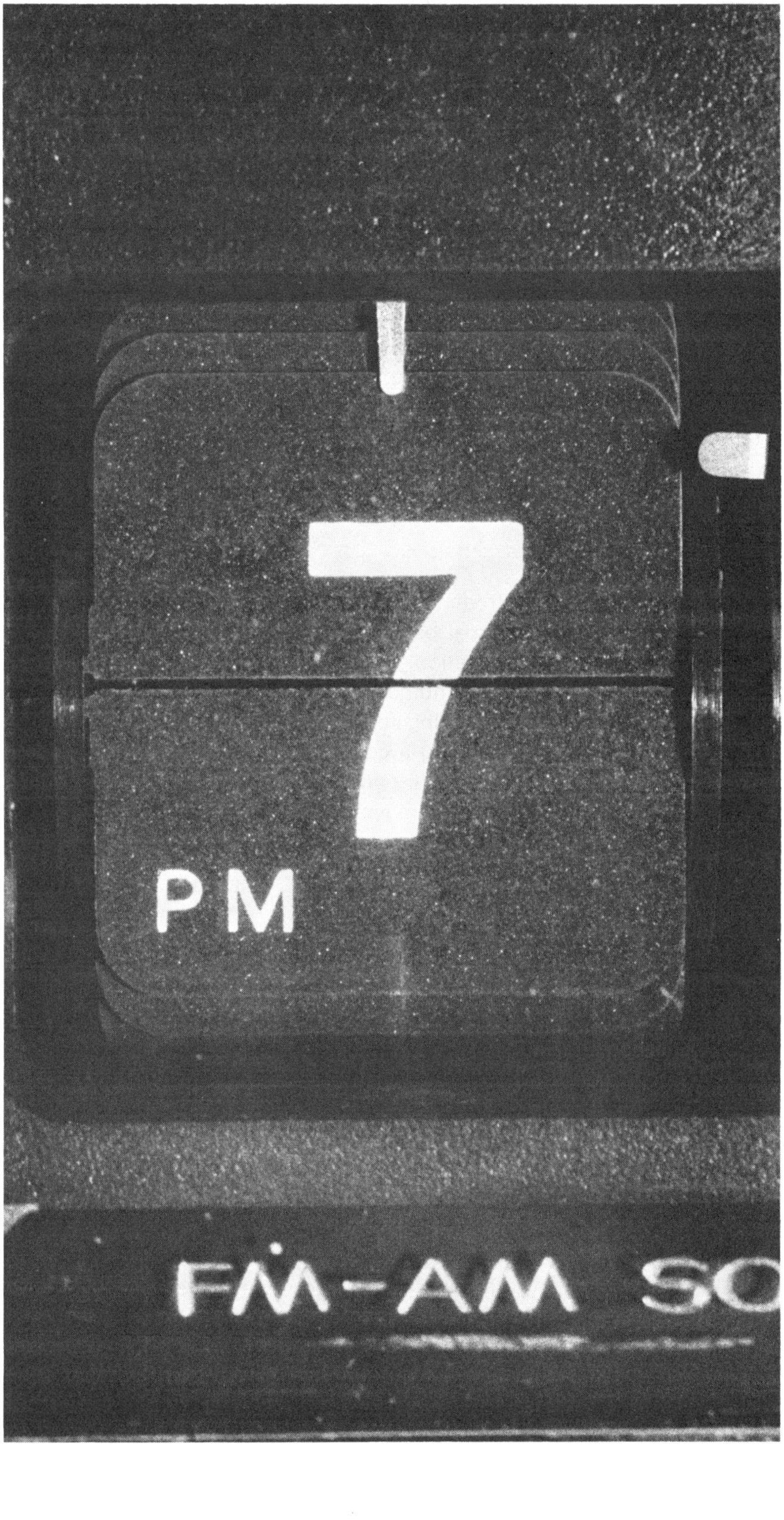
7
PM
FM-AM SO

7 Accounting for professional enterprises

It's uphill all the way for minority-group members who try to go into business on their own. And too few realize that you start making money in your business *only* when you know how to keep books correctly. Earl Graves, Publisher and Editor, *Black Enterprise*

Key points
- Accrual basis of accounting
- Modified cash basis of accounting
- Use of the combined journal
- Accounting procedure for a dentist, a typical professional enterprise

Chapter contents
- Introduction
- Accrual basis versus cash basis of accounting
- Illustration: records of a dentist
- The combined journal
- Accounting for other professional enterprises
- Designing a combined journal
- Illustration: combined journal used for a service-type enterprise
- Summary
- Glossary
- Exercises
- Problems

Specific objectives
After you have completed this chapter, you will be able to:
- Define the following methods of accounting: cash-receipts-and-disbursements basis, modified cash basis, accrual basis.
- Record transactions for both a professional and a service-type enterprise in a combined journal.
- Complete the entire accounting cycle for a professional enterprise.

Introduction
Professional enterprises include the practice of medicine, dentistry, law, architecture, engineering, optometry, and so forth. Naturally the knowledge of accounting procedures that you have acquired can be readily applied to professional enterprises. Generally, the accounting records for professional enterprises are kept on a modified cash basis. To obtain the background setting for this basis, we shall digress briefly in order to define the bases of accounting currently in use and officially recognized.

**Accrual basis versus
cash basis of
accounting**

Accrual basis Up to this time we have been dealing with the accrual basis of accounting, and therefore we shall look at it first in this section. When we use the accrual basis, we record revenue when it is earned and expenses when they are incurred. For example, the books of Dale's Cleaners were recorded on the accrual basis; as proof, let us recall two transactions.

(k) Received the bill for newspaper advertising, $90.

Advertising Expense		Accounts Payable	
(k) 90		**(k)** 90	

The expense was recorded before it was paid in cash.

(p) Entered into a contract with Ace Rental to clean their for-hire garments on a credit basis. Accordingly, we billed Ace Rental $40 for services performed.

Accounts Receivable		Income from Services	
(p) 40		**(p)** 40	

The revenue was recorded before it was received in cash.

Incidentally, accountants feel strongly that this accrual basis gives the most realistic picture of the revenue and expense accounts, and hence the net income, which is derived by subtracting total expenses from total revenue. We shall depart from this basis temporarily, because we are now concerned with professional enterprises, and their accounting records, as we said, are typically kept on a modified cash basis.

Cash basis The *cash basis* is used primarily for convenience and simplicity. As a practical matter, it is divided into two types: the *cash-receipts-and-disbursements basis* and the *modified cash basis.*

**Cash-receipts-and-
disbursements basis**

The term *disbursements* refers to cash payments. A firm which uses the cash-receipts-and-disbursements basis records revenue only when it is received in cash, and generally records expenses only when they are paid in cash. For business firms, this basis is usually limited to enterprises in which very little equipment is involved. In the case of cash expenditures, the Internal Revenue Service makes an exception when expenses are paid in advance, as the expenses are deductible only in the year to which they apply. For example, only one year would be deductible on a 3-year insurance premium that was paid in advance. However, the cash-receipts-and-disbursements basis is used by most individuals in filing their personal income tax returns. Revenue in the form of salaries, wages, dividends, etc., is recorded in the year in which it is received. Likewise, expenditures—to be counted as employee business expenses or personal deductions—are recorded in the year in which they are paid.

Modified cash basis

Not only professional enterprises use a modified cash basis, but also many small business firms use it; in addition, it is useful in accounting for income from rental units. In Internal Revenue Service publications, the modified cash basis is referred to as the *hybrid method*. In addition to the prorating of expenses paid in advance, such as the costs of insurance and supplies, one can also use a modified cash basis by initially recording as assets cash expenditures for long-lived assets that are clearly going to last over a number of years. The cost of these assets is then spread out over a number of years through the medium of depreciation, in the same manner in which we spoke of depreciation earlier. As a result, it is necessary to make adjustments in the work sheet for depreciation, expired insurance, and supplies expense. This is the extent of the adjustments under the modified cash basis. The accrual basis, by comparison, would necessitate an additional adjustment for accrued wages, as well as a number of other adjustments that we shall introduce later.

Illustration: records of a dentist

To understand the accounting system used for a professional enterprise, let us look at the records of Dr. John A. Tanner, a dentist.

Chart of Accounts

	Assets
111	Cash
112	X-ray Supplies
113	Dental Supplies
114	Office Supplies
115	Prepaid Insurance
121	Dental Equipment
122	Accumulated Depreciation, Dental Equipment
123	Office Furniture and Equipment
124	Accumulated Depreciation, Office Furniture and Equipment

	Liabilities
221	Notes Payable

	Owner's Equity
311	J. A. Tanner, Capital
312	J. A. Tanner, Drawing
313	Revenue and Expense Summary

	Revenue
411	Professional Fees

Chart of Accounts (cont.)

	Expenses
511	Dental Supplies Expense
512	Dental Instruments Expense
513	X-ray Supplies Expense
514	Laundry and Cleaning Expense
515	Office Salary Expense
516	Laboratory Expense
517	Rent Expense
518	Insurance Expense
519	Office Supplies Expense
520	Depreciation Expense, Dental Equipment
521	Depreciation Expense, Office Furniture and Equipment
522	Telephone Expense
523	Utilities Expense
524	Repairs and Maintenance Expense
525	Miscellaneous Expense

Appointment record

The dentist's receptionist keeps a daily appointment record, showing the time of appointment and the name of each patient, and gives a copy of the appointment record to the doctor the day before the scheduled appointments. An example appears on page 152.

Patient's ledger record

The dentist's receptionist also maintains a patient's ledger record card for each patient. One side of this card shows a daily record of the services performed, amount of any cost estimate given, plan of payment, information regarding collections, etc.; the card looks like the example shown at the top of page 153.

The other side of the card contains a diagram of the patient's teeth and a space for personal information about the patient.

After the dentist has completed the work, he or she (or an assistant) records a description of the services performed and the amount of the fees in the debit column. The card is returned to the receptionist, who records on the original appointment record the services rendered and the fees charged.

When a patient sends in a payment, the receptionist records the amount in the appointment record and on the patient's ledger record card in the credit column. Remember that the fees charged are not recorded in the Professional Fees account until they are received in cash. The record showing the amounts patients owe is much like Accounts Receivable, except that these amounts are not officially recorded in the books. This record does resemble Accounts Receivable in that debits mean increases in the amounts owed by patients and credits mean decreases in the amounts owed by patients. The balance columns show the final amounts owed by patients.

Appointment Record

Date _12/1_

Hour	Patient	Service Rendered	Fees		Receipts
8 00	Donald Rankin				
15	Patricia Fischer				
30					
45	Cecil Hansen				
9 00					
15					
30					
45	Donna Heller				
10 00	C. F. Elliott				
15					
30					
45	Ralph Simons				
11 00	Peter Smithson				
15					
30					
45					
1 00	Donald C. Kraft				
15					
30	N. C. Byers				
45					
2 00	Mrs. N. D. Silversmith				
15					
30	John F. Piper				
45	Nolan F. Sanderson				
3 00					
15	Nancy Stacy				
30					
45	C. D. Harper				
4 00	Ardis Newell				
15					
30					
45					
5 00					
15					

Name
Elliott, C. H.

Address
1629 S.W. Arbor St., Denver

Telephone
365-2619

Ledger Record

Date	Service Rendered	Time	Debit		Date	Credit		Balance	
6/15	#31 – MOD (3)	10:00	20	00				20	00
6/15	#30 – OCC (1)		7	00				27	00
7/4	CK				7/4	27	00	—	
7/16	#27 – DO (amal.)	9:15	7	00				7	00
7/16	#27 – M (Porc.)		15	00				22	00
8/5	CK				8/5	22	00	—	
9/24	#25 (porcelain jacket)	10:00	125	00				125	00
10/6	CK				10/6	50	00	75	00
10/18	#24 – M (Porc.)	9:00	10	00				85	00
10/18	#24 – D (Porc.)		10	00				95	00
11/3	CK				11/3	50	00	45	00
11/9	#18 full gold crown	10:00	100	00				145	00
12/1	#19 MOD – BU	10:00	20	00				165	00
12/1	Bitewing x-rays (6)		8	00				173	00
12/1	Scale and polish		20	00				193	00
12/1	Impression upper F/1		225	00				418	00
12/1	CS				12/1	60	00	358	00

Plan of Service	Plan of Payments	Collection Effort
1-2 surf.) amalgam 2-3 surf.) 1 full gold crown 1-1 surf.) 1 ceramic crown 2 anterior porcelain Estimate if any $273 upper denture (6 appt.)	30-day basis or $50 per month $60 per month	

The services to be performed may require a number of appointments. Some patients may make partial payments each time they have appointments. Others may pay the entire amount at—or after—the last appointment. Patients' bills are compiled directly from the ledger cards. The dentist or receptionist keeps a constant watch on the patients' ledger records to determine those accounts that are past due and to take the necessary measures to speed up collections. The following statement was mailed to a patient at the end of the month.

STATEMENT

John A. Tanner, D.D.S.
1620 South Canton Place
Denver, Colorado 80226

C. F. Elliott
1629 S. W. Arbor Street
Denver, Colorado 80232

DATE	PATIENT	PROFESSIONAL SERVICE	CHARGE	PAYMENT	BALANCE
6/15	Mr. E.	#31 — MOD (3)	20.00		20.00
6/15	"	#30 — OCC (1)	7.00		27.00
7/4		CK		27.00	—
7/16	"	#27 — DO (Amal.)	7.00		7.00
7/16	"	#27 — M (Porc.)	15.00		22.00
8/5		CK		22.00	—
9/24	"	#25 — PJC	125.00		125.00
10/6		CK		50.00	75.00
10/18	"	#24 — M (Porc.)	10.00		85.00
10/18	"	#24 — D (Porc.)	10.00		95.00
11/3	"	CK		50.00	45.00
11/9	"	#18 — FC (Gold)	100.00		145.00
12/1	"	#19 — MOD — BU	20.00		165.00
12/1	"	Bitewing x-rays (6)	8.00		173.00
12/1	"	Scale and polish	20.00		193.00
12/1	"	Impression upper 7/1	225.00		418.00
12/1		CS		60.00	358.00

PLEASE PAY LAST AMOUNT IN THIS COLUMN ▶

BU.—BUCCAL	MO.—MESIAL OCCLUSAL	BO.—BUCCAL-OCCLUSAL
D.—DISTAL	MOD.—MESIAL OCCLUSAL DISTAL	B.W.—X-RAYS
M.—MESIAL	PJC.—PORCELAIN JACKET CROWN	CS.—CASH
LA.—LABIAL	FC.—FULL CROWN	CK.—CHECK
DO.—DISTAL OCCLUSAL	LI.—LINGUAL	CB.—CEMENT BASE
		¾ CROWN

PAYMENT PLAN— $60.00 per month

Receipt of payments from patients

Depending on the size of the office, the person who receives payments may be the receptionist or the cashier in the accounting office. Whoever receives them issues a written receipt for all incoming cash, filled out in duplicate, sending the first copy to the patient and filing the second copy as evidence of the transaction. Receipts should be prenumbered, so that they can all be accounted for by number. The payment is recorded in the receipts column of the appointment record.

On page 156 is a typical appointment record for a day, showing services rendered, fees (recorded by the dentist on the patients' ledger records), and payments received (recorded by the receptionist). The receptionist deposits $408 in the bank.

Summary of procedures

1 Patients request appointments.
2 Receptionist records appointments on appointment record: date, time, and name of patient.
3 Receptionist furnishes dentist with appointment record for the day, plus the patients' ledger records.
4 Dentist performs services, and records on each patient's ledger record descriptions of the services and the fees to be charged, in the debit column.
5 Receptionist accepts payments from patients both in the office and through the mail, and records receipt of payments in the receipts column of the appointment record.
6 At the end of the day, receptionist deposits in the bank any cash received.
7 Receptionist records on the appointment record the description of services and the amount charged.
8 Receptionist records the payments received from patients on the patients' ledger records, in the credit column. The source of information is the appointment record.
9 The receptionist compiles monthly statements directly from the patients' ledger records.

This procedure may vary, depending on the size of the office staff. It could be further abbreviated by avoiding the repetition of description of services. For the sake of security or internal control, if the size of the office staff is sufficiently large, the function of accepting and depositing money should be separated from the function of recording payments.

Here is a list of Dr. Tanner's transactions for December, the last month of the fiscal period. To save time and space, the receipts of cash are recorded on a weekly basis.

Dec.	1	Paid rent for the month, $500.
	1	Paid telephone bill, $16.
	1	Paid electric bill, $33.
	3	Issued check to Superior Printing for patient statement forms, $66.
	5	Bought drills for cash, $127, from Anderson Dental Supply.
	5	Total cash received from patients during the week, $2,762.

Appointment Record

Date _12/1_

Hour	Patient	Service Rendered	Fees		Receipts	
8 00	Donald Rankin	Extraction	15	00		
15	Patricia Fischer	Three amalgam fillings DO(3)	46	00	16	00
30						
45	Cecil Hansen	Gold inlay filling	65	00		
9 00						
15						
30						
45	Donna Heller	Amalgam filling DO	12	00		
10 00	C. F. Elliott	Denture – full upper	273	00	60	00
15		(6 appointments)				
30						
45	Ralph Simons	Prophylaxis	16	00	16	00
11 00	Peter Smithson	Endodontia treatment	80	00	10	00
15						
30						
45						
1 00	Donald C. Kraft	Amalgam filling MOD	18	00	15	00
15						
30	N. C. Byers	Porcelain jacket crown	115	00		
45						
2 00	Mrs. N. D. Silversmith	Extraction	17	00		
15						
30	John F. Piper	Amalgam filling 1 surf.	9	00		
45	Nolan F. Sanderson	Prophylaxis and full-mouth				
3 00		x-ray (14)	18	00		
15	Nancy Stacy	Fixed bridge 3 unit (Gold)	360	00	40	00
30		(5 appointments)				
45	C. D. Harper	Prophylaxis & bitewing x-rays	20	00		
4 00	Ardis Newell	Periodontal treatment	41	00		
15						
30						
45						
5 00						
15						
	Ronald J. McCaw				40	00
	Helen Bower				35	00
	Eugene Sampson				48	00
	Sidney Weeks				18	00
	C. D. Sanderson				66	00
	Roger Lindsay				18	00
	Gilbert Rae				26	00
			1,105	00	408	00

Dec.	8	Paid bill for repair of office typewriter to Johnson Office Supply, $29.	
	9	Tanner withdrew $200 for personal use.	
	11	Paid Dan-Dee Building Maintenance Company for janitorial service, $60.	
	12	Total cash received from patients during the week, $921.	
	16	Paid Pacific Dental Supply for miscellaneous dental supplies, $216.	
	16	Paid salaries of dental assistant and receptionist, $490.	
	19	Bought new dental chair from Anderson Dental Supply, $617, $217 down, the balance to be paid in eight monthly payments of $50 each.	
	19	Total cash received from patients during the week, $310.	
	22	Tanner withdrew $260 for personal use.	
	23	Paid bill for laboratory expense to Rogers Dental Laboratory, $148.	
	23	Paid Pacific Dental Supply $160 as a contract payment on dental equipment purchased in October.	
	27	Total cash received from patients during the week, $196.	
	29	Tanner wrote check to garage for repairing his car, $64 (to be recorded as Drawing).	
	31	Paid Anderson Dental Supply for miscellaneous dental supplies, $96.	
	31	Paid salaries of dental assistant and receptionist, $490.	
	31	Tanner withdrew $390 for personal use.	
	31	Paid $27 to Manson Publishers Service for magazines for the office.	
	31	Paid Quality Linen Supply for laundry service, $42.	
	31	Total cash received from patients up until last day of year, $133.	

The entries for the first nine of these transactions are now recorded in general journal form.

General Journal				Page 67	
Date		Description	Debit	Credit	
19 __					
Dec.	1	Rent Expense	500 00		
		Cash		500 00	
		Rent for December			
	1	Telephone Expense	16 00		
		Cash		16 00	
		Telephone bill for November			
	1	Utilities Expense	33 00		
		Cash		33 00	
		Electric bill for November			

General Journal			Page 67 (cont.)	
Date		Description	Debit	Credit
Dec.	3	Office Supplies	66 00	
		Cash		66 00
		Superior Printing for statement forms		
	5	Dental Instruments Expense	127 00	
		Cash		127 00
		Anderson Dental Supply for drills		
	5	Cash	2,762 00	
		Professional Fees		2,762 00
		For period December 1 through 5		
	8	Repairs and Maintenance Expense	29 00	
		Cash		29 00
		Johnson Office Supply, typewriter		
	9	J. A. Tanner, Drawing	200 00	
		Cash		200 00
		For personal use		
	11	Laundry and Cleaning Expense	60 00	
		Cash		60 00
		Dan-Dee Building Maintenance Company		

The combined journal

One can obtain more efficiency in the recording and posting of transactions by using a type of journal that is employed for both professional and service-type operations: a *combined journal*. The person keeping records may record each transaction on one line, and use special columns to record transactions that occur often. One can use the Sundry columns to record accounts for which special columns are not available. Compare the recording of the first nine transactions in the combined journal shown on pages 160–161 with the same transactions recorded in the general journal just shown. When you use a combined journal, you don't need any other journal.

After you have added all columns at the end of the month, prove on scratch paper that the sum of the debit totals equals the sum of the credit totals, as shown in the following example.

Column	Debit totals	Credit totals
Cash	$4,322.00	$3,631.00
Dental Supplies	312.00	
J. A. Tanner, Drawing	914.00	
Professional Fees		4,322.00
Laundry and Cleaning Expense	102.00	
Office Salary Expense	980.00	
Laboratory Expense	148.00	
Miscellaneous Expense	27.00	
Sundry	1,548.00	400.00
	$8,353.00	$8,353.00

Posting from the combined journal

The person who is keeping records posts items in the Sundry columns individually, usually daily. After posting the ledger account, the person records the ledger account number in the Posting Reference column of the combined journal. He or she puts a check mark (✓) below the totals of the Sundry columns to indicate that the totals are not to be posted.

Special columns, used only for the debit or credit to specific accounts, are posted as totals. When the person who is keeping the books has posted the total, he or she indicates this by writing the account number in parentheses immediately below the total, then putting the page number of the combined journal in the Posting Reference column of the ledger accounts in the usual manner.

Work sheet for a professional enterprise

Assume that Dr. Tanner's receptionist has posted the journal entries to the ledger accounts, and has recorded the trial balance in the first two columns of the work sheet. Dr. Tanner uses the modified cash basis of accounting, recording revenue only when he has received it in cash, and recording expenses only when he has paid for them in cash. In addition, when Dr. Tanner buys an item that is going to last a number of years, he records this item as an asset, and writes it off or depreciates it in the form of an adjusting entry, made each year over the duration of its useful life. He also makes adjusting entries for expired insurance, as well as for supplies used.

Data for the adjustments are as follows.
a Additional depreciation on dental equipment, $4,200.
b Additional depreciation on office furniture and equipment, $760.
c Inventory of x-ray supplies, $309.
d Inventory of dental supplies, $808.
e Inventory of office supplies, $98.
f Insurance expired, $360.

The work sheet is now completed. On pages 162–163 the work sheet with the adjusting entries is shown.

Combined Journal

Date		Account Name	Post. Ref.	Cash Debit		Cash Credit		Dental Supplies Debit		J. A. Tanner, Drawing Debit		Professional Fees Credit	
19__													
Dec.	1	Rent Expense	517			500	00						
	1	Telephone Expense	522			16	00						
	1	Utilities Expense	523			33	00						
	3	Office Supplies	114			66	00						
	5	Dental Instruments Expense	512			127	00						
	5	Professional Fees	✓	2,762	00							2,762	00
	8	Repairs and Maintenance Expense	524			29	00						
	9	J. A. Tanner, Drawing				200	00			200	00		
	11	Laundry and Cleaning Expense				60	00						
	12	Professional Fees		921	00							921	00
	16	Dental Supplies				216	00	216	00				
	16	Office Salary Expense				490	00						
	19	Dental Equipment	121			217	00						
		Notes Payable	221										
	19	Professional Fees		310	00							310	00
	22	J. A. Tanner, Drawing				260	00			260	00		
	23	Laboratory Expense				148	00						
	23	Notes Payable	221			160	00						
	27	Professional Fees		196	00							196	00
	29	J. A. Tanner, Drawing				64	00			64	00		
	31	Dental Supplies				96	00	96	00				
	31	Office Salary Expense				490	00						
	31	J. A. Tanner, Drawing				390	00			390	00		
	31	Miscellaneous Expense				27	00						
	31	Laundry and Cleaning Expense				42	00						
	31	Professional Fees		133	00							133	00
				4,322	00	3,631	00	312	00	914	00	4,322	00
				(111)		(111)		(113)		(312)		(411)	

Laundry and Cleaning Expense Debit	Office Salary Expense Debit	Laboratory Expense Debit	Misc. Expense Debit	Sundry Debit	Credit
				500 00	
				16 00	
				33 00	
				66 00	
				127 00	
				29 00	
60 00					
	490 00				
				617 00	
					400 00
		148 00			
				160 00	
	490 00				
			27 00		
42 00					
102 00	980 00	148 00	27 00	1,548 00	400 00
(514)	(515)	(516)	(525)	(√)	(√)

J. A. Tanner, D.D.S.
Work Sheet
For year ended December 31, 19___

Account Name	Trial Balance Debit	Trial Balance Credit	Adjustments Debit	Adjustments Credit
Cash	3,893 00			
X-ray Supplies	1,381 00			(c) 1,072 00
Dental Supplies	2,740 00			(d) 1,932 00
Office Supplies	654 00			(e) 556 00
Prepaid Insurance	424 00			(f) 360 00
Dental Equipment	42,617 00			
Accumulated Deprecia-tion, Dental Equip.		8,600 00		(a) 4,200 00
Office Furniture and Equipment	3,900 00			
Accum. Depreciation, Office Furniture and Equipment		2,100 00		(b) 760 00
Notes Payable		3,800 00		
J. A. Tanner, Capital		26,279 00		
J. A. Tanner, Drawing	16,640 00			
Professional Fees		56,012 00		
Dental Instruments Expense	991 00			
Laundry and Cleaning Expense	1,512 00			
Office Salary Expense	11,760 00			
Laboratory Expense	2,928 00			
Rent Expense	6,000 00			
Telephone Expense	206 00			
Utilities Expense	389 00			
Repairs and Main-tenance Expense	444 00			
Miscellaneous Expense	312 00			
	96,791 00	96,791 00		
Depreciation Expense, Dental Equipment			(a) 4,200 00	
Depreciation Expense, Office Furniture and Equipment			(b) 760 00	
X-ray Supp. Expense			(c) 1,072 00	
Dental Supp. Expense			(d) 1,932 00	
Office Supp. Expense			(e) 556 00	
Insurance Expense			(f) 360 00	
			8,880 00	8,880 00
Net Income				

Adjusted Trial Balance		Income Statement		Balance Sheet	
Debit	Credit	Debit	Credit	Debit	Credit
3,893 00				3,893 00	
309 00				309 00	
808 00				808 00	
98 00				98 00	
64 00				64 00	
42,617 00				42,617 00	
	12,800 00				12,800 00
3,900 00				3,900 00	
	2,860 00				2,860 00
	3,800 00				3,800 00
	26,279 00				26,279 00
16,640 00				16,640 00	
	56,012 00		56,012 00		
991 00		991 00			
1,512 00		1,512 00			
11,760 00		11,760 00			
2,928 00		2,928 00			
6,000 00		6,000 00			
206 00		206 00			
389 00		389 00			
444 00		444 00			
312 00		312 00			
4,200 00		4,200 00			
760 00		760 00			
1,072 00		1,072 00			
1,932 00		1,932 00			
556 00		556 00			
360 00		360 00			
101,751 00	101,751 00	33,422 00	56,012 00	68,329 00	45,739 00
		22,590 00			22,590 00
		56,012 00	56,012 00	68,329 00	68,329 00

Financial statements for a professional enterprise

From the work sheet, Dr. Tanner's accountant prepares the following financial statements.

J. A. Tanner, D.D.S Income Statement For year ended December 31, 19__		
Revenue		
Professional Fees		$56,012 00
Expenses		
Office Salary Expense	$11,760 00	
Rent Expense	6,000 00	
Depreciation Expense, Dental Equipment	4,200 00	
Laboratory Expense	2,928 00	
Dental Supplies Expense	1,932 00	
Laundry and Cleaning Expense	1,512 00	
X-ray Supplies Expense	1,072 00	
Dental Instruments Expense	991 00	
Depreciation Expense, Office Furniture and Equipment	760 00	
Office Supplies Expense	556 00	
Repairs and Maintenance Expense	444 00	
Utilities Expense	389 00	
Insurance Expense	360 00	
Telephone Expense	206 00	
Miscellaneous Expense	312 00	
Total Expenses		33,422 00
Net Income		$22,590 00

J. A. Tanner, D.D.S. Statement of Owner's Equity For year ended December 31, 19__		
J. A. Tanner, Capital, Jan. 1, 19__		$26,279 00
Add: Net Income for year	$22,590 00	
Less: Withdrawals for year	16,640 00	
Increase in Capital		5,950 00
J. A. Tanner, Capital, Dec. 31, 19__		$32,229 00

J. A. Tanner, D.D.S.
Balance Sheet
December 31, 19___

Assets			
Cash			$ 3,893 00
X-ray Supplies			309 00
Dental Supplies			808 00
Office Supplies			98 00
Prepaid Insurance			64 00
Dental Equipment	$42,617 00		
Less Accumulated Depreciation	12,800 00	29,817 00	
Office Furniture and Equipment	3,900 00		
Less Accumulated Depreciation	2,860 00	1,040 00	
Total Assets			$36,029 00
Liabilities			
Notes Payable			$ 3,800 00
Owner's Equity			
J. A. Tanner, Capital			32,229 00
Total Liabilities and Owner's Equity			$36,029 00

Adjusting and closing entries

Dr. Tanner (or his receptionist) records the adjusting and closing entries in the Sundry columns of the combined journal. These entries must be posted separately. For example, the adjusting entries are shown on page 166 in an abbreviated page of the combined journal.

There are a number of aspects of the accounting for a professional enterprise which we have not yet dealt with:

1 Special funds, such as the change fund and the petty cash fund. (We shall discuss these in Chapter 13.)
2 Payroll deductions, such as withholdings for employees' income taxes, Social Security taxes, and other salary deductions. (We shall discuss these in Chapter 14.)
3 Payroll taxes levied on the employer, such as the matching for Social Security, and unemployment taxes. (We shall discuss these in Chapter 15.)

Accounting for other professional enterprises

Accounting records for other professional enterprises are similar to our dentist's records. Professional people use the modified cash basis, recording revenue when it is received in cash, and recording expenses when they are paid in cash. Adjusting entries are also made for supplies used, expired insurance, and depreciation on specialized equipment. Ledger cards for patients or clients are used, although they may be given special titles. For example, lawyers call the ledger cards of their clients Collection Dockets.

Combined Journal

Date		Account Name	Post. Ref.	Cash Debit	Cash Credit	Sundry Debit	Sundry Credit
19__		**Adjusting Entries**					
Dec.	31	Deprec. Expense,					
		Dental Equipment	520			4,200 00	
		Accum. Deprec.,					
		Dental Equipment	122				4,200 00
	31	Deprec. Expense,					
		Office Furniture and					
		Equipment	521			760 00	
		Accum. Deprec.,					
		Office Furniture and					
		Equipment	124				760 00
	31	X-ray Supplies					
		Expense	513			1,072 00	
		X-ray Supplies	112				1,072 00
	31	Dental Supplies					
		Expense	511			1,932 00	
		Dental Supplies	113				1,932 00
	31	Office Supplies					
		Expense	519			556 00	
		Office Supplies	114				556 00
	31	Insurance Expense	518			360 00	
		Prepaid Insurance	115				360 00
						8,880 00	8,880 00

Lawyers have an additional asset account, Advances for Clients, representing amounts they have paid on behalf of their clients. Advances for Clients is consequently a receivable, similar to Accounts Receivable. Lawyers also have an additional liability account, Collections for Clients, representing amounts they receive on behalf of their clients. Collections for Clients is consequently a payable, similar to Accounts Payable. All in all, therefore, you can see that the same general accounting principles and procedures prevail in all professional enterprises.

Designing a combined journal

As we have said, the combined journal is widely used in professional offices and service-type business firms. It is interesting to look over the varieties of combined journals that are available at stores that sell office supplies. Some are bound journals, and others are loose-leaf-type books. The number of columns may vary from six to twenty, and they are available with or without column headings. Those which do have printed column headings represent a "canned" type of combined journal; in other words, they are all set up for a particular kind of business enterprise, with descriptions of how to channel routine transactions into the journal. For example, these journals are available for service stations, dry cleaners, doctors' offices, etc.

A person with even a limited knowledge of accounting can keep books as long as the transactions remain routine and fall into the established channels. However, in every business, unusual or nonroutine transactions do seem to pop up from time to time, and therefore you need to have enough knowledge and background to be able to handle them. Understanding the entire accounting system is also essential if you are ever going to see *why* transactions are recorded as they are.

Combined journals with blank columns can be customized to meet specific requirements of a given business. One first studies the operations of the business and makes up a chart of accounts. Next one chooses those accounts that are likely to be used frequently in recording typical transactions of the business. Naturally, if these accounts are used over and over again, one needs to set up special columns for them.

Illustration: combined journal used for a service-type enterprise

As an example of the combined journal for a service-type business, let us return to Dale's Cleaners, the business discussed in Chapters 1 through 6.

The person keeping the records first establishes the chart of accounts, then looks over the accounts to see how frequently each is used. She or he decides at the outset to use special columns for Cash debit and credit, Accounts Receivable debit and credit, Accounts Payable debit and credit, Wages Expense debit, and Income from Services credit. She or he then writes the transactions carried out during the first month of operations.

Observe the way each transaction is recorded in the combined journal shown on pages 168–169. One may use the combined journal in conjunction with either the accrual basis or the cash basis of accounting. You will recognize that the accrual basis is used by Dale's Cleaners.

June	1	Dale Armstrong invests $16,000 cash in his new business.
	2	Armstrong buys $9,000 worth of equipment in cash.
	2	Armstrong buys $2,000 worth of equipment on credit.
	4	Pays $500 to be applied against the firm's liability of $2,000.
	4	Buys cleaning fluids for $200 on credit.
	7	Receives cash income for first week, $300.
	8	Pays $200 rent for the month.
	10	Pays wages to employees, $120.
	10	Pays $160 for a 2-year insurance policy.
	14	Receives cash income for second week, $380.
	14	Receives bill for newspaper advertising, $90.
	15	Pays $900 to creditor as part payment on account.
	15	Receives and pays bill for utilities, $110.
	15	Pays $90 to newspaper for advertising. (This bill has previously been recorded.)

Combined Journal

Date	Ck. No.	Account Name	Post. Ref.	Cash Debit	Cash Credit	Accounts Receivable Debit	Accounts Receivable Credit
19__							
June 1		Dale Armstrong, Capital	311	16,000 00			
2	1	Equipment	121		9,000 00		
2		Equipment, Hansen, Inc.	121				
4	2	Hansen, Inc.			500 00		
4		Supplies, Taylor & Co.	113				
7		Income from Services		300 00			
8	3	Rent Expense	512		200 00		
10	4	Wages Expense			120 00		
10	5	Prepaid Insurance	114		160 00		
14		Income from Services		380 00			
14		Advertising Expense, *Daily Chronicle*	513				
15	6	Hansen, Inc.			900 00		
15	7	Utilities Expense	514		110 00		
15	8	*Daily Chronicle*			90 00		
21		Income from Services		415 00			
23		Ace Rental				40 00	
24	9	Wages Expense			195 00		
26		Equipment, Hansen, Inc.	121				
30		Income from Services		480 00			
30		Ace Rental		30 00			30 00
30	10	Dale Armstrong, Drawing	312		500 00		
				17,605 00	11,775 00	40 00	30 00
				(111)	(111)	(112)	(112)

June 21 Receives cash income for third week, $415.

23 Enters into a contract with Ace Rental to clean their for-hire formal clothes on a credit basis. Accordingly, bills Ace Rental for $40.

24 Pays wages of employees, $195.

26 Buys additional equipment on account, $140.

30 Receives cash income for fourth week, $480.

30 Receives $30 from Ace Rental to apply on the amount previously billed.

30 Withdraws $500 for personal use.

The combined journal above shows all these transactions at a glance.

Summary

A person may keep accounting records for any business by the following methods: cash-receipts-and-disbursements basis, modified cash basis, or

Accounts Payable		Wages Expense	Income from Services	Sundry	
Debit	Credit	Debit	Credit	Debit	Credit
					16,000 00
				9,000 00	
	2,000 00			2,000 00	
500 00					
	200 00			200 00	
			300 00		
				200 00	
		120 00			
				160 00	
			380 00		
	90 00			90 00	
900 00					
				110 00	
90 00					
			415 00		
			40 00		
		195 00			
	140 00			140 00	
			480 00		
				500 00	
1,490 00	2,430 00	315 00	1,615 00	12,400 00	16,000 00
(211)	(211)	(511)	(411)	(✓)	(✓)

accrual basis. The most popular method for a professional enterprise is the modified cash basis, because it is practical and realistic. All three bases are acceptable for income tax purposes, but the business must consistently follow the chosen basis. Professional persons and service-type businesses most often use the combined journal.

Glossary

o **Accrual basis** An accounting method by which revenue is recorded when it is earned, regardless of when it is received. Expenses are recorded when they are incurred, regardless of when they are paid.

o **Cash-receipts-and-disbursements basis** An accounting method by which revenue is recorded only when it is received in cash, and expenses, consisting of all expenditures, are recorded only when they are paid in cash.

o **Modified cash basis** An accounting method by which revenue is recorded only when it is received in cash. Expenditures classified as expenses are recorded only when they are paid in cash. An exception is expenses paid in advance and affecting more than one fiscal period. For example, expenditures for supplies and insurance premiums are *prorated,* or apportioned over the fiscal periods covered. Expenditures for long-lived items are recorded as assets, and later depreciated or written off as an expense during their useful lives.

Exercises

Exercise 1 Using the straight-line method, calculate the depreciation for 1 year on the following assets of a dentist.

a Dental equipment, life 8 years, cost $4,800; trade-in value at end of 8 years, zero.

b Electric typewriter, life 5 years, cost $190; trade-in value at end of 5 years, $40.

Exercise 2 On the appointment record for the dentist, the total of the fees column is $624, and the total of the receipts column is $386. The dentist deposits $386 in the bank at the end of the day. Record the journal entry for the deposit.

Exercise 3 In the following T accounts, record the plus and minus signs and $418 depreciation for the fiscal period.

Depreciation Expense, Equipment	Accumulated Depreciation, Equipment

Exercise 4 Record the depreciation in Exercise 3 in the following work sheet.

Account Name	Trial Balance		Adjustments		Adjusted Trial Balance	
	Debit	Credit	Debit	Credit	Debit	Credit
Equipment	12,000 00				12,000 —	
Accumulated Deprec., Equipment		4,650 00		418 —		5068 —
	56,720 00	56,720 00				
Deprec. Expense, Equipment						

Exercise 5 Record the proper account or classification of accounts in the blank spaces on the next page. Number **1** is given as an example.

1 Assets
2 Expenses
3 Revenue
4 Liabilities

5 Drawing
6 Accumulated Depreciation
7 Owner's Equity

Account Name	Trial Balance		Adjustments		Adjusted Trial Balance		Income Statement		Balance Sheet	
	Debit	Credit	Debit	Credit	Debit	Credit	Debit	Credit	Debit	Credit
	1	7			1	3		3	1	4
	2	6			2	4			8	6
	5	3			5	6				7
		1				7				

Exercise 6 Journalize the closing entries in the proper sequence for the following ledger accounts.

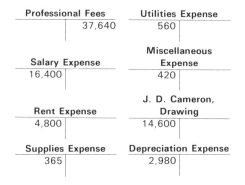

Professional Fees		Utilities Expense	
	37,640	560	

Salary Expense		Miscellaneous Expense	
16,400		420	

Rent Expense		J. D. Cameron, Drawing	
4,800		14,600	

Supplies Expense		Depreciation Expense	
365		2,980	

Exercise 7 The Standifer Insurance Agency uses a combined journal, which has the following columns.

Date
Account Name
Post. Ref.
Cash debit
Cash credit
Accounts Receivable debit
Accounts Receivable credit
Accounts Payable debit
Accounts Payable credit
Commissions Income credit
Salary Expense debit
Miscellaneous Expense debit
Sundry debit
Sundry credit

Answer the following.
a Which money column totals are not posted?
b How do you record an investment of additional cash in the business by C. T. Standifer?
c How do you determine the balance of Cash at any time during the month?
d Which columns are used to record the payment of rent for the month?

Exercise 8 Arrange the steps in the accounting cycle in the appropriate sequence.

6 Financial statements
3 Trial balance
7 Journalizing adjusting entries
1 Journalizing transactions
8 Journalizing closing entries
5 Completing the work sheet
4 Formulating the data for the adjustments
2 Posting to the ledger accounts
9 Post-closing trial balance

Problem 7-1 G. E. Howard, M.D., uses the following chart of accounts.

	Assets
111	Cash
112	Medical Supplies
113	X-ray Supplies
114	Office Supplies
115	Medical Equipment
116	Accumulated Depreciation, Medical Equipment
117	Office Furniture and Equipment
118	Accumulated Depreciation, Office Furniture and Equipment
119	Automobile
120	Accumulated Depreciation, Automobile

	Liabilities
211	Notes Payable

	Owner's Equity
311	G. E. Howard, Capital
312	G. E. Howard, Drawing
313	Revenue and Expense Summary

	Revenue
411	Professional Fees

	Expenses
511	Nurses' Salaries Expense
512	Office Salaries Expense
513	Rent Expense
514	Equipment Rental Expense
515	Medical Supplies Expense
516	X-ray Supplies Expense
517	Laboratory Expense
518	Laundry and Cleaning Expense
519	Office Supplies Expense
520	Depreciation Expense, Medical Equipment
521	Depreciation Expense, Office Furniture and Equipment
522	Depreciation Expense, Automobile
523	Automobile Expense
524	Insurance Expense
525	Telephone Expense
526	Utilities Expense
527	Miscellaneous Expense

Dr. Howard's records consist of an appointment record book, examination and charge reports, patients' ledger records, a general journal, and a general ledger. The doctor fills out an examination and charge report each time a patient visits. The reports contain a description or listing of the treatments and tests administered and the amount of the charges. The charges are then recorded in the patient's ledger record. Monthly statements based on the patient's ledger record are mailed to the patient. Dr. Howard's books are kept on the modified cash basis. These transactions took place during April.

April	1	Paid rent for the month, $900, to Jennings and Logan.
	3	Bought medical supplies for cash from Rogers Surgical Supply, $260.
	4	Paid office salaries, $520, for the month.
	6	Received cash from patients during week, $4,160.
	10	Paid telephone bill, $54.
	12	Paid for laboratory expense to Quality Laboratories, $210.
	13	Total cash received from patients during week, $2,932.
	16	Paid for x-ray supplies to Tempo Supply Company, $122.
	17	Dr. Howard withdrew $520 for personal use.
	19	Bought postage stamps, $26 (Miscellaneous Expense); paid cash.
	20	Received cash from patients during week, $1,184.
	23	Paid for gas and oil to Roy's Service Station, $62.
	24	Paid Speedy News Service for magazines, $41.
	27	Paid $56 for laundry service to Modern Laundry.
	30	Paid nurses' salaries, $1,260, for the month.
	30	Dr. Howard withdrew $680 for personal use.
	30	Paid Johnson Janitorial Service, $82.
	30	Received cash from patients (April 21 through 30), $917.

Instructions

1 Journalize these transactions in the combined journal.
2 Prove the equality of the debit and credit totals.

Problem 7-2 Dr. S. R. Weiss owns and operates the Valley Chiropractic Clinic. The trial balance section of the work sheet as of December 31 of this year is as shown at the top of the next page. (December 31 is the end of the fiscal year.)

Data for the adjustments are as follows.

a Additional depreciation of chiropractic equipment for the year, $2,400.
b Additional depreciation of office furniture and equipment for year, $620.
c Inventory of x-ray supplies, $542.
d Inventory of office supplies, $57.
e Expired insurance, $544.
Instructions Complete the work sheet.

Account Name	Trial Balance Debit	Trial Balance Credit
Cash	6,160 00	
X-ray Supplies	1,262 00	
Office Supplies	427 00	
Prepaid Insurance	621 00	
Chiropractic Equipment	41,600 00	
Accumulated Depreciation, Chiropractic Equipment		16,720 00
Office Furniture and Equipment	3,870 00	
Accumulated Depreciation, Office Furniture and Equipment		2,810 00
Notes Payable		3,990 00
S. R. Weiss, Capital		25,304 00
S. R. Weiss, Drawing	14,500 00	
Professional Fees		30,716 00
Laundry and Cleaning Expense	840 00	
Office Salary Expense	5,600 00	
Rent Expense	3,400 00	
Telephone Expense	280 00	
Utilities Expense	372 00	
Repairs and Maintenance Expense	416 00	
Miscellaneous Expense	192 00	
	79,540 00	79,540 00

Problem 7-3 The trial balance section of the work sheet for R. C. Bowen, architect, as of December 31, the end of the current fiscal year, is as follows.

Account Name	Trial Balance Debit	Trial Balance Credit
Cash	4,280 00	
Supplies	1,426 00	
Office Equipment	23,700 00	
Accumulated Depreciation, Office Equipment		10,870 00
R. C. Bowen, Capital		12,541 00
R. C. Bowen, Drawing	16,200 00	
Professional Fees		50,680 00
Salary Expense	18,720 00	
Blueprint Expense	2,172 00	
Rent Expense	4,200 00	
Automobile Expense	920 00	
Travel Expense	1,480 00	
Entertainment Expense	564 00	
Miscellaneous Expense	429 00	
	74,091 00	74,091 00

Data for the adjustments are as follows.
a Additional depreciation of office equipment, $3,410.
b Inventory of supplies, $212.
Instructions
1 Complete the work sheet.
2 Prepare an income statement.
3 Prepare a statement of owner's equity.
4 Prepare a balance sheet.
5 Journalize the adjusting entries.
6 Journalize the closing entries.

Problem 7-4 Donna D. Pickett, M.D., completed the following transactions during November of this year. Her chart of accounts is as follows.

	Assets
111	Cash
112	Accounts Receivable
113	Supplies
114	Prepaid Insurance
121	Equipment

	Liabilities
211	Accounts Payable

	Owner's Equity
311	Donna D. Pickett, Capital
312	Donna D. Pickett, Drawing
313	Revenue and Expense Summary

	Revenue
411	Professional Fees

	Expenses
511	Salary Expense
512	Rent Expense
513	Laboratory Expense
514	Utilities Expense

Nov.	2	Bought laboratory equipment on account, $940.
	2	Paid office rent for the month, $460.
	2	Received cash on account from patients, $470; A. L. Lawrence, $160; Thomas Dennis, $190; Anthony Anderson, $120. (Dr. Pickett is on the accrual basis, so use Accounts Receivable. Use three lines.)
	4	Received cash for professional services rendered, $125.
	6	Received and paid telephone bill for month, $24.
	6	Received and paid electric bill, $85.
	9	Recorded fees charged to patients on account for professional services rendered, $545: Steven T. Darling, $260; Robert Hastings, $285.
	16	Paid salary of nurse, $315.
	19	Received cash for professional services, $310.
	23	Returned part of equipment purchased on November 2 and received a reduction on the bill, $60.
	27	Billed patients on account for professional services rendered, $390: T. R. Russell, $90; Noah Baker, $160; Alan MacTavish, $140.
	30	Paid salary of nurse, $315.
	30	Paid salary of receptionist, $380, for the month.
	30	Dr. Pickett withdrew $840 cash for personal use.

Instructions

1 Record these transactions in a combined journal.

2 On scratch paper, prove the equality of the debit and credit totals.

Problem 7-1A The following chart of accounts is used by T. J. Bowen, M.D.

	Assets
111	Cash
112	Medical Supplies
113	X-ray Supplies
114	Office Supplies
115	Medical Equipment
116	Accumulated Depreciation, Medical Equipment
117	Office Furniture and Equipment
118	Accumulated Depreciation, Office Furniture and Equipment
119	Automobile
120	Accumulated Depreciation, Automobile

	Liabilities
211	Notes Payable

	Owner's Equity
311	T. J. Bowen, Capital
312	T. J. Bowen, Drawing
313	Revenue and Expense Summary

	Revenue
411	Professional Fees

	Expenses
511	Salaries Expense
512	Rent Expense
513	Equipment Rental Expense
514	Medical Supplies Expense
515	X-ray Supplies Expense
516	Laboratory Expense
517	Laundry and Cleaning Expense
518	Office Supplies Expense
519	Depreciation Expense, Medical Equipment
520	Depreciation Expense, Office Furniture and Equipment
521	Depreciation Expense, Automobile
522	Automobile Expense
523	Insurance Expense
524	Telephone Expense
525	Utilities Expense
526	Miscellaneous Expense

Dr. Bowen's records consist of an appointment record book, examination and charge reports, patients' ledger records, a general journal, and a general ledger.

The doctor fills out an examination and charge report each time a patient visits. The reports contain a description or listing of the treatments and tests administered and the amount of the charges. The charges are then recorded in the patient's ledger record. Monthly statements based on the patients' ledger records are mailed to patients. Dr. Bowen's books are kept on the modified cash basis.

The following transactions took place during September.

Sept.	1	Bought medical supplies for cash from Porter Surgical Supply, $285.
	1	Paid rent for the month, $850, to Dolan Realty.
	5	Paid office salaries, $590, for the month.
	6	Received cash from patients during the week, $4,916.
	7	Bought an examination table from Porter Surgical Supply, costing $420, paying $120 in cash and agreeing by contract to pay the balance in three monthly installments of $100 each. (Credit Notes Payable.)
	8	Paid telephone bill, $62.
	9	Paid for laboratory expense to Superior Laboratories, $216.
	13	Total cash received from patients during the week, $3,114.
	16	Paid for x-ray supplies to Modern Supply Company, $129.
	16	Dr. Bowen withdrew $615 for personal use.
	20	Total cash received from patients during the week, $1,222.
	23	Bought postage stamps, $60 (Miscellaneous Expense); paid cash.
	25	Paid for gas and oil to Stan's Service Station, $65.50.
	29	Paid $40 to United Building Maintenance for janitorial service.
	30	Paid nurses' salaries, $1,342.
	30	Dr. Bowen withdrew $920 for personal use.
	30	Paid $61.40 to Economy Laundry for laundry service through September 30.

Instructions

1 Journalize these transactions in the combined journal.
2 Prove the equality of the debit and credit totals.

Problem 7-2A Dr. Arthur P. Lincoln owns and operates the Lincoln Pet Clinic. The trial balance section of the work sheet as of December 31 of this year is as shown at the top of the next page. (December 31 is the end of the fiscal year.) The data for the adjustments are as follows.

a Additional depreciation of veterinary equipment for the year, $2,860.
b Additional depreciation of office furniture and equipment for year, $418.
c Inventory of x-ray supplies, $129.
d Inventory of medical supplies, $273.
e Expired insurance, $861.

Account Name	Trial Balance	
	Debit	Credit
Cash	1,962 00	
X-ray Supplies	621 00	
Medical Supplies	1,219 00	
Prepaid Insurance	926 00	
Veterinary Equipment	37,720 00	
Accumulated Depreciation, Veterinary Equipment		14,910 00
Office Furniture and Equipment	1,684 00	
Accumulated Depreciation, Office Furniture and Equipment		1,220 00
Notes Payable		871 00
Arthur P. Lincoln, Capital		20,340 00
Arthur P. Lincoln, Drawing	15,600 00	
Professional Fees		38,519 00
Laundry and Cleaning Supplies Expense	968 00	
Wages Expense	8,727 00	
Rent Expense	5,200 00	
Utilities Expense	624 00	
Telephone Expense	144 00	
Repair Expense	329 00	
Miscellaneous Expense	136 00	
	75,860 00	75,860 00

Instructions Complete the work sheet.

Problem 7-3A The trial balance section of the work sheet for H. C. Kurtz, architect, as of December 31, the end of this fiscal year, is as follows.

Account Name	Trial Balance	
	Debit	Credit
Cash	3,179 00	
Supplies	2,172 00	
Office Equipment	31,718 00	
Accumulated Depreciation, Office Equipment		9,760 00
H. C. Kurtz, Capital		22,496 56
H. C. Kurtz, Drawing	15,780 00	
Professional Fees		46,758 00
Salary Expense	17,164 00	
Blueprint Expense	2,008 64	
Rent Expense	4,200 00	
Automobile Expense	886 19	
Travel Expense	1,292 00	
Entertainment Expense	416 53	
Miscellaneous Expense	198 20	
	79,014 56	79,014 56

The data for the adjustments are as follows:
a Additional depreciation of office equipment, $2,982.
b Inventory of supplies, $979.
Instructions
1 Complete the work sheet.
2 Prepare an income statement.
3 Prepare a statement of owner's equity.
4 Prepare a balance sheet.
5 Journalize the adjusting entries.
6 Journalize the closing entries.

Problem 7-4A Donna D. Pickett, M.D., completed the transactions described below during November of this year. Her chart of accounts is as follows.

	Assets
111	Cash
112	Accounts Receivable
113	Supplies
114	Prepaid Insurance
121	Equipment
122	Accumulated Depreciation, Equipment

	Liabilities
211	Accounts Payable

	Owner's Equity
311	Donna D. Pickett, Capital
312	Donna D. Pickett, Drawing
313	Revenue and Expense Summary

	Revenue
411	Professional Fees

	Expenses
511	Salary Expense
512	Rent Expense
513	Laboratory Expense
514	Utilities Expense

May	2	Bought laboratory equipment on account, $936.
	2	Paid office rent for month, $460.
	2	Received cash on account from patients, $470: A. C. Cummings, $85; Agnes Denton, $148; Frank Curtis, $192; Simon Russell, $45. (Dr. Pickett operates on the accrual basis, so use Accounts Receivable. Use four lines.)
	4	Received cash for professional services rendered, $142.
	6	Received and paid telephone bill for the month, $26.
	6	Received and paid electric bill, $82.38.
	9	Recorded fees charged to patients on account for professional services rendered, $469: Derek Stevens, $249; Mildred Wendt, $220.
	16	Paid salary of nurse, $335.
	19	Received cash for professional services, $316.
	23	Returned part of equipment purchased on May 2 and received a reduction on the bill, $42.
	27	Billed patients on account for professional services rendered, $640: Emerson Schultz, $360; Mary MacIntyre, $145; David Allen, $135.
	30	Paid salary of nurse, $335.

May 30 | Paid salary of receptionist, $420.
30 | Dr. Pickett withdrew $985 cash for personal use.

Instructions
1 Record these transactions in the combined journal.
2 On scratch paper, prove the equality of the debit and credit totals.

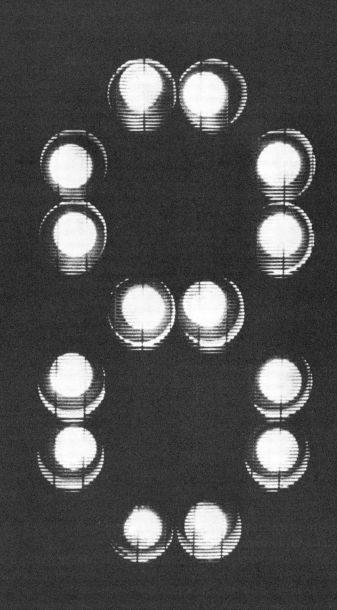

8 Accounting for merchandise: sales

Never anticipate a profit, but provide for all losses. Anonymous

Key points
- Classifications and functions of specific accounts pertaining to merchandise-type enterprises
- Posting from sales journals
- Relationship of controlling account and subsidiary ledger

Chapter contents
- Introduction
- Special journals
- Specific accounts for merchandising firms
- Procedures for handling of sales on account
- The sales journal
- The accounts receivable ledger
- Sales Returns and Allowances
- Posting directly from sales invoices
- Summary
- Glossary
- Exercises
- Problems

Specific objectives

After you have completed this chapter, you will be able to:
- Record transactions in sales journals.
- Post from sales journals to an accounts receivable ledger and a general ledger.
- Prepare a schedule of accounts receivable.
- Post directly from sales invoices to an accounts receivable ledger and a general ledger.

Introduction

By now you've had enough experience to complete the full accounting cycle for a service-type as well as a professional enterprise. To enlarge your accounting knowledge, let us now introduce accounting systems for merchandising enterprises. You will immediately realize that the same general principles of double-entry accounting prevail. This chapter describes specific accounts of merchandising firms (such a merchandising firm could be anything from a dress shop to a supermarket). The sales journal and the accounts receivable ledger are also presented. Just as we used Dale's Cleaners as a continuous illustration of a service-type business, we shall use North Central

Plumbing Supply as an illustration of a merchandising business.

Special journals

In our previous descriptions of the accounting process, we have intentionally shown the entire procedure. In other words, we have taken the long way home, but there are certain shortcuts that you can use. Moreover, as far as understanding accounting is concerned, if you fully understand the long way, it's relatively easy to learn the shortcuts. The reverse is not true, in that you cannot readily understand the entire system if you are exposed to shortcuts only.

Any accounting system must be as efficient as possible. As a matter of fact, accounting is a means, or tool, by which to measure efficiency in a business. Consequently, one should take shortcuts wherever one can do so without sacrificing internal control (discussed in detail in Chapter 9).

As we shall see, using special journals is a form of shortcut. Using a two-column general journal for recording transactions which take place day after day is extremely time-consuming, because each individual debit and credit entry must be posted separately. The combined journal introduced in Chapter 7 improves the efficiency of the posting process. Special journals represent further improvement because they make possible the handling of specialized transactions and delegation of the work.

Here's a list of the special journals that we shall introduce separately in the next few chapters.

Chapter	Special journal	Letter designation	Specialized transaction
8	Sales journal	S	Sales of merchandise on account only
9	Purchases journal	P	Purchase of merchandise on account only
10	Cash receipts journal	CR	All cash received from any source
10	Cash payments journal	CP	All cash paid out for any purpose

When one uses any of these four journals, one must also use the general journal to record any *non*specialized transactions—in other words, any transactions that the special journals cannot handle. In this case the letter designation for the general journal is J.

Specific accounts for merchandising firms

A service or professional enterprise, such as the ones we have encountered, depends for its revenue on the rendering of services; for example, a service or professional enterprise uses such accounts as Income from

Services or Professional Fees. A merchandising business, however, depends for its revenue on the sale of goods or merchandise, recording the amount of the sale under the account titled Sales.

Merchandise consists of a stock of goods that a firm buys and intends to resell, in the same physical condition, at a profit. Merchandise should be differentiated from other assets, such as equipment and supplies, which are acquired for use in the business and are not for resale.

Since the merchandising firm has to record transactions involving the purchase, handling, and sale of its merchandise, it also has to use some specific accounts and procedures that we have not yet discussed. As an introduction to these accounts, we now present the Trial Balance Equation with the new T accounts which are introduced in this chapter, as well as in Chapters 9 and 10.

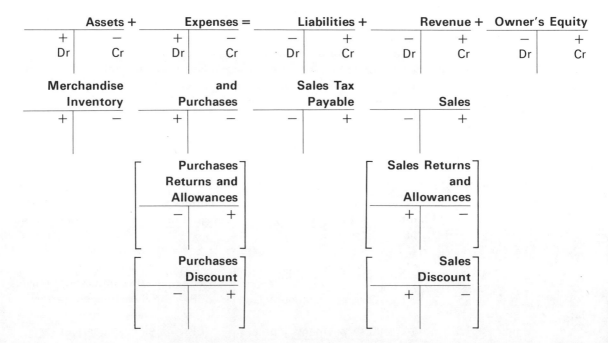

The Sales account, as we have said, is a revenue account, and records the sale of merchandise.

The Purchases account records the cost of merchandise acquired for resale. Remember that the Purchases account is used strictly for the buying of merchandise. The plus and minus signs are the same as the signs for Merchandise Inventory. Purchases is placed under the heading of Expenses merely because the accountant closes it at the end of the fiscal period, along with the expense accounts. Also, Purchases is similar to Expenses, in that it is a temporary decrease in owner's equity.

The Sales Returns and Allowances account records the physical return of merchandise by customers, or a reduction in a bill due to the fact that merchandise was damaged. It is treated as a deduction from Sales.

The Purchases Returns and Allowances account records the firm's return of merchandise previously purchased, or a reduction in the bill due to damaged merchandise. It is treated as a deduction from Purchases.

The Sales Discount and Purchases Discount accounts record cash discounts granted for prompt payments, in accordance with the credit terms. We shall discuss these in connection with the cash journals.

The firm's accountant makes entries involving Merchandise Inventory only when the firm takes an actual physical count of the goods in stock; otherwise the accountant leaves this account strictly alone.

The brackets around the account titles emphasize that we are treating these accounts as deductions from the related accounts placed above them. The reason we list these accounts as deductions is that they appear as deductions in the financial statements. This is similar to the relationship between the Drawing account and the Capital account; remember that we deduct Drawing from Capital in the statement of owner's equity.

The type of transaction most frequently encountered in a merchandising business is the sale of merchandise. Some businesses sell on a cash-and-carry basis only; others sell on a credit basis only. Many firms offer both arrangements. The same general types of entries could pertain to both retail and wholesale enterprises. Here are some examples.

Sale of merchandise for cash, $100.

Cash		Sales	
+	−	−	+
100			100

Debit Cash and credit Sales; record this in the cash receipts journal.

Sale of merchandise on account, $200.

Accounts Receivable		Sales	
+	−	−	+
200			200

Debit Accounts Receivable and credit Sales; then record this in the sales journal.

Procedures for handling of sales on account

All sales are recorded in response to an order received from a customer. The routines for processing orders and recording sales vary with the type and size of the business.

In a retail business, a salesperson usually prepares a sales ticket—either in duplicate or triplicate—for a sale on account. One copy is given to the customer, and another copy to the accounting department, where it will be used as the basis for an entry in the sales journal. A third copy may be used for a record of sales as, for example, when one is computing sales commissions or is involved in inventory control.

In a wholesale business, the company usually receives a written order from a customer, or from a salesperson who obtained the order from the customer. The order must then be approved by the credit department, after which it is sent to the billing department, where the sales invoice is prepared. As in the case of the sales ticket, the sales invoice may be made out either in duplicate or in triplicate.

For our illustration we shall use North Central Plumbing Supply, a wholesaler. One of their invoices follows.

Invoice   No. __320__

North Central Plumbing Supply
1968 Arrow St., N.W.
Seattle, Washington 98111

Sold to:

T. L. Long Co.
18160 Federal St., S. W.
Seattle, Wash. 98110

Date _____ August 1, 19__

Terms _____ 2/10, n/30 _____

Shipped via __Their truck__

Quantity	Description	Price	Total
100'	3/4" galv. pipe, 10' lengths	.235	235.00
50	1½" cast-iron 90° reg. elbow	.90	45.00
40	1½" cast-iron 90° street elbow	1.125	45.00
			325.00

As a basis for the introduction to the sales journal, we shall use three transactions as illustrations.

Aug.	1	Sold merchandise on account to T. L. Long Company, $325, invoice no. 320.
	3	Sold merchandise on account to Macon, Inc., $116, invoice no. 321.
	6	Sold merchandise on account to Acme Plumbing and Heating, $94, invoice no. 322.

We can use T accounts to visualize these transactions.

Accounts Receivable		Sales	
+	−	−	+
325			325
116			116
94			94

If they were recorded in a general journal, they would appear as follows.

General Journal					Page 23
Date	Description	Post. Ref.	Debit		Credit
19__					
Aug. 1	Accounts Receivable	113	325	00	
	Sales	411			325 00
	Invoice no. 320,				
	T. L. Long Company				
3	Accounts Receivable	113	116	00	
	Sales	411			116 00
	Invoice no. 321,				
	Macon, Inc.				
6	Accounts Receivable	113	94	00	
	Sales	411			94 00
	Invoice no. 322, Acme				
	Plumbing and Heating				

Next the journal entries would be posted to the accounts in the general ledger, as shown at the top of the next page.

Obviously, there is a great deal of repetition in both journalizing and posting. The credit sales require three separate journal entries, three debit postings to Accounts Receivable, and three credit postings to Sales. Using a *sales journal* avoids all this repetition. We have presented all of this to show the advantages of the sales journal.

Accounts Receivable				Post. Ref.	Debit	Credit	Balance Debit	Balance Credit	Account No. 113

Accounts Receivable — Account No. 113

Date		Item	Post. Ref.	Debit	Credit	Balance Debit	Balance Credit
19__ Aug.	1		23	325 00		325 00	
	3		23	116 00		441 00	
	6		23	94 00		535 00	

Sales — Account No. 411

Date		Item	Post. Ref.	Debit	Credit	Balance Debit	Balance Credit
19__ Aug.	1		23		325 00		325 00
	3		23		116 00		441 00
	6		23		94 00		535 00

The sales journal

The sales journal records *sales of merchandise on account only.* This special-ized type of transaction would result in debits to Accounts Receivable and credits to Sales. We shall now record the three transactions for North Central Plumbing Supply in the sales journal as a substitute for recording them in the general journal.

Sales Journal — Page 38

Date		Invoice No.	Customer's Name	Post. Ref.	Accts. Rec. Dr Sales Cr
19__ Aug.	1	320	T. L. Long Company		325 00
	3	321	Macon, Inc.		116 00
	6	322	Acme Plumbing and Heating		94 00

Note that the one money column is headed *Accounts Receivable Debit* and *Sales Credit.* Each transaction requires only a single line. Repetition is avoided, and one can now find all entries for sales of merchandise on account in one place. Listing the invoice number is useful in case one should later want to make a further check on the details of a particular sale.

Posting from the sales journal

Using the sales journal also enables one to save time and space when one is posting to the ledger accounts. The transactions involving the sales of merchandise on account for the month of August are as shown at the top of the next page.

Since all the entries are a debit to Accounts Receivable and a credit to Sales,

Sales Journal
Page 38

Date		Invoice No.	Customer's Name	Post. Ref.	Accts. Rec. Dr Sales Cr
19__					
Aug.	1	320	T. L. Long Company		325 00
	3	321	Macon, Inc.		116 00
	6	322	Acme Plumbing and Heating		94 00
	9	323	Manning Service Company		961 00
	11	324	Clark and Keller Hardware		86 00
	16	325	Home Hardware Company		215 00
	20	326	Henning's Plumbing		293 00
	23	327	Baker Building Supplies		560 00
	24	328	Clark and Keller Hardware		286 00
	28	329	Home Hardware Company		75 00
	30	330	Baker Building Supplies		387 00
	31	331	T. L. Long Company		56 00
	31	332	Robert D. Bishop, Inc.		871 00
					4,325 00
					(113)(411)

one can now make a single posting to these accounts for the amount of the total as of the last day of the month. (In each of the following ledger accounts, assume there was no balance in the account prior to the transaction.)

Accounts Receivable
Account No. 113

Date	Item	Post. Ref.	Debit	Credit	Balance Debit	Balance Credit
19__						
Aug. 31		S38	4,325 00		4,325 00	

Sales
Account No. 411

Date	Item	Post. Ref.	Debit	Credit	Balance Debit	Balance Credit
19__						
Aug. 31		S38		4,325 00		4,325 00

In the Posting Reference columns of the ledger accounts, the letter S designates the sales journal.

After posting to the ledger accounts, go back to the sales journal and record the account numbers in parentheses directly below the totals. Write the account number of the account that was debited (in this case, Accounts Receivable) on the left side of the column. Again, as a precaution, don't record these account numbers until you have completed the postings.

Sales journal provision for sales tax

In most states there's a sales tax on retail sales of goods and services. The retailer collects the sales tax from customers and then later pays it to the tax authorities.

When goods or services are sold on a credit basis, the sales tax is charged to the customer and recorded at the time of the sale. The sales journal has to be redesigned to handle this type of transaction. For example, if a retail store sells an item for $100 and the sales tax is 4%, then, by T accounts, it would be recorded like this.

Accounts Receivable	Sales	Sales Tax Payable
+ −	− +	− +
104	100	4

The accountant debits Sales Tax Payable and credits Cash when the sales tax is paid to the government.

The following sales journal is for Clark and Keller Hardware, a retail enterprise.

Sales Journal   Page 96

Date		Sales Slip	Customer's Name	Post. Ref.	Accounts Receivable Debit	Sales Tax Payable Credit	Sales Credit
19__							
Apr.	1	9382	N. T. George		16 64	64	16 00
	1	9383	Culver Apartments		22 88	88	22 00
	1	9384	Richard Gladdon		52 00	2 00	50 00
	2	9385	T. R. Sears		12 48	48	12 00
	30	10121	Paul Murphy		124 80	4 80	120 00
					2,516 80	96 80	2,420 00
					(113)	(214)	(411)

Each column is posted to the ledger accounts as a total at the end of the month. After posting the figures, the accountant records the account numbers in parentheses immediately below the total.

Accounts Receivable   Account No. 113

Date	Item	Post. Ref.	Debit	Credit	Balance Debit	Balance Credit
19__						
Apr. 30		S96	2,516 80		2,516 80	

Sales Tax Payable						Account No. 214	
		Post.			Balance		
Date	Item	Ref.	Debit	Credit	Debit	Credit	
19 __							
Apr. 30		S96		96 80		96 80	

Sales						Account No. 411	
		Post.			Balance		
Date	Item	Ref.	Debit	Credit	Debit	Credit	
19 __							
Apr. 30		S96		2,420 00		2,420 00	

**The accounts
receivable ledger**

The Accounts Receivable account, as we have seen, represents the total amount owed to a business by its charge customers.

But there is a deficiency of information here, in that the business can't tell at a glance *how much* each individual charge customer owes. This handicaps the credit department. To correct this shortcoming, one must keep a separate account for each charge customer.

For a business having very few charge customers, it is possible to have a separate Accounts Receivable account in the general ledger for each charge customer. However, if there are many charge customers (which is the usual case), this would be too cumbersome. The trial balance, with each charge customer's account included, would be very long. Of course, the possibility for errors would also increase accordingly.

So it is more practical to have a separate book containing a list of all the charge customers and each one's respective balance. This is called the *accounts receivable ledger.* The Accounts Receivable account should still be maintained in the general ledger; when all the postings are up to date, the balance of this account should equal the total of all the individual balances of the charge customers. The Accounts Receivable account in the general ledger is called a *controlling account.* The accounts receivable *ledger,* containing the accounts or listing of all the charge customers, is really a special ledger, and it is called a *subsidiary ledger.* The interrelationship of these books is illustrated on page 192.

The accountant posts the individual amounts daily to the accounts receivable ledger, so that this ledger will have up-to-date information. At the end of the month, the accountant posts the total of the sales journal (in this case, $1,800) to the general ledger accounts as a debit to the Accounts Receivable (controlling) account and a credit to the Sales account. As indicated in the illustration on page 192, the balance of the Accounts Receivable (controlling)

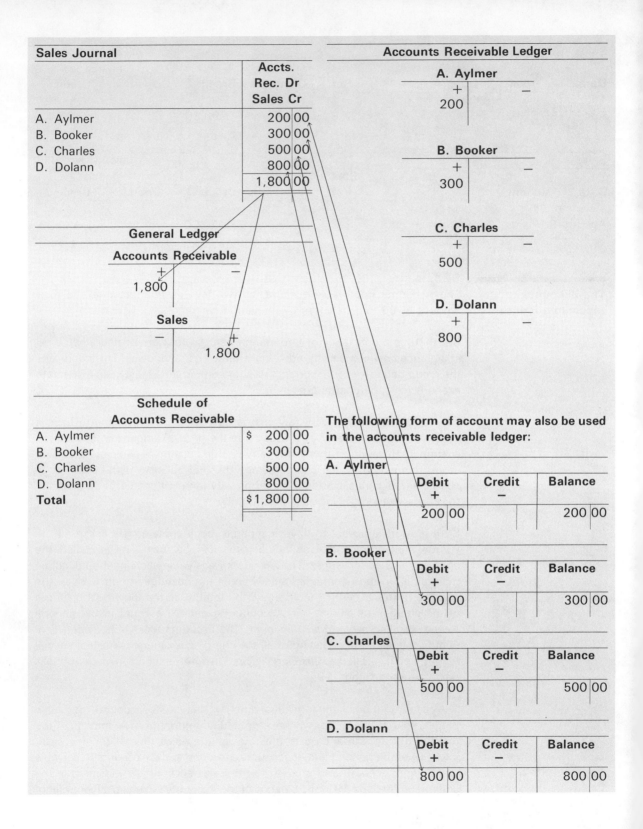

Sales Journal

	Accts. Rec. Dr Sales Cr
A. Aylmer	200 00
B. Booker	300 00
C. Charles	500 00
D. Dolann	800 00
	1,800 00

General Ledger

Accounts Receivable

+	−
1,800	

Sales

−	+
	1,800

Schedule of Accounts Receivable

A. Aylmer	$ 200 00
B. Booker	300 00
C. Charles	500 00
D. Dolann	800 00
Total	$1,800 00

Accounts Receivable Ledger

A. Aylmer

+	−
200	

B. Booker

+	−
300	

C. Charles

+	−
500	

D. Dolann

+	−
800	

The following form of account may also be used in the accounts receivable ledger:

A. Aylmer

Debit +	Credit −	Balance
200 00		200 00

B. Booker

Debit +	Credit −	Balance
300 00		300 00

C. Charles

Debit +	Credit −	Balance
500 00		500 00

D. Dolann

Debit +	Credit −	Balance
800 00		800 00

account at the end of the month must equal the total of the balances of the charge customer accounts in the accounts receivable ledger. The schedule of accounts receivable, which is merely a listing and total of the individual balances, shows this.

After you post the amount from the sales journal to the charge customer's account in the accounts receivable ledger, put a check mark (√) in the Posting Reference column of the sales journal.

Let us now look at North Central Plumbing Supply's sales journal for August, with the daily postings that their accountant has made to the accounts receivable ledger, as well as the schedule of accounts receivable.

Sales Journal   Page 38

Date		Invoice No.	Customer's Name	Post. Ref.	Accts. Rec. Dr Sales Cr
19__					
Aug.	1	320	T. L. Long Company	√	325 00
	3	321	Macon, Inc.	√	116 00
	6	322	Acme Plumbing and Heating	√	94 00
	9	323	Manning Service Company	√	961 00
	11	324	Clark and Keller Hardware	√	86 00
	16	325	Home Hardware Company	√	215 00
	20	326	Henning's Plumbing	√	293 00
	23	327	Baker Building Supplies	√	560 00
	24	328	Clark and Keller Hardware	√	286 00
	28	329	Home Hardware Company	√	75 00
	30	330	Baker Building Supplies	√	387 00
	31	331	T. L. Long Company	√	56 00
	31	332	Robert D. Bishop, Inc.	√	871 00
					4,325 00
					(113)(411)

Accounts Receivable Ledger
Acme Plumbing and Heating
1015 Broadway, S.W.
Seattle, Washington 98102

Date		Invoice No.	Item	Post. Ref.	Debit	Credit	Balance
19__							
Aug.	6	322		S38	94 00		94 00

Baker Building Supplies
17 No. Second St.
Renton, Washington 98055

Date		Invoice No.	Item	Post. Ref.	Debit		Credit		Balance	
19—										
Aug.	23	327		S38	560	00			560	00
	30	330		S38	387	00			947	00

Robert D. Bishop, Inc.
2168 Main St.
Kent, Washington 98031

Date		Invoice No.	Item	Post. Ref.	Debit		Credit		Balance	
19—										
Aug.	31	332		S38	871	00			871	00

Clark and Keller Hardware
2005 N. Powder St.
Everett, Washington 98201

Date		Invoice No.	Item	Post. Ref.	Debit		Credit		Balance	
19—										
Aug.	11	324		S38	86	00			86	00
	24	328		S38	286	00			372	00

Henning's Plumbing
21680 S.E. Twelfth Ave.
Portland, Oregon 97208

Date		Invoice No.	Item	Post. Ref.	Debit		Credit		Balance	
19—										
Aug.	20	326		S38	293	00			293	00

Home Hardware Company
2810 Pender St. N.W.
Seattle, Washington 98101

Date		Invoice No.	Item	Post. Ref.	Debit		Credit		Balance	
19—										
Aug.	16	325		S38	215	00			215	00
	28	329		S38	75	00			290	00

T. L. Long Company
18160 Federal St., S.W.
Seattle, Washington, 98110

Date		Invoice No.	Item	Post. Ref.	Debit		Credit		Balance	
19__										
Aug.	1	320		S38	325	00			325	00
	31	331		S38	56	00			381	00

Macon, Inc.
1720 Ninth St., N.W.
Seattle, Washington 98107

Date		Invoice No.	Item	Post. Ref.	Debit		Credit		Balance	
19__										
Aug.	3	321		S38	116	00			116	00

Manning Service Company
2720 N.W. 43rd Ave.
Portland, Oregon 97210

Date		Invoice No.	Item	Post. Ref.	Debit		Credit		Balance	
19__										
Aug.	9	323		S38	961	00			961	00

North Central Plumbing Supply
Schedule of Accounts Receivable
August 31, 19__

Acme Plumbing and Heating	$	94 00
Baker Building Supplies		947 00
Robert D. Bishop, Inc.		871 00
Clark and Keller Hardware		372 00
Henning's Plumbing		293 00
Home Hardware Company		290 00
T. L. Long Company		381 00
Macon, Inc.		116 00
Manning Service Company		961 00
Total Accounts Receivable		$4,325 00

In the accounts receivable ledger, the individual charge customer accounts are listed in alphabetical order. Most accountants prefer a loose-leaf binder so that they can insert accounts for new customers and remove other accounts; they do not use account numbers.

Assuming that these were the only transactions involving charge customers, the accountant prepares a schedule of accounts receivable, listing the balance of each charge customer.

Again we assume that there were no previous balances in the customer's accounts. So the Accounts Receivable (controlling) account in the general ledger will have the same balance, $4,325.

Accounts Receivable						Account No. 113		
			Post.				Balance	
Date		Item	Ref.	Debit	Credit	Debit	Credit
19__							
Aug.	31		S38	4,325 00		4,325 00	

Sales Returns and Allowances

This account handles two types of transactions having to do with merchandise that has previously been sold. A *return* means a physical return of the goods. An *allowance* means allowing a reduction from the original price due to the fact that the goods were defective or damaged. It may not be economically worthwhile to return the goods; each situation is a special case. In order to avoid writing a separate letter each time, one uses a special form which is called a *credit memorandum*. A typical one might look like this.

Credit Memorandum   No. __69__

North Central Plumbing Supply
1968 Arrow St., N.W.
Seattle, Washington 98111

Credit to:

⌐   ¬
    Clark and Keller Hardware   Date ____August 25, 19__
    2005 N. Powder St.
    Everett, Wash. 98201
∟   ⌙

WE CREDIT YOUR ACCOUNT AS FOLLOWS:

1 pedestal sump pump (Randall) 1/3 h.p., 1 1/4" discharge tap   45.00

The Sales Returns and Allowances account is considered to be a deduction from Sales. In order to have a better record of the total returns and allowances, accountants use an account separate from Sales, and they deduct Sales Returns and Allowances from Sales in the income statement, as we shall see later. Let's consider this situation by using T accounts.

(a) On August 24, North Central sold merchandise on account to Clark and Keller Hardware, $286, and recorded this in the sales journal.
(b) On August 25, Clark and Keller Hardware returned $45 worth of the merchandise, and North Central issued a credit memorandum.

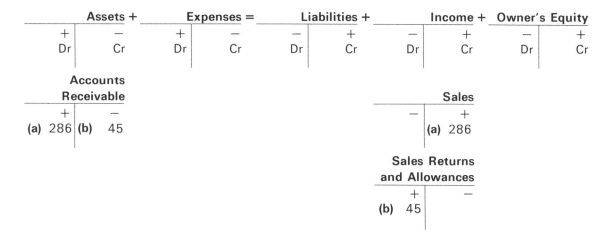

North Central's accountant debits Sales Returns and Allowances because North Central has greater returns and allowances than they did before, and credits Accounts Receivable because the charge customer (Clark and Keller) owes less than before.

One uses the word *credit* in "credit memorandum" because one credits Accounts Receivable. During August, North Central Plumbing Supply issues two credit memorandums, and records the entries in the general journal as follows.

General Journal				Page 27	
Date	Description	Post. Ref.	Debit		Credit
19__					
Aug.	25 Sales Returns and Allowances		45 00		
	Accounts Receivable, Clark				
	and Keller Hardware	/			45 00
	Credit memorandum				
	no. 69				

General Journal   **Page 27 (cont.)**

Date		Description	Post. Ref.	Debit		Credit	
Aug.	31	Sales Returns and Allowances		116	00		
		Accounts Receivable, Home					
		Hardware Company	/			116	00
		Credit memorandum					
		no. 70					

Note that Accounts Receivable is not the only thing recorded in the general journal entry; it is followed by the name of the charge customer's account in the accounts receivable ledger. If the balance of the Accounts Receivable (controlling) account is to equal the total of the individual balances in the accounts receivable ledger, one must post to *both* the Accounts Receivable account in the general ledger *and* the account of Clark and Keller Hardware in the accounts receivable ledger. To take care of this double posting, one puts a slant line in the Posting Reference column. When the amount has been posted as a credit to this account, the accountant puts the account number of Accounts Receivable in the left part of the Posting Reference column. After the account of Clark and Keller Hardware has been posted as a credit, the accountant puts a check mark in the right portion of the Posting Reference column, then posts Sales Returns and Allowances in the usual manner. Here are the entries with posting completed. (No balance was recorded in the Accounts Receivable account because a credit balance would not be a normal balance for the account.)

General Journal   **Page 27**

Date		Description	Post. Ref.	Debit		Credit	
19__							
Aug.	25	Sales Returns and Allowances	412	45	00		
		Accounts Receivable, Clark					
		and Keller Hardware	113/√			45	00
		Credit memorandum					
		no. 69					
	31	Sales Returns and Allowances	412	116	00		
		Accounts Receivable, Home					
		Hardware Company	113/√			116	00
		Credit memorandum					
		no. 70					

General Ledger

Accounts Receivable　　　　　　　　　　　　　　　　　　　　　　　　Account No. 113

Date		Item	Post. Ref.	Debit	Credit	Balance Debit	Balance Credit
19__							
Aug.	25		J27		45 00	——	
	31		J27		116 00	——	

Sales Returns and Allowances　　　　　　　　　　　　　　　　　Account No. 412

Date		Item	Post. Ref.	Debit	Credit	Balance Debit	Balance Credit
19__							
Aug.	25		J27	45 00		45 00	
	31		J27	116 00		161 00	

Accounts Receivable Ledger

Clark and Keller Hardware
2005 N. Powder St.
Everett, Washington 98201

Date		Invoice No.	Item	Post. Ref.	Debit	Credit	Balance
19__							
Aug.	11	324		S38	86 00		86 00
	24	328		S38	286 00		372 00
	25			J27		45 00	327 00

Home Hardware Company
2810 Pender St. N.W.
Seattle, Washington 98101

Date		Invoice No.	Item	Post. Ref.	Debit	Credit	Balance
19__							
Aug.	16	325		S38	215 00		215 00
	28	329		S38	75 00		290 00
	31			J27		116 00	174 00

Posting directly from sales invoices

An accountant can take a further shortcut by posting directly from the sales invoices or sales slips. The accountant posts to the charge customers' accounts in the accounts receivable ledger daily, directly from carbon copies of the sales invoices or sales slips. He or she writes the invoice number in the Posting Reference column in place of the journal page number. Then, at the end of the month, he or she brings the Accounts Receivable (controlling) account in the general ledger up to date, by totaling all the sales invoices for the month, then making a general journal entry debiting Accounts Receivable and crediting Sales.

For a change, let us use a different firm as an illustration. The Mendozo Sports Equipment Company posts directly from its sales invoices; the total of their sales invoices for December is $17,296. Their accountant journalizes and posts the entry as follows.

General Journal   **Page 36**

Date		Description	Post. Ref.	Debit	Credit
19__					
Dec.	31	Accounts Receivable		17,296 00	
		Sales			17,296 00
		Summarizing entry for the total of the sales invoices for the month			

General Ledger

Accounts Receivable   **Account No. 113**

Date		Item	Post. Ref.	Debit	Credit	Balance Debit	Balance Credit
19__							
Dec.	31		J36	17,296 00		17,296 00	

Sales   **Account No. 411**

Date		Item	Post. Ref.	Debit	Credit	Balance Debit	Balance Credit
19__							
Dec.	31		J36		17,296 00		17,296 00

This is called a *summarizing entry* because it summarizes the credit sales for 1 month. Their accountant posts the entry to the accounts in the general ledger, which does away with the need for a sales journal, since the one summarizing entry in the general journal records the total sales for the month.

One invoice and the corresponding entry in the accounts receivable ledger might look like those shown at the top of the next page.

The $168 figure would, of course, be posted to the general ledger as a part of the total comprising the summarizing entry.

Summary

Keeping special journals is a shortcut in the accounting process, which makes it possible to record a transaction on one line and to post column totals rather than individual figures. This chapter introduced three new kinds of accounts:

Invoice   No. 6075

Mendozo
Sports Equipment Company
1610 Alhambra Blvd.
San Diego, California 92002

Sold to:
Reams and Son, Sporting Goods
1600 S.W. Santa Clara Ave.
Portland, Oregon 97216

Date ___Dec. 4, 19___

Terms ___2/10, n/30___

Shipped via ___Express Collect___

Quantity	Description	Price	Total
10	Molded unicellular foam ski/life vest (Davis) lg.	16.80	168.00

Accounts Receivable Ledger
Reams and Son, Sporting Goods
1600 S.W. Santa Clara Ave.
Portland, Oregon 97216

Date	Item	Post. Ref.	Debit	Credit	Balance
19___ Dec. 4		6075	168 00		168 00

Sales is a revenue account like Income from Services; *Sales Returns and Allowances* is a deduction from Sales; and *Sales Tax Payable* is a liability account, since the company has to pay the balance to a state or local government.

The sales journal takes care of sales of merchandise on account only. The entries are posted *daily* to the accounts receivable ledger. At the end of the month the total is posted to the general ledger as a debit to the Accounts Receivable (controlling) account and a credit to the Sales account. When a customer returns merchandise that he or she has bought, or when his/her bill is reduced due to an allowance for defective or damaged merchandise, the Sales Returns and Allowances account is increased, and the Accounts

Receivable account is decreased. The entry is recorded in the general journal and posted to both the general ledger and the accounts receivable ledger.

Another shortcut is using sales invoices or sales slips as a sales journal, thereby doing away with the sales journal. One posts to the charge-customer accounts in the accounts receivable ledger directly from the sales invoices. At the end of the month, one adds all the sales invoices and makes a summarizing entry in the general journal for the amount of the total. This entry is a debit to Accounts Receivable and a credit to Sales.

Glossary

o **Controlling account** An account in the general ledger which summarizes the balances of a subsidiary ledger.
o **Credit memorandum** A written statement indicating a seller's willingness to reduce the amount of a buyer's debt. The seller records the amount of the credit memorandum under the Sales Returns and Allowances account.
o **Merchandise inventory** A stock of goods that a firm buys with the intent of reselling in the same physical condition.
o **Sales discount** A deduction from the original price, granted by the seller to the buyer for the prompt payment of an invoice.
o **Sales Returns and Allowances** The account a seller uses to record the amount of a reduction granted to a customer either for the physical return of merchandise previously sold to the customer, or as compensation for merchandise that is damaged. This account is usually evidenced by a credit memorandum issued by the seller.
o **Sales tax** A tax levied by a state or local government on the sale of goods. The tax is paid by the consumer, but collected by the merchant.
o **Special journal** A book of original entry in which one records specialized types of transactions; each transaction is recorded on one line.
o **Subsidiary ledger** A group of accounts representing individual subdivisions of a controlling account.

Exercises

Exercise 1 Describe the transactions recorded in the following T accounts.

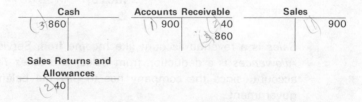

Exercise 2 Record the following transactions in general journal form.
a Sold merchandise on account to L. B. Simpson, $120, invoice no. 318.
b Issued credit memo no. 18 to L. B. Simpson for merchandise returned, $20.
c Received full payment from L. B. Simpson.

Exercise 3 Post the following entry to the general ledger and subsidiary ledger accounts.

General Journal   **Page 43**

Date		Description	Post. Ref.	Debit	Credit
19__					
May	1	Sales Returns and Allowances	412	121 16	
		Accounts Receivable, J. B.			
		Stokes	113		121 16
		Issued credit			
		memo no. 129			

General Ledger

Accounts Receivable   **Account No. 113**

Date		Item	Post. Ref.	Debit	Credit	Balance Debit	Balance Credit
19__							
May	1	Balance	✓		121 16	6,321 70	
			743			6200 54	

Sales Returns and Allowances   **Account No. 412**

Date		Item	Post. Ref.	Debit	Credit	Balance Debit	Balance Credit
May	1		J43	121 16		121 16	

Accounts Receivable Ledger   ✓

J. B. Stokes

Date		Invoice No.	Item	Post. Ref.	Debit	Credit	Balance
19__							
Apr.	30	761		S26	492 60	121 16	492 60
May	1						

Exercise 4 Describe the transactions recorded in the following T accounts.

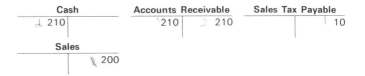

Cash		Accounts Receivable		Sales Tax Payable
1. 210		`210	2. 210		1. 10

Sales	
	1. 200

Exercise 5 Label the blanks as debit or credit.

Sales Journal   **Page __**

Date	Sales Slip	Customer's Name	Post. Ref.	Accounts Receivable (debit)	Sales Tax Payable (CR)	Sales (CR)

Exercise 6 Record the following transactions in general journal form.

a Sold merchandise for cash to Axel Bremmer, $100 plus 5% sales tax.

b Bremmer returned $20 of the merchandise, issued credit memo no. 323, and paid Bremmer $21 in cash, $20 for the amount of the returned merchandise plus $1 for the amount of the sales tax.

Exercise 7 A business firm uses carbon copies of its sales invoices to record sales of merchandise on account and carbon copies of its credit memorandums to record its sales returns and allowances. During September, the firm issued 214 invoices for $82,729.82 and 12 credit memorandums for $1,768.20. Present the summarizing entries, dated September 30, in general journal form, to record the sales and sales returns for the month.

Exercise 8 On Monday morning a sleepy accountant made the following errors in journalizing sales of merchandise on account in a single-column sales journal and posting to the general ledger and accounts receivable ledger. The errors were discovered at the end of the month before the closing entries were journalized and posted. Describe the means of correcting the errors.

a He footed the sales journal correctly as $34,760, but posted it as a debit and credit of $34,670.

b He posted a sale of $56 to T. R. Standifer to his account as $5.60.

c He recorded a sale of $72 to A. C. Piazza in the sales journal correctly, but posted it to Piazza's account as $27.

Problems

Problem 8-1 Fanning Wholesale Electric Company, which opened for business during October of this year, had the following sales of merchandise on account and sales returns and allowances during the month.

Oct.	6	Sold merchandise on account to Danforth Electric, invoice no. 1, $260.
	9	Sold merchandise on account to N. T. Bremmer Company, invoice no. 2, $315.
	11	Sold merchandise on account to Baker and Martin, Inc., invoice no. 3, $870.
	16	Sold merchandise on account to Francis Hardware, invoice no. 4, $776.
	17	Issued credit memorandum no. 1, $48, to N. T. Bremmer Company for merchandise returned.
	21	Sold merchandise on account to Danforth Electric, invoice no. 5, $964.
	23	Issued credit memorandum no. 2 to Baker and Martin, Inc., for merchandise returned, $120.
	27	Sold merchandise on account to Francis Hardware, invoice no. 6, $229.
	29	Sold merchandise on account to N. T. Bremmer Company, invoice no. 7, $694.
	30	Sold merchandise on account to Danforth Electric, invoice no. 8, $161.
	31	Issued credit memorandum no. 3, to Baker and Martin, Inc., for damage done to merchandise during shipping, $40.

Instructions
1 Record the above sales of merchandise on account in the sales journal. Record the sales returns and allowances in the general journal.
2 Immediately after recording each transaction, post to the accounts receivable ledger.

3 At the end of the month, post the entries from the general journal and the sales journal to the general ledger. Post the sales journal amount as a total.

4 Prepare a schedule of accounts receivable.

5 Compare the balance of the Accounts Receivable control account with the total of the schedule of accounts receivable.

Problem 8-2 McFadden Brothers sells welding equipment on a wholesale basis. The following transactions took place during March of this year.

Mar.	1	Sold merchandise on account to Danton Construction Company, Invoice no. 621, $457.
	6	Sold merchandise on account to R. T. Grover Company, invoice no. 622, $353.
	7	Issued credit memorandum no. 30 to Raymond Farm Supply for merchandise returned, $34.
	12	Sold merchandise on account to Stan's Hardware, invoice no. 623, $98.
	14	Sold merchandise on account to Singleton and Graves, invoice no. 624, $921.
	19	Sold merchandise on account to Stanton School District No. 23, invoice no. 625, $469.
	23	Issued credit memorandum no. 31 to Singleton and Graves for merchandise returned, $96.
	25	Sold merchandise on account to Raymond Farm Supply, invoice no. 626, $392.
	29	Sold merchandise on account to Stan's Hardware, invoice no. 627, $872.
	31	Issued credit memorandum no. 32 to Stan's Hardware for damage to merchandise, $29.

Instructions

1 Record these sales of merchandise on account in the sales journal. Record the sales returns and allowances in the general journal.

2 Immediately after recording each transaction, post to the accounts receivable ledger.

3 At the end of the month, post the entries from the general journal and the sales journal to the general ledger.

4 Prepare a schedule of accounts receivable.

Problem 8-3 Sunset Florists sells flowers on a retail basis. Most of the sales are for cash; however, a few steady customers have charge accounts. Sunset salespersons fill out sales slips for each sale. The state government levies a 5% retail sales tax, which is collected by the retailer. The following represent Sunset Florists' charge sales for November.

Nov.	3	Sold floral arrangement to A. T. Anderson, sales slip no. 238, $16, plus sales tax of $.80, total $16.80.
	5	Sold potted plant to Neil Nolan, sales slip no. 263, $8, plus sales tax of $.40, total $8.40.

Nov. 10	Sold corsage to Florence Scott, sales slip no. 271, $6, plus sales tax of $.30.
15	Sold wreath to American Legion for $24, plus sales tax, sales slip no. 282.
16	Givens Funeral Home bought several floral arrangements on account, sales slip no. 296, $60, plus sales tax.
19	Givens Funeral Home returned a flower spray, from sales slip no. 296. Delivery of the spray occurred after the funeral was over, so Sunset allowed full credit on the sale of $18 and the sales tax of $.90.
20	First Federal Savings and Loan Association bought flower arrangements for their anniversary for $90, plus sales tax, sales slip no. 303.
22	Allowed First Federal Savings and Loan credit, $8, plus tax, because of withered blossoms in floral arrangements bought on sales slip no. 303.

Instructions

1 Record the transactions in either the sales journal or the general journal.
2 Immediately after recording each transaction, post to the accounts receivable ledger.
3 At the end of the month, post the entries from the general journal and the sales journal to the general ledger.
4 Prepare a schedule of accounts receivable.

Problem 8-4 Wear-Ever Leather Goods Company uses carbon copies of its charge sales invoices as a sales journal, and posts to the accounts receivable ledger directly from the sales invoices. At the end of the month, the accountant totals the invoices and makes an entry in the general journal summarizing the charge sales for the month. The charge sales invoices are as follows.

Mar. 3	T. R. Timmins Company, invoice no. 2016, $360.
9	Northern Novelty Company, invoice no. 2019, $789.
12	Harold J. Townsend, invoice no. 2021, $219.
16	Vance and Harris, invoice no. 2024, $1,068.
17	Coolidge and Roe, Inc., invoice no. 2025, $724.
19	Prentice and Thomas, Inc., invoice no. 2027, $191.
25	Perez Specialty Company, invoice no. 2028, $783.
29	Singleton Amusement Company, invoice no. 2039, $860.
30	Northern Novelty Company, invoice no. 2040, $1,216.

Instructions

1 Post to the accounts receivable ledger directly from the sales invoices, listing the invoice number in the Posting Reference column.
2 Record the summarizing entry in the general journal for the total amount of the sales invoices.
3 Post the general journal entry to the appropriate accounts in the general ledger.
4 Prepare a schedule of accounts receivable.

Problem 8-1A Fanning Wholesale Electric, which opened for business during May of this year, had the following sales of merchandise on account and sales returns and allowances during the month.

May	3	Sold merchandise on account to Danforth Electric, invoice no. 1, $272.65.
	9	Sold merchandise on account to N. T. Bremmer Company, invoice no. 2, $318.
	11	Sold merchandise on account to Baker and Martin, Inc., invoice no. 3, $864.20.
	16	Sold merchandise on account to Francis Hardware, invoice no. 4, $788.16.
	17	Issued credit memorandum no. 1, $26, to N. T. Bremmer Company for merchandise returned.
	22	Sold merchandise on account to Danforth Electric, invoice no. 5, $976.70.
	24	Issued credit memorandum no. 2, $118.10, to Baker and Martin, Inc. for merchandise returned.
	27	Sold merchandise on account to Francis Hardware, invoice no. 6, $227.18.
	29	Sold merchandise on account to N. T. Bremmer Company, invoice no. 7, $698.
	30	Sold merchandise on account to Danforth Electric, invoice no. 8, $163.72.
	31	Issued credit memorandum no. 3, $44, to Baker and Martin, Inc. for merchandise damaged in transit.

Instructions
1 Record these sales of merchandise on account in the sales journal. Record the sales returns and allowances in the general journal.
2 Immediately after recording each transaction, post to the accounts receivable ledger.
3 At the end of the month, post the entries from the general journal and the sales journal to the general ledger; post the sales journal amount as a total.
4 Prepare a schedule of accounts receivable.
5 Compare the balance of the Accounts Receivable control account with the total of the schedule of accounts receivable.

Problem 8-2A McFadden Brothers sells welding equipment on a wholesale basis. The following transactions took place during March of this year.

Mar.	1	Sold merchandise on account to Danton Construction Company, invoice no. 623, $482.
	7	Sold merchandise on account to R. T. Grover Company, invoice no. 624, $386.
	8	Issued credit memorandum no. 41 to Raymond Farm Supply for merchandise returned, $46.
	13	Sold merchandise on account to Stan's Hardware, invoice no. 625, $106.

Mar.	15	Sold merchandise on account to Singleton and Graves, invoice no. 626, $933.
	20	Sold merchandise on account to Stanton School District No. 23, invoice no. 627, $481.
	24	Issued credit memorandum no. 42 to Singleton and Graves for merchandise returned, $97.
	26	Sold merchandise on account to Raymond Farm Supply, invoice no. 628, $398.
	29	Sold merchandise on account to Stan's Hardware, invoice no. 629, $861.
	30	Issued credit memorandum no. 43 to Stan's Hardware for damage to merchandise, $43.

Instructions

1 Record these sales of merchandise on account in the sales journal. Record the sales returns and allowances in the general journal.
2 Immediately after recording each transaction, post to the accounts receivable ledger.
3 At the end of the month, post the entries from the general journal and the sales journal to the general ledger.
4 Prepare a schedule of accounts receivable.

Problem 8-3A Sunset Florists sells flowers on a retail basis. Most sales are for cash; however, a few steady customers have charge accounts. Sunset salespersons fill out sales slips for each sale. The state government levies a 5% retail sales tax, which is collected by the retailer. Sunset Florists' charge sales for November are as follows:

Nov.	3	Sold floral arrangement to A. T. Anderson, sales slip no. 238, $18, plus sales tax of $.90, total $18.90.
	5	Sold potted plant to Neil Nolan, sales slip no. 263, $7, plus sales tax of $.35, total $7.35.
	10	Sold corsage to Florence Scott, sales slip no. 271, $4.80, plus sales tax of $.24.
	15	Sold wreath to American Legion for $26, plus sales tax, sales slip no. 282.
	16	Givens Funeral Home bought several floral arrangements on account, sales slip no. 296, $80, plus sales tax.
	19	Givens Funeral Home returned a flower spray, from sales slip no. 296. Delivery of the spray occurred after the funeral was over, so Sunset allowed full credit on the sale of $14, and the sales tax of $.70.
	20	First Federal Savings and Loan Association bought flower arrangements for their anniversary for $110, plus sales tax, sales slip no. 303.
	22	Allowed First Federal Savings and Loan credit, $11, plus tax, because of withered blossoms in floral arrangements bought on sales slip no. 303.

Instructions

1 Record these sales of merchandise on account in either the sales journal or the general journal.

2 Immediately after recording each transaction, post to the accounts receivable ledger.

3 At the end of the month, post the entries from the general journal and the sales journal to the general ledger.

4 Prepare a schedule of accounts receivable.

Problem 8-4A Wear-Ever Leather Goods Company uses carbon copies of its charge sales invoices as a sales journal, and posts to the accounts receivable ledger directly from the sales invoices. The invoices are totaled at the end of the month, and an entry is made in the general journal which summarizes the charge sales for the month. The charge sales invoices for March are as follows.

Mar.	2	T. R. Timmins Company, invoice no. 3912, $348.
	7	Northern Novelty Company, invoice no. 3925, $104.
	9	Harold J. Townsend, invoice no. 3936, $542.
	11	Vance and Harris, invoice no. 3944, $744.
	16	Coolidge and Roe, Inc., invoice no. 3962, $148.
	21	Prentice and Thomas, Inc., invoice no. 3978, $432.
	25	Perez Specialty Company, invoice no. 3989, $539.
	27	Singleton Amusement, invoice no. 3999, $268.
	31	Northern Novelty Company, invoice no. 4011, $189.

Instructions

1 Post to the accounts receivable ledger directly from the sales invoices, listing the invoice number in the Posting Reference column.

2 Record the summarizing entry in the general journal for the total amount of the sales invoices.

3 Post the general journal entry to the appropriate accounts in the general ledger.

4 Prepare a schedule of accounts receivable.

9

Accounting for merchandise: purchases

O money, money, money, I'm not necessarily
  one of those who think thee holy,
But I often stop to wonder how thou
  canst go out so fast when thou
  comest in so slowly.

Ogden Nash, "Hymn to the Thing That Makes the Wolf Go"

Key points
- The Purchases account is used exclusively for the buying of merchandise.
- How to post from a purchases journal
- How to handle transportation charges on incoming goods

Chapter contents
- Introduction
- Purchasing procedures
- Purchases journal
- The accounts payable ledger
- Purchases Returns and Allowances
- Posting directly from purchase invoices
- Transportation charges on incoming merchandise and other assets
- Internal control
- Summary
- Glossary
- Exercises
- Problems

Specific objectives
After you have completed this chapter, you will be able to:
- Record transactions in a one-column purchases journal.
- Post from a one-column purchases journal to an accounts payable ledger and a general ledger.
- Prepare a schedule of accounts payable.
- Post directly from purchase invoices to an accounts payable ledger and a general ledger.
- Journalize transactions involving transportation charges on incoming goods.

Introduction

We've been talking about the procedures, accounts, and special journals used to record the *selling* of merchandise. Now let's talk about those same elements as they apply to the *buying* of merchandise. This means that we'll be dealing with the Purchases account as well as Purchases Returns and Allowances. You'll see in this chapter that Accounts Payable is a controlling account, just as you saw in Chapter 8 that Accounts Receivable is a controlling account.

Purchasing procedures

When you think of the great variety in types and sizes of merchandising firms, it comes as no surprise to learn that there is also considerable variety in the procedures used to buy goods for resale. Some purchases may be for cash; however, in most cases, purchases are on a credit basis. In a small retail store, the owner may do the buying. In large retail and wholesale concerns, department heads or division managers do the buying, after which the purchasing department goes into action: placing purchase orders, following up the orders, receiving the goods, and seeing that deliveries are made to the right departments. The purchasing department also acts as a source of information on current prices, price trends, quality of goods, prospective suppliers, and reliability of suppliers.

The purchasing department as a rule requires that any buying orders be in writing, in the form of a purchase requisition. After the purchase requisition is approved, the purchasing department sends a *purchase order* to the supplier. A purchase order is the company's written offer to buy certain goods. The accountant does not make any entry at this point, because the supplier has not yet indicated acceptance of the order. A purchase order is made out in triplicate: One copy goes to the supplier, one stays in the purchasing department (as proof of what was ordered), and one goes to the department that sent out the requisition (this tells them that the goods they wanted have indeed been ordered.)

To continue with the illustration of North Central Plumbing Supply: The pipe department submits a purchase requisition to the purchasing department as shown at the top of page 214.

The purchasing department completes the bottom part of the purchase requisition and sends out a purchase order (bottom of page 214).

The seller now sends an *invoice* to the buyer. This invoice should arrive in advance of the goods (or at least *with* the goods). From the seller's point of view, this is a sales invoice. If the sale is on credit, as we saw in Chapter 8, the seller's accountant makes an entry debiting Accounts Receivable and crediting Sales. To the buyer, this is a purchase invoice, so the buyer's accountant makes an entry debiting Purchases and crediting Accounts Payable. North Central Plumbing Supply receives from Danton, Inc., the invoice we see on page 215.

Purchase Requisition   No. C-726

North Central Plumbing Supply
1968 Arrow St., N.W.
Seattle, Washington 98111

Department ____Pipe_____   Date of Request ___July 2, 19___
Advise on delivery ___Mr. Holloway___   Date Required ___Aug. 5, 19___

Quantity	Description
1,000'	Flexible copper tubing 5/8", Type L (50' roll)

Approved by ___Steven Thompson___   Requested by ___J. H. Holloway___

For Purchasing Dept. Use Only

Purchase Order No. __7918__   Issued to: Danton, Inc.
Date ___July 5, 19___   1616 Madlyn Ave.
                                                  Los Angeles, Calif. 90026

Purchase Order   No. 7918

North Central Plumbing Supply
1968 Arrow St., N.W.
Seattle, Washington 98111

To: Date ____July 5, 19___
┌   ┐   Deliver by __Aug. 1, 19___
   Danton, Inc.   Ship via ___Freight Truck___
   1616 Madlyn Ave.   F.O.B. ____Los Angeles___
   Los Angeles, Calif. 90026   Terms ___2/10, n/30___
└   ┘

Quantity	Description	Unit Price
1,000'	Flexible copper tubing 5/8", Type L (50' roll)	.285

Steven Thompson

Danton, Inc.

1616 Madlyn Ave.
Los Angeles, California
90026

Invoice no. _____ **2706**
Invoice date _July 31, 19___
Terms _2/10, n/30_
Cust. order no. _____ 7918
Contract no. _____

Sold to

┌   ┐
    North Central Plumbing Supply
    1968 Arrow St., N.W.
    Seattle, Wash. 98111
└   ┘

Destination _Seattle_
Date shipped _July 28, 19__
How shipped _Western_
            Freight Line

Ship to

┌   ┐
    same

└   ┘

F.O.B. _Los Angeles_

Quantity	Description	Unit price	Amount
1,000'	Flexible copper tubing 5/8", Type L (50' roll)	.285	285.00

Let us now extract, from the Trial Balance Equation (recall Chapter 8), the T accounts involved in buying merchandise (see page 216). The brackets indicate that these accounts are deductions from Purchases. Bear in mind that the Purchases account is used exclusively for the buying of merchandise intended for resale. If the firm buys anything else, the accountant records the amount under the appropriate asset or expense account. At the end of the fiscal period, the balance in the Purchases account represents the total cost of merchandise bought during the period. As we said in Chapter 8, Purchases is classified as an expense only for the sake of convenience, because it is closed at the end of the fiscal period along with the expense accounts. Also, the Purchases account is like expenses in that it is a temporary decrease in owner's equity.

Purchases Returns and Allowances is a deduction from Purchases. So that we can keep track of the amount of the returns, we set up a separate account for them. In the income statement, we treat Purchases Returns and Allowances and Purchases Discount as deductions from Purchases; so, for consistency they are presented right below Purchases in the Trial Balance Equation just shown. (We'll talk about Purchases Discount in Chapter 10.)

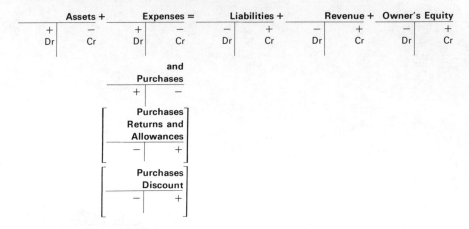

To get back to North Central Plumbing Supply: As in the pattern of Chapter 8, we'll record three transactions in the general journal. Then—just to point up again the advantage of special journals as opposed to the general journal—we'll record the same three transactions in a special journal.

During the first week in August, the following transactions took place.

Aug. 2	Bought merchandise on account from Danton, Inc., $285, their invoice no. 2706, dated July 31, terms 2/10, n/30.
3	Bought merchandise on account from Rogers and Simon Company, $760, their invoice no. 982, dated August 2, terms net 30 days.
5	Bought merchandise on account from Argel Manufacturing Company, $692, their invoice no. 10611, dated August 3, terms 2/10, n/30.

Let's visualize these transactions in terms of T accounts. ("2/10, n/30" refers to the purchase or cash discount, meaning that a 2% discount is allowed if the bill is paid within 10 days after the date of the invoice, and the bill must be paid within 30 days after the date of invoice.)

Purchases		Accounts Payable	
+	−	−	+
285			285
760			760
692			692

If these transactions were recorded in the general journal, they would be:

General Journal   **Page 22**

Date		Description	Post. Ref.	Debit	Credit
19__					
Aug.	2	Purchases	511	285 00	
		Accounts Payable	211		285 00
		Danton Inc., their invoice no. 2706, terms 2/10, n/30, dated July 31			
	3	Purchases	511	760 00	
		Accounts Payable	211		760 00
		Rogers and Simon Company, their invoice no. 982, terms net 30 days, dated Aug. 2			
	5	Purchases	511	692 00	
		Accounts Payable	211		692 00
		Argel Manufacturing Company, their invoice no. 10611, terms 2/10, n/30, dated Aug. 3			

Next the general journal entries would be posted to the general ledger.

Purchases   **Account No. 511**

Date		Item	Post. Ref.	Debit	Credit	Balance Debit	Balance Credit
19__							
Aug.	2		22	285 00		285 00	
	3		22	760 00		1,045 00	
	5		22	692 00		1,737 00	

Accounts Payable   **Account No. 211**

Date		Item	Post. Ref.	Debit	Credit	Balance Debit	Balance Credit
19__							
Aug.	2		22		285 00		285 00
	3		22		760 00		1,045 00
	5		22		692 00		1,737 00

Purchases journal

The above repetition could have been avoided if the accountant had used a *purchases journal* instead of the general journal. The purchases journal is used for the *purchase of merchandise on account only*. In each case, with this special type of transaction, the accountant debits Purchases and credits Accounts Payable.

Purchases Journal							Page 29
Date	Supplier's Name	Invoice No.	Invoice Date	Terms	Post. Ref.	Purch. Dr Accts. Pay. Cr	
19__							
Aug.	2 Danton, Inc.	2706	7/31	2/10 n/30		285	00
	3 Rogers and Simon Company	982	8/2	n/30		760	00
	5 Argel Manufacturing Company	10611	8/3	2/10 n/30		692	00

Note that the one money column is headed Purchases Debit and Accounts Payable Credit. Each transaction can thus be recorded on one line.

Posting from the purchases journal

The accountant has now journalized the transactions involving the purchase of merchandise on account for August.

Purchases Journal							Page 29
Date	Supplier's Name	Invoice No.	Invoice Date	Terms	Post. Ref.	Purch. Dr Accts. Pay. Cr	
19__							
Aug.	2 Danton, Inc.	2706	7/31	2/10 n/30		285	00
	3 Rogers and Simon Company	982	8/2	n/30		760	00
	5 Argel Manufacturing Company	10611	8/3	2/10 n/30		692	00
	9 Sinclair Manufacturing Company	B643	8/6	1/10 n/30		165	00
	18 Tru-Fit Valve, Inc.	46812	8/17	n/60		228	00
	25 Donaldson and Farr	1024	8/23	2/10 n/30		376	00
	26 Danton, Inc.	2801	8/25	n/30		406	00
						2,912	00
						(511)(211)	

Since all the entries are debits to Purchases and credits to Accounts Payable, one can post these accounts as totals at the end of the month.

Purchases							Account No. 511	
		Post.				Balance		
Date	Item	Ref.	Debit		Credit	Debit		Credit
Aug.	31	P29	2,912	00		2,912	00	

Accounts Payable							Account No. 211	
		Post.				Balance		
Date	Item	Ref.	Debit		Credit	Debit		Credit
19__								
Aug.	1 Balance	✓					356	00
	31	P29			2,912 00		3,268	00

In the Posting Reference column of the ledger accounts, P designates the purchases journal. After posting to the ledger accounts, the accountant goes back to the purchases journal and records the account numbers in parentheses right below the totals, placing on the left the account that was debited.

The accounts payable ledger

In Chapter 8 we called the Accounts Receivable account in the general ledger the *controlling* account, and explained that the accounts receivable ledger consisted of individual accounts for each charge customer, and that the accountant posts to the accounts receivable ledger every day.

Now, Accounts Payable is a parallel case, since it is also a controlling account in the general ledger. The accounts payable ledger is also a subsidiary ledger, and consists of individual accounts for each creditor. Again, in the accounts payable ledger, posting is daily. After posting to the individual creditors' accounts, the accountant puts a check mark (✓) in the Posting Reference column of the purchases journal. After he or she has finished all the posting to the controlling account and the accounts payable ledger, the total of the schedule of accounts payable should equal the balance of the Accounts Payable (controlling) account. Incidentally, one always uses the three-column form for the accounts payable ledger. Since the T account for Accounts Payable is

it follows that the three-column form is like this:

Accounts Payable Ledger

	Debit	Credit	Balance
	−	+	+

Let's now recapitulate what the purchases journal looks like, and show how daily postings are made to the accounts payable ledger.

Purchases Journal — Page 29

Date	Supplier's Name	Invoice No.	Invoice Date	Terms	Post. Ref.	Purch. Dr Accts. Pay. Cr
19—						
Aug. 2	Danton, Inc.	2706	7/31	2/10 n/30	✓	285 00
3	Rogers and Simon Company	982	8/2	n/30	✓	760 00
5	Argel Manufacturing Company	10611	8/3	2/10 n/30	✓	692 00
9	Sinclair Manufacturing Company	B643	8/6	1/10 n/30	✓	165 00
18	Tru-Fit Valve, Inc.	46812	8/17	n/60	✓	228 00
25	Donaldson and Farr	1024	8/23	2/10 n/30	✓	376 00
26	Danton, Inc.	2801	8/25	n/30	✓	406 00
						2,912 00
						(511) (211)

Accounts Payable Ledger

Argel Manufacturing Company
2510 Madeira Ave.
San Francisco, California 94130

Date		Invoice No.	Item	Post. Ref.	Debit		Credit		Balance	
19__										
Aug.	5	10611		P29			692	00	692	00

Danton, Inc.
1616 Madlyn Ave.
Los Angeles, California 90026

Date		Invoice No.	Item	Post. Ref.	Debit		Credit		Balance	
19__										
Aug.	2	2706		P29			285	00	285	00
	26	2801		P29			406	00	691	00

Donaldson and Farr
1600 S.W. Yelm St.
Portland, Oregon 97216

Date		Invoice No.	Item	Post. Ref.	Debit		Credit		Balance	
19__										
Aug.	25	1024		P29			376	00	376	00

Rogers and Simon Company
21325 186th Ave. No.
Seattle, Washington 98101

Date		Invoice No.	Item	Post. Ref.	Debit		Credit		Balance	
19__										
July	27	899		P28			180	00	180	00
Aug.	3	982		P29			760	00	940	00

Sinclair Manufacturing Company
1068 Casino Ave.
Los Angeles, California 90023

Date		Invoice No.	Item	Post. Ref.	Debit	Credit	Balance
19__							
Aug.	9	B643		P29		165 00	165 00

Tru-Fit Valve, Inc.
1620 Minard St.
San Francisco, California 94130

Date		Invoice No.	Item	Post. Ref.	Debit	Credit	Balance
19__							
July	29	45981		P28		176 00	176 00
Aug.	18	46812		P29		228 00	404 00

Note that in the accounts payable ledger—as in the accounts receivable ledger—the accounts of the individual creditors are listed in alphabetical order. In addition, one usually uses a loose-leaf binder, and there are no page numbers or account numbers.

Purchases Returns and Allowances

This account, as the title implies, handles either a return of merchandise previously purchased or an allowance made for merchandise that arrived in damaged condition. In both cases there is a reduction in the amount owed to the supplier. The buyer sends a letter or printed form to the supplier, who acknowledges the reduction by sending a *credit memorandum.* It is wise for the buyer to wait for the notice of the agreed deduction from the supplier before making an accounting entry.

The Purchases Returns and Allowances account is considered to be a deduction from Purchases. In order to have a better record of the total returns and allowances, one uses a separate account. Purchases Returns and Allowances is deducted from the Purchases account in the income statement. (We'll get around to discussing this later.) For now, let's look at an illustration consisting of two entries on the books of North Central Plumbing Supply.

(a) On August 5, bought merchandise on account from Argel Manufacturing Company, $692, their invoice no. 10611, dated August 3, terms 2/10, n/30. Recorded this as a debit to Purchases and a credit to Accounts Payable. On August 6, returned $70 worth of the merchandise. Made no entry.

(b) On August 8, received credit memorandum no. 629 from Argel Manufacturing Company for $70. Recorded this as a debit to Accounts Payable and a credit to Purchases Returns and Allowances.

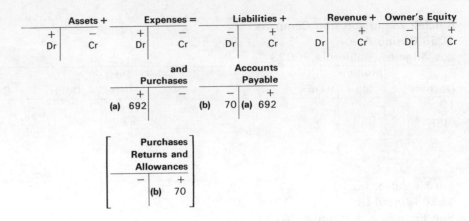

North Central credits Purchases Returns and Allowances because it has greater returns and allowances than before, and debits Accounts Payable because it owes the creditor less than before.

Suppose that North Central Plumbing Supply returned merchandise on two occasions during August, and received credit memorandums from the suppliers; the entries are recorded in the general journal.

General Journal					Page 27	
Date		Description	Post. Ref.	Debit		Credit
19__						
Aug.	8	Accounts Payable, Argel Manufacturing Company		70	00	
		Purchases Returns and Allowances				70 00
		Credit memo 629, invoice no. 10611				
	12	Accounts Payable, Sinclair Manufacturing Company		36	00	
		Purchases Returns and Allowances				36 00
		Credit memo 482, invoice no. B643				

In this entry, Accounts Payable is followed by the name of the individual creditor's account. The accountant must post to both the Accounts Payable controlling account and the individual creditor's account in the accounts payable ledger. The journal entries are now repeated, and the posting is completed, as shown by the Posting Reference column on page 223, in which the account numbers indicate postings to the accounts in the general ledger and the check marks indicate postings to the accounts in the accounts payable ledger.

General Journal

Date		Description	Post. Ref.	Debit	Credit
19__					
Aug.	8	Accounts Payable, Argel	211/	70 00	
		Manufacturing Company			
		Purchases Returns and			
		Allowances	512		70 00
		Credit memo 629,			
		invoice no. 10611			
	12	Accounts Payable, Sinclair	211/	36 00	
		Manufacturing Company			
		Purchases Returns and			
		Allowances	512		36 00
		Credit memo 482,			
		invoice no. B643			

General Ledger

Accounts Payable

Account No. 211

Date		Item	Post. Ref.	Debit	Credit	Balance Debit	Balance Credit
19__							
Aug.	1	Balance	✓				356 00
	8		J27	70 00			286 00
	12		J27	36 00			250 00

Purchases Returns and Allowances

Account No. 512

Date		Item	Post. Ref.	Debit	Credit	Balance Debit	Balance Credit
19__							
Aug.	8		J27		70 00		70 00
	12		J27		36 00		106 00

Accounts Payable Ledger

Argel Manufacturing Company
2150 Madeira Ave.
San Francisco, California 94130

Date		Invoice No.	Item	Post. Ref.	Debit	Credit	Balance
19__							
Aug.	5	10611		P29		692 00	692 00
	8			J27	70 00		622 00

Sinclair Manufacturing Company
1068 Casino Ave.
Los Angeles, California 90023

Date		Invoice No.	Item	Post. Ref.	Debit		Credit		Balance	
19—										
Aug.	9	B643		P29			165	00	165	00
	12			J27	36	00			129	00

Assuming that there were no other transactions involving Accounts Payable, the schedule of accounts payable would appear as follows.

North Central Plumbing Supply		
Schedule of Accounts Payable		
August 31, 19__		
Argel Manufacturing Company	$ 622	00
Danton, Inc.	691	00
Donaldson and Farr	376	00
Rogers and Simon Company	940	00
Sinclair Manufacturing Company	129	00
Tru-Fit Valve, Inc.	404	00
Total Accounts Payable	$3,162	00

The Accounts Payable controlling account in the general ledger is now posted up to date.

Accounts Payable   **Account No. 211**

Date		Item	Post. Ref.	Debit		Credit		Balance Debit		Balance Credit	
19—											
Aug.	1	Balance	✓							356	00
	8		J27	70	00					286	00
	12		J27	36	00					250	00
	31		P29			2,912	00			3,162	00

Posting directly from purchase invoices

Posting from purchase invoices is just like posting from sales invoices (described in Chapter 8), in that it's also a shortcut. The accountant posts to the individual creditors' accounts daily, directly from the purchase invoices. The suppliers' invoice numbers are recorded in the Posting Reference column in place of the journal page number. The Accounts Payable controlling account in the general ledger is brought up to date at the end of the month by making a summarizing entry in the general journal, debiting

Purchases and any asset accounts that may be involved, and crediting Accounts Payable.

Since posting directly from purchase invoices is a variation of the accounting system, we shall use a different illustration: Ron's Towing and Trailer Service. This firm sorts out its invoices for the month, and finds that the totals are as follows: purchase of merchandise, $8,610; store supplies, $168; office supplies, $126; store equipment, $520. The accountant then makes a summarizing entry in the general journal, as follows.

General Journal			Post. Ref.	Debit	Credit	Page 37
Date		Description				
19—						
Oct.	31	Purchases		8,610 00		
		Store Supplies		168 00		
		Office Supplies		126 00		
		Store Equipment		520 00		
		Accounts Payable			9,424 00	
		Summarizing entry for				
		total purchases of goods				
		on account				

The accountant posts the above entry to the general ledger accounts.

Store Supplies   **Account No. 114**

Date	Item	Post. Ref.	Debit	Credit	Balance Debit	Balance Credit
19—						
Oct. 31		J37	168 00		168 00	

Office Supplies   **Account No. 115**

Date	Item	Post. Ref.	Debit	Credit	Balance Debit	Balance Credit
19—						
Oct. 31		J37	126 00		126 00	

Store Equipment   **Account No. 121**

Date	Item	Post. Ref.	Debit	Credit	Balance Debit	Balance Credit
19—						
Oct. 31		J37	520 00		520 00	

Accounts Payable   Account No. 211

Date		Item	Post. Ref.	Debit		Credit		Balance Debit		Balance Credit	
19__											
Oct.	31		J37			9,424	00			9,424	00

Purchases   Account No. 511

Date		Item	Post. Ref.	Debit		Credit		Balance Debit		Balance Credit	
19__											
Oct.	31		J37	8,610	00			8,610	00		

This procedure not only does away with the need for a purchases journal, but also includes the buying of any assets on account in the same summarizing entry. An example of an invoice follows.

Invoice No. **13168**

Superior Electronics

9600 Alhambra St.
San Francisco, California 94132

Sold to
┌ Ron's Towing and Trailer Service ┐
   2716 Brighton Road
   Burlingame, Calif. 94011
└   ┘

Ship to
┌   ┐
   Same
└   ┘

Invoice Date 10/4
Terms 1/10, n/30
Cust. Order No. 1635

Shipped via Pacific Express Co.

F.O.B. San Francisco

Quantity	Stock No.	Description	Unit Price	Amount
20	AD732	Mobile home antenna – TV	8.80	176.00

Ron's Towing and Trailer Service posts the amount of the invoice to the account of the supplier in the accounts payable ledger.

Accounts Payable Ledger
Superior Electronics
9600 Alhambra St.
San Francisco, California 94132

Date		Item	Post. Ref.	Debit	Credit	Balance
19__ Oct.	7		13168		176 00	176 00

Ron's Towing and Trailer Service will also include the $176 figure in the summarizing entry recorded in the general journal, debiting Purchases and crediting Accounts Payable.

Transportation charges on incoming merchandise and other assets	When a firm buys merchandise, the total of the purchase invoice may include the transportation charges. If it does, this means that the supplier is selling on the basis of *FOB destination*. In other words, the supplier loads the goods *free on board* (FOB) the carrier and ships them to the customer without charge. The supplier is, of course, paying the freight charges, and naturally has to add these charges to the selling price of the goods.

For example, North Central Plumbing Supply (remember it's in Seattle) buys pipe fittings from a supplier in Chicago, with a note on the invoice that the terms are FOB Seattle. The total of the invoice is $1,200, and North Central knows that this figure includes the freight charges. We can show this by T accounts as follows.

Purchases		Accounts Payable	
+	−	−	+
1,200			1,200

What happens when the transportation charges are separate? In that case, there's a note on the invoice that the terms are FOB shipping point. This means that the supplier will load the goods free on board the carrier at the shipping point, but any freight charges from there on have to be paid by the buyer.

Suppose, for example, that North Central Plumbing Supply buys lavatories from a manufacturer in Detroit with terms FOB Detroit. Now the total of the invoice is $1,750, but in this case North Central Plumbing Supply has to pay the freight charges from Detroit to Seattle. The lavatories are shipped by rail, and North Central pays the railroad $125. In our minds we can picture the T accounts this way.

Purchases		Accounts Payable		Cash	
+	−	−	+	+	−
1,750			1,750		125
125					

Any merchandising concern must base its markups on the *delivered* cost of the merchandise. So, for this reason, the buyer debits any freight charges on incoming merchandise to Purchases. Thus the Purchases account represents both the *cost* of the merchandise and the *freight charges* the buyer has to pay for transporting the goods. In the case of FOB destination, the buyer has already paid the freight charges. So in the case of FOB shipping point, the buyer debits the Purchases account for the amount of the freight charges—which amounts to the same thing.

Any firm which sells on the basis of FOB destination must be able to cover all its costs, which of course include freight costs. Therefore the firm must include freight costs when it quotes the price for its goods. There is an interesting legal point here. Ordinarily, unless the title is expressly reserved, whoever pays the freight charges on the goods has title to the goods.

Some business firms, instead of debiting Purchases for freight charges on incoming merchandise, set up an expense account entitled Freight In or Transportation In. In the income statement, the accountant adds the balances of these accounts to the balance of the Purchases account in order to determine the *delivered* cost of the Purchases. However, here we shall follow the policy of debiting Purchases for freight charges on incoming merchandise.

Any shipping charges involved in the buying of any other assets, such as supplies or equipment, are debited to the account of the respective asset. For example, North Central Plumbing Supply bought display cases on account, at a cost of $2,700 plus freight charges of $90. As a convenience, the seller of the display cases paid the transportation costs for North Central Plumbing Supply and then added the $90 onto the invoice price of the cases. Let's visualize this by means of T accounts.

Store Equipment		Accounts Payable	
+	−	−	+
2,790			2,790

On the other hand, if North Central had paid the freight charges separately, the entry for the payment would be a debit to Store Equipment for $90 and a credit to Cash for $90.

Internal control

We spoke briefly about internal control in Chapter 7 when we were talking about the receipt and deposit of cash from the patients of Dr. Tanner. When there is internal control, plans and procedures are injected into the accounting system in order to control operations. This is, of course, necessary when the owner or management must delegate authority. So the owner takes measures to (1) protect the assets against fraud and waste, (2) provide for accurate accounting data, (3) promote an efficient operation, and (4) encourage adherence to management policies. We'll be talking about the concept of internal control quite often throughout the text.

Internal control of purchases

Efficiency and security require that most companies work out careful procedures for buying and paying for goods. This is understandable, as large sums of money are usually involved. The control aspect generally involves the following measures.

1 Purchases are made only after proper authorization is given. Purchase requisitions and purchase orders are all prenumbered, so that each form may be accounted for.
2 The receiving department carefully checks and counts all goods upon receipt. Later the report of the receiving department is verified against the purchase order and the purchase invoice.
3 The person who authorizes the payment is someone other than the person doing the ordering, and other than the person actually writing the check. This person authorizes payment only after the verifications have been made.
4 The person who actually writes the check has not been involved in any of the foregoing purchasing procedures.

Summary

In this chapter, we introduced two new accounts: the Purchases account, which records the cost of merchandise acquired for resale, and the Purchases Returns and Allowances account, which is deducted from Purchases.

The purchases journal handles the purchase of merchandise *on account only*, and entries from it are posted daily to the accounts payable ledger. At the end of the month, the total is posted to the general ledger as a debit to the Purchases account and a credit to the Accounts Payable controlling account.

When merchandise is returned, the firm credits Purchases Returns and Allowances. If the customer had bought the goods on a charge-account basis, the firm debits Accounts Payable and records the entry in the general journal.

As a further shortcut, the firm may post to the accounts of the individual creditors in the accounts payable ledger directly from invoices of purchases of merchandise bought on credit. At the end of the month, the accountant makes a summarizing entry in the general journal, debiting Purchases and debiting any assets that were acquired, and crediting Accounts Payable for the total of the invoices.

When a firm lists transportation charges on incoming goods separately, it debits them to the related accounts. For example, freight charges on merchandise bought are debited to Purchases, freight charges on office equipment bought are debited to Office Equipment, and so forth.

Glossary

o **FOB** Free on board; the goods are loaded on the carrier with no additional charge levied on the buyer.

o **FOB destination** The seller pays the freight charges.

o **FOB shipping point** The buyer pays the freight charges between the point of shipment and the destination.

o **Internal control** Plans and procedures inherent in the accounting system with the following objectives: (1) to protect assets against fraud and waste, (2) to yield accurate accounting data, (3) to promote an efficient operation, and (4) to encourage adherence to management policies.

o **Purchase discount** A cash discount allowed for prompt payment of an invoice; for example, 2% if the bill is paid within 10 days.

o **Purchase invoice** A business form prepared by the seller that lists the items shipped, their cost, and the mode of shipment. The buyer considers it a purchase invoice; the seller considers it a sales invoice.

o **Purchase order** A written order from the buyer of goods to the supplier, listing items wanted as well as terms of the transaction.

o **Purchase requisition** A form used to request the purchasing department to buy something. This form is intended for internal use within a company.

o **Purchases Returns and Allowances** The account used by the buyer to record a reduction granted by the supplier for either the return of merchandise or compensation for damage to the merchandise. The entry in the buyer's account is based on a credit memorandum received from the supplier.

Exercises

Exercise 1 Describe the transactions in the following T accounts.

Cash	Purchases	Purchases Returns and Allowances	Accounts Payable	
670	720	50	50	720
			670	

Exercise 2 Record the following transactions in general journal form.

a Bought merchandise on account from Bingham and Harvey, $640, invoice no. D716.

b Received credit memo no. 216 from Bingham and Harvey for merchandise returned, $30.

c Issued a check to Bingham and Harvey in full payment of invoice no. D716.

Exercise 3 Label the blanks as debit or credit.

Purchases Journal							Page ___
Date	Supplier's Name	Invoice No.	Invoice Date	Terms	Post. Ref.	Purchases (____) Accts. Pay. (____)	

Exercise 4 Post the following entry to the general ledger and subsidiary ledger accounts.

General Journal   **Page 44**

Date		Description	Post. Ref.	Debit	Credit
19__					
June	15	Accounts Payable,	✓	37 40	
		L. B. Dixon Company			
		Purchases Returns and			
		Allowances			37 40
		Received credit memo			
		no. 1087			

General Ledger

Accounts Payable   **Account No. 212**

Date		Item	Post. Ref.	Debit	Credit	Balance Debit	Balance Credit
19__							
June	1	Balance	✓				1,654 20

Purchases Returns and Allowances   **Account No. 512**

Date		Item	Post. Ref.	Debit	Credit	Balance Debit	Balance Credit
19__							
June	1	Balance	✓				84 20

Accounts Payable Ledger

L. B. Dixon Company

Date	Invoice No.	Item	Post. Ref.	Debit	Credit	Balance
19__						
May	27		G729 J440	37 40	128 00	128 00

Exercise 5 A business firm which posts directly from its purchase invoices sorts the invoices for the month and finds that the totals are as follows: purchases of merchandise, $7,624; store supplies, $118; office supplies, $97; office equipment, $136. Record the summarizing entry in general journal form.

Exercise 6 Record the following transactions in general journal form.
a Bought merchandise on account from City Bindery, $416, invoice no. 7197, FOB shipping point.
b Paid Eastern Fast Freight for shipping charges on the above purchase, $36.

Exercise 7 On the above purchase, the Varsity Bookstore uses a markup of 20% of cost. Determine the selling price of the new merchandise. $342.40

Exercise 8 Record the following transactions in general journal form.
a Bought a desk for use in the office from Modern Office Supply, invoice no. D419, $240.
b Paid Mountain States Freight Company for shipping the desk, $9.

Problem 9-1 The Atlas Cycle and Toy Company uses a single-column purchases journal. On January 1 of this year, the balances of the ledger accounts are: Accounts Payable, $539.06; Purchases, zero. In addition to a general ledger, they also use an accounts payable ledger. Transactions for January related to the buying of merchandise are as follows.

Jan. 3	Bought forty 10-speed bicycles from Super Bicycle Company, invoice no. 3916C, dated January 2; terms net 60 days; $2,376.
5	Bought locks from Security Lock Company, invoice no. 27615, dated January 2; terms 2/10, n/30; $325.
8	Bought hand brakes from Temple, Inc., invoice no. 298AC, dated January 5; terms 1/10, n/30; $264.
11	Bought tires from Ultra Tire and Rubber, invoice no. C8729, dated January 10; terms 2/10, n/30; $480.
15	Bought handle grips from Forester Products Company, invoice no. 2782, dated January 14; terms net 30 days; $98.
23	Bought twenty 5-speed bicycles from Super Bicycle Company, invoice no. 4013C, dated January 21; terms net 60 days; $980.
29	Bought bicycle lights and reflectors from Forester Products Company, invoice no. 28183, dated January 28; terms net 30 days; $263.
30	Bought knapsacks from Paragon Manufacturing Company, invoice no. 721AX, dated January 27; terms 2/10, n/30; $286.

Instructions

1 Open the following accounts in the accounts payable ledger and record the balances as of January 1: Forester Products Company; Paragon Manufacturing Company, $143.17; Security Lock Company, $167.19; Super Bicycle Company; Temple, Inc., $228.70; Ultra Tire and Rubber.
2 Record balance of $539.06 in the Accounts Payable controlling account as of January 1.
3 Record the transactions in the purchases journal beginning with page 81.
4 Post to the accounts payable ledger and the Accounts Payable controlling account.
5 Prepare a schedule of accounts payable.
6 Compare the balance of the Accounts Payable controlling account with the total of the schedule of accounts payable.

Problem 9-2 The Novel Gift Shop bought the following merchandise and supplies and had the following returns and allowances during May of this year.

May 2	Bought merchandise on account from Tenning Pottery Company, invoice no. 9761, dated May 1; terms 2/10, n/30; $680.
4	Bought merchandise on account from Novel Card Company, invoice no. 16728, dated May 1; terms 1/10, n/30; $268.
6	Bought merchandise on account from Dow Supply Company, invoice no. 21792D, dated May 5; terms net 30 days; $586.

May 10	Bought office supplies on account from Drexel and Son, invoice no. 2995C, dated May 10; terms net 30 days; $162.
12	Received a credit memorandum from Novel Card Company for merchandise returned, $26.
16	Bought merchandise on account from Axel Printing Company, invoice no. 99821, dated May 15; terms 1/10, n/30; $580.
21	Bought office equipment on account from Dalton Equipment Company, invoice no. 6616, dated May 18; terms net 30 days; $624.
26	Bought merchandise on account from Novel Card Company, invoice no. 17118, dated May 23; terms 1/10, n/30; $982.
27	Received a credit memorandum from Dow Supply Company for merchandise returned, $76.
28	Bought merchandise on account from Tenning Pottery Company, invoice no. 10096, dated May 27; terms 2/10, n/30; $1,642.
29	Bought store supplies on account from Towne and Truvall, invoice no, 98621, dated May 29; terms net 30 days; $32.

Instructions

1 Open the following accounts in the general ledger and enter the balances as of May 1.

113	Store Supplies	$ 210
114	Office Supplies	121
121	Office Equipment	4,680
211	Accounts Payable	2,788
511	Purchases	6,984
512	Purchases Returns and Allowances	270

2 Open the following accounts in the accounts payable ledger and enter the balances in the Balance columns as of May 1: Axel Printing Company; Dalton Equipment Company; Dow Supply Company, $1,800; Drexel and Son; Novel Card Company, $28; Tenning Pottery Company, $960; Towne and Truvall.

3 Record the transactions in either the general journal, page 27, or the purchases journal, page 6.

4 Post the entries to the creditors' accounts in the accounts payable ledger immediately after you make each journal entry.

5 Post the entries in the general journal immediately after you make each journal entry.

6 Post the total of the purchases journal at the end of the month.

7 Prepare a schedule of accounts payable.

8 Compare the balance of the Accounts Payable controlling account with the total of the schedule of accounts payable.

Problem 9-3 The Arizona Products Company records sales of merchandise daily, by posting directly from its sales invoices to the accounts receivable ledger. At the end of the month, a summarizing entry is made in the general journal. The purchase of goods on account is recorded in a similar manner, with the posting each day done directly from the invoices to the accounts payable ledger, and a summarizing entry is made in the general journal at the end of the month. Sales of merchandise and purchases of goods on account during September of this year were as follows.

Sales of merchandise

Sept. 3	Arnold Store Corp., no. 2611, $2,300.
6	T. D. Mitchell, no. 2612, $3,400.
10	C. A. Howard and Company, no. 2613, $1,612.
14	Bartor and Bartell, no. 2614, $2,680.
21	Franklin P. Ellis, no. 2615, $1,470.
23	George H. Anderson, no. 2616, $424.
24	Daniel B. Tyne, no. 2617, $2,900.
27	Marshall and Miner, no. 2618, $640.
28	T. D. Mitchell, no. 2619, $1,876.
30	Bartor and Bartell, no. 2620, $1,920.
30	Marshall and Miner, no. 2621, $3,268.

Purchases of goods on account

Sept. 2	Lanham Corp., merchandise, no. 6382, $2,170.
6	Unique Wood Products, merchandise, no. 2198A, $1,800.
8	Modern Manufacturing Company, merchandise, no. 82116, $4,620.
16	Slessor and Smith, store supplies, no. D9682, $210.
25	B. R. Rogers and Company, store supplies, no. 9621, $180.
28	Lanham Corp., merchandise, no. B726, $3,960.
30	Unique Wood Products, merchandise, no. 2716A, $4,215.
30	Johnson Equipment Company, store equipment, no. 72116, $325.

Instructions

1 Record the summarizing entry for sales of merchandise on account in the general journal.

2 Record the summarizing entry for the purchase of goods on account in the general journal.

Problem 9-4 The following transactions relate to the Modern Fixture Company during March of this year. Terms of sale are 2/10, n/30.

Mar. 1	Sold merchandise on account to Arthur Yeager, invoice no. 16116, $800.
3	Bought merchandise on account from Newton Manufacturing Company, invoice no. A1121, $450; 1/10, n/30; dated March 1.
9	Sold merchandise on account to Anderson and Low, invoice no. 16117, $1,250.
11	Bought merchandise on account from N. D. Stonewall Company, invoice no. 7892, $4,300; 2/10, n/30; dated March 10.
14	Received credit memo 84 for merchandise returned from N. D. Stonewall Company, for $110, related to invoice no. 7892.
17	Sold merchandise on account to Martin Dahl, invoice no. 16118, $840.
17	Issued credit memo no. 26 to Anderson and Low, for merchandise returned, $80, related to invoice no. 16117.

Mar. 26	Bought merchandise on account from George T. Williams and Son, invoice no. 9986, $1,600; 2/10, EOM (within 10 days after the end of the month); dated March 25.
28	Bought office supplies on account from Freeport Stationery Company, invoice no. R2686, dated March 28, $65; 30 days net.
29	Sold merchandise on account to Sutton and Thomas, invoice no. 16119, $2,960.
30	Issued credit memo no. 27 to Sutton and Thomas for merchandise returned, $190, related to invoice no. 16119.

Instructions

1 Open the following accounts in the accounts payable ledger: Freeport Stationery Company; Newton Manufacturing Company; N. D. Stonewall Company, $378; George T. Williams and Son.
2 Open the following accounts in the accounts receivable ledger: Anderson and Low, $417; Dahl, Martin; Sutton and Thomas, $983; Yeager, Arthur.
3 Record the transactions in the sales, purchases, and general journals.
4 Post purchases to the accounts payable ledger daily.
5 Post sales to the accounts receivable ledger daily.

Problem 9-1A The Suburban Bicycle Shop uses a single-column purchases journal. On January 1 of this year the balances of the ledger accounts are: Accounts Payable, $400.86; Purchases, zero. In addition to a general ledger, the shop also uses an accounts payable ledger. Transactions for January related to the purchase of merchandise are as follows.

Jan. 5	Bought sixty 10-speed bicycles from Standard Bicycle Company, invoice no. 2918D, dated January 4; terms net 60 days; $5,920.
7	Bought tires from Amalgamated Tire Company, invoice no. D4926, dated January 7; terms 2/10, n/30; $482.
8	Bought bicycle lights and reflectors from Fancher Products Company, invoice no. 16183, dated January 8; terms net 30 days; $268.
11	Bought hand brakes from J. T. Conners, Inc., invoice no. 361DE, dated January 9; terms 1/10, n/30; $282.
19	Bought handle grips from Fancher Products Company, invoice no. 16482, dated January 18; terms net 30 days; $73.60.
24	Purchased thirty 5-speed bicycles from Standard Bicycle Company, invoice no. 3062D, dated January 23; terms net 60 days; $1,326.
29	Bought knapsacks from Canfield Manufacturing Company, invoice no. 832JB, dated January 27; terms 2/10, n/30; $293.16.
31	Bought locks from Safety Lock Company, invoice no. 36192, dated January 28; terms 2/10, n/30; $326.82.

Instructions

1 Open the following accounts in the accounts payable ledger: Amalgamated Tire Company, $128; Canfield Manufacturing Company, $74.16; J. T. Connors, Inc.; Fancher Products Company; Safety Lock Company, $198.70; Standard Bicycle Company.

2 Record the balance of $400.86 in the Accounts Payable controlling account as of January 1.

3 Record the transactions in the purchases journal beginning with page 72.

4 Post to the accounts payable ledger and the Accounts Payable controlling account.

5 Prepare a schedule of accounts payable.

6 Compare the balance of the Accounts Payable controlling account with the total of the schedule of accounts payable.

Problem 9-2A The Briarcliff Gift Shop had the following purchases of merchandise and supplies and related returns and allowances during March.

Mar.	3	Bought merchandise on account from Mueller Pottery Company, invoice no. 8792, dated March 1; terms 2/10, n/30; $682.
	4	Bought merchandise on account from Danville Supply Company, invoice no. 21863D, dated March 2; terms net 30 days; $583.20.
	7	Bought merchandise on account from Dumas and Son, invoice no. 28860, dated March 7; terms net 30 days; $291.72.
	11	Bought office supplies on account from Nielson Office Supply, invoice no. 3849, dated March 11; terms net 30 days; $169.48.
	13	Received a credit memo from Mueller Pottery Company for merchandise returned, $22.
	15	Bought merchandise on account from Unique Card Company, invoice no. 77281, dated March 15; terms 1/10, n/30; $789.60.
	20	Bought office equipment on account from Carlton Equipment Company, invoice no. 6582, dated March 18; terms net 30 days; $717.
	25	Bought merchandise on account from Unique Card Company, invoice no. 77472, dated March 25; terms 1/10, n/30; $989.60.
	28	Received a credit memo from Danville Supply Company for merchandise returned, $73.
	29	Bought merchandise on account from Mueller Pottery Company, invoice no. 8871, dated March 28; terms 2/10, n/30; $1,273.10.
	30	Bought store supplies on account from Lassiter and Foss, invoice no. 87616, dated March 30; terms net 30 days; $41.
	30	Bought merchandise on account from Dumas and Son, invoice no. 29143, dated March 29; terms net 30 days; $142.30.
	30	Bought merchandise on account from Danville Supply Company, invoice no. 21914D, dated March 28; terms net 30 days; $348.16.

Instructions

1 Open the following accounts in the general ledger and enter the balances as of March 1.

113	Store Supplies	$ 315.18
114	Office Supplies	136.32
121	Office Equipment	4,775.00
211	Accounts Payable	2,744.01
511	Purchases	6,881.19
512	Purchases Returns and Allowances	262.46

2 Open the following accounts in the accounts payable ledger and enter the balances in the Balance columns as of March 1: Carlton Equipment Company; Danville Supply Company; Dumas and Son, $924.18; Lassiter and Foss; Mueller Pottery Company, $1,480; Nielson Office Supply; Unique Card Company, $339.83.

3 Record the transactions either in the general journal, page 31, or the purchases journal, page 9.

4 Post the entries to the creditors' accounts in the accounts payable ledger immediately after you record each journal entry.

5 Post the entries to the general ledger after you record each general journal entry.

6 Post the total of the purchases journal at the end of the month.

7 Prepare a schedule of accounts payable.

8 Compare the balance of the Accounts Payable controlling account with the total of the schedule of accounts payable.

Problem 9-3A California Products Company records sales of merchandise daily by posting directly from its sales invoices to the accounts receivable ledger. At the end of the month they make a summarizing entry in the general journal. They record purchases of goods on account the same way, daily, posting directly from the invoices to the accounts payable ledger and making a summarizing entry in the general journal at the end of the month. Sales of merchandise and purchases of goods on account during October of this year were as follows.

Sales of merchandise

Oct.		
	4	Ardenvoir Specialty Shop, no. 3216, $348.17.
	7	I. D. Miller, no. 3217, $548.19.
	11	R. D. Blanchard and Company, no. 3218, $918.65.
	15	Myron and Nelson, no. 3219, $1,080.72.
	22	Lane P. Jackson, no. 3220, $877.25.
	24	Eldon P. Wenzel, no, 3221, $967.60.
	25	Rex P. Ruller, no. 3222, $1,110.
	28	Dante and Rubin, no. 3223, $540.35.
	30	Myron and Nelson, no. 3224, $318.
	31	I. D. Miller, no. 3225, $225.70.

Purchases of goods on account

Oct.		
	3	Denham and Lancaster, merchandise, no. C1189, $566.
	7	Dugan Wood Products, merchandise, no. 23229, $1,400.
	9	Precision Manufacturing Company, merchandise, no. 83118, $3,870.
	10	Singleton Supply Company, office supplies, no. AD716, $112.
	19	C. C. Russo and Company, merchandise, no. C1146, $129.76.
	26	Nelson and Nelson, store supplies, no. S9825, $54.60.
	28	Dugan Wood Products, merchandise, no. 23313, $2,874.
	31	Denton Equipment Company, store equipment, no. 31192, $210.

Instructions

1 Record the summarizing entry for the sales of merchandise on account in the general journal.

2 Record the summarizing entry for the purchase of goods on account in the general journal.

Problem 9-4A The transactions described below relate to the Alpine Supply Company during April of this year. Terms of sale are 2/10, n/30.

Apr.	1	Sold merchandise on account to Spangler Hardware, invoice no. 36442, $762.
	4	Bought merchandise on account from Northern Manufacturing Company, invoice no. C1149, $320; 1/10, n/30; dated April 4.
	8	Sold merchandise on account to Meadowland Department Store, invoice no. 36443, $942.
	10	Bought merchandise on account from Superior Products Company, invoice no. 9119, $3,776.75; 2/10, n/30; dated April 10.
	13	Received credit memo no. 96 for merchandise returned from Roxford and Son for $341, related to invoice no. D1198.
	16	Sold merchandise on account to Nancy Girard, invoice no. 36444, $442.70.
	17	Issued credit memo no. 31 to Meadowland Department Store for merchandise related to invoice no. 36443, $96.
	25	Bought merchandise on account from Danforth Manufacturing Company, invoice no. B4491, $1,562; 2/10, n/30; dated April 23.
	27	Bought store supplies on account from Hosford and Randall Company, invoice no. D3179, dated April 26, $56.20; 30 days net.
	27	Sold merchandise on account to Hadley Specialty Company, invoice no. 36445, $3,006.
	30	Issued credit memo no. 32 to Hadley Specialty Company for merchandise related to invoice no. 36445, $258.

Instructions

1 Open the following accounts in the accounts payable ledger: Danforth Manufacturing Company; Hosford and Randall; Northern Manufacturing Company; Roxford and Son, $984; Superior Products Company.

2 Open the following accounts in the accounts receivable ledger: Girard, Nancy; Hadley Specialty Company, $459; Meadowland Department Store; Spangler Hardware.

3 Record the transactions in the sales, purchases, and general journals.

4 Post the purchases to the accounts payable ledger daily.

5 Post the sales to the accounts receivable ledger daily.

10 Cash receipts and cash payments

Cash In must exceed Cash Out. Robert Heller, *The Great Executive Dream*

Key points

- Use of a cash receipts journal
- Posting from the cash receipts journal
- Sales discounts treated as deductions from Sales
- Use of a cash payments journal
- Use of a check register
- Posting from a cash payments journal
- Purchases discounts treated as deductions from Purchases
- Transactions involving trade discounts are recorded at the net amount.

Chapter contents

- Introduction
- Cash receipts journal
- Credit terms
- Cash payments journal: service enterprise
- Cash payments journal: merchandising enterprise
- Check register
- Trade discounts
- Summary
- Glossary
- Exercises
- Problems

Specific objectives

After you have completed this chapter, you will be able to:

- Record transactions for a retail merchandising business in a cash receipts journal.
- Record transactions for a wholesale merchandising business in a cash receipts journal.
- Post from a cash receipts journal to a general ledger and an accounts receivable ledger.
- Determine cash discount according to credit terms, and record cash receipts from charge customers who are entitled to deduct the cash discount.
- Record transactions in a cash payments journal for a service enterprise.
- Record transactions in a cash payments journal for a merchandising enterprise.
- Record transactions in a check register.
- Post from a cash payments journal and a check register to a general ledger and an accounts payable ledger.
- Record transactions involving trade discounts.

Introduction

We have seen that using the sales journal and the purchases journal enables an accountant to carry out the journalizing and posting processes much more efficiently. These special journals make it possible to record an entry on one line, and to post column totals rather than individual figures. This can also make possible a division of labor, because the journalizing functions can be delegated to different persons. The *cash receipts journal* and *cash payments journal* carry these advantages further.

Cash receipts journal

The cash receipts journal records all transactions in which cash comes in, or increases. When the cash receipts journal is used, all transactions in which cash is debited *must* be recorded in it. It may be used for a service as well as a merchandising business. To get acquainted with the cash receipts journal, let's list some typical transactions of a retail merchandising business which result in an increase in cash. So that you'll see the transactions at a glance, let's record them immediately in T accounts.

May 3: Sold merchandise for cash, $100, plus $4 sales tax.

Cash		Sales		Sales Tax Payable	
+	−	−	+	−	+
104			100		4

May 4: Sold merchandise, $100 plus $4 sales tax; but the customer used a bank charge card. The firm deposits the bank credit card receipts, and the bank *deducts a discount* and credits the firm's account with cash. This discount is often 6% of the sale, exclusive of the sales tax. The firm therefore records the amount of the discount under Credit Card Expense. (From the amount that would ordinarily be debited to Cash, deduct the bank charge, consisting of 6% of the sale, and debit this amount to Credit Card Expense instead of to Cash: $100 × .06 = $6.00, so $100 + $4 − $6 = $98.)

Cash		Credit Card Expense		Sales Tax Payable		Sales	
+	−	+	−	−	+	−	+
98		6			4		100

May 5: Collected $208 cash on account from John Oatey, a charge customer.

Cash		Accounts Receivable	
+	−	+	−
208			208

May 7: The owner, Eric Adams, invested cash in the business, $3,000.

Cash		Eric Adams, Capital	
+	−	−	+
3,000			3,000

May 8: Sold equipment for cash at cost, $150.

Cash		Equipment	
+	−	+	−
150			150

Now let's appraise these four transactions: The first two would be very frequent; the last two could conceivably take place, but they would be rather infrequent. If one were designing a cash receipts journal, it would be logical to include a Cash debit column because all the transactions involve an increase in cash. If a business regularly collects cash from charge customers, there should be an Accounts Receivable credit column. If a firm often sells merchandise for cash and collects a sales tax, there should be a Sales credit column and a Sales Tax Payable credit column. If the business honors bank charge cards, there should be a Credit Card Expense debit column to take care of the amount deducted by the bank.

However, the credit to Eric Adams, Capital, and the credit to Equipment occur very seldom, so it wouldn't be practical to set up special columns for them, as they can be handled adequately by a Sundry credit column, which can be used for credits to all other accounts that have no special column.

Now let's record the same transactions in a cash receipts journal. First we repeat the transactions.

May 3 | Sold merchandise for cash, $100, plus $4 sales tax.
4 | Sold merchandise, $100 plus $4 sales tax, and the customer used a bank charge card. Discount charged by the bank is 6% of the amount of the sale.
5 | Collected cash from John Oatey, a charge customer, on account, $208.
7 | The owner, Eric Adams, invested cash in the business, $3,000.
8 | Sold equipment for cash, at cost, $150.

At the end of the month we can post the special columns in the cash receipts journal as totals to the general ledger accounts. These include Accounts Receivable credit, Sales credit, Sales Tax Payable credit, Credit Card Expense debit, and Cash debit. We post the items in the Sundry Accounts credit column individually, and post the figures in the Accounts Receivable credit column separately to the accounts in the accounts receivable ledger. The posting letter designation for the cash receipts journal is CR.

Cash Receipts Journal

Date		Account Name	Post. Ref.	Sundry Accounts Credit		Accts. Rec. Credit		Sales Credit		Sales Tax Payable Credit		Credit Card Expense Debit		Cash Debit	
19—															
May	3	Sales						100	00	4	00			104	00
	4	Sales						100	00	4	00	6	00	98	00
	5	John Oatey				208	00							208	00
	7	Eric Adams, Capital		3,000	00									3,000	00
	8	Equipment		150	00									150	00

Here are some other transactions made during the month that involve increases in cash. (Remember that these transactions are for a retail business.)

May 11	Borrowed $300 from the bank, receiving cash and giving the bank a promissory note.
16	Sold merchandise for cash, $200, plus $8 sales tax.
21	Sold merchandise for cash, $50, plus $2 sales tax; customer used a bank charge card.
26	Collected cash from Kenneth Ralston, a charge customer, on account, $62.40.
28	Sold merchandise for cash, $40, plus $1.60 sales tax.
31	Sold merchandise for cash, $150, plus $6 sales tax; customer used a bank charge card.
31	Collected cash from Donald Madden, a charge customer, on account, $26.

Let us assume that all the month's transactions involving debits to Cash have now been recorded in the cash receipts journal. The cash receipts journal and charts on page 244 illustrate the postings to the general ledger and the accounts receivable ledger.

Posting from the cash receipts journal

In the Posting Reference column, the Check marks (✓) stand for the fact that one has posted the amounts in the Accounts Receivable credit column to the individual charge customers' accounts as credits. The account numbers indicate that one has posted the amounts in the Sundry Accounts credit column separately to the accounts described in the Account Name column. One also puts a check mark (✓) under the total of the Sundry column. This means "do not post," as the figures are posted separately, as described above. A check mark in accounting thus has two meanings: (1) *that the individual account has been posted in the subsidiary ledger,* as in the Accounts Receivable credit column; and (2) *that the total is not to be posted,* as in the case of the Sundry column.

Date	Account Name	Post. Ref.	Sundry Accounts Credit	Accounts Receivable Credit	Sales Credit	Sales Tax Payable Credit	Credit Card Expense Debit	Cash Debit
19__								
May 3	Sales				100 00	4 00		104 00
4	Sales				100 00	4 00	6 00	98 00
5	John Oatey	✓		208 00				208 00
7	Eric Adams, Capital	311	3,000 00					3,000 00
8	Equipment	121	150 00					150 00
11	Notes Payable	211	300 00					300 00
16	Sales				200 00	8 00		208 00
21	Sales				50 00	2 00	3 00	49 00
26	Kenneth Ralston	✓		62 40				62 40
28	Sales				40 00	1 60		41 60
31	Sales				150 00	6 00	9 00	147 00
31	Donald Madden	✓		26 00				26 00
31			3,450 00	296 40	640 00	25 60	18 00	4,394 00
			(✓)	(113)	(411)	(213)	(513)	(111)

Individual amounts in the Accounts Receivable credit column are posted daily.

Accounts Receivable Ledger

Donald Madden

Date	Debit	Credit	Balance
May 21			26 00
31		26 00	—

John Oatey

Date	Debit	Credit	Balance
May 1			208 00
5		208 00	—

Kenneth Ralston

Date	Debit	Credit	Balance
May 1			62 40
26		62 40	—

Individual amounts in the Sundry credit column are posted daily.

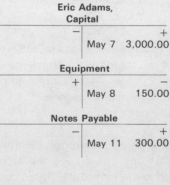

Eric Adams, Capital

−	+
	May 7 3,000.00

Equipment

+	−
May 8 150.00	

Notes Payable

−	+
	May 11 300.00

Totals are posted at the end of the month.

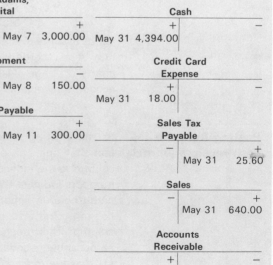

Cash

+	−
May 31 4,394.00	

Credit Card Expense

+	−
May 31 18.00	

Sales Tax Payable

−	+
	May 31 25.60

Sales

−	+
	May 31 640.00

Accounts Receivable

+	−
	May 31 296.40

Let's say it's the end of the month. We total the columns, then check the accuracy of the footings by proving that the sum of the debit totals equals the sum of the credit totals.

	Debit totals
Cash	$4,394.00
Credit Card Expense	18.00
	$4,412.00

	Credit totals
Sundry Accounts	$3,450.00
Accounts Receivable	296.40
Sales	640.00
Sales Tax Payable	25.60
	$4,412.00

Credit terms

The seller always stipulates credit terms: How much credit can be allowed to a customer? And how much time should the customer be given to pay the full amount? The *credit period* is the time the seller allows the buyer before full payment has to be made. Retailers generally allow 1 month.

Wholesalers and manufacturers often have a *cash discount* specified in their credit terms. A cash discount is the amount a customer can deduct if she or he pays the bill within a short time. Naturally this discount acts as an incentive for charge customers to pay their bills promptly.

For example, say that a wholesaler offers customers credit terms of 2/10, n/30. This means that the customer gets a 2% discount if he or she pays the bill within 10 days after the invoice date. If the customer can't pay the bill within the 10 days, then he or she has to pay the entire amount within 30 days after the invoice date. Other cash discounts that may be used are:

- **1/15, n/60** *Translation:* The seller offers a 1% discount if the bill is paid within 15 days after the invoice date, and the whole bill must be paid within 60 days after the invoice date.
- **2/10, EOM, n/60** *Translation:* The seller offers a 2% discount if the bill is paid within 10 days after the end of the month, and the whole bill must be paid within 60 days after the invoice date.

A wholesaler or manufacturer offering a cash discount adopts one cash discount as a credit policy, and makes this available to all its customers.

The seller considers cash discounts to be sales discounts; the buyer, on the other hand, considers cash discounts as purchases discounts. In this section we are concerned with the sales discount. The Sales Discount account, like Sales Returns and Allowances, is a deduction from Sales.

To illustrate, we return to North Central Plumbing Supply. The following transactions take place, and we'll record them in T accounts so we can see them at a glance.

(a) August 1: Sold merchandise on account to T. L. Long Company, invoice no. 320, $325, terms 2/10, n/30.

(b) August 10: T. L. Long Company paid invoice no. 320, less cash discount ($325.00 − $6.50 = $318.50).

Assets +		Expenses =		Liabilities +		Revenue +	Owner's Equity	
+	−	+	−	−	+	−	+	−	+
Dr	Cr	Dr	Cr	Dr	Cr	Dr	Cr	Dr	Cr

Accounts Receivable

+	−
(a) 325	(b) 325

Sales

−	+
	(a) 325

Cash

+	−
(b) 318.50	

Sales Discount

+	−
(b) 6.50	

Since North Central Plumbing Supply offers this cash discount to all customers, and since charge customers often pay their bills within the discount period, North Central sets up a Sales Discount debit column in the cash receipts journal.

Cash Receipts Journal   Page 18

Date		Account Name	Post. Ref.	Sundry Accounts Credit	Accounts Receivable Credit	Sales Credit	Sales Discount Debit	Cash Debit
19___								
Aug.	10	T. L. Long Company			325 00		6 50	318 50

Here are some more transactions of North Central Plumbing Supply involving increases in cash during August of this year. Remember that the standard credit terms for all charge customers are 2/10, n/30.

Aug. 15	Cash sales for first half of the month, $460.
16	Acme Plumbing and Heating paid invoice no. 322, less cash discount, $1.88 ($94.00 − $1.88 = $92.12).
17	Received payment on a promissory note given by John R. Stokes, $300 principal, plus $3 interest. (The amount of the interest is recorded in the Interest Income account.)

Aug. 21 Clark and Keller Hardware paid invoice no. 324, $86, less cash
discount, $1.72 ($86.00 − $1.72 = $84.28).

23 Sold store equipment for cash at cost, $126.

26 Robert C. Randall, the owner, invested an additional $4,000 cash
in the business.

26 Home Hardware Company paid invoice no. 325, less the amount
of credit memorandum no. 70, less cash discount ($215 −
$116 = $99 net, $99 − $1.98 = $97.02).

30 Henning's Plumbing paid invoice no. 326, less cash discount
($293 − $5.86 = $287.14).

31 Cash sales for second half of the month, $620.

31 Macon, Inc., paid invoice no. 321, $116. (This is longer than the
10-day period, so they missed the cash discount.)

North Central records these transactions in their cash receipts journal.

Cash Receipts Journal						Page 18	
Date	Account Name	Post. Ref.	Sundry Accounts Credit	Accounts Receivable Credit	Sales Credit	Sales Discount Debit	Cash Debit
19__							
Aug. 10	T. L. Long Company			325 00		6 50	318 50
15	Sales				460 00		460 00
16	Acme Plumbing and Heating			94 00		1 88	92 12
17	Notes Receivable		300 00				
	Interest Income		3 00				303 00
21	Clark and Keller Hardware			86 00		1 72	84 28
23	Store Equipment		126 00				126 00
26	Robert C. Randall, Capital		4,000 00				4,000 00
26	Home Hardware Company			99 00		1 98	97 02
30	Henning's Plumbing			293 00		5 86	287 14
31	Sales				620 00		620 00
31	Macon, Inc.			116 00			116 00
31			4,429 00	1,013 00	1,080 00	17 94	6,504 06

North Central's accountant proves the equality of debits and credits:

	Debit totals
Cash debit	$6,504.06
Sales Discount debit	17.94
	$6,522.00

	Credit totals
Sundry Accounts credit	$4,429.00
Accounts Receivable credit	1,013.00
Sales credit	1,080.00
	$6,522.00

**Cash payments
journal:
service enterprise**

The cash payments journal, as the name implies, records all transactions in which cash goes out, or decreases. When the cash payments journal is used, all transactions in which cash is credited *must* be recorded in it. It may be used for a service as well as a merchandising business.

To get acquainted with the cash payments journal, let's list some typical transactions of a service firm (such as a dry cleaners or a bowling alley) or of a professional enterprise which result in a decrease in cash. So that you'll see the transactions at a glance, let's record them directly in T accounts.

May 2: Paid Henry Moore Company, a creditor, on account, check no. 63, $220.

Accounts Payable		**Cash**	
−	+	+	−
220			220

May 4: Bought supplies for cash, $90, check no. 64.

Supplies		**Cash**	
+	−	+	−
90			90

May 5: Paid wages for 2 weeks, check no. 65, $1,216.

Wages Expense		**Cash**	
+	−	+	−
1,216			1,216

May 6: Paid rent for the month, $350, check no. 66.

Rent Expense		**Cash**	
+	−	+	−
350			350

Now let's appraise these four transactions. The first one would occur very often, as payments to creditors would be made several times a month. Of the last three transactions, the debit to Wages Expense might occur twice a month, the debit to Rent Expense once a month, and the debit to Supplies every now and then.

If one were designing a cash payments journal, it would be logical to include a Cash credit column because all the transactions involve a decrease in cash. Since payments are made to creditors often, there should be an Accounts Payable debit column. One could set up any other column if it were used often enough to warrant it. Otherwise, a Sundry debit column would take care of all the other transactions.

Now let's record these same transactions in a cash payments journal, and include a column entitled Check Number. If you think a moment, you'll see that this is consistent with good management of cash, in that all expenditures should be paid for by check, except for Petty Cash, which we'll talk about later. First let's repeat the transactions.

May 2	Paid Henry Moore Company, a creditor, on account, $220, check no. 63.
4	Bought supplies for cash, $90, check no. 64.
5	Paid wages for the first 2 weeks, $1,216, check no. 65.
6	Paid rent for the month, $350, check no. 66.

Cash Payments Journal   **Page 62**

Date		Ck. No.	Account Name	Post. Ref.	Sundry Accounts Debit	Accounts Payable Debit	Cash Credit
19—							
May	2	63	Henry Moore Company			220 00	220 00
	4	64	Supplies		90 00		90 00
	5	65	Wages Expense		1,216 00		1,216 00
	6	66	Rent Expense		350 00		350 00

Note that you list all checks in consecutive order, even those checks which must be voided. In this way, every check is accounted for, which is necessary for internal control.

At the end of the month, post the special columns as totals to the general ledger accounts, but not the total of the Sundry Accounts debit column. Post the figures in this column individually, after which you place the account number in the Posting Reference column. Post the figures in the Accounts Payable debit column separately to the individual accounts in the accounts payable ledger, and after posting, put a check mark (√) in the Posting Reference column. The posting letter designation for the cash payments journal is CP. Other transactions involving decreases in cash during May are as follows.

May	7	Paid $360 for a 3-year premium for fire insurance, check no. 67.
	9	Paid Treadwell, Inc., a creditor, on account, $418, check no. 68.
	11	Issued check no. 69 in payment of delivery expense, $62.
	14	Paid Johnson and Son, a creditor, on account, $110, check no. 70.
	16	Issued check no. 71 to the Melton State Bank, for Note Payable, $660, $600 on the principal and $60 interest.
	19	Voided check no. 72.
	19	Bought equipment for $800, paying $200 down. Issued check no. 73. The other part of this entry will be recorded in the general journal as a debit to Equipment and a credit to Accounts Payable, for $600 each.
	20	Paid wages for 2 weeks, check no. 74, $1,340.
	22	Issued check no. 75 to Peter R. Morton Advertising Agency for advertising, $94.
	26	Paid telephone bill, $26, check no. 76.
	31	Issued check for freight bill on equipment purchased on May 19, $28, check no. 77.
	31	Paid Teller and Noble, a creditor, on account, $160, check no. 78.

On the following page the postings to the accounts payable ledger and the general ledger are illustrated. Here is the cash payments journal.

Cash Payments Journal							Page 62			
Date		Ck. No.	Account Name	Post. Ref.	Sundry Accounts Debit		Accounts Payable Debit		Cash Credit	
19___										
May	2	63	Henry Moore Company	✓			220	00	220	00
	4	64	Supplies	113	90	00			90	00
	5	65	Wages Expense	411	1,216	00			1,216	00
	6	66	Rent Expense	412	350	00			350	00
	7	67	Prepaid Insurance	114	360	00			360	00
	9	68	Treadwell, Inc.	✓			418	00	418	00
	11	69	Delivery Expense	413	62	00			62	00
	14	70	Johnson and Son	✓			110	00	110	00
	16	71	Notes Payable	211	600	00				
			Interest Expense	414	60	00			660	00
	19	72	Void	✓						
	19	73	Equipment	121	200	00			200	00
	20	74	Wages Expense	411	1,340	00			1,340	00
	22	75	Advertising Expense	415	94	00			94	00
	26	76	Telephone Expense	416	26	00			26	00
	31	77	Equipment	121	28	00			28	00
	31	78	Teller and Noble	✓			160	00	160	00
	31				4,426	00	908	00	5,334	00
					(✓)		(212)		(111)	

Individual amounts in the Accounts Payable debit column are posted daily.

Individual amounts in the Sundry debit column are posted daily.

Totals are posted at the end of the month.

Accounts Payable Ledger

Johnson and Son

Date		Debit	Credit	Balance
May	1			110
	14	110		——

Henry Moore Company

Date		Debit	Credit	Balance
May	1			220
	2	220		——

Teller and Noble

Date		Debit	Credit	Balance
May	1			160
	31	160		——

Treadwell, Inc.

Date		Debit	Credit	Balance
May	1			418
	9	418		——

Supplies

	+		−
May 4	90		

Wages Expense

	+		−
May 5	1,216		
20	1,340		

Rent Expense

	+		−
May 6	350		

Prepaid Insurance

	+		−
May 7	360		

Delivery Expense

	+		−
May 11	62		

Notes Payable

	−		+
May 16	600		

Interest Expense

	+		−
May 16	60		

Equipment

	+		−
May 19	200		
31	28		

Advertising Expense

	+		−
May 22	94		

Telephone Expense

	+		−
May 26	26		

Cash

	+		−
		May 31	5,334

Accounts Payable

	−		+
May 31	908		

At the end of the month, after totaling the columns, check the accuracy of the footings by proving that the sum of the debit totals equals the sum of the credit totals. Since you have posted the individual amounts in the Sundry debit column to the general ledger, the posting that remains to be done consists of the credit to the Cash account for $5,334 and the debit to the Accounts Payable (controlling) account for $908.

	Debit totals
Sundry debit	$4,426.00
Accounts Payable debit	908.00
	$5,334.00

	Credit totals
Cash credit	$5,334.00

Cash payments journal: merchandising enterprise

There is one slight difference between the cash payments journal for a merchandising enterprise and that for a service enterprise. This difference has to do with the cash discounts that are available to a merchandising business. Recall that cash discounts are the amount that the buyer may deduct from the bill; this acts as an incentive to make the buyer pay the bill promptly. The buyer considers the cash discount to be a Purchases Discount, because it relates to his or her purchase of merchandise. The Purchases Discount account, like Purchases Returns and Allowances, is a deduction from Purchases, so the buyer, in his or her income statement, treats it as such.

Let us return to North Central Plumbing Supply, and assume that the following transactions take place. To demonstrate the debits and credits, let's show some typical transactions in the form of T accounts.

(a) August 2: Bought merchandise on account from Danton, Inc., their invoice no. 2706, $285; terms 2/10, n/30; dated July 31.

(b) August 8: Issued check no. 76, $279.30, to Danton, Inc., in payment of invoice no. 2706, less the cash discount, $5.70.

Assets +		Expenses =		Liabilities +		Revenue +		Owner's Equity	
+	−	+	−	−	+	−	+	−	+
Dr	Cr	Dr	Cr	Dr	Cr	Dr	Cr	Dr	Cr

Cash		and Purchases		Accounts Payable	
+	−	+	−	−	+
	(b) 279.30	(a) 285		(b) 285	(a) 285

Purchases Discount	
−	+
	(b) 5.70

Any well-managed business takes advantage of a purchases discount whenever possible. So if a discount is available to the business, it is worthwhile to set up a special Purchases Discount credit column in the cash payments journal.

Cash Payments Journal — Page 26

Date	Ck. No.	Account Name	Post. Ref.	Sundry Accounts Debit	Accounts Payable Debit	Purchases Discount Credit	Cash Credit
19__							
Aug. 8	76	Danton, Inc.			285 00	5 70	279 30

Here are some other transactions of North Central Plumbing Supply involving decreases in cash during August. Note that credit terms vary among the different creditors.

Aug. 10	Paid wages for 2-week period, $1,680, check no. 77.
11	Issued check no. 78, $609.56, to Argel Manufacturing Company, in payment of invoice no. 10611, $692; less return of $70, less cash discount, 2/10, n/30 ($692 − $70 = $622; $622 × .02 = $12.44; $622 − $12.44 = $609.56).
12	Bought supplies for cash, $70, issued check no. 79 payable to Davenport Office Supplies.
15	Paid Sinclair Manufacturing Company, their invoice no. B643, check no. 80, $127.71; $165 less return of $36, less cash discount, $1.29 ($165 − $36 = $129; $129 × .01 = $1.29; $129.00 − $1.29 = $127.71).
16	Bought merchandise for cash, $200, check no. 81, payable to Jones Sheet and Tube.
19	Paid freight bill for merchandise to Reliable Express Company, $60, check no. 82.
23	Voided check no. 83.
23	Issued check no. 84 to American Fire Insurance Company for insurance premium for 1 year, $120.
25	Paid wages for 2-week period, $1,750, check no. 85.
27	Paid T. R. Waller $46 for merchandise he returned on a cash sale, check no. 86.
31	Issued check no. 87, $760, to Rogers and Simon Company in payment of invoice no. 982 (net 30 days).

Let us now record these transactions in the cash payments journal at the top of the next page.

Check register

Instead of using a cash payments journal as a book of original entry, one can use a check register. The check register is merely a large checkbook with perforations so that it is easy to tear out the checks. The page opposite the checks has columns which may be labeled for special accounts, such as bank

Date		Ck. No.	Account Name	Post. Ref.	Sundry Accounts Debit		Accounts Payable Debit		Purchases Discount Credit		Cash Credit	
19__												
Aug.	8	76	Danton, Inc.				285	00	5	70	279	30
	10	77	Wages Expense		1,680	00					1,680	00
	11	78	Argel Manufacturing Company				622	00	12	44	609	56
	12	79	Supplies		70	00					70	00
	15	80	Sinclair Manufacturing Company				129	00	1	29	127	71
	16	81	Purchases		200	00					200	00
	19	82	Purchases		60	00					60	00
	23	83	Void									
	23	84	Prepaid Insurance		120	00					120	00
	25	85	Wages Expense		1,750	00					1,750	00
	27	86	Sales Returns and Allowances		46	00					46	00
	31	87	Rogers and Simon Company				760	00			760	00
	31				3,926	00	1,796	00	19	43	5,702	57

credit (in place of Cash), Accounts Payable debit, etc. The checks are pre-numbered, and one records each check issued on the columnar sheet. This is common practice for a small business in which the owner writes the checks himself or herself. One posts directly from the check register.

Suppose North Central Plumbing Supply had used a check register instead of the cash payments journal. Their August transactions would appear as shown on the next page.

You can see for yourself that the difference between the cash payments journal and the check register is minor. Recall that one substitutes the bank credit column for the Cash credit column. The check register lists the payee of the check. The Accounts Payable debit column and the Purchases Discount credit column are included to handle payments to creditors.

Two additional columns, Deposits and Bank Balance, could be added, to give a current balance of the First National Bank or Cash account. The posting process for each book of original entry would be the same.

In a small business, the owner or manager usually signs all the checks. However, if the owner delegates the authority to sign checks to some other person, that person should *not* have access to the accounting records. Why?

Check Register

Date	Ck. No.	Payee	Account Debited	Post. Ref.	Sundry Accounts Debit	Accounts Payable Debit	Purchases Discount Credit	Valley National Bank Credit
19—								
Aug. 8	76	Danton, Inc.	Danton, Inc.			285 00	5 70	279 30
10	77	Payroll	Wages Exp.		1,680 00			1,680 00
11	78	Argel Mfg.	Argel Mfg.			622 00	12 44	609 56
12	79	Davenport	Supplies		70 00			70 00
15	80	Sinclair Mfg.	Sinclair Mfg.			129 00	1 29	127 71
16	81	Jones Sheet	Purchases		200 00			200 00
19	82	Reliable Exp.	Purchases		60 00			60 00
23	83	Void						
23	84	American Fire	Prepaid Ins.		120 00			120 00
25	85	Payroll	Wages Exp.		1,750 00			1,750 00
27	86	F. R. Waller	Sales Ret. and Allow.		46 00			46 00
31	87	Rogers & Simon Co.	Rogers & Simon Co.			760 00		760 00
31					3,926 00	1,796 00	19 43	5,702 57

Well, this helps to prevent fraud, because a dishonest employee could conceal a cash disbursement in the accounting records. In other words, for a medium-to large-size business, it's worth a manager's while to keep a separate book, which in this case is the cash payments journal. One person writes the checks, and another person records the checks in the cash payments journal. This means that one person acts as a check on the other, and there would have to be collusion between the two people for embezzlement to take place. Again, this precaution is consistent with a good system of internal control.

Trade discounts

Manufacturers and wholesalers of many lines of products publish annual catalogs listing their products at retail prices. These concerns offer their customers substantial reductions (often as much as 40%) from the list or catalog prices. The reductions from the list prices are called *trade discounts*. Firms grant sales discounts and purchases discounts for prompt payment of invoices, but trade discounts are not related to cash payments. Manufacturers and wholesalers use trade discounts to avoid reprinting catalogs when selling prices change. They simply change the selling prices in the catalogs by issuing a new list of trade discounts to be applied to the catalog prices.

Firms may quote trade discounts as a single percentage. Example: A distributor of furnaces grants a single discount of 40% off the listed catalog price of $8,000. In this case, the selling price is calculated as follows.

List or catalog price	$8,000
Less: Trade discount of 40% ($8,000 × .4)	3,200
Selling price	$4,800

Neither the seller nor the buyer records trade discounts in the accounts; they enter only the selling price. By T accounts, the furnace distributor records the sale as:

Accounts Receivable		Sales	
+	−	−	+
4,800			4,800

The buyer records the purchase as:

Purchases		Accounts Payable	
+	−	−	+
4,800			4,800

Firms may also quote trade discounts as a chain or series of percentages. For example, a distributor of automobile parts grants discounts of 30%, 10%, and 10% off the listed catalog price of $900. In this case, the selling price is calculated as follows.

List or catalog price	$900.00
Less: First trade discount of 30% ($900 × .3)	270.00
Remainder after first discount	$630.00
Less: Second trade discount of 10% ($630 × .1)	63.00
Remainder after second discount	$567.00
Less: Third discount of 10% ($567 × .1)	56.70
Selling price	$510.30

By T accounts, the automobile parts distributor records the sale as:

Accounts Receivable		Sales	
+	−	−	+
510.30			510.30

The buyer records the purchase as shown on the next page.

Purchases			Accounts Payable	
+	−		−	+
510.30				510.30

In the situation involving a chain of discounts, the additional discounts are granted for large-volume transactions, either in dollar amounts or in sizes of shipments, such as carload lots.

Cash discounts could also apply in situations involving trade discounts. Example: Suppose that the credit terms of the above sale included a cash discount of 2/10, n/30, and that the buyer pays the invoice within 10 days. The seller applies the cash discount to the selling price. By T accounts, the seller records the transaction as:

Cash		Sales Discount		Accounts Receivable	
+	−	+	−	+	−
500.09		10.21			510.30

The buyer records the transaction as:

Cash		Purchases Discount		Accounts Payable	
+	−	−	+	−	+
	500.09		10.21	510.30	

Summary

When a business entity uses a cash receipts journal, it *must* record every transaction which results in a debit to cash in this journal. The person handling the books sets up special columns in the journal to take care of debits or credits to accounts that are used frequently. In accounting, *Sundry* means miscellaneous, so one records entries in the Sundry column when there is no appropriate special column. The accountant posts daily from the Accounts Receivable credit column to the individual charge customers' accounts in the accounts receivable ledger. After posting, he or she puts a check mark (✓) in the Posting Reference column. The accountant also posts the amounts in the Sundry credit column daily. After these entries are posted, the account numbers are recorded in the Posting Reference column. The special columns are posted as totals at the end of the month. After posting, the accountant writes the account numbers in parentheses under the totals.

When a business entity uses a cash payments journal, it *must* record every transaction which results in a credit to cash in this journal. This enables the accountant to determine quickly the balance of the Cash account. It follows that if all incoming cash is recorded in the cash receipts journal, and if all outgoing cash is recorded in the cash payments journal, then one can readily determine the current balance of cash at any time during the month by adding the receipts to the beginning balance of cash and deducting the outgoing payments.

Smaller firms often use a check register as a substitute for the cash payments journal. Either book of original entry may be used by service as well as merchandising enterprises. The posting procedure for both a cash payments journal and a check register is just like the posting procedure for a cash receipts journal.

In transactions involving trade discounts, one deducts the trade discounts from the list prices to arrive at the selling prices. Both sellers and buyers record the transactions at the selling prices.

Glossary

o **Bank charge card** A bank credit card, like the credit cards used by millions of private citizens. The card holder pays what she or he owes directly to the issuing bank. The business firm deposits the credit card receipts; the amount of the deposit equals the total of the receipts, less a discount deducted by the bank.

o **Trade discount** A substantial reduction from the list or catalog prices of goods, granted by the seller.

Exercises

Exercise 1 Describe the transactions recorded in the following T accounts.

Cash		Sales Tax Payable		Accounts Receivable		Sales	
208			8	208	208		200

Exercise 2 Record the transactions listed below in general journal form.

Aug. 2 | Sold merchandise on account to T. Clancy, $800, 2/10, n/30.
4 | Issued credit memo no. 493 to T. Clancy for damaged merchandise, $35.
22 | Received a check from Clancy in full payment of bill.

Exercise 3 Describe the transactions recorded in the following T accounts.

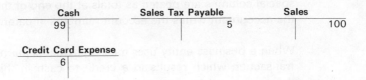

Cash		Sales Tax Payable		Sales	
99			5		100

Credit Card Expense	
6	

Exercise 4 Label the blanks on the next page as debit or credit.

Cash Receipts Journal								Page __
Date	Account Name	Post. Ref.	Sundry Accounts (d)	Accounts Receivable (R)	Sales (CR)	Sales Discount (d R)	Cash (R)	

Exercise 5 Describe the transactions recorded in the following T accounts.

Cash		Accounts Payable			Purchases Discount	
	588	600	Bal. 600			12

Exercise 6 Record the transactions listed here in general journal form.

Mar.	9	Bought merchandise on account from Columbia Electrical Supply, $1,500, 2/10, n/30.
	21	Received a credit memo for $100 for defective goods returned.
Apr.	8	Paid Columbia Electrical Supply in full of account.

Exercise 7 Label the blanks as debit or credit.

Cash Payments Journal								Page __
Date	Ck. No.	Account Name	Post. Ref.	Sundry Accounts ( )	Accounts Payable ( )	Purchases Discount (R)	Cash (C)	

Exercise 8 Describe the transactions recorded in the following T accounts.

Cash		Accounts Payable		Purchases	
	1,372	200	1,600	1,600	
		1,400			

Purchases Returns and Allowances		Purchases Discount	
	200		28

Problems

Problem 10-1 The Exclusive Luggage Company, a retail sales concern, sells on the basis of (1) cash, (2) charge accounts, and (3) bank credit cards. The following transactions involved cash receipts for the firm during April of this year. The state imposes a 4% sales tax on retail sales.

Apr.	7	Total cash sales for the week, $900, plus $36 sales tax.
	7	Total sales for the week paid for by bank credit cards, $800, plus $32 sales tax. The bank charges 6% on the total of the actual sales ($800 × .06 = $48).

Apr.	8	N. T. Nolan, the owner, invested an additional $2,000.
	11	Collected cash from Robert Stone, a charge customer, $47.80.
	12	Sold store equipment for cash, at cost, $160.
	14	Total cash sales for the week, $1,100, plus $44 sales tax.
	14	Total sales for the week paid for by bank credit cards, $600, plus $24 sales tax.
	18	Borrowed $1,600 from the bank, receiving cash and giving the bank a promissory note.
	20	Collected cash from Ted Bacon, a charge customer, $52.
	21	Total sales for the week paid for by bank credit cards, $700, plus $28 sales tax.
	21	Total cash sales for the week, $1,400, plus $64 sales tax.
	23	Received cash as refund for return of merchandise bought, $90.
	25	Collected cash from J. R. Finch, a charge customer, $104.
	30	Total sales for the week paid for by bank credit cards, $160, plus $6.40 sales tax.
	30	Collected cash from Nathan Turnbull, a charge customer, $72.80.
	30	Total cash sales for the week, $1,550, plus $62 sales tax.

Instructions

1 Record the transactions in the cash receipts journal.
2 Total and rule the cash receipts journal.
3 Prove the equality of debit and credit totals.

Problem 10-2 Randolph Company sells candy wholesale, primarily to vending machine operators. Terms of sales on account are 2/10, n/30, FOB shipping point. The following transactions involving cash receipts and sales of merchandise took place in May of this year.

May	1	Received $980 cash from G. Payne in payment of April 22 invoice of $1,000, less cash discount.
	3	Received $660 cash in payment of a $600 note receivable and interest of $60.
	6	Received $588 cash from J. R. Potter in payment of April 29 invoice of $600, less cash discount.
	7	Sold merchandise on account to N. Olson, invoice no. 286, $400.
	15	Cash sales for first half of May, $2,160.
	16	Received cash from N. Olson in payment of invoice no. 286, less discount.
	19	Received $160 cash from Ralph Porter in payment of April 16 invoice; no discount.
	20	Sold merchandise on account to P. R. Thresher, invoice no. 298, $810.
	23	Received $216 cash refund for return of defective equipment bought in April for cash.
	26	Sold merchandise on account to T. E. Bannister, invoice no. 306, $460.
	31	Cash sales for second half of May, $3,290.

Instructions

1 Journalize the transactions for May in the cash receipts journal and the sales journal.

2 Total and rule the journals.

Problem 10-3 The Campus Bookshop uses a check register to keep track of expenditures. The following transactions occurred during February of this year.

Feb.	2	Issued check no. 6210, $627.20, to Amalgamated Publishers for the amount of their invoice no. 68172 for $640, less 2% cash discount.
	3	Paid freight bill to Midway Express Company, $40, for books purchased, issuing check no. 6211.
	5	Paid rent for the month, $190, check no. 6212, to Beale Land Company.
	10	Paid for advertising in *Campus News,* $40, check no. 6213.
	11	Paid New England Book Company $851.40, check no. 6214, for their invoice no. A3322 for $860 less 1% cash discount.
	16	Paid wages for first half of February, $320, check no. 6215.
	20	N. D. Thomas, the owner, withdrew $200 for personal use, check no. 6216.
	25	Made payment on bank loan, $440, check no. 6217, consisting of $400 on the principal and $40 interest, Coast National Bank.
	28	Paid Midwest Publishing Company $940, check no. 6218, for their invoice no. 7768 (no discount).
	28	Voided check no. 6219.
	28	Paid wages expense for second half of February, $320, check no. 6220.

Instructions

1 Record the transactions in the check register.

2 Total and rule the check register.

3 Prove the equality of the debit and credit totals.

Problem 10-4 The following transactions were completed by Valley Electronics Supply during January, the first month of this fiscal year. Terms of sale are 2/10, n/30.

Jan.	2	Paid rent for the month, $520, check no. 6891.
	2	H. R. Drummond, the owner, invested an additional $2,000 in the business.
	4	Bought merchandise on account from Tracy and Company, $2,720, their invoice no. A961, 2/10, n/30, dated January 2.
	4	Received check from Danner Appliance for $980 in payment of $1,000 invoice, less discount.
	4	Sold merchandise on account to N. D. Miller, $640, invoice no. 8643.

Jan.	6	Received check from Everett and Rollins for $735 in payment of $750 invoice, less discount.
	7	Issued check no. 6892, $490, to Murphy and Logan, in payment of their invoice no. T1172 for $500, less discount.
	7	Bought supplies on account from Jensen Office Supply, $96, their invoice no. 1023A.
	7	Sold merchandise on account to Tredder and Adams, $820, invoice no. 8644.
	9	Issued credit memo no. 33 to N. D. Miller, $40, for merchandise returned.
	11	Cash sales for January 1 to 10, $4,336.
	11	Paid Tracy and Company $2,665.60, check no. 6893, in payment of $2,720 invoice, less discount.
	14	Sold merchandise on account to Danner Appliance, $1,900, invoice no. 8645.
	14	Received check from N. D. Miller, $588, in payment of $640 invoice, less return of $40 and less discount.
	15	Paid salaries for first half of month, $2,400, check no. 6894.
	18	Bought merchandise on account from Stanton Products, $4,870, their invoice no. 8712G, 2/10 EOM, n/60, dated January 16.
	21	Issued check no. 6895, $260, for advertising.
	21	Cash sales for January 11 to 20, $3,980.
	23	Paid Able Fast Freight, check no. 6896, $80, for transportation of merchandise purchased.
	23	Received credit memo no. 316, $400, from Stanton Products, for merchandise returned.
	29	Sold merchandise on account to Union Supply, $1,810, invoice no. 8646.
	31	Issued check no. 6897, $2,400, for salaries for second half of month.
	31	Cash sales, January 21 to 31, $4,316.
	31	H. R. Drummond, the owner, withdrew $600 for personal use, check no. 6898.
	31	Issued check no. 6899, $46, for miscellaneous expenses.

Instructions

1 Record the balances of the following accounts in the general ledger.

111	Cash	$ 8,610
113	Accounts Receivable	1,750
114	Merchandise Inventory	19,436
115	Supplies	462
116	Prepaid Insurance	380
121	Equipment	3,224
211	Accounts Payable	500
311	H. R. Drummond, Capital	33,362
312	H. R. Drummond, Drawing	
411	Sales	
412	Sales Returns and Allowances	

413   Sales Discount
511   Purchases
512   Purchases Returns and Allowances
513   Purchases Discounts
521   Salaries Expense
522   Rent Expense
523   Miscellaneous Expense

2 Open the following accounts in the accounts receivable ledger, entering the balances as of January 1 in the Balance columns: Danner Appliance, $1,000; Everett and Rollins, $750; N. D. Miller; Tredder and Adams; Union Supply.

3 Open the following accounts in the accounts payable ledger, entering the balances as of January 1 in the Balance columns: Jensen Office Supply; Murphy and Logan, $500; Stanton Products; Tracy and Company.

4 Record the transactions for January, using a sales journal, page 79; a purchases journal, page 62; a cash receipts journal, page 44; a cash payments journal, page 51; and a general journal, page 106.

5 Post *daily* those entries involving the Sundry columns and the general journal to the accounts receivable ledger, the accounts payable ledger, and the general ledger; also post daily the entries in the Sundry columns of the special journals.

6 Add the columns of the special journals, and prove the equality of debit totals and credit totals.

7 Post the appropriate totals of the special journals to the general ledger.

8 Prepare a trial balance.

9 Prepare a schedule of accounts receivable and a schedule of accounts payable. Do the totals equal the balances of the related controlling accounts?

Problem 10-1A The Durable Luggage Company, a retail store, sells on the basis of (1) cash, (2) charge accounts, and (3) bank credit cards. The following transactions involve cash receipts for the firm for March of this year. The state imposes a 4% sales tax on retail sales. (Durable Luggage uses a tax table to determine the amount of sales tax for cash sales, so the sales tax they collect does not *exactly* equal 4% of taxable sales.)

Mar.	8	Total cash sales for the week, $850, plus $34 sales tax.
	8	Total sales from bank credit cards for the week, $900, plus $36 sales tax. The bank charges 6% on the total of the actual sale ($900 × .06 = $54).
	12	C. T. Kohler, the owner, invested an additional $2,364.
	13	Sold office equipment for cash, at cost, $183.
	13	Collected cash from Robert Alston, a charge customer, $46.92.
	15	Total cash sales for the week, $1,296.52, plus $51.12 sales tax.
	15	Total sales for the week on the basis of bank credit cards, $720, plus $28.80 sales tax.
	19	Collected cash from Douglas Lowe, a charge customer, $39.26.
	20	Borrowed $2,780 from the bank, receiving cash and giving the bank a promissory note.
	22	Total cash sales for the week, $1,627, plus $65.22 sales tax.

Mar. 22	Total sales from bank credit cards for the week, $740, plus $29.60 sales tax.
23	Collected cash from T. E. French, a charge customer, $116.76.
25	Durable Luggage received cash as a refund for the return of merchandise they purchased, $186.
28	Collected cash from Norbert Truman, a charge customer, $71.56.
31	Total sales from bank credit cards for the week, $176.40, plus $7.06 sales tax.
31	Total cash sales for the week, $1,927.84, plus $77.24 sales tax.

Instructions

1 Record the transactions in the cash receipts journal.
2 Total and rule the cash receipts journal.
3 Prove the equality of debit and credit totals.

Problem 10-2A The H. G. Stassen Company sells candy wholesale, primarily to vending-machine operators. Terms of sales on account are 2/10, n/30, FOB shipping point. The following transactions involving cash receipts and sales of merchandise took place in May of this year.

May 1	Received $490 cash from P. Kline in payment of April 23 invoice of $500, less cash discount.
4	Received $840 cash in payment of $800 note receivable and interest of $40.
7	Sold merchandise on account to F. Stevens, invoice no. 871, $360.
8	Received $686 in cash from Donald Pihl in payment of April 30 invoice of $700, less cash discount.
14	Received cash from F. Stevens in payment of invoice no. 871, less discount.
15	Cash sales for first half of May, $2,772.
18	Received $152 in cash from Randy Sims in payment of April 14 invoice, no discount.
21	Sold merchandise on account to S. T. Thompson, invoice no. 898, $416.
24	Received $218 cash refund for return of defective equipment bought in April for cash.
27	Sold merchandise on account to C. C. Cummins, invoice no. 921, $432.
31	Cash sales for the second half of May, $2,027.

Instructions

1 Journalize the transactions for May in the cash receipts journal and the sales journal.
2 Total and rule the journals.

Problem 10-3A The Cranston Bookstore uses a check register to keep track of expenditures. The following transactions occurred during February of this year.

Feb.	2	Issued check no. 3118 to National Book Company for their invoice no. 1113B, $520, less cash discount of $10.40, $509.60.
	3	Paid freight bill to Newton Express Company, $47, for merchandise purchased, issuing check no. 3119.
	5	Paid rent for month of February, $215, check no. 3120, to Standard Realty.
	10	Paid for advertising in *Campus News*, $42, check no. 3121.
	11	Paid Piedmont Publishing Company $990, check no. 3122, for their invoice no. C755 in the amount of $1,000 less 1% cash discount.
	16	Paid wages for first half of month, $426, check no, 3123.
	20	R. Cranston, the owner, withdrew $425 for personal use, check no. 3124.
	26	Made payment on bank loan, $620, check no. 3125, consisting of $600 on principal and $20 interest, Fenway National Bank.
	28	Issued to Southern Publishing Company $358, check no. 3126, for their invoice no. 3126 (no discount).
	28	Voided check no. 3127.
	28	Paid wages for second half of month, $426, check no. 3128.
	28	Received and paid telephone bill, $32, check no. 3129, payable to Nationwide Telephone Company.

Instructions

1 Record the transactions in the check register.
2 Total and rule the check register.
3 Prove the equality of the debit and credit totals.

Problem 10-4A The following transactions were completed by Valley Electronics Supply during January, the first month of this fiscal year. Terms of sale are 2/10, n/30.

Jan.	2	Paid rent for month, $515, check no. 6891.
	2	H. R. Drummond, the owner, invested an additional $2,160 in the business.
	4	Bought merchandise on account from Tracy and Company, $2,690, their invoice no. A961, 2/10, n/30, dated January 2.
	4	Received check from Danner Appliance for $980 in payment of invoice for $1,000, less discount.
	4	Sold merchandise on account to N. D. Miller, $620, invoice no. 8643.
	6	Received check from Everett and Rollins for $735 in payment of $750 invoice, less discount.
	7	Issued check no. 6892, $490, to Murphy and Logan, in payment of their invoice no. T1172 for $500, less discount.
	7	Bought supplies on account from Jensen Office Supply, $78.20, their invoice no. 1023A.
	7	Sold merchandise on account to Tredder and Adams, $810, their invoice no. 8644.

Jan.	9	Issued credit memo no. 33 to N. D. Miller, $20, for merchandise returned.
	11	Cash sales for January 1 to 10, $4,228.20.
	11	Paid Tracy and Company $2,636.20, check no. 6893, in payment of their $2,690 invoice, less discount.
	14	Sold merchandise on account to Danner Appliance, $1,800, invoice no. 8645.
	14	Received check from N. D. Miller, $588, in payment of $620 invoice, less return of $20 and less discount.
	15	Paid salaries for first half of month, $2,370, check no. 6894.
	18	Bought merchandise on account from Stanton Products, $3,680, their invoice no. 8712G, 2/10, EOM, dated January 16.
	21	Issued check no. 6895, $258, for advertising.
	21	Cash sales for January 11 to 20, $3,498.
	23	Paid Able Fast Freight, check no. 6896, $72, for transporting of merchandise purchased.
	23	Received credit memo no. 316, $51, from Stanton Products Company, for merchandise returned.
	29	Sold merchandise on account to Union Supply, $1,742, invoice no. 8646.
	31	Issued check no. 6897, $2,370, for salaries for second half of month.
	31	Cash sales, January 21 to 31, $4,298.
	31	H. R. Drummond, the owner, withdrew $650 for personal use, check no. 6898.
	31	Issued check no. 6899, $43, for miscellaneous expense.

Instructions

1 Record the balances of the following accounts in the general ledger.

111	Cash	$ 8,610
113	Accounts Receivable	1,750
114	Merchandise Inventory	19,436
115	Supplies	462
116	Prepaid Insurance	380
121	Equipment	3,224
211	Accounts Payable	500
311	H. R. Drummond, Capital	33,362
312	H. R. Drummond, Drawing	
411	Sales	
412	Sales Returns and Allowances	
413	Sales Discount	
511	Purchases	
512	Purchases Returns and Allowances	
513	Purchases Discount	
521	Salaries Expense	
522	Rent Expense	
523	Miscellaneous Expense	

2 Open the following accounts in the accounts receivable ledger, entering the balances as of January 1 in the Balance columns: Danner Appliance, $1,000; Everett and Rollins, $750; N. D. Miller; Tredder and Adams; Union Supply.

3 Open the following accounts in the accounts payable ledger, entering the balances as of January 1 in the Balance columns: Jensen Office Supply; Murphy and Logan, $500; Stanton Products; Tracy and Company.

4 Record the transactions for January, using a sales journal, page 44; a cash payments journal, page 51; and a general journal, page 106.

5 Post entries daily to the accounts receivable ledger and the accounts payable ledger. Also post daily the entries in the Sundry columns of the special journals, as well as the entries in the general journal.

6 Add the columns of the special journals, and prove the equality of debit totals and credit totals.

7 Post the appropriate totals of the special journals to the general ledger.

8 Prepare a trial balance.

9 Prepare a schedule of accounts receivable and a schedule of accounts payable. Do the totals equal the balances of the related controlling accounts?

11 Work sheet and adjusting entries for a merchandising business

Once a business gets too big for one brain to handle, accounting takes over the job. Norton M. Bedford, *Income Determination Theory*

Specific objectives

After you have completed this chapter, you will be able to:
- Complete a work sheet for a merchandising business involving adjustments for merchandise inventory, depreciation, expired insurance, supplies used, accrued wages or salaries, and unearned revenue.
- Journalize the adjusting entries for a merchandising business.

Introduction

For quite some time we've been talking about the way to keep special journals and accounts when one is dealing with a merchandising enterprise. Now let's take another step forward in the accounting cycle for a merchandising business: *adjustments* and *work sheets*.

The columnar classifications and procedures for completing the work sheet are basically like those described in Chapter 5. A merchandising business—like a service business—requires adjustments for supplies used, expired insurance, depreciation, and accrued wages. However, there is an additional adjustment that applies exclusively to a merchandising enterprise: the adjustment for merchandise inventory. Still another adjustment, which could apply to either a merchandising or a service business, is the adjustment for unearned revenue. Note that doing away with the Adjusted Trial Balance columns reduces the size of the work sheet. This chapter will also discuss the work sheet with respect to the handling of the specialized accounts of a merchandising business.

Adjustment for merchandise inventory

In Chapter 8, when we introduced the Merchandise Inventory account, we put it under the heading of assets, and said that the balance of the account should be changed only when a physical inventory has been taken. This is consistent with a system of periodic inventories in which one records purchase of merchandise as a debit to Purchases, for the amount of the cost, and sale of merchandise as a credit to Sales, for the amount of the selling price.

Consider this example: A firm has a balance of Merchandise Inventory of $18,000, which represents the value of the inventory at the beginning of the fiscal period. Then at the end of the fiscal period, the firm takes an actual count of the stock on hand, and determines the value of the ending inventory to be $22,000. Naturally, in any business, goods are constantly being bought, sold, and replaced. Evidently the reason why the value of the ending inventory is larger than that of the beginning inventory is that the firm bought a greater amount than it sold. When we adjust the Merchandise Inventory account, we want to install the new figure of $22,000 in the account. We do this by a two-step process.

Step 1 Eliminate or close the Merchandise Inventory account into Revenue and Expense Summary by the amount of the beginning inventory.

Let's look at this entry in the form of T accounts.

We handle this the same way we handle the closing of any other account, by balancing off the account, or making the balance equal to zero. This is why we enter it as a credit to Merchandise Inventory. Now we do the opposite to Revenue and Expense Summary, which is a debit to this account.

Step 2 Enter the ending Merchandise Inventory, because one must record on the books the cost of the asset remaining on hand.

Let's repeat the T accounts and Step 1.

Here we debit Merchandise Inventory because this is the plus side of the account, and we do the opposite to Revenue and Expense Summary, which is, of course, a credit.

The reason we adjust the Merchandise Inventory account in these two steps is that both the beginning and the ending figures appear separately in the income statement, which is prepared directly from the Income Statement columns of the work sheet. Adjusting the inventory this way is considered to be more meaningful than taking a shortcut and adjusting for the difference between the beginning and the ending inventory values, since the amount of the difference does not appear as a distinct figure in the income statement.

Adjustment for unearned revenue

Let us now introduce another adjusting entry: unearned revenue. As we said, this entry could pertain to a service as well as to a merchandising business. Occasionally, cash is received in advance for services to be performed in the future. For example, a dormitory receives a semester's rent in advance, a dining hall sells meal tickets in advance, a concert association sells season tickets in advance, a magazine receives subscriptions in advance, or an insurance company receives premiums in advance. Let's assume that the entry for each transaction was recorded as a debit to Cash and a credit to a revenue account. If the period of time for which the cash was paid in advance does not entirely expire within the current fiscal period, the revenue will be overstated.

To illustrate, assume that Mary Curtis, a magazine publisher, receives $60,000 in cash for subscriptions, and records them originally as debits to Cash and credits to Subscriptions Income. At the end of the year, she finds that $4,000 of the subscriptions have been paid for in advance for the following year. Accordingly, she records an adjusting entry, debiting Subscriptions Income and crediting Unearned Subscriptions. Unearned Subscriptions is classified as a current liability, because the publisher is liable for the money; in other words, she is obligated to supply the magazines until the subscriptions run out. By T accounts, the situation looks like this.

Cash		Subscriptions Income		Unearned Subscriptions	
+	−	−	+	−	+
60,000		Adj. 4,000	60,000		Adj. 4,000

As another example, suppose that North Central Plumbing Supply rents an office to a manufacturer's representative for $150 per month. On November 1, he pays North Central $450 for 3 months' rent in advance, and North Central's accountant records this as a debit to Cash of $450 and a credit to Rent Income of $450. North Central's fiscal period ends on December 31, and since only 2 months' rent has been earned, the accountant must make an adjusting entry to transfer $150 from Rent Income to Unearned Rent. By T accounts, the situation looks like this.

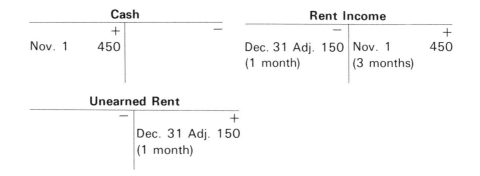

Let's demonstrate these adjustments by first looking at the trial balance section of North Central Plumbing Supply's work sheet.

North Central Plumbing Supply
Work Sheet
For year ended December 31, 19___

Account Name	Trial Balance Debit	Trial Balance Credit
Cash	10,961 00	
Notes Receivable	2,000 00	
Accounts Receivable	14,680 00	
Merchandise Inventory	31,500 00	
Supplies	720 00	
Prepaid Insurance	480 00	
Equipment	16,800 00	
Accumulated Depreciation, Equipment		8,200 00
Building	50,000 00	
Accumulated Depreciation, Building		16,000 00
Land	6,000 00	
Notes Payable		1,500 00
Accounts Payable		18,200 00
Mortgage Payable		4,000 00
Robert C. Randall, Capital		73,287 00
Robert C. Randall, Drawing	9,600 00	
Sales		88,090 00
Sales Discount	940 00	
Sales Returns and Allowances	420 00	
Rent Income		450 00
Interest Income		60 00
Purchases	42,800 00	
Purchases Discount		624 00
Purchases Returns and Allowances		416 00
Wages Expense	22,900 00	
Taxes Expense	980 00	
Interest Expense	46 00	
	210,827 00	210,827 00

Data for the adjustments

a-b Ending merchandise inventory, $29,400
c Unearned rent income, $150
d Ending supplies inventory, $206
e Insurance expired, $160
f Additional year's depreciation of equipment, $2,400
g Additional year's depreciation of building, $2,000
h Additional wages owed to employees but not paid at end of year, $610

At first glance, listing the adjustment data appears to be a relatively minor task. However, in a business situation, as we said before, one must take actual physical counts of the inventories, and match them up with the costs. One has to check insurance policies to determine the amount of insurance that has expired. Finally, one has to write off or depreciate, in a systematic manner, the cost of equipment and building. Incidentally, for income tax purposes, land cannot be depreciated. Even if the building and the lot were bought as one package for one price, one must separate the value of the building from the value of the land. For real estate taxes, the county assessor appraises the building and the land separately. If there is no other qualified appraisal available, one can use the assessor's ratio or percentage as a basis for separating building value and land value.

Now let's look at the data for these adjustments in the form of T accounts.

Merchandise Inventory				Revenue and Expense Summary			
+		−		(a)	31,500	(b)	29,400
Bal.	31,500	(a)	31,500				
(b)	29,400						

Rent Income				Unearned Rent			
−		+		−		+	
(c)	150	Bal.	450			(c)	150

Supplies				Supplies Expense			
+		−		+		−	
Bal.	720	(d)	514	(d)	514		

Prepaid Insurance				Insurance Expense			
+		−		+		−	
Bal.	480	(e)	160	(e)	160		

Accumulated Depreciation, Equipment				Depreciation Expense, Equipment			
−		+		+		−	
		Bal.	8,200	(f)	2,400		
		(f)	2,400				

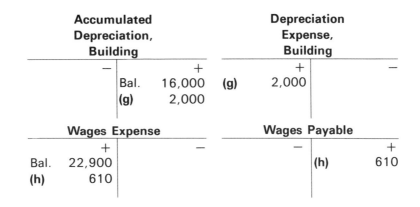

	Accumulated Depreciation, Building		Depreciation Expense, Building	
−	+		+	−
	Bal. 16,000	(g)	2,000	
	(g) 2,000			

	Wages Expense		Wages Payable	
+	−		−	+
Bal. 22,900			(h)	610
(h) 610				

We now record these in the Adjustments column of the work sheet, using the same letters in identifying the adjustments, as follows.

North Central Plumbing Supply
Work Sheet
For year ended December 31, 19___

Account Name	Trial Balance		Adjustments	
	Debit	Credit	Debit	Credit
Cash	10,961 00			
Notes Receivable	2,000 00			
Accounts Receivable	14,680 00			
Merchandise Inventory	31,500 00		(b) 29,400 00	(a) 31,500 00
Supplies	720 00			(d) 514 00
Prepaid Insurance	480 00			(e) 160 00
Equipment	16,800 00			
Accumulated Depreciation, Equipment		8,200 00		(f) 2,400 00
Building	50,000 00			
Accumulated Depreciation, Building		16,000 00		(g) 2,000 00
Land	6,000 00			
Notes Payable		1,500 00		
Accounts Payable		18,200 00		
Mortgage Payable		4,000 00		
Robert C. Randall, Capital		73,287 00		
Robert C. Randall, Drawing	9,600 00			
Sales		88,090 00		
Sales Discount	940 00			
Sales Returns and Allowances	420 00			
Rent Income		450 00	(c) 150 00	
Interest Income		60 00		
Purchases	42,800 00			
Purchases Discount		624 00		
Purchases Returns and Allowances		416 00		
Wages Expense	22,900 00		(h) 610 00	
Taxes Expense	980 00			
Interest Expense	46 00			
	210,827 00	210,827 00		
Revenue and Expense Summary			(a) 31,500 00	(b) 29,400 00
Unearned Rent				(c) 150 00
Supplies Expense			(d) 514 00	
Insurance Expense			(e) 160 00	
Depreciation, Expense, Equipment			(f) 2,400 00	
Depreciation Expense, Building			(g) 2,000 00	
Wages Payable				(h) 610 00
			66,734 00	66,734 00

Completion of the work sheet

Now we carry the account balances from the Trial Balance and Adjustments columns directly to the Income Statement and Balance Sheet columns. In the interest of efficiency, we do away with the Adjusted Trial Balance columns. It was worth our while to include these columns in the earlier presentation because they acted as a teaching device, and as an intermediate checkpoint to prove that the accounts were in balance before we carried them forward to the Income Statement and Balance Sheet columns. However, obviously the Adjusted Trial Balance columns are not necessary in order for one to complete the work sheet. Business practice requires that accounting be done by the most efficient and economical means, and therefore one eliminates the Adjusted Trial Balance columns.

Observe in particular the way we carry forward the figures for Merchandise Inventory and Revenue and Expense Summary. *Revenue and Expense Summary is the only account in which we don't combine the debit and credit figures;* instead we carry them into the Income Statement columns as *two distinct figures.* As we said, the reason is that both figures appear in the income statement itself. We'll talk about this more in Chapter 12.

When you are developing the work sheet, complete one stage at a time, as in the following illustration:

1 Record the trial balance, and make sure that the total of the Debit column equals the total of the Credit column.
2 Record the adjustments in the Adjustments columns, and make sure that the totals are equal.
3 Complete the Income Statement and Balance Sheet columns by recording the adjusted balance of each account, as indicated by the following classification of accounts.

Income Statement		Balance Sheet	
Debit	**Credit**	**Debit**	**Credit**
		A	L
		+	+
E	R	Drawing	OE
			+
			Accum.
			Deprec.

The completed work sheet would look like the one we have illustrated on the next page.

Please note especially the way we treat the special accounts for a merchandising business. For emphasis, look again at these accounts and their placement in the Income Statement and Balance Sheet columns at the top of page 278.

North Central Plumbing Supply
Work Sheet
For year ended December 31, 19___

Account Name	Trial Balance Debit	Trial Balance Credit	Adjustments Debit	Adjustments Credit	Income Statement Debit	Income Statement Credit	Balance Sheet Debit	Balance Sheet Credit
Cash	10,961						10,961	
Notes Receivable	2,000						2,000	
Accounts Receivable	14,680						14,680	
Merchandise Inventory	31,500		(b) 29,400	(a) 31,500			29,400	
Supplies	720			(d) 514			206	
Prepaid Insurance	480			(e) 160			320	
Equipment	16,800						16,800	
Accumulated Depreciation, Equipment		8,200		(f) 2,400				10,600
Building	50,000						50,000	
Accumulated Depreciation, Building		16,000		(g) 2,000				18,000
Land	6,000						6,000	
Notes Payable		1,500						1,500
Accounts Payable		18,200						18,200
Mortgage Payable		4,000						4,000
Robert C. Randall, Capital		73,287						73,287
Robert C. Randall, Drawing	9,600						9,600	
Sales		88,090				88,090		
Sales Discount	940				940			
Sales Returns and Allowances	420				420			
Rent Income		450	(c) 150			300		
Interest Income		60				60		
Purchases	42,800				42,800			
Purchases Discount		624				624		
Purchases Returns and Allowances		416				416		
Wages Expense	22,900		(h) 610		23,510			
Taxes Expense	980				980			
Interest Expense	46				46			
	210,827	210,827						
Revenue and Expense Summary			(a) 31,500	(b) 29,400	31,500	29,400		
Unearned Rent				(c) 150				150
Supplies Expense			(d) 514		514			
Insurance Expense			(e) 160		160			
Depreciation Expense, Equipment			(f) 2,400		2,400			
Depreciation Expense, Building			(g) 2,000		2,000			
Wages Payable				(h) 610				610
			66,734	66,734	105,270	118,890	139,967	126,347
Net Income					13,620			13,620
					118,890	118,890	139,967	139,967

277 Completion of the work sheet

Account Name	Income Statement		Balance Sheet	
	Debit	Credit	Debit	Credit
Merchandise Inventory			29,400 00	
Sales		88,090 00		
Sales Discount	940 00			
Sales Returns and Allowances	420 00			
Purchases	42,800 00			
Purchases Discount		624 00		
Purchases Returns and Allowances		416 00		
Revenue and Expense Summary	31,500 00	29,400 00		

Adjusting entries

Here's the way the adjusting entries look, as taken from the Adjustments column of the work sheet.

General Journal					Page 96	
Date		Description	Post. Ref.	Debit		Credit
19__		**Adjusting Entries**				
Dec.	31	Revenue and Expense Summary		31,500 00		
		Merchandise Inventory				31,500 00
	31	Merchandise Inventory		29,400 00		
		Revenue and Expense Summary				29,400 00
	31	Rent Income		150 00		
		Unearned Rent				150 00
	31	Supplies Expense		514 00		
		Supplies				514 00
	31	Insurance Expense		160 00		
		Prepaid Insurance				160 00
	31	Depreciation Expense, Equipment		2,400 00		
		Accumulated Depreciation, Equipment				2,400 00
	31	Depreciation Expense, Building		2,000 00		
		Accumulated Depreciation, Building				2,000 00

General Journal				Page 96 (cont.)	
Date	Description	Post. Ref.	Debit	Credit	
Dec. 31	Wages Expense		610 00		
	Wages Payable			610 00	

Summary

The work sheet is a device accountants use to organize the account balances so that they can prepare the income statement and the balance sheet. Typical adjustments that affect both service and merchandising firms are the recording of supplies used, insurance expired, depreciation of equipment and buildings, accrued wages, and unearned revenue. Merchandising firms have an additional adjustment for Merchandise Inventory. The companion account in this adjusting entry is Revenue and Expense Summary. Adjusting the Merchandise Inventory account is a two-step process. First, eliminate or close the beginning inventory. Second, restate, or add on, the ending inventory, in order to record the current balance of the account. In the work sheet, carry the Revenue and Expense Summary account as two separate figures from the Adjustments columns into the Income Statement columns.

Glossary

o **Physical inventory** An actual count of the stock of goods on hand; also referred to as a *periodic inventory*.
o **Unearned revenue** Revenue received in advance for services to be performed later; considered to be a liability until the revenue is earned.

Exercises

Exercise 1 The beginning inventory of a merchandising business was $27,000, and the ending inventory is $31,000. What entries are needed at the end of the fiscal period to adjust Merchandise Inventory?

Exercise 2 List the following in all the columns in which they appear in the work sheet (with the exception of the Adjustments column): Expenses, Accumulated Depreciation, Liabilities, Drawing, Assets, Net Income. (*Example:* Owner's Equity.)

Trial Balance		Adjustments		Income Statement		Balance Sheet	
Debit	Credit	Debit	Credit	Debit	Credit	Debit	Credit
	Owner's Equity						Owner's Equity

Exercise 3 From the ledger account for Supplies shown at the top of the next page, journalize the complete entries from which each of the items identified by journal reference was posted.

Supplies   Account No. 126

Date		Item	Post. Ref.	Debit	Credit	Balance Debit	Balance Credit
19__							
Jan.	1	Balance	✓			960 00	
Apr.	16		CP41	320 00		1,280 00	
Sept.	22		CP63	210 00		1,490 00	
Dec.	31	Adjusting	J91		590 00	900 00	

Exercise 4 Determine the annual amount of depreciation on each of the following:

a A building costing $40,000, expected life of 20 years, no salvage value at the end of 20 years; use the straight-line method.

b Office equipment costing $8,000, expected life of 5 years, trade-in value of $500 at the end of 5 years; use the straight-line method.

Exercise 5 Determine the amount of expired insurance for the fiscal year, January 1 through December 31, from the following account.

Prepaid Insurance   Account No. 118

Date		Item	Post. Ref.	Debit	Credit	Balance Debit	Balance Credit
19__							
Jan.	1	Balance (4 months)	✓			420 00	
May	1	(12 months)	CP59	1,680 00		2,100 00	

Exercise 6 In the Income Statement columns of the work sheet, we record the Revenue and Expense Summary account as $68,000 in the debit column and $72,000 in the credit column. Identify the beginning and ending merchandise inventory.

Exercise 7 From the ledger account for Wages Expense, journalize the complete entry from which each of the items identified by number was posted.

Wages Expense   Account No. 514

Date		Item	Post. Ref.	Debit	Credit	Balance Debit	Balance Credit
19__							
Dec.	28	(1)	CP39	2,200 00		91,700 00	
	31	(2)	J42	600 00		92,300 00	
	31	(3)	J43		92,300 00	——	——

Exercise 8 Complete each horizontal line in the following work sheet. (*Examples:* Equipment; Insurance Expense)

Account Name	Trial Balance Debit	Trial Balance Credit	Adjustments Debit	Adjustments Credit	Income Statement Debit	Income Statement Credit	Balance Sheet Debit	Balance Sheet Credit
Accounts Receivable	18,000							
Merchandise Inventory	60,000							
Prepaid Insurance	1,620							
Equipment	26,000						26,000	
Accumulated Depreciation		15,200						
Sales		80,000						
Sales Returns and Allowances	300							
Purchases	42,000							
Purchases Discount		1,050						
Wages Expense	29,000							
Revenue and Expense Summary			60,000	56,000				
Wages Payable				200				
Depreciation Expense			2,400					
Insurance Expense			820		820			
Rent Income		1,200						
Unearned Rent				300				

Problems

Problem 11-1 The trial balance of Sinclair Variety as of December 31, the end of their current fiscal year, is as follows.

Sinclair Variety
Trial Balance
December 31, 19___

	Debit	Credit
Cash	4,781 96	
Merchandise Inventory	31,761 42	
Store Supplies	720 56	
Prepaid Insurance	480 00	
Store Equipment	18,740 00	
Accumulated Depreciation, Store Equipment		12,160 00
Accounts Payable		7,289 40
Sales Tax Payable		121 68
J. K. Sinclair, Capital		27,815 00
J. K. Sinclair, Drawing	14,720 00	
Sales		89,518 37
Sales Returns and Allowances	721 52	
Purchases	40,621 73	
Purchases Discount		748 95
Purchases Returns and Allowances		939 47
Salary Expense	18,329 40	
Rent Expense	7,200 00	
Miscellaneous Expense	516 28	
	138,592 87	138,592 87

Here are the data for the adjustments.

a Merchandise Inventory at December 31, $33,416.28.

b Supplies inventory, $198.20.

c Insurance expired, $360.

d Salaries accrued, $281.50.

e Depreciation of store equipment, $1,940.

Instructions Complete the work sheet.

Problem 11-2 The balances of the ledger accounts of Ordway Sporting Goods as of December 31, the end of their fiscal year, are as follows.

Cash	$ 5,796
Accounts Receivable	21,481
Merchandise Inventory	60,919
Supplies	785
Prepaid Insurance	814
Store Equipment	18,462
Accumulated Depreciation, Store Equipment	14,710
Office Equipment	4,718
Accumulated Depreciation, Office Equipment	860
Accounts Payable	15,411
Notes Payable	2,000
Wages Payable	——
Unearned Rent	——
N. T. Ordway, Capital	60,266
N. T. Ordway, Drawing	14,000
Revenue and Expense Summary	——
Sales	326,000
Sales Returns and Allowances	4,874
Rent Income	1,600
Purchases	271,549
Purchases Discount	3,817
Purchases Returns and Allowances	6,720
Wages Expense	27,600
Depreciation Expense, Store Equipment	——
Depreciation Expense, Office Equipment	——
Supplies Expense	——
Insurance Expense	——
Interest Expense	386

Data for the adjustments are as follows.
a Merchandise Inventory at December 31, $50,838.
b Wages accrued at December 31, $978.
c Supplies inventory at December 31, $372.
d Depreciation of store equipment, $2,934.
e Depreciation of office equipment, $866.
f Insurance expired during the year, $316.
g Unearned rent, $400.
Instructions
1 Complete the work sheet.
2 Journalize the adjusting entries.

Problem 11-3 A portion of the work sheet of Morris Dow and Company for the year ending December 31 is as follows.

Account Name	Income Statement Debit	Income Statement Credit	Balance Sheet Debit	Balance Sheet Credit
Cash			4,670 00	
Merchandise Inventory			38,470 00	
Supplies			128 00	
Prepaid Insurance			120 00	
Store Equipment			19,640 00	
Accumulated Depreciation, Store Equip.				13,110 00
Accounts Payable				7,300 00
Morris Dow, Capital				34,470 00
Morris Dow, Drawing			13,800 00	
Sales		86,710 00		
Sales Returns and Allowances	760 00			
Purchases	42,130 00			
Purchases Discount		800 00		
Purchases Returns and Allowances		470 00		
Salary Expense	18,780 00			
Rent Expense	7,400 00			
Revenue and Expense Summary	32,840 00	38,470 00		
Depreciation Expense, Store Equipment	2,020 00			
Insurance Expense	380 00			
Supplies Expense	472 00			
Salaries Payable				280 00
	104,782 00	126,450 00	76,828 00	55,160 00

Instructions

1 Determine the entries that appeared in the Adjustments columns, and present them in general journal form.
2 Determine the net income for the year and the amount of the owner's capital at the end of the year.

Problem 11-4 The accounts in the ledger of Roberts Variety, with the balances as of December 31, the end of their fiscal year, are as follows.

Cash	$ 4,200
Accounts Receivable	680
Merchandise Inventory	40,200
Store Supplies	540
Prepaid Insurance	980
Store Equipment	18,700
Accumulated Depreciation, Store Equipment	4,200
Building	30,000
Accumulated Depreciation Building	12,200
Land	6,000
Notes Payable	3,600
Accounts Payable	6,420
Sales Tax Payable	1,980
Salaries Payable	——

F. T. Roberts, Capital	$ 57,000
F. T. Roberts, Drawing	18,000
Revenue and Expense Summary	——
Sales	156,000
Sales Returns and Allowances	2,900
Purchases	101,000
Purchases Discount	1,600
Purchases Returns and Allowances	2,300
Salaries Expense	17,500
Advertising Expense	2,050
Depreciation Expense, Store Equipment	——
Depreciation Expense, Building	——
Store Supplies Expense	——
Insurance Expense	——
Utilities Expense	1,870
Sales Tax Expense	90
Miscellaneous Expense	330
Interest Expense	260

Data for the adjustments are as follows.
a Merchandise Inventory at December 31, $41,600.
b Store supplies inventory at December 31, $180.
c Depreciation of store equipment, $1,200.
d Depreciation of building, $1,400.
e Salaries accrued at December 31, $550.
f Insurance expired during the year, $760.
Instructions
1 Complete the work sheet.
2 Journalize the adjusting entries.

Problem 11-1A The trial balance of Slocum Variety as of December 31, the end of their fiscal year, is shown at the top of the next page. Here are the data for the adjustments.
a Merchandise Inventory at December 31, $32,874.90.
b Supplies inventory, $202.16.
c Insurance expired, $368.00.
d Salaries accrued, $293.40.
e Depreciation of store equipment, $1,960.00.
Instructions Complete the work sheet.

Problem 11-2A The balances of the ledger accounts of Collins Office Supplies as of June 30, the end of their fiscal year, are as follows.

Cash	$ 9,850
Accounts Receivable	34,200
Merchandise Inventory	48,600

Slocum Variety
Trial Balance
December 31, 19___

Cash	4,568 27	
Merchandise Inventory	31,427 41	
Store Supplies	733 42	
Prepaid Insurance	510 00	
Store Equipment	18,670 00	
Accumulated Depreciation, Store Equipment		12,418 00
Accounts Payable		7,143 48
Sales Tax Payable		123 49
J. C. Slocum, Capital		27,529 92
J. C. Slocum, Drawing	14,500 00	
Sales		88,983 17
Sales Returns and Allowances	746 92	
Purchases	40,718 92	
Purchases Discount		751 82
Purchases Returns and Allowances		928 91
Salary Expense	18,284 43	
Rent Expense	7,200 00	
Miscellaneous Expense	519 42	
	137,878 79	137,878 79

Supplies	$ 980
Prepaid Insurance	720
Store Equipment	17,860
Accumulated Depreciation, Store Equipment	10,800
Office Equipment	6,400
Accumulated Depreciation, Office Equipment	3,210
Accounts Payable	28,600
Notes Payable	2,400
Salaries Payable	———
Unearned Rent	———
T. C. Collins, Capital	63,560
T. C. Collins, Drawing	16,000
Revenue and Expense Summary	———
Sales	311,000
Sales Returns and Allowances	2,140
Rent Income	1,800
Purchases	261,000
Purchases Discount	1,520
Purchases Returns and Allowances	4,780
Salaries Expense	29,500
Depreciation Expense, Store Equipment	———
Depreciation Expense, Office Equipment	———
Insurance Expense	———
Supplies Expense	———
Interest Expense	420

Here are the data for the adjustments.

a Merchandise Inventory at June 30, $76,400.
b Salaries accrued at June 30, $960.
c Insurance expired during the year, $600.
d Supplies inventory at June 30, $190.
e Depreciation of store equipment, $2,500.
f Depreciation of office equipment, $1,300.
g Unearned rent income, $300.

Instructions

1 Complete the work sheet.
2 Journalize the adjusting entries.

Problem 11-3A Here is a portion of the work sheet of Stanley Morton & Company for the year ending December 31.

Account Name	Income Statement Debit	Income Statement Credit	Balance Sheet Debit	Balance Sheet Credit
Cash			3,868 00	
Merchandise Inventory			37,149 00	
Supplies			149 00	
Prepaid Insurance			125 00	
Store Equipment			18,980 00	
Accumulated Depreciation, Store Equip.				14,720 00
Accounts Payable				6,880 00
Stanley Morton, Capital				37,571 00
Stanley Morton, Drawing			15,400 00	
Sales		85,908 00		
Sales Returns and Allowances	717 00			
Purchases	44,296 00			
Purchases Discount		818 00		
Purchases Returns and Allowances		482 00		
Salary Expense	18,926 00			
Rent Expense	7,200 00			
Revenue and Expense Summary	34,114 00	37,149 00		
Depreciation Expense, Store Equipment	2,180 00			
Insurance Expense	276 00			
Supplies Expense	442 00			
Salaries Payable				294 00
	108,151 00	124,357 00	75,671 00	59,465 00

Instructions

1 Determine the entries that appeared in the Adjustments columns and present them in general journal form.
2 Determine the net income for the year and the amount of the owner's capital at the end of the year.

Problem 11-4A Here are the accounts in the ledger of Reiner's Health Foods Store, with the balances as of December 31, the end of their fiscal year.

Cash	$ 3,760
Accounts Receivable	518
Merchandise Inventory	38,700
Store Supplies	428
Prepaid Insurance	762

Store Equipment	$ 25,830
Accumulated Depreciation, Store Equipment	5,720
Building	26,000
Accumulated Depreciation, Building	9,780
Land	5,000
Accounts Payable	4,690
Sales Tax Payable	928
Salaries Payable	——
Mortgage Payable	14,620
C. C. Reiner, Capital	50,610
C. C. Reiner, Drawing	15,500
Revenue and Expense Summary	——
Sales	126,418
Sales Returns and Allowances	1,296
Purchases	87,656
Purchases Discount	1,470
Purchases Returns and Allowances	1,087
Salaries Expense	7,800
Advertising Expense	642
Depreciation Expense, Store Equipment	——
Depreciation Expense, Building	——
Store Supplies Expense	——
Insurance Expense	——
Utilities Expense	386
Sales Tax Expense	54
Miscellaneous Expense	271
Interest Expense	720

Here are the data for the adjustments.

a Merchandise Inventory at December 31, $37,690.
b Insurance expired during the year, $418.
c Depreciation of store equipment, $2,860.
d Depreciation of building, $1,400.
e Salaries accrued at December 31, $140.
f Store supplies inventory at December 31, $106.

Instructions
1 Complete the work sheet
2 Journalize the adjusting entries.

12

Financial statements and closing entries for a merchandising firm

A business with an income at its heels
Furnishes always oil for its own wheels.

William Cowper, ''Retirement''

Key points
- Outline of the income statement
- Determination of cost of merchandise sold
- Order of listing accounts in the balance sheet
- Steps in the closing procedure

Chapter contents
- Introduction
- The income statement
- The balance sheet
- Closing entries
- Reversing entries
- Summary
- Glossary
- Exercises
- Problems

Specific objectives

After you have completed this chapter, you will be able to:
- Prepare a classified income statement for a merchandising firm.
- Prepare a classified balance sheet for any type of business.
- Journalize the closing entries for a merchandising firm.
- Determine which adjusting entries should be reversed.

Introduction

Chapters 5 and 8 discussed at length the income statements for a service and a professional enterprise, respectively. Then, in Chapters 9 through 11, we discussed the specialized accounts and journals for merchandising enterprises; in Chapter 11 we also explained the work sheet.

This chapter will formulate financial statements directly from work sheets. We will also explain the functions of closing entries and reversing entries as means of completing the accounting cycle. To do this, we'll reproduce part of the work sheet for North Central Plumbing Supply that we presented in

Chapter 11. First we look at the financial statements in their entirety, and then we'll explain their various subdivisions.

North Central Plumbing Supply
Work Sheet
For year ended December 31, 19___

Account Name	Trial Balance Debit	Trial Balance Credit	Income Statement Debit	Income Statement Credit
Cash	10,961 00			
Notes Receivable	2,000 00			
Accounts Receivable	14,680 00			
Merchandise Inventory	31,500 00			
Supplies	720 00			
Prepaid Insurance	480 00			
Equipment	16,800 00			
Accumulated Depreciation, Equipment		8,200 00		
Building	50,000 00			
Accumulated Depreciation, Building		16,000 00		
Land	6,000 00			
Notes Payable		1,500 00		
Accounts Payable		18,200 00		
Mortgage Payable		4,000 00		
Robert C. Randall, Capital		73,287 00		
Robert C. Randall, Drawing	9,600 00			
Sales		88,090 00		88,090 00
Sales Discount	940 00		940 00	
Sales Returns and Allowances	420 00		420 00	
Rent Income		450 00		300 00
Interest Income		60 00		60 00
Purchases	42,800 00		42,800 00	
Purchases Discount		624 00		624 00
Purchases Returns and Allowances		416 00		416 00
Wages Expense	22,900 00		23,510 00	
Taxes Expense	980 00		980 00	
Interest Expense	46 00		46 00	
	210,827 00	210,827 00		
Revenue and Expense Summary			31,500 00	29,400 00
Unearned Rent				
Supplies Expense			514 00	
Insurance Expense			160 00	
Depreciation Expense, Equipment			2,400 00	
Depreciation Expense, Building			2,000 00	
Wages Payable				
			105,270 00	118,890 00
Net Income			13,620 00	
			118,890 00	118,890 00

The income statement

As you know, each of the figures that appears in the Income Statement columns of the work sheet will be used in the income statement. Incidentally, this is why we kept the figures for the beginning and ending Merchandise Inventory separate; each now appears on the Revenue and Expense Summary line. Now we show the entire income statement. Pause for awhile and look it over; then we'll break it down into its component parts.

North Central Plumbing Supply Income Statement For year ended December 31, 19___				
Revenue from Sales				
Sales			$88,090 00	
Less: Sales Returns and				
Allowances	$ 940 00			
Sales Discount	420 00		1,360 00	
Net Sales				$86,730 00
Cost of Merchandise Sold				
Merchandise Inventory, Jan. 1, 19___			$31,500 00	
Purchases	$42,800 00			
Less: Purchases Returns and Allowances $624.00				
Purchases Discount 416.00	1,040 00			
Net Purchases			41,760 00	
Merchandise Available for Sale			$73,260 00	
Less Merchandise Inventory, Dec. 31, 19___			29,400 00	
Cost of Merchandise Sold				43,860 00
Gross Profit				$42,870 00
Operating Expenses				
Wages Expense			$23,510 00	
Depreciation Expense, Equipment			2,400 00	
Depreciation Expense, Building			2,000 00	
Taxes Expense			980 00	
Supplies Expense			514 00	
Insurance Expense			160 00	
Total Operating Expenses				29,564 00
Net Income from Operations				$13,306 00
Other Income				
Rent Income			$ 300 00	
Interest Income			60 00	
Total Other Income			$ 360 00	
Other Expenses				
Interest Expense			46 00	314 00
Net Income				$13,620 00

The outline of the income statement follows a logical pattern, and it is pretty much the same for any type of merchandising business. Being able to use the income statement and extract parts from it is very useful when one is assembling information in order to make decisions. But, to be able to realize the full use of an income statement, you need to know the skeleton outline of an income statement backward and forward, so that you can visualize it at a moment's notice. So, let's look at the statement piece by piece.

Sales	$86,730
— Cost of Merchandise Sold	43,860
= Gross Profit	$42,870
— Operating Expenses	29,564
= Net Income from Operations	$13,306

To hammer home the concepts of *gross* and *net,* let's take a simple case of a transaction that takes place many thousands of times a day, all over the world: selling a house.

Cynthia Jones, a few years back, bought a house and lot for $12,000. Last week she sold the house and lot for $20,000; The real estate agent who did the actual selling gets a sales commission of 6%. How much did Jones make as clear profit?

Sale price of property	$20,000
— Cost of property sold	12,000
= Gross Profit (or Gross Margin)	$ 8,000
— Agent's commission expense	1,200
= Net Income or Net Profit	
(gain on the sale)	$ 6,800

Gross profit is the profit on the sale of the property before any expense has been deducted; it may also be called *gross margin*. *Net income* or *net profit* is the final or clear profit after all the *expenses* have been deducted. On a single-sale situation such as this, we refer to the final outcome as the net profit. But for a business having a number of sales and expenses, most accountants use the term *net income*. However, regardless of whether one uses the word *profit* or the word *income, net* refers to clear profit.

Revenue from sales

All right, now let's look at the Revenue from Sales section in the accounts of North Central Plumbing Supply.

Revenue from Sales				
Sales			$88,090 00	
Less: Sales Returns and				
Allowances	$	940 00		
Sales Discount		420 00	1,360 00	
Net Sales				$86,730 00

When we introduced Sales Returns and Allowances and Sales Discounts, we treated them as deductions from Sales. You can see that we needed to do this because this is the way they are treated in the income statement.

Cost of merchandise sold

The section of the income statement that requires the greatest amount of concentration is the Cost of Merchandise Sold. Let us therefore repeat it in its entirety.

Cost of Merchandise Sold					
Merchandise Inventory, Jan. 1, 19___			$31,500 00		
Purchases	$42,800 00				
Less: Purchases Returns and Allowances $624.00					
Purchases Discount 416.00	1,040 00				
Net Purchases			41,760 00		
Merchandise Available for Sale			$73,260 00		
Less Merchandise Inventory, Dec. 31, 19___			29,400 00		
Cost of Merchandise Sold				43,860 00	

First let's look closely at the Purchases section.

Purchases	$42,800 00			
Less: Purchases Returns and Allowances $624.00				
Purchases Discount 416.00	1,040 00			
Net Purchases			41,760 00	

Note a parallel here to the Sales section, in that, in order to arrive at Net Purchases, we deduct both Purchases Returns and Allowances and Purchases Discount from Purchases.

Now let's take in the full Cost of Merchandise Sold section. Does this seem like a reasonable summing up of the situation?

Amount we started with (beginning inventory)	$31,500
+ Net amount we purchased	41,760
= Total amount that could have been sold (available)	$73,260
− Amount left over (ending inventory)	29,400
= Cost of the merchandise that was actually sold	$43,860

Or

Merchandise Inventory,	
Jan. 1, 19____	$31,500
Net Purchases	41,760
Merchandise Available for Sale	$73,260
Less Merchandise Inventory,	
Dec. 31, 19____	29,400
Cost of Merchandise Sold	$43,860

Remember that *net purchases* means total Purchases less both Purchases Returns and Allowances and Purchases Discount.

Operating expenses

Operating expenses, as the name implies, are the regular expenses of doing business. They may be listed in descending order, with the largest amount first. If one has a Miscellaneous Expense account, one always places it last, regardless of its amount. We shall follow this order in this text. There's another way of handling it, though; many accountants list the accounts and their respective balances in the order that the accounts appear in the ledger.

Many firms may use subclassifications of operating expenses, such as the following.

Selling expenses Any expenses directly connected with the selling activity, such as:
- Sales Salaries Expense
- Sales Commissions Expense
- Advertising Expense
- Store Supplies Expense
- Delivery Expense
- Depreciation Expense, Store Equipment

General expenses Any expenses related to the office or the administration, or any expense that cannot be directly connected with a selling activity:
- Office Salaries Expense
- Taxes Expense
- Depreciation Expense, Office Equipment
- Rent Expense
- Insurance Expense
- Office Supplies Expense

Classifying expense accounts as selling expenses or general expenses is a matter of judgment. The only reason we're not using this breakdown here is that we're trying to keep the number of accounts to a minimum. In other words, we don't want you to get bogged down in a large number of accounts, making it more difficult to understand the main concepts. We don't want you to lose sight of the forest on account of the trees.

Net income from operations

Now let's repeat the skeleton outline.

Sales
— Cost of Merchandise Sold
= Gross Profit
— Operating Expenses
= Net Income from Operations

If the Operating Expenses are the sort that are regular, recurring types of expenses of doing business, then Net Income from Operations should be the regular or recurring net income. When you are comparing the results of operations over a number of years, the net income from operations is a most significant figure to use each year as a basis for comparison.

Other income

The Other Income classification, as the name implies, records any revenue account other than revenue from Sales. What we are trying to do is to isolate Sales at the top of the income statement as the major revenue account, so that the gross profit figure represents the profit made on the sale of merchandise *only.* Additional accounts that may appear under the heading of Other Income are: Rent Income (the firm is subletting part of its premises); Interest Income (the firm is the holder of an interest-bearing note or contract); Gain on Disposal of Plant and Equipment (the firm makes a profit on the sale of plant and equipment).

Other expenses

The classification of Other Expenses records any nonrecurring expenses, such as Interest Expense and Loss on Disposal of Plant and Equipment.

The balance sheet

Again we show a partial work sheet for North Central Plumbing Supply (recall Chapter 11) on the opposite page.

Now here again we find that each figure that appears in the Balance Sheet columns of the work sheet will be used in the statement of owner's equity and the balance sheet. These two statements appear below and on page 298.

North Central Plumbing Supply Statement of Owner's Equity For year ended December 31, 19__		
Robert C. Randall, Capital, Jan. 1, 19__		$69,287 00
Additional Investment, Aug. 26, 19__		4,000 00
Total		$73,287 00
Add: Net Income for the Year	$13,620 00	
Less: Withdrawals for the Year	9,600 00	
Increase in Capital		4,020 00
Robert C. Randall, Capital, Dec. 31, 19__		$77,307 00

North Central Plumbing Supply
Work Sheet
For year ended December 31, 19___

Account Name	Trial Balance Debit	Trial Balance Credit	Balance Sheet Debit	Balance Sheet Credit
Cash	10,961 00		10,961 00	
Notes Receivable	2,000 00		2,000 00	
Accounts Receivable	14,680 00		14,680 00	
Merchandise Inventory	31,500 00		29,400 00	
Supplies	720 00		206 00	
Prepaid Insurance	480 00		320 00	
Equipment	16,800 00		16,800 00	
Accumulated Depreciation, Equipment		8,200 00		10,600 00
Building	50,000 00		50,000 00	
Accumulated Depreciation, Building		16,000 00		18,000 00
Land	6,000 00		6,000 00	
Notes Payable		1,500 00		1,500 00
Accounts Payable		18,200 00		18,200 00
Mortgage Payable		4,000 00		4,000 00
Robert C. Randall, Capital		73,287 00		73,287 00
Robert C. Randall, Drawing	9,600 00		9,600 00	
Sales		88,090 00		
Sales Discount	940 00			
Sales Returns and Allowances	420 00			
Rent Income		450 00		
Interest Income		60 00		
Purchases	42,800 00			
Purchases Discount		624 00		
Purchases Returns and Allowances		416 00		
Wages Expense	22,900 00			
Taxes Expense	980 00			
Interest Expense	46 00			
	210,827 00	210,827 00		
Revenue and Expense Summary				
Unearned Rent				150 00
Supplies Expense				
Insurance Expense				
Depreciation Expense, Equipment				
Depreciation Expense, Building				
Wages Payable				610 00
			139,967 00	126,347 00
Net Income				13,620 00
			139,967 00	139,967 00

North Central Plumbing Supply
Balance Sheet
December 31, 19___

Assets			
Current Assets			
Cash		$10,961 00	
Notes Receivable		2,000 00	
Accounts Receivable		14,680 00	
Merchandise Inventory		29,400 00	
Supplies		206 00	
Prepaid Insurance		320 00	
Total Current Assets			$ 57,567 00
Plant and Equipment			
Equipment	$16,800 00		
Less Accumulated Depreciation	10,600 00	$ 6,200 00	
Building	$50,000 00		
Less Accumulated Depreciation	18,000 00	32,000 00	
Land		6,000 00	
Total Plant and Equipment			44,200 00
Total Assets			$101,767 00
Liabilities			
Current Liabilities			
Notes Payable		$ 1,500 00	
Mortgage Payable			
(current portion)		1,000 00	
Accounts Payable		18,200 00	
Wages Payable		610 00	
Unearned Rent		150 00	
Total Current Liabilities			$ 21,460 00
Long-term Liabilities			
Mortgage Payable			3,000 00
Total Liabilities			$ 24,460 00
Owner's Equity			
Robert C. Randall, Capital			77,307 00
Total Liabilities and			
Owner's Equity			$101,767 00

We have already discussed the statement of owner's equity. North Central Plumbing Supply's statement of owner's equity shows why the balance of the Capital account has changed from the beginning of the fiscal period to the end of it, and also includes the feature of an additional investment made during the period. After one has added the additional investment to the beginning capital, the remainder of the statement is the same as our previous illustrations. If there is no additional investment, then one can just go ahead and record the net income, less withdrawals, and the resulting increase or decrease in capital.

This is the first time that a classified balance sheet has been presented. Classifications in accounting are generally uniform for all types of business enterprises. You are strongly urged to take the time to learn the following definitions of the classifications and the order of accounts within them. If you do, you will forever after have a standard routine for compiling the balance sheet, and this will save you a lot of grief and time.

Current assets

Current Assets consist of cash and any other assets or resources which are expected to be realized in cash, or to be sold or consumed during the normal operating cycle of the business.

Accountants list Current Assets in the order of their convertibility into cash, or in other words, their *liquidity.* (If you've got an asset such as a car or a diamond, and you sell it quickly and turn it into cash, you are said to be turning it into a *liquid* state.) If the first four accounts under Current Assets (see North Central Plumbing Supply's balance sheet) are present, always record them in the same order: (1) Cash, (2) Notes Receivable, (3) Accounts Receivable, and (4) Merchandise Inventory.

Notes Receivable are promissory notes held by the firm, or promise-to-pay notes. (*Example:* Suppose you are the owner of a lumber yard, and you sell lumber to a builder who does not have enough cash to pay for it, but has a ready buyer for the finished house. The builder therefore gives you a *promissory note,* stating that you will be paid within 90 days.) Notes Receivable is placed ahead of Accounts Receivable, because promissory notes are considered to be more liquid than Accounts Receivable. (Reason: The holder of the note can raise more cash by borrowing from a bank, pledging the notes as security for the loan.) Supplies and Prepaid Insurance are considered to be prepaid items that will be used up or expire eventually over time; that's why they appear at the bottom of the Current Assets section. [There is no particular reason to list Supplies before Prepaid Insurance. Prepaid Insurance could just as easily have preceded Supplies.]

Plant and equipment

Plant and equipment are relatively long-lived assets that one holds for use in the production or sale of other assets or services; some accountants refer to them as *fixed assets*. The three types of accounts that usually appear in this category are equipment, buildings, and land (refer to the balance sheet for North Central Plumbing Supply once again). Note that the Equipment and Building accounts are followed by their respective Accumulated Depreciation accounts. (Remember how we spoke of Accumulated Depreciations as being deductions from assets?) Plant and equipment are listed in the order of their length of life, with the shortest-lived asset (equipment) recorded first. A firm which has some delivery equipment, for example, lists it first, because of its relatively short life. In other words, Plant and Equipment go in order from the least fixed to the most fixed. Land is placed last in this category, because no matter where land is located, *it lasts.*

299   The balance sheet

Current liabilities

Current liabilities are debts that will become due within a short period, usually within 1 year, and will normally be paid, when due, from current assets. List current liabilities in the order of their urgency of payment, putting the most pressing obligation first. Notes Payable precedes Accounts Payable, just as Notes Receivable precedes Accounts Receivable. The Mortgage Payable (current portion), which also may precede Accounts Payable, is the payment one makes to reduce the principal of the mortgage in a given year. Wages Payable follows the other three current liabilities; this is true of any accrued liabilities such as Commissions Payable. Any unearned revenue accounts fall at the bottom of the list of current liabilities.

Long-term liabilities

Long-term liabilities are debts that are payable over a comparatively long period, usually more than 1 year. Ordinarily the only account that would be in this category for a sole-proprietorship (or one-owner) type of business is Mortgage Payable. One single amount in a category can be recorded in the column on the extreme right.

Chart of accounts

In Chapter 4, when we introduced the chart of accounts and the account-number arrangement, we said that the first digit represents the classification of the accounts:

Assets	1 _ _
Liabilities	2 _ _
Owner's Equity	3 _ _
Revenue	4 _ _
Expenses	5 _ _

The second digit stands for the *sub*classification.

Assets	1 _ _
Current Assets	11 _
Plant and Equipment	12 _
Liabilities	2 _ _
Current Liabilities	21 _
Long-term Liabilities	22 _
Revenue	4 _ _
Revenue from Sales	41 _
Other Income	42 _
Expenses	5 _ _
Cost of Merchandise Sold	51 _
Selling Expenses	52 _
General Expenses	53 _
Other Expenses	54 _

The third digit indicates the placement of the account within the subclassification.

Closing entries

In Chapter 6 we discussed closing entries for a service business; now let's discuss closing entries for a merchandising business. The same methods apply to both types of business. That is, you want to balance off the revenue, expense, and Drawing accounts. So you go through the same four steps as in a service business. At the end of this fiscal period, close the revenue and expense accounts in order to start the next fiscal period with a clean slate. Also close the Drawing account, because it too applies to one fiscal period only. These accounts are called *temporary equity* accounts.

When you're working out your closing entries, you can take a shortcut by balancing off each figure in the Income Statement columns of the work sheet. For example, if the figure is recorded as a $900 credit in the Income Statement column of the work sheet, then, in the closing entries, debit the account $900.

The work sheet on the next page shows the Income Statement columns. After you have looked them over, let's take up those four steps and see how we came out.

Four steps in the closing procedure

1 Close the revenue accounts into Revenue and Expense Summary. (Debit the figures that are credited in the Income Statement column of the work sheet, except the figures in the Revenue and Expense Summary line.)

General Journal					Page 97
Date		Description	Post. Ref.	Debit	Credit
19__		**Closing Entries**			
Dec.	31	Sales		88,090 00	
		Rent Income		300 00	
		Interest Income		60 00	
		Purchases Discount		624 00	
		Purchases Returns and			
		Allowances		416 00	
		Revenue and Expense			
		Summary			89,490 00

North Central Plumbing Supply
Work Sheet
For year ended September 31, 19___

Account Name	Trial Balance Debit	Trial Balance Credit	Income Statement Debit	Income Statement Credit
Cash	10,961 00			
Notes Receivable	2,000 00			
Accounts Receivable	14,680 00			
Merchandise Inventory	31,500 00			
Supplies	720 00			
Prepaid Insurance	480 00			
Equipment	16,800 00			
Accumulated Depreciation, Equipment		8,200 00		
Building	50,000 00			
Accumulated Depreciation, Building		16,000 00		
Land	6,000 00			
Notes Payable		1,500 00		
Accounts Payable		18,200 00		
Mortgage Payable		4,000 00		
Robert C. Randall, Capital		73,287 00		
Robert C. Randall, Drawing	9,600 00			
Sales		88,090 00		88,090 00
Sales Discount	940 00		940 00	
Sales Returns and Allowances	420 00		420 00	
Rent Income		450 00		300 00
Interest Income		60 00		60 00
Purchases	42,800 00		42,800 00	
Purchases Discount		624 00		624 00
Purchases Returns and Allowances		416 00		416 00
Wages Expense	22,900 00		23,510 00	
Taxes Expense	980 00		980 00	
Interest Expense	46 00		46 00	
	210,827 00	210,827 00		
Revenue and Expense Summary			31,500 00	29,400 00
Unearned Rent				
Supplies Expense			514 00	
Insurance Expense			160 00	
Depreciation Expense, Equipment			2,400 00	
Depreciation Expense, Building			2,000 00	
Wages Payable				
			105,270 00	118,890 00
Net Income			13,620 00	
			118,890 00	118,890 00

2 Close the expense accounts into Revenue and Expense Summary. (Credit the figures that are debited in the Income Statement column of the work sheet, except the figures in the Revenue and Expense Summary line.)

Dec.	31	Revenue and Expense			
		Summary		73,770 00	
		Sales Discount			940 00
		Sales Returns and			
		Allowances			420 00
		Purchases			42,800 00
		Wages Expense			23,510 00
		Taxes Expense			980 00
		Interest Expense			46 00
		Supplies Expense			514 00
		Insurance Expense			160 00
		Depreciation Expense,			
		Equipment			2,400 00
		Depreciation Expense,			
		Building			2,000 00

3 Close the Revenue and Expense Summary account into Robert C. Randall, Capital (by the amount of the Net Income).

Dec.	31	Revenue and Expense			
		Summary		13,620 00	
		Robert C. Randall, Capital			13,620 00

Revenue and Expense Summary

Adjusting	31,500	Adjusting	29,400
(Beginning		(Ending	
Merchandise		Merchandise	
Inventory)		Inventory)	
(Expenses)	73,770	(Revenue)	89,490
Clos. (Net Inc.)	13,620		

Robert C. Randall, Capital

−		+
	Balance	73,287
	(Net Inc.)	13,620

4 Close the Drawing account into the Capital account.

Dec.	31	Robert C. Randall, Capital		9,600	00		
		Robert C. Randall, Drawing				9,600	00

Robert C. Randall, Drawing

	+		−	
Balance	9,600	Closing	9,600	

Robert C. Randall, Capital

	−		+	
(Drawing)	9,600	Balance	73,287	
		(Net Inc.)	13,620	

Note that you close Purchases Discount and Purchases Returns and Allowances in Step 1 along with the revenue accounts. Note also that, in Step 2, you close Sales Discount and Sales Returns and Allowances along with the expense accounts. Finally, bear in mind that the Revenue and Expense Summary account already contains adjusting entries for merchandise inventory.

Reversing entries

Reversing entries are general journal entries which are the exact reverse of certain adjusting entries. A reversing entry enables the accountant to record routine transactions in the usual manner, *even though* an adjusting entry affecting one of the accounts involved in the transaction has intervened. We can see this concept best by looking at an example.

Suppose there's an adjusting entry for accrued wages owed to employees at the end of the fiscal year. (Recall that we talked about this in Chapter 5.) Assume that the employees of a certain firm are paid altogether $100 per day for a 5-day week, and that payday occurs every Friday throughout the year. When the employees get their checks at 5:00 P.M. on Friday, the checks include their wages for that day as well as the preceding 4 days. And say that one year the last day of the fiscal period happens to fall on Wednesday, December 31. A diagram of this situation would look like this:

				Dec. 26	Dec. 29	Dec. 30	Dec. 31	End of Fiscal Year	Jan. 2
Mon	Tue	Wed	Thur	Fri	Mon	Tue	Wed	Thur	Fri
100	100	100	100	100	100	100	100	100	100
←————Payroll period————→					←————Payroll period————→				
				Payday $500			Accrued $300		Payday $500

Each Friday during the year, the payroll has been debited to the Wages Expense account and credited to the Cash account. As a result, Wages Expense has a debit balance of $25,700. Here is the adjusting entry in T account form.

Wages Expense		Wages Payable	
+	−	−	+
Bal. 25,700			12/31 Adj. 300
12/31 Adj. 300			

After the accountant completes the closing process, he or she clears the Wages Expense account, which yields a zero balance. However, the Wages Payable account continues to have a credit balance. In this case, the only way out is to record the $500 payroll on January 2 as a debit of $300 to Wages Payable, a debit of $200 to Wages Expense, and a credit of $500 to Cash. This means that the employee who records the payroll not only has to record this particular payroll differently from all other weekly payrolls for the year, but also has to refer back to the adjusting entry to determine the portion of the $500 to be debited to Wages Payable and Wages Expense, respectively. But in the company's delegation of responsibility, the employee who records the payroll may not have access to the adjusting entries.

One can avoid the necessity of referring to the earlier entry and of dividing the debit total between the two accounts by *recording a reversing entry as of the first day of the following fiscal period.* One makes an entry which is the exact reverse of the adjusting entry, as follows.

General Journal				Page 118	
Date		Description	Post. Ref.	Debit	Credit
19__		**Reversing Entries**			
Jan.	1	Wages Payable		300 00	
		Wages Expense			300 00

Let us now bring the T accounts up to date.

Wages Expense				Wages Payable			
+		−		−		+	
Bal.	25,700	12/31 Clos.	26,000	1/1 Rev.	300	12/31 Adj.	300
12/31 Adj.	300						
		1/1 Rev.	300				

The reversing entry has the effect of transferring the $300 liability from Wages Payable to the credit side of Wages Expense. Wages Expense will temporarily have a credit balance until the next payroll is recorded in the routine manner. In the above illustration, this occurs on January 2, for $500. Here are the T accounts for this.

305 Reversing entries

Wages Expense				Wages Payable			
+		**−**		**−**		**+**	
Bal.	25,700	12/31 Clos.	26,000	1/1 Rev.	300	12/31 Adj.	300
12/31 Adj.	300						
1/2	500	1/1 Rev.	300				

There is now a *net debit balance* of $200 in Wages Expense. To see this, look at the following ledger accounts.

Wages Expense   Account No. 514

Date		Item	Post. Ref.	Debit		Credit		Balance Debit		Credit	
19__											
Dec.	26		CP16	500	00			25,700	00		
	31	Adjusting	J116	300	00			26,000	00		
	31	Closing	J117			26,000	00	———			
19__											
Jan.	1	Reversing	J118			300	00			300	00
	2		CP17	500	00			200	00		

Wages Payable   Account No. 213

Date		Item	Post. Ref.	Debit		Credit		Balance Debit		Credit	
19__											
Dec.	31	Adjusting	J116			300	00			300	00
19__											
Jan.	1	Reversing	J118	300	00			———		———	

The reversing entry for accrued salaries or wages applies to service companies as well as to merchandising ones. You can see that a reversing entry consists of simply switching around an adjusting entry. The question is, which adjusting entries should be reversed? Here's a handy rule of thumb that will help you decide.

▸ **If an adjusting entry increases an asset account or liability account (except Merchandise Inventory or a contra account, such as Accumulated Depreciation), then reverse the adjusting entry.**

Let's apply this rule to the adjusting entries for North Central Plumbing Supply.

From the following adjusting entries, note two things: (1) *An adjusting entry always involves an income statement account and a balance sheet account.* (2) *Reversing entries involve balance sheet accounts that had no previous balance.*

Revenue and Expense Summary	
Adj. 31,500	

Merchandise Inventory	
+	−
Bal. 31,500	Adj. 31,500

(Do not reverse; Merchandise Inventory is an exception.)

Merchandise Inventory	
+	−
Bal. 31,500	Adj. 31,500
Adj. 29,400	

Revenue and Expense Summary	
Adj. 31,500	Adj. 29,400

(Do not reverse; Merchandise Inventory is an exception.)

Rent Income	
−	+
Adj. 150	Bal. 450

Unearned Rent	
−	+
	Adj. 150

(Reverse; Unearned Rent is a *liability* account, and it was *increased*.)

Supplies Expense	
+	−
Adj. 514	

Supplies	
+	−
Bal. 720	Adj. 514

(Do not reverse; Supplies is an asset account, but it was decreased.)

Insurance Expense	
+	−
Adj. 160	

Prepaid Insurance	
+	−
Bal. 480	Adj. 160

(Do not reverse; Prepaid Insurance is an asset account, but it was decreased.)

Depreciation Expense, Equipment	
+	−
Adj. 2,400	

Accumulated Depreciation, Equipment	
−	+
	Bal. 8,200
	Adj. 2,400

(Do not reverse; Accumulated Depreciation is an exception.)

Depreciation Expense, Building	
+	−
Adj. 2,000	

Accumulated Depreciation, Building	
−	+
	Bal. 16,000
	Adj. 2,000

(Do not reverse; Accumulated Depreciation is an exception.)

Wages Expense	
+	−
Bal. 22,900	
Adj. 610	

Wages Payable	
−	+
	Adj. 610

(Reverse; Wages Payable is a *liability* account, and it was *increased*.)

Whenever we introduce additional adjusting entries, we'll make it a point to state whether these adjusting entries should be reversed.

The skeleton outline of the income statement is as follows.

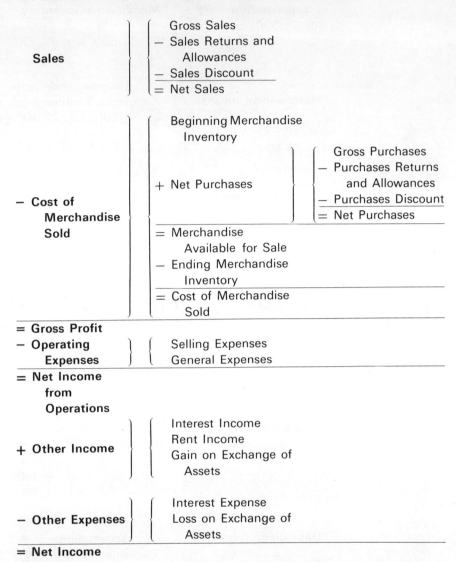

```
Sales ⎰ ⎱  Gross Sales
              − Sales Returns and
                  Allowances
              − Sales Discount
              = Net Sales

− Cost of     Beginning Merchandise
  Merchandise   Inventory
  Sold        + Net Purchases ⎰ ⎱  Gross Purchases
                                   − Purchases Returns
                                       and Allowances
                                   − Purchases Discount
                                   = Net Purchases
              = Merchandise
                  Available for Sale
              − Ending Merchandise
                  Inventory
              = Cost of Merchandise
                  Sold

= Gross Profit
− Operating   ⎰ ⎱  Selling Expenses
  Expenses           General Expenses

= Net Income
    from
    Operations

+ Other Income  ⎰ ⎱  Interest Income
                     Rent Income
                     Gain on Exchange of
                         Assets

− Other Expenses ⎰ ⎱  Interest Expense
                      Loss on Exchange of
                          Assets

= Net Income
```

The skeleton outline of the balance sheet looks like this.

Assets
Current Assets (Listed in the order of their convertibility into cash.)
1 Cash
2 Notes Receivable
3 Accounts Receivable
4 Prepaid items (Supplies; Prepaid Insurance)
Plant and Equipment (Listed in the order of their length of life; the asset with the shortest life is placed first. Land is placed last.)

1 Equipment
2 Buildings
3 Land

Liabilities
Current Liabilities (Listed in the order of their urgency of payment, the most pressing obligation is placed first.)
1 Notes Payable
2 Mortgage Payable or Contracts Payable (current portion)
3 Accounts Payable
4 Accrued liabilities (Wages Payable; Commissions Payable)
5 Unearned revenue
Long-term Liabilities (Contracts Payable; Mortgage Payable)

Owner's Equity
Capital balance at end of the fiscal year

There are four steps in making closing entries for a merchandising business.

Step 1
Close all revenue accounts, Purchases Discount, and Purchases Returns and Allowances into Revenue and Expense Summary.

Step 2
Close all expense accounts, Sales Discount, and Sales Returns and Allowances into Revenue and Expense Summary.

Step 3
Close revenue and Expense Summary into Capital.

Step 4
Close Drawing into Capital.

When you make reversing entries, record them as of the first day of the period following the adjusting entries.

Glossary

○ **Cost of merchandise sold** Merchandise Inventory at beginning of fiscal period, plus net purchases, minus Merchandise Inventory at end of fiscal period. Terms often used to describe the same thing are *cost of goods sold* and *cost of sales.*

    Merchandise Inventory (beginning)
+ Net Purchases
= Merchandise Available for Sale
− Merchandise Inventory
= Cost of Merchandise Sold

o **Current assets** Cash and any other assets or resources which are expected to be realized in cash or sold or consumed during the normal operating cycle of the business.

o **Current liabilities** Debts that are due within a short period, usually 1 year, and which are normally paid from current assets.

o **General expenses** Expenses incurred in the administration or operation of a business, including office expenses and any expenses that are not wholly classified as Selling Expenses or Other Expenses.

o **Gross profit** Net sales minus Cost of Merchandise Sold, or profit before deducting expenses. Gross profit may also be called *gross margin.*

> Net Sales
> — Cost of Merchandise Sold
> = Gross Profit

o **Liquidity** The ability of an asset to be quickly turned into cash, either by selling it or by putting it up as security for a loan.

o **Long-term liabilities** Debts that you don't have to pay right away, but can pay over a comparatively long period, usually more than 1 year.

o **Net income** The final figure on an income statement after all expenses have been deducted from revenues.

o **Net purchases** Total purchases, minus Purchases Returns and Allowances and minus Purchases Discount.

> Purchases
> — Purchases Returns and Allowances
> — Purchases Discount
> = Net Purchases

o **Net sales** Total sales, minus Sales Returns and Allowances and minus Sales Discount.

> Sales
> — Sales Returns and Allowances
> — Sales Discount
> = Net Sales

o **Notes receivable** Written promises to pay received from customers and due in a period of less than 1 year.

o **Plant and equipment** Long-lived assets that are held for use in the production or sale of other assets or services. They may also be called *fixed assets.*

o **Reversing entry** The reverse of certain adjusting entries, recorded as of the first day of the following fiscal year.

o **Selling expenses** Expenses directly related to the sale of merchandise, such as salaries of sales staff, expenses for advertising, and expenses for delivery.

o **Temporary equity** Accounts whose balances apply to one fiscal period only, such as revenues, expenses, and the Drawing account. Temporary-equity accounts are also called nominal accounts.

Exercise 1 R. M. Rawling bought a house for $22,000. Nine years later, after spending $4,000 on permanent improvements, he sold it for $34,000. The real estate agent who sold the house charged a 6% commission. What is Rawling's net profit?

Exercise 2 Arrange the following accounts as they would appear in the Current Assets section of the balance sheet.

Supplies	$ 410
Accounts Receivable	18,000
Merchandise Inventory	36,000
Cash	6,900
Prepaid Insurance	360
Notes Receivable	2,400
Prepaid Advertising	220

Exercise 3 The Sherwood Music Company, at the beginning of the year, held merchandise valued at $39,000. Their net purchases during the year amounted to $168,000. The merchandise inventory at the end of the year is $34,600. Determine (1) merchandise available for sale, and (2) cost of merchandise sold.

Exercise 4 Calculate the missing items in the following.

	Sales	Sales Returns	Net Sales	Beginning Inventory	Net Purchases	Merch. Available	Ending Inventory	Cost of Merch. Sold	Gross Profit
a	$62,000	$1,500		$37,000	$42,500	$ 79,500	$34,000	$45,500	
b	76,000		$ 74,000	36,000	65,000		49,000	52,000	
c		3,000	157,000	21,000		124,000	23,000		$56,000

Exercise 5 During the year just past, Johnson and Company had net sales of $196,000 and net purchases of $163,000. Their ending merchandise inventory was $32,000, and their beginning merchandise inventory was $29,000. How much is their gross profit?

Exercise 6 From the following information, present a statement of owner's equity.

D. C. Collier, Capital

16,500	Bal.	60,000	
		18,000	

Revenue and Expense Summary

Adj.	48,000	Adj.	51,000
	105,000		120,000
Closing	18,000		

D. C. Collier, Drawing

Bal.	16,500	Closing	10,500

Exercise 7 From the following T accounts, record the closing entries.

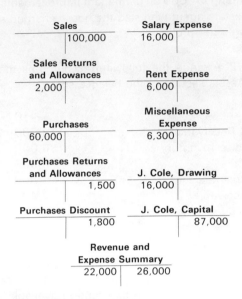

Sales	
	100,000

Salary Expense	
16,000	

Sales Returns and Allowances	
2,000	

Rent Expense	
6,000	

Purchases	
60,000	

Miscellaneous Expense	
6,300	

Purchases Returns and Allowances	
	1,500

J. Cole, Drawing	
16,000	

Purchases Discount	
	1,800

J. Cole, Capital	
	87,000

Revenue and Expense Summary	
22,000	26,000

Exercise 8 The following items appeared in the Income Statement columns of a work sheet prepared for Ormsby Sales and Service. W. E. Ormsby withdrew $10,200 from the business during the fiscal period. Prepare entries to close the revenue and expense accounts, Revenue and Expense Summary, and W. E. Ormsby, Drawing.

Ormsby Sales and Service
Work Sheet
For year ended June 30, 19___

Account Name	Income Statement	
	Debit	Credit
Sales		100,000 00
Sales Returns and Allowances	3,000 00	
Purchases	60,000 00	
Purchases Discount		1,200 00
Purchases Returns and Allowances		800 00
Salaries Expense	9,600 00	
Commissions Expense	6,400 00	
Rent Expense	3,600 00	
Miscellaneous Expense	600 00	
Revenue and Expense Summary	18,000 00	26,000 00
	101,200 00	128,000 00
Net Income	26,800 00	
	128,000 00	128,000 00

Problems

Problem 12-1 On the next page we see a partial work sheet for Duncan Electrical Supply. The merchandise inventory at the beginning of the fiscal period is $26,600. A. C. Duncan is the owner.

Duncan Electrical Supply
Work Sheet
For year ended December 31, 19___

Account Name	Income Statement	
	Debit	Credit
Sales		164,000 00
Sales Discount	1,854 00	
Sales Returns and Allowances	2,240 00	
Interest Income		920 00
Purchases	106,120 00	
Purchases Returns and Allowances		1,490 00
Wages Expense	21,600 00	
Rent Expense	4,800 00	
Commissions Expense	5,160 00	
Interest Expense	482 00	
Revenue and Expense Summary	26,600 00	22,180 00
Supplies Expense	416 00	
Insurance Expense	520 00	
Depreciation Expense, Equipment	1,800 00	
Depreciation Expense, Building	2,400 00	
	173,992 00	188,590 00
Net Income	14,598 00	
	188,590 00	188,590 00

Instructions

1 Prepare an income statement.
2 Journalize the closing entries.

Problem 12-2 At the top of the next page is a partial work sheet for Midway Electronics.

Instructions

1 Prepare a statement of owner's equity (no additional investment).
2 Prepare a balance sheet.

Problem 12-3 The following accounts appear in the ledger of the Moore-house Company on December 31, the end of this fiscal year.

Cash	$ 3,600
Accounts Receivable	9,400
Merchandise Inventory	37,000
Store Supplies	460
Prepaid Insurance	720
Store Equipment	18,600
Accumulated Depreciation, Store Equipment	1,800
Accounts Payable	7,200
Wages Payable	___
T. R. Moorehouse, Capital	49,080
T. R. Moorehouse, Drawing	24,000
Sales	156,000

Midway Electronics
Work Sheet
For year ended December 31, 19___

Account Name	Balance Sheet Debit	Balance Sheet Credit
Cash	8,610 00	
Notes Receivable	4,200 00	
Accounts Receivable	22,180 00	
Merchandise Inventory	36,896 00	
Supplies	280 00	
Prepaid Taxes	420 00	
Prepaid Insurance	360 00	
Delivery Equipment	3,600 00	
Accumulated Depreciation, Delivery Equipment		2,980 00
Testing Equipment	4,820 00	
Accumulated Depreciation, Testing Equipment		3,616 00
Store Equipment	2,928 00	
Accumulated Depreciation, Store Equipment		1,116 00
Building	40,000 00	
Accumulated Depreciation, Building		12,600 00
Land	5,200 00	
Notes Payable		2,810 00
Accounts Payable		18,760 00
Mortgage Payable (current portion)		1,200 00
Mortgage Payable		36,800 00
J. T. Rogers, Capital		44,876 00
J. T. Rogers, Drawing	14,960 00	
Wages Payable		656 00
	144,454 00	125,414 00
Net Income		19,040 00
	144,454 00	144,454 00

Sales Returns and Allowances	$ 2,000
Purchases	98,000
Purchases Discount	1,600
Purchases Returns and Allowances	2,300
Wages Expense	16,000
Advertising Expense	2,600
Depreciation Expense, Store Equipment	____
Store Supplies Expense	____
Rent Expense	5,600
Insurance Expense	____

The data needed for adjustments on December 31 are as follows.

a Merchandise Inventory, December 31 $35,600
b Store Supplies inventory, December 31   260
c Insurance expired   410
d Depreciation for the year   930
e Accrued wages on December 31   180

Instructions

1 Prepare a work sheet for the fiscal year ended December 31.
2 Prepare an income statement.

3 Prepare a statement of owner's equity.
4 Prepare a balance sheet.
5 Journalize the adjusting entries.
6 Journalize the closing entries.
7 Journalize the reversing entry.

Problem 12-4 The partial work sheet for Johnson and Company for the year ending June 30 is as follows.

Johnson and Company
Work Sheet
For year ended June 30, 19___

Account Name	Income Statement		Balance Sheet	
	Debit	Credit	Debit	Credit
Cash			14,100 00	
Accounts Receivable			46,000 00	
Merchandise Inventory			56,200 00	
Supplies			420 00	
Prepaid Insurance			610 00	
Delivery Equipment			6,200 00	
Accumulated Depreciation, Delivery Equipment				2,900 00
Store Equipment			16,700 00	
Accumulated Depreciation, Store Equipment				4,800 00
Accounts Payable				30,100 00
Salaries Payable				620 00
N. C. Johnson, Capital				83,910 00
N. C. Johnson, Drawing			14,000 00	
Revenue and Expense Summary	54,600 00	56,200 00		
Sales		260,000 00		
Purchases	202,000 00			
Purchases Discount		2,400 00		
Purchases Returns and Allowances		3,800 00		
Salaries Expense	24,000 00			
Truck Expense	4,300 00			
Supplies Expense	1,100 00			
Depreciation Expense, Delivery Equipment	1,200 00			
Depreciation Expense, Store Equipment	1,400 00			
Insurance Expense	920 00			
Miscellaneous Expense	980 00			
	290,500 00	322,400 00	154,230 00	122,330 00
Net Income	31,900 00			31,900 00
	322,400 00	322,400 00	154,230 00	154,230 00

Instructions
1 Journalize the seven adjusting entries.
2 Journalize the closing entries.
3 Journalize the reversing entry.

Problem 12-1A The partial work sheet on the next page is for the Allen Cycle and Toy Company. The merchandise inventory at the beginning of the fiscal period is $24,792. D. A. Allen is the owner.
Instructions
1 Prepare an income statement.
2 Journalize the closing entries.

Allen Cycle and Toy Company
Work Sheet
For year ended December 31, 19___

Account Name	Income Statement	
	Debit	Credit
Sales		163,296 40
Sales Discount	954 00	
Sales Returns and Allowances	2,614 60	
Interest Income		162 49
Purchases	104,728 00	
Purchases Returns and Allowances		828 00
Wages Expense	19,762 00	
Rent Expense	4,680 00	
Commissions Expense	4,720 00	
Interest Expense	328 16	
Revenue and Expense Summary	24,792 00	21,986 00
Supplies Expense	318 60	
Insurance Expense	468 00	
Depreciation Expense, Equipment	1,670 00	
Depreciation Expense, Building	2,400 00	
	167,435 36	186,272 89
Net Income	18,837 53	
	186,272 89	186,272 89

Problem 12-2A The following partial work sheet is for the Rolfe Novelty Company.

Rolfe Novelty Company
Work Sheet
For year ended December 31, 19___

Account Name	Balance Sheet	
	Debit	Credit
Cash	6,482 00	
Notes Receivable	2,400 00	
Accounts Receivable	28,586 40	
Merchandise Inventory	37,798 00	
Supplies	316 00	
Prepaid Taxes	409 00	
Prepaid Insurance	420 00	
Delivery Equipment	3,710 00	
Accumulated Depreciation, Delivery Equipment		2,870 00
Store Equipment	4,380 00	
Accumulated Depreciation, Store Equipment		3,330 00
Office Equipment	3,616 00	
Accumulated Depreciation, Office Equipment		2,780 00
Building	42,000 00	
Accumulated Depreciation, Building		14,400 00
Land	5,600 00	
Notes Payable		3,620 00
Accounts Payable		19,727 80
Mortgage Payable (current portion)		1,800 00
Mortgage Payable		37,142 00
J. T. Rolfe, Capital		43,372 60
J. T. Rolfe, Drawing	16,796 00	
Wages Payable		852 00
	152,513 40	129,894 40
Net Income		22,619 00
	152,513 40	152,513 40

Instructions

1 Prepare a statement of owner's equity (no additional investment).
2 Prepare a balance sheet.

Problem 12-3A The following accounts appear in the ledger of the Granning Company as of December 31, the end of this fiscal year.

Cash	$ 2,900
Accounts Receivable	9,940
Merchandise Inventory	34,320
Store Supplies	490
Prepaid Insurance	650
Store Equipment	19,760
Accumulated Depreciation, Store Equipment	1,920
Accounts Payable	6,990
Wages Payable	——
C. A. Granning, Capital	48,130
C. A. Granning, Drawing	18,840
Sales	148,420
Sales Returns and Allowances	1,760
Purchases	97,540
Purchases Discount	1,710
Purchases Returns and Allowances	2,930
Wages Expense	15,400
Advertising Expense	2,100
Depreciation Expense, Store Equipment	——
Store Supplies Expense	——
Rent Expense	6,400
Insurance Expense	——

The data needed for adjustments on December 31 are as follows.

a	Merchandise Inventory, December 31	$32,160
b	Store Supplies inventory, December 31	180
c	Insurance expired for the year	420
d	Depreciation for the year	860
e	Accrued wages on December 31	110

Instructions

1 Prepare a work sheet for the fiscal year ended December 31.
2 Prepare an income statement.
3 Prepare a statement of owner's equity.
4 Prepare a balance sheet.
5 Journalize the adjusting entries.
6 Journalize the closing entries.
7 Journalize the reversing entry.

Problem 12-4A The following partial work sheet covers the affairs of Smithwick and Company for the year ending June 30.

Smithwick and Company
Work Sheet
For year ended June 30, 19___

Account Name	Income Statement Debit	Income Statement Credit	Balance Sheet Debit	Balance Sheet Credit
Cash			16,192 17	
Accounts Receivable			52,317 27	
Merchandise Inventory			61,728 72	
Supplies			516 00	
Prepaid Insurance			660 00	
Delivery Equipment			6,460 00	
Accumulated Depreciation, Delivery Equipment				3,240 00
Store Equipment			18,250 00	
Accumulated Depreciation, Store Equipment				5,180 00
Accounts Payable				33,718 67
Salaries Payable				426 00
C. T. Smithwick, Capital				99,961 29
C. T. Smithwick, Drawing			18,720 00	
Revenue and Expense Summary	57,613 00	59,728 00		
Sales		268,176 20		
Purchases	208,640 00			
Purchases Discount		2,873 00		
Purchases Returns and Allowances		3,914 00		
Salaries Expense	25,700 00			
Truck Expense	4,671 00			
Supplies Expense	1,282 00			
Depreciation Expense, Delivery Equipment	1,350 00			
Depreciation Expense, Store Equipment	1,448 00			
Insurance Expense	960 00			
Miscellaneous Expense	709 00			
	302,373 00	334,691 20	174,844 16	142,525 96
Net Income	32,318 20			32,318 20
	334,691 20	334,691 20	174,844 16	174,844 16

Instructions

1 Journalize the adjusting entries.
2 Journalize the closing entries.
3 Journalize the reversing entry.

13

Bank accounts and petty cash

Those who despair of ever being rich make little account of small expenses, thinking that a little added to a little will never make any great sum. Plutarch, *Of Man's Progress in Virtue*

Key points

- The bank account as an independent record of cash
- Procedure for reconciling bank statement
- Journal entries based on bank reconciliation
- Petty Cash and Change Fund are debited only once, unless it is necessary to increase or decrease the size of the funds.
- In reimbursing the Petty Cash Fund, debit the accounts on whose behalf the money was spent, and credit Cash.
- A debit balance in Cash Short and Over represents a net shortage.
- A credit balance in Cash Short and Over represents a net overage.

Specific objectives

After you have completed this chapter, you will be able to:
- Reconcile a bank statement.
- Journalize the requisite entries directly from the bank reconciliation.
- Journalize entries to establish and reimburse Petty Cash Fund.
- Complete petty cash vouchers and petty cash payments records.
- Journalize the entries to establish a Change Fund.
- Journalize transactions involving Cash Short and Over.

Introduction

As we have said before, internal control is very important in any system of financial accounting. And one aspect of internal control is the efficient management of cash. For a business of any size, all cash received during a working day should be deposited at the end of the day, and all disburse-ments—with the exception of payments from Petty Cash—should be made by check. When we talk about cash, we mean currency, coins, checks, money orders, and bank drafts or bank cashier's checks. Personal checks are accepted on a conditional-payment status, that is, based on the condition that they're valid. In other words, we give checks the benefit of the doubt, and consider them to be good until they are proved to be no good.

In this chapter, we're also going to talk about petty cash funds and change funds. A cash fund, in this sense, is a separate kitty of cash.

Making deposits

Although you may be familiar with the process of making deposits and writing checks, let's review these procedures for a business.

Signature card

When Robert C. Randall founded North Central Plumbing Supply (yes, we're back with them again), he opened a checking account in the name of the business. When he made his first deposit, he filled out a *signature card* for the bank's files. Randall gave his accountant the right to sign checks too, so the accountant also signed the card. This card gives the bank a copy of the official signatures of any persons authorized to sign checks. The bank can use it as a verification of any signatures on checks of North Central Plumbing Supply presented for payment. This, of course, helps the bank detect forgeries. See the example of a signature card.

NAME & ADDRESS

North Central Plumbing Supply
1968 Arrow St., N.W.
Seattle, Wash. 98111

AUTHORIZED SIGNATURES
1. *Robert C. Randall*
2. *Ronald R. Hoffman*
3. _____
(   ) SIGNATURE(S) REQUIRED

TYPE OF DEPOSITOR

☑ Individual(s)   ☐ Partnership   ☐ Corporation   ☐ Association   ☐ Fiduciary

TYPE OF ACCOUNT

☐ Regular Checking   ☑ Business Checking   ☐ Savings

TERMS OF ACCOUNT

☑ One Name   ☐ Joint with right of Survivorship
☐ Joint without right of Survivorship

The above signed hereby agree to the terms of account for the account designated above and to the rules and regula-tions and changes or additions thereto of Valley National Bank, applicable to the type of account designated above. The applicable terms and rules and regulations, receipt of a copy of which is hereby acknowledged, are incorporated herein by this reference as if set forth in full. The rules and regulations are posted at all times in the lobby of the bank.

[Ordinarily, for purposes of internal control, an employee who has access to the records should not have access to the cash. However, in the case of a small business, it may be necessary for one person to have access to both.]

Deposit slips

The bank provides deposit slips on which the customer records the amount of coins and currency he or she is depositing, and lists each individual check being deposited. A typical deposit slip is shown on page 323. Each check should be listed according to its American Bankers Association (ABA) transit number, which has two parts: The numerator indicates the city or state in which the bank is located and the specific bank in that area; the denominator indicates the Federal Reserve District in which the check is cleared and the routing number used by the Federal Reserve Bank. For example,

$$\frac{98\text{-}420}{1214}$$

The 98 identifies the city or state, and the 420 indicates the specific bank within that area. It would be enough just to list the top part only on the deposit slip. However, for your own information, in the denominator, the 12 represents the Twelfth Federal Reserve District, and 14 is the routing number used by the Federal Reserve Bank.

The depositor fills out the deposit slip in duplicate, giving one copy to the bank teller, and keeping the other copy. (This procedure occasionally varies from bank to bank.)

When the bank receives the deposited checks, it prints the amount of each check on the lower right side of the check in a very distinctive-looking script. The script is called "MICR," which stands for *magnetic ink character recognition*. The routing number used by the Federal Reserve Bank was previously printed on the lower left side of the blank check. The reason they use this MICR script is that electronic equipment, used by banks to process the checks, is able to read the script identifying the bank on which the check is drawn, and the amount of the check.

Night deposits

Most banks provide night depositories so that firms can make deposits after regular banking hours. Depositories are steel-lined chutes into which a firm's representative can drop a bag of cash, knowing that their day's receipts will be safe until the bank opens in the morning. The bank gives the firm canvas deposit bags with locks and keys. The business owner can put locked bags down the night deposit chute, and go home with a calm mind. The next day—whenever it's convenient—the owner or her or his representative can drop by the bank and unlock the bag (or bags). Since it is the owner (or the firm's representative) who has the only keys to the bags, he or she is the one who has to go to the bank on the next banking day and make the actual deposit.

DEPOSITED WITH

VALLEY NATIONAL BANK

FOR ACCOUNT OF

North Central Plumbing Supply

SEATTLE, WASH., *March 1*   19

In receiving items for deposit or collection, this bank acts only as depositor's collecting agent and assumes no responsibility beyond the exercise of due care. All items are credited subject to final payment in cash or solvent credits. This bank will not be liable for default or negligence of its duly selected correspondents nor for losses in transit, and each correspondent so selected shall not be liable except for its own negligence. This bank or its correspondents may send items, directly or indirectly, to any bank including the payor, and accept its draft or credit as conditional payment in lieu of cash; it may charge back any item at any time before final payment, whether returned or not, also any item drawn on this bank not good at close of business on day deposited.

	DOLLARS	CENTS
CURRENCY	117	00
SILVER	14	65
CHECKS AS FOLLOWS		
98–420	16	20
96–164	37	29
98–837	146	82
92–111	107	96
96–722	98	37
TOTAL $	538	29

SEE THAT ALL CHECKS AND DRAFTS ARE ENDORSED

NOT NEGOTIABLE
ORIGINAL DEPOSIT TICKET

Received by _____

Endorsements

The bank refuses to accept for deposit a check made out to a firm until someone from the firm has endorsed the check. The endorsement may be made by signature or by using a stamp. The endorsement (1) transfers title to the money, and (2) guarantees the payment of the check. In other words, if the check is not good, NSF (not sufficient funds), then the bank, in order to protect itself, is able to deduct the amount of the check from the depositor's account.

Note in the illustration on page 324 how an endorsement is written on the back of a check, on the left side.

Our model company, North Central Plumbing Supply, endorses all incoming checks by putting its stamp on the back of the checks: ''Pay to the Order of Valley National Bank, For Deposit Only, North Central Plumbing Supply.''

This is called a *restrictive endorsement,* because it restricts or limits any further negotiation of the check; it forces the deposit of the check, since the endorsement is not valid for any other purpose.

Writing checks

As you of course know, you have to use a check to withdraw money from a checking account. A check represents an order by the depositor, directing the bank to pay money to a designated person or firm: the *payee.*

The checks may be attached to check stubs. The stub has spaces to record the check number and amount, the date and payee, the purpose of the check, and the beginning and ending balances. *Note well:* The information recorded on the check stub is the basis for the journal entry. So check stubs are vitally important. A person in a hurry, or working under pressure, can sometimes neglect to fill in the check stubs; it is therefore best to record all the information on the check stub *before one makes out the check.*

A variation of this system is the check register, which, as we have said, may be used as a substitute for the cash payments journal. But again, as a precaution, one should record all the details in the check register *before* one writes the check itself.

It goes without saying that all checks should be written carefully, so that no dishonest person can successfully alter them. The payee's name goes on the first long line. Write the amount in figures next to the dollar sign, then write the amount in words at the extreme left of the line provided for this information. Write cents as a fraction of 100. For example, write $727.50 as ''seven hundred twenty-seven and 50/100,'' or $69.00 as ''sixty-nine and 00/100.'' From a legal standpoint, if there is a discrepancy between the amount in figures and the written amount, it is the written amount that prevails. However, as a general practice, the bank gets in touch with the depositor and asks what the correct amount should be.

Many firms use a *check writer,* which is a machine used to record, on the check itself, the amount in figures and in words. This neatly prevents anyone from altering the amount of the check.

In the illustration we see checks, with the accompanying stubs, drawn on the account of North Central Plumbing Supply.

NO. 2023	$ 827.00
DATE Oct 11	19 ___
TO Argel Mfg. Co.	
FOR Merchandise	

	DOLLARS	CENTS
BAL. BRO'T. FOR'D.	6,952	95
AMT. DEPOSITED		
" "		
TOTAL		
AMT. THIS CHECK	827	00
BAL. CAR'D. FOR'D.	6,125	95

VALLEY NATIONAL BANK   98-461 / 1252

1728 BIRCH STREET
SEATTLE, WASH. 98110

NORTH CENTRAL PLUMBING SUPPLY
1968 ARROW STREET N.W.
SEATTLE, WASHINGTON 98111   SEATTLE, WASHINGTON Oct. 11 19 ___   No. 2023

PAY TO THE ORDER OF __Argel Manufacturing Co.__ $ 827.00

__Eight hundred twenty-seven and 00/100__ ———— DOLLARS

Robert C. Randall

⑆1252⑆0461⑆

NO. 2024	$ 67.00
DATE Oct. 12	19 ___
TO Davenport	
FOR Supplies	

	DOLLARS	CENTS
BAL. BRO'T. FOR'D.	6,125	95
AMT. DEPOSITED		
TOTAL		
AMT. THIS CHECK	67	00
BAL. CAR'D. FOR'D.	6,058	95

VALLEY NATIONAL BANK   98-461 / 1252

1728 BIRCH STREET
SEATTLE, WASH. 98110

NORTH CENTRAL PLUMBING SUPPLY
1968 ARROW STREET N.W.
SEATTLE, WASHINGTON 98111   SEATTLE, WASHINGTON Oct. 12 19 ___   No. 2024

PAY TO THE ORDER OF __Davenport Office Supplies__ $ 67.00

__Sixty-seven and 00/100__ ———— DOLLARS

Robert C. Randall

⑆1252⑆0461⑆

Bank statements

Once a month the bank sends all customers a statement of their accounts, giving them the following information.
- The balance at the beginning of the month
- Deductions in the form of checks and debit memos
- Additions in the form of deposits and credit memos
- The final balance at the end of the month

A bank statement for North Central Plumbing Supply is shown on page 326.

The code symbols for this statement are explained directly below it.

VALLEY NATIONAL BANK

1728 BIRCH STREET
SEATTLE, WASH. 98110

STATEMENT OF ACCOUNT

North Central Plumbing Supply
1968 Arrow Street, N.W.
Seattle, Washington 98111

ACCOUNT NO.
172-381-02
STATEMENT DATE
October 31, 19__

CHECKS AND OTHER DEBITS			DEPOSITS	DATE	BALANCE
BALANCE BROUGHT FORWARD FROM LAST STATEMENT				Oct. 1, 19__	7,495.13
50.00	200.00	400.00	921.00	Oct. 1	7,766.13
46.00	174.23	671.74	1,476.22	Oct. 2	8,350.38
846.20	664.56		463.62	Oct. 3	7,303.24
719.00	61.68	591.84	789.43	Oct. 4	6,720.15
36.92	817.22	DM 125.00	1,063.14	Oct. 7	6,804.15
523.00	786.40	374.00	1,211.96	Oct. 8	6,332.71
	943.64		CM 606.00	Oct. 30	7,812.62
			873.19	Oct. 30	8,685.81
843.17	21.92	SC 5.50	946.78	Oct. 31	8,762.00

PLEASE EXAMINE THIS STATEMENT CAREFULLY. REPORT ANY POSSIBLE ERRORS IN 10 DAYS.

CODE SYMBOLS

CM Credit Memo	OD Overdraft
DM Debit Memo	SC Service Charge
EC Error Correction	

CM Credit memo Increases or credits to the account, such as notes or accounts left with the bank for collection.

DM Debit memo Decreases or debits to the account, items returned such as NSF checks, special charges levied by the bank against the account.

EC Error correction Corrections of errors made by the bank, such as mistakes in transferring figures.

OD Overdraft An overwithdrawal, resulting in a negative balance in the account.

SC Service charge The amount charged by the bank for servicing the account, based on the number of items processed and the average balance of the account.

The bank statement is a valuable aid to internal control, because it gives a double record of the Cash account. If a business entity deposits all cash receipts and makes all payments by check, then the bank is keeping an independent record of the firm's cash. Offhand, you might think that the two balances—the firm's and the bank's—should be equal, but this is most unlikely, because some transactions may have been recorded in the firm's account before being recorded in the bank's. Also there are often unavoidable delays (by either the firm or the bank) in recording transactions. There is generally a time lag of at least 2 days between the bank's cutoff date and the time it takes the post office to deliver the bank statement to the depositor. During this time, deposits made or checks written are recorded in the firm's checkbook, but are not yet recorded on the bank statement.

The bank usually mails statements to its depositors shortly after the end of the month. In the same envelope with the statement are the canceled checks (the firm's checks that have been cashed or cleared by the bank) and debit or credit memos. As we mentioned before, debit memos represent deductions and credit memos represent additions to a bank account. Each business entity keeps its accounts from its *own* point of view, and the customer's deposits, as far as the bank is concerned, are liabilities, in that the bank owes the customer the amount of the deposits. By T accounts, it looks like this.

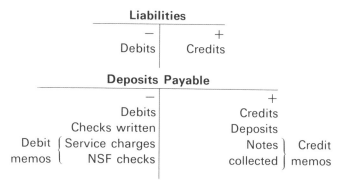

On the customer's books, of course, this comes under the account titled Cash, or Cash in Bank, or simply the name of the bank. Regardless of what title is used for the account, however, the balance of the account is referred to as the *book balance of Cash.*

Need for reconciling bank balance and book balance

The *book balance* is the balance of the Cash account in the general ledger. Since the bank statement balance and the book balance are not equal, a firm makes a *reconciliation* to discover the reasons for the difference between the two balances, and to correct any errors that may have been made by either the bank or the firm. This makes it possible to wind up with the same balance in each account, which is called the *adjusted balance,* or *true balance,* of the Cash account.

A variety of reasons or errors may cause the difference between the bank statement balance and the customer's cash balance. Some of the more usual ones are as follows.

1 **Outstanding checks** Checks that have been written but which have not yet been received for payment by the time the bank sends out its statement. But the depositor, when writing out his or her checks, deducted the amounts from the Cash account in his/her books.

2 **Late deposits** Deposits made after the bank statement was issued. Many accountants call these *deposits in transit.* The depositor has naturally already added them to the Cash account in his or her books, however.

3 **Service charges** The bank charges for services rendered: for issuing checks, for collecting money, for receiving payment of notes turned over to it by the customer for collection, and for other such services. The bank notifies the depositor with a debit memorandum, and immediately deducts the fee from the balance of the bank account.

4 **Collections** When the bank acts as a collection agent for its customers by accepting payments on promissory notes, installment accounts, and charge accounts, it adds the proceeds to the customer's bank account and sends a credit memorandum to notify the customer of the transaction.

5 **NSF checks (not sufficient funds)** When a bank customer deposits a check, she or he counts it as cash. However, occasionally a check bounces, and then the bank sends the customer notice to that effect. The customer must then make a deduction from the Cash account.

6 **Errors** In spite of internal control and systems designed to double-check against errors, sometimes either the customer or the bank may make a mistake. Often these errors do not become evident until the bank reconciliation is performed.

Steps in reconciling the bank statement

1 **Canceled checks** The bank stacks canceled checks returned to it in the order in which it paid them, and lists them in the same way on the bank statement. *While they are still stacked in this order,* compare each check with the bank statement, and note any discrepancies.

2 **Deposits** Look over the late deposits, or unrecorded deposits listed on the bank reconciliation of the previous month. Compare these with the deposits listed on this month's bank statement. These deposits should all be accounted for; note any discrepancy. Now compare the remaining deposits listed on the current bank statement with deposits written in the firm's accounting records. Consider any deposits not shown on the bank statement as late deposits, or deposits in transit.

3 **Outstanding checks** Next, arrange the canceled checks in the order of the check numbers. Look over the list of outstanding checks left over from the bank reconciliation of the previous month, and note the checks that have now been returned. Compare each canceled check with the entry in the cash payments journal or check register; if these books are not available, then compare the canceled checks with the check stubs. In either case, use a check mark ($\checkmark$) to indicate that the check has been paid and that the amount is correct. To further verify that money has been sent to the right payee, review the endorsements on the backs of the checks. Any payments that have *not* been checked off, including the outstanding checks from the previous bank reconciliation, are the present outstanding checks. In other words, they were not presented for payment by the time of the cutoff date of the bank statement.

4 **Bank memorandums** Trace the credit memos to the cash receipts journal, and the debit memos to the cash payments journal or check register. If the memos have not been recorded, make separate journal entries for them.

As you can see, a bank can be an accountant's best friend. A large firm interested in maintaining internal control should require that the reconciliation be prepared by an employee who is not involved in recording business transactions.

<table>
<tr><td>Form of bank
reconciliation</td><td>Let's look at the standard form of a bank reconciliation for a hypothetical company.</td></tr>
</table>

Bank statement balance (last figure on the bank statement)		$4,000
Add		
Late deposits (they have already been added to the Cash account)	$300	
Bank errors	20	320
		$4,320
Deduct		
Outstanding checks (they have already been deducted from the Cash account)	$960	
Bank errors	40	1,000
Adjusted balance (the true balance of Cash)		$3,320

Book balance of Cash (the latest balance of the Cash account if it has been posted up to date; otherwise take the beginning balance of Cash, plus cash receipts and minus cash payments)		$2,850
Add		
Credit memos (additions by the bank not recorded in the Cash account, such as collections of notes)	$500	
Book errors (that understate balance)	40	540
		$3,390
Deduct		
Debit memos (deductions by the bank not recorded in the Cash account, such as service charges or collection charges)	$ 20	
Book errors (that overstate balance)	50	70
Adjusted balance (the true balance of Cash)		$3,320

<table>
<tr><td>Illustrations of
bank reconciliations</td><td>As a more elementary illustration, let's take the case of J. P. Caldwell and Company, followed by the case of North Central Plumbing Supply.</td></tr>
</table>

J. P. Caldwell and Company The bank statement of J. P. Caldwell and Company indicates a balance of $2,119 as of March 31. The balance of the Cash account in their ledger as of that date is $1,552. Caldwell's accountant has taken the steps we've listed.

1 Recorded canceled checks correctly on the bank statement.

2 Noted that deposit made on March 31 was not recorded on the bank statement, $762.

3 Noted outstanding checks: no. 921, $626; no. 985, $69; no. 986, $438.

4 Noted credit memo: note collected by the bank, $200, not recorded in cash receipts journal. Noted debit memo: collection charge and service charge not recorded in cash payments journal, $4.

The bank reconciliation may be made on a separate sheet of paper, or on the back of the bank statement, since some banks print the main headings on the form. Here are Caldwell's bank reconciliation and journal entries.

J. P. Caldwell and Company		
Bank Reconciliation		
March 31, 19___		
Bank Statement Balance		$2,119.00
Add: Late deposit (March 31)		762.00
		$2,881.00
Deduct: Outstanding checks		
No. 921	$626.00	
No. 985	69.00	
No. 986	438.00	1,133.00
Adjusted Balance		$1,748.00
Book Balance of Cash		$1,552.00
Add: Note collected by bank		200.00 ←
		$1,752.00
Deduct: Bank service and		
collection charges		4.00 ←
Adjusted Balance		$1,748.00

Require journal entries

Note that journal entries should be based on the bank reconciliation, since the true balance of Cash is $1,748, whereas the current balance on the firm's books is $1,552. You have undoubtedly seen that you can't change the balance of an account unless you first make a journal entry and then post the entry to the accounts involved. Consequently, you have to make journal

19___						
Mar.	31	Cash	200	00		
		Notes Receivable			200	00
		Non-interest-bearing note signed by S. Alden was collected by the bank				
	31	Miscellaneous General Expense	4	00		
		Cash			4	00
		Service charge and collection charge levied by the bank				

entries only from the Book Balance of Cash section of the bank reconciliation. Debit additions to Cash and credit deductions from Cash. J. P. Caldwell and Company records the entries on page 330 in their general journal.

Here service charges and collection charges are recorded in the same account, as the amounts are relatively small. However, some accountants may use separate expense accounts.

North Central Plumbing Supply North Central Plumbing Supply's bank statement shows a final balance of $8,762 as of October 31. The present balance of the Cash account in the ledger, after North Central's accountant has posted the cash receipts journal and the cash payments journal, is $7,806.50. The accountant took the following steps:

1 Verified that canceled checks were recorded correctly on the bank statement.
2 Discovered that a deposit of $1,003 made on October 31 was not recorded on the bank statement.
3 Noted outstanding checks: no. 1916, $461; no. 2022, $119; no. 2023, $827; no. 2024, $67.
4 Noted that a credit memo for a note collected by the bank from Acme Plumbing and Heating, $600 principal plus $6 interest, was not recorded in the cash receipts journal.
5 Found that check no. 2001 for $523, payable to Mahon, Inc., on account was recorded in the cash payments journal as $532. (The correct amount is $523.)
6 Noted that a debit memo for a collection charge and service charge of $5.50 was not recorded in the cash payments journal.
7 Noted that debit memo for an NSF check for $125 from T. L. Long Company was not recorded.

The reconciliation is shown at the top of the next page.

The accountant has to make the journal entries shown below the reconciliation in order to change the Cash account from the present balance of $7,806.50 to the true balance of $8,291. Let us assume that she or he has previously posted the cash receipts journal and the cash payments journal to the Cash account in the ledger. Otherwise the entries could be recorded directly in the cash journals. ·

The Petty Cash Fund

Day after day, business firms are confronted with transactions involving small immediate payments, such as the cost of a telegram, delivery charges, postage due for mail, a new typewriter ribbon, etc. If the firm had to go through the usual procedure of making all payments by check, the time consumed would be frustrating, and the whole process unduly expensive. For many firms, just the cost of writing each check is more than $.50; this includes the cost of an employee's time in writing and reconciling the check. Suppose the mail carrier is at the door with a letter on which there is $.10 postage due. To write a check would be ridiculous. It only makes sense to

North Central Plumbing Supply
Bank Reconciliation
October 31, 19___

Bank Statement Balance		$8,762.00
Add: Late deposit (October 31)		1,003.00
		$9,765.00
Deduct: Outstanding checks		
No. 1916	$461.00	
No. 2022	119.00	
No. 2023	827.00	
No. 2024	67.00	1,474.00
Adjusted Balance		$8,291.00
Book Balance of Cash		$7,806.50
Add: Note collected (principal $600.00, interest $6.00, Acme Plumbing and Heating)	$606.00	
Error in recording check no. 2001 payable to Mahon, Inc.	9.00	615.00
		$8,421.50
Deduct: Bank service and collection charges	$5.50	
NSF check from T. L. Long Company	125.00	130.50
Adjusted Balance		$8,291.00

Do not require journal entries

Require journal entries

19___					
Oct.	31	Cash		606 00	
		Notes Receivable			600 00
		Interest Income			6 00
		Bank collected note signed by Acme Plumbing and Heating			
	31	Cash		9 00	
		Accounts Payable, Mahon, Inc.			9 00
		Error in recording check no. 2001			
	31	Miscellaneous General Expense		5 50	
		Cash			5 50
		Bank service charge and collection charge			
	31	Accounts Receivable, T. L. Long		125 00	
		Cash			125 00
		NSF check			

pay in cash, out of the Petty Cash Fund. *Petty* means small; so the firm sets a maximum amount that can be paid out of the Petty Cash Fund. Payments larger than this maximum must be processed by regular check through the cash payments journal or check register.

Establishing the Petty Cash Fund

After the firm has decided on the maximum amount of a payment from petty cash, the next step is to estimate how much cash will be needed during a given period of time, such as a month. Small payments are made during the month from the Petty Cash Fund. At the end of the month, when the fund is nearly exhausted, the accountant reimburses the fund for expenditures made, to bring the fund back up to the original amount. Consequently, it may be considered to be a revolving fund. For example, say the amount initially put in the Petty Cash Fund is $50, and at the end of the month all that's left is $4. So the accountant puts $46 in the fund as a reimbursement, thereby bringing it back up to $50 to start the new month.

When keeping cash in the office, one also has to consider the element of security. If risk is great, the amount of the fund should be kept small, and the fund should be reimbursed at intervals of perhaps 1 week, or 2 weeks. One can also set a predetermined minimum amount for the fund, and reimburse it whenever the balance falls to this minimum.

North Central Plumbing Supply decided to establish a Petty Cash Fund of $50, and put it under the control of the secretary. Accordingly, their accountant writes a check, cashes it at the bank, and records this in the cash payments journal as follows.

Cash Payments Journal

Date	Ck. No.	Account Name	Post. Ref.	Sundry Accounts Debit	Sundry Accounts Credit	Cash Credit
19__ Sept. 1	88	Petty Cash Fund		50 00		50 00

Because the Petty Cash Fund is a current-asset account, it is listed in the balance sheet immediately below Cash.

▶ **Note: The Petty Cash Fund account is debited only once, and this happens when the fund is established initially.**

The only exception would be a case in which the original amount was not large enough to handle the necessary transactions, and therefore the accountant had to make the Petty Cash Fund bigger—maybe change the $50 to $75. But, barring such a change in the size of the fund, Petty Cash is debited only once.

After the accountant cashes that original $50 check, he or she converts it into convenient denominations, such as quarters, dimes, etc., and puts the money in a locked drawer, in the secretary's desk, telling the secretary not to pay for anything larger than $5 out of Petty Cash.

Payments from the Petty Cash Fund

The secretary now takes the responsibility for the Petty Cash Fund; he or she is designated as the only person who can make payments from it. In case of his or her illness, some other employee should be named as stand-in. There has to be a *petty cash voucher* to account for every payment from the fund, in other words, a receipt signed by the person who authorized the payment and by the person receiving payment. This is another illustration of internal control. Even for these small payments of $5 or less, there would have to be collusion between the payee and the secretary in order for any theft to occur. The following illustration shows what a petty cash voucher looks like.

PETTY CASH VOUCHER

No. *1*   Date *September 2, 19—*

Paid to *Excell Delivery Service* $ *2.00*

For *Delivery*

Account *Delivery Expense*

Approved by   Payment received by

R. Jason   *C. J. Comstock*

Reimbursement of the Petty Cash Fund

The procedure for reimbursing the Petty Cash Fund, or bringing it up to the original amount, may vary according to the size of the business. Every method involves sorting out the petty cash vouchers and gathering them together by accounts, as recorded on the face of each voucher.

For example, take voucher no. 1 (as shown in the illustration), in which $2 is charged to Delivery Expense. Let's say that, as the month goes by, $12 more is charged to Delivery Expense on other petty cash vouchers. Assume that the total amount spent from the fund during the month is $43. At the end of the month, the accountant makes a summarizing entry, debiting the accounts which have been recorded on the petty cash vouchers, and crediting Cash. For this month, she or he debits Delivery Expense for $14, debits other accounts for $29, and credits Cash for $43. By doing this, she/he officially journalizes the transactions so that they can be posted to the ledger accounts. The accountant writes a check for $43, cashes it, and has the secretary put the money in the drawer, bringing the fund up to the original $50. Some firms like a written record on one sheet of paper, so they keep a *petty cash payments record,* with columns in the Distribution of Accounts section labeled with the types of expenditures they make most often. Note that the vouchers are listed consecutively.

North Central Plumbing Supply made the following payments from its Petty Cash Fund during September.

Sept.	2	Paid $2 to Excell Delivery Service, voucher no. 1.
	3	Bought pencils and pens, $3.20, voucher no. 2.
	5	Paid high school annual for advertising, $5, voucher no. 3.
	7	Paid for mailing packages, $2.90, voucher no. 4.
	10	Robert C. Randall, the owner, withdrew $5 for personal use, voucher no. 5.
	14	Postage due on incoming mail, $.16, voucher no. 6.
	21	Bought typewriter ribbons, $4.10, voucher no. 7.
	22	Paid $3 to Excell Delivery Service, voucher no. 8.
	26	Paid for mailing packages, $3.80, voucher no. 9.
	27	Paid $3.50 to Fast Way Delivery, voucher no. 10.
	29	Bought memo pads, $4.40, voucher no. 11.
	29	Paid for collect telegram, $2.60, voucher no. 12.
	30	Paid $3.20 to Excell Delivery Service, voucher no. 13.
	30	Paid for having windows cleaned, $5, voucher no. 14.

North Central Plumbing Supply uses a petty cash payments record to keep track of the payments according to purpose. This is only a supplementary record, *not* a journal. It is merely used as a basis for compiling the journal entry to reimburse the fund. North Central's petty cash payments record is shown at the top of the next page.

Now the accountant makes the summarizing entry in order to officially journalize the transactions that have taken place. He or she takes the information directly from the petty cash payments record.

Cash Payments Journal

Date	Ck. No.	Account Name	Post. Ref.	Sundry Accounts Debit	Sundry Accounts Credit	Cash Credit
19__						
Sept.	30 136	Office Supplies		11 70		47 86
		Delivery Expense		18 40		
		Miscellaneous General Expense		7 76		
		Advertising Expense		5 00		
		Robert C. Randall, Drawing		5 00		

Note that in the summarizing entry the accountant debits the accounts on whose behalf the payments were made, and credits the Cash account. *He or she leaves the Petty Cash Fund strictly alone.* Then she or he cashes a check for $47.86, and puts the cash in the secretary's desk drawer, thereby

Petty Cash Payments Record
Month of September 19___

Date	Vou. No.	Explanation	Payments	Office Supplies	Delivery Expense	Misc. Gen. Exp.	Sundry Account	Amount
							Distribution of Payments	
Sept. 1		Established fund, check no. 88, $50						
2	1	Excell Delivery Service	2 00		2 00			
3	2	Pencils and pens	3 20	3 20				
5	3	High school annual	5 00				Advertising Expense	5 00
7	4	Postage for mailings	2 90		2 90			
10	5	Robert C. Randall	5 00				R.C. Randall, Drawing	5 00
14	6	Postage on incoming mail	16			16		
21	7	Typewriter ribbons	4 10	4 10				
22	8	Excell Delivery Service	3 00		3 00			
26	9	Postage for mailings	3 80		3 80			
27	10	Fastway Delivery	3 50		3 50			
29	11	Memo pads	4 40	4 40				
29	12	Collect telegram	2 60			2 60		
30	13	Excell Delivery Service	3 20		3 20			
30	14	Cleaning windows	5 00			5 00		
		Totals	47 86	11 70	18 40	7 76		10 00
		Balance in Fund $ 2.14						
		Reimbursed, ck. no. 136 47.86						
		Total $50.00						

restoring the amount in the Petty Cash Fund to the original $50.

The Change Fund

Anyone who has ever tried to pay for a small item by handing the clerk a $20 bill knows that a firm which carries out numerous cash transactions needs a Change Fund.

Establishing the Change Fund

Before setting up a Change Fund, one has to decide on two things: (1) how much money needs to be in the fund, and (2) what denominations of bills and coins are needed. The Change Fund is like the Petty Cash Fund in that *it is debited only once: when it is established.* It is left at the initial figure unless the person in charge decides to make it larger. The Change Fund account, like the Petty Cash account, is also a current asset, and is recorded in the balance sheet immediately below Cash. If the Change Fund account is larger than the Petty Cash account, it precedes Petty Cash.

The owner of North Central Plumbing Supply, Mr. Randall, decides to establish a Change Fund; he decides this at the same time he sets up his Petty Cash Fund. The entries for both transactions look like this.

Cash Payments Journal

Date		Ck. No.	Account Name	Post. Ref.	Sundry Accounts Debit	Sundry Accounts Credit	Cash Credit
19__							
Sept.	1	88	Petty Cash Fund		50 00		50 00
	1	89	Change Fund		200 00		200 00

So Randall cashes a check for $200, gets the money in several denominations, and he's prepared to make change in any normal business transactions.

Depositing cash

At the end of each business day, Randall deposits the cash taken in during the day, but he holds back the amount of the Change Fund, being sure that it's in convenient denominations. The *time* he makes up the Change Fund depends on what time his shop closes for the day, and what time the bank closes. Let's say that on September 1, North Central Plumbing Supply has $925 on hand at the end of the day. The T accounts look like this.

Cash			Sales	
+	−		−	+
725				725

Randall records this in the cash receipts journal as follows.

Cash Receipts Journal

Date		Account Name	Post. Ref.	Sundry Accounts Debit	Sundry Accounts Credit	Sales Credit	Cash Debit
19__							
Sept.	1	Sales				725 00	725 00

Now recall that the amount of the cash deposit is the total cash count less the amount of the Change Fund, so that's how the deposit happens to be $725. On another day the cash count is $1,027. So Randall deposits $827 (get the picture?), and the deposit is as shown at the top of the next page.

Some business firms label the Cash account as *Cash in Bank,* and label the Change Fund as *Cash on Hand.*

Cash Receipts Journal

Date		Account Name	Post. Ref.	Sundry Accounts		Sales Credit	Cash Debit
				Debit	Credit		
19__ Sept.	9	Sales				827 00	827 00

Cash Short and Over

An inherent danger in making change is the human factor: Human beings make mistakes, especially when there are many customers to be waited on or when the business is temporarily short-handed. Ideally, mistakes should be eliminated. However, since mistakes do happen, accounting records must be set up so that they can cope with the situation. Both shortages and overages are recorded in the same account, which is called *Cash Short and Over.* (The Cash Short and Over account may also be used to handle shortages and overages in the Petty Cash Fund.)

For example, let's say that on September 14 North Central Plumbing Supply is faced with the following situation.

Cash Register Tape	Cash Count	Amount of the Change Fund
$781	$978	$200

After deducting the $200 in the Change Fund, Randall ought to deposit $778. The T accounts show how Randall actually handled the deposit.

Cash		Sales		Cash Short and Over
+	−	−	+	3
778			781	

The next day, September 15, the pendulum happens to swing in the other direction.

Cash Register Tape	Cash Count	Amount of the Change Fund
$856	$1,057	$200

So Randall deposits $857, which we can show by T accounts this way.

Cash		Sales		Cash Short and Over
+	−	−	+	1
857			856	

Now let's draw some conclusions from these illustrations.

1 At the close of the business day, the firm deposits the total day's receipts, retaining the Change Fund.

2 The firm records its sales as being the amount shown on the cash register tape.

3 If the amount of cash actually received disagrees with the record of receipts, Cash Short and Over takes up the difference. In the first situation just described, there was a shortage of $3, so there was a debit to Cash Short and Over. In the second situation, there was an overage of $1, so there was a credit to Cash Short and Over.

It is apparent that the account looks like this.

Cash Short and Over

Shortage 3	Overage 1

Since the Cash Short and Over account is used quite frequently, the accountant may provide for it in the cash receipts journal. Many firms include a Cash Short and Over *debit* column for the shortages and a Cash Short and Over *credit* column for the overages. Here's how North Central Plumbing Supply's cash sales for September 14 and 15 look when recorded in the cash receipts journal.

Cash Receipts Journal

Date	Account Name	Post. Ref.	Sales Credit	Cash Short and Over Debit	Cash Short and Over Credit	Sales Discount Debit	Cash Debit
19__ Sept. 14	Sales		781 00	3 00			778 00
15	Sales		856 00		1 00		857 00

As far as errors are concerned, one would think that shortages would be offset by overages. However, customers are more likely to report shortages than overages. Consequently, shortages predominate. For purposes of internal control, a firm may set a tolerance level for the cashiers; if the shortages consistently exceed the level of tolerance, either there is fraud involved or somebody is making entirely too many careless mistakes.

Throughout any fiscal period, the accountant continually has to record shortages and overages in the Cash Short and Over account. Let's say that North Central's final balance is $21 on the debit side.

So North Central winds up with a net shortage of $21. Therefore, *at the end of the fiscal period, if the final account has a debit balance or net shortage, the accountant classifies it as an expense, and puts it in the income*

statement under Miscellaneous General Expense or Miscellaneous Expense.
The T account would look like this.

Cash Short and Over

Short			Over	
	3		1	
	4		1	
	3		2	
	7		2	
	5		1	
	2		2	
	3		1	
	4		10	
21	31			

Conversely, if the final account has a credit balance or net overage, the accountant classifies it as a revenue account, and puts it in the income statement under Miscellaneous Income. This is an exception to the policy of recording accounts in financial statements under the name of their exact account title. Rather than attaching plus and minus signs to the Cash Short and Over account immediately, we wait until we find out its final balance.

Summary

A business firm has a valuable ally in its bank, because the bank maintains a record of cash which is independent of the firm's record of cash. That is, the bank does this if the business deposits all incoming cash in the bank, and makes all cash payments by check. The only exception to this—and it is a minor one—is the case of transactions involving Petty Cash.

The bank sends its statement accompanied by canceled checks, debit memos, and credit memos. Debit memos cover service and collection charges, as well as NSF checks. Credit memos cover the collection of notes or other items left for collection.

Each month the firm's accountant has to make a reconciliation between the bank account balance and the firm's Cash account balance because some transactions might not have been recorded by either the bank or the depositor, or errors might have been made by either. The steps in reconciling the bank statement are as follows.

1 **Canceled checks** Verify that the amount of each check tallies with the amount listed on the bank statement.
2 **Late deposits** Determine the deposits that the bank has not yet recorded.
3 **Outstanding checks** Determine the checks that the bank has not yet reported as being cashed.
4 **Bank memos** Trace bank memos to the cash receipts journal and cash payments journal to see whether they have been recorded.

Form of Bank Reconciliation (a hypothetical situation)

Bank Statement Balance		$4,000	
Add: Late deposits	$300		Do not
Bank errors	20	320	require
		$4,320	journal
Deduct: Outstanding checks	$960		entries
Bank errors	40	1,000	
Adjusted Balance		$3,320	
(true balance of Cash)			
Book Balance of Cash		$2,850	
Add: Credit memos	$500 ←		
Book errors	40 ←	540	Require
		$3,390	journal
Deduct: Debit memos	$ 20 ←		entries
Book errors	50 ←	70	
Adjusted Balance		$3,320	
(true balance of Cash)			

In this chapter, we discussed two special funds: the Petty Cash Fund and the Change Fund. A fund, in every case, is a separate kitty of cash. When one establishes a fund, one makes a check payable to the particular fund, then cashes it, and converts it into convenient denominations. The original entry in each case is a debit to the fund account and a credit to Cash. The journal entry to reimburse Petty Cash is a debit to the accounts for which the money was expended (as shown by the petty cash payments record or a summary of the petty cash vouchers) and a credit to Cash. The Petty Cash Fund account is debited only at the time it is established, and remains at the same level, unless the firm decides to change the account's size. Whenever a firm makes a bank deposit, it holds back the amount of the Change Fund and converts it into the proper change.

The Cash Short and Over account takes care of errors in making change. A debit to Cash Short and Over denotes a shortage; a credit to Cash Short and Over denotes an overage.

Glossary

o **ABA number** The number assigned by the American Bankers Association to a given bank. The first part of the numerator denotes the city or state in which the bank is located; the second part denotes the bank on which the check is drawn. The denominator indicates the Federal Reserve District and the routing number used by the Federal Reserve Bank.

o **Bank reconciliation** A process by which an accountant determines whether there is a difference between the balance as shown on the bank statement and the balance of the Cash account in the firm's general ledger. The object is to determine the adjusted (or true) balance of the Cash account.

- **Bank statement** Periodic statement which a bank sends to the holder of a checking account listing deposits received and checks paid by the bank, as well as debit and credit memorandums.
- **Canceled checks** Checks issued by the depositor that have been paid by the bank and listed on the bank statement. They are called canceled checks because they are canceled by a stamp or perforation, indicating that they have been paid.
- **Cash fund** A sum of money set aside for a specific purpose.
- **Change Fund** A cash fund used by a firm to make change for customers who pay cash for goods or services.
- **Deposit slip** A printed form provided by a bank so that a customer can list in detail all the items being deposited; also known as a *deposit ticket.*
- **Endorsement** The process by which the payee (party to whom the check is made payable) transfers ownership of the check to a bank or another party. A check must be endorsed when deposited in a bank because the bank must have legal title to it in order to collect payment from the drawer of the check (the person or firm who wrote the check). In case the check cannot be collected, the endorser guarantees all subsequent holders (*Exception:* an endorsement ''without recourse'').
- **Late deposit** Deposit not recorded on the bank statement because the deposit was made between the time of the bank's closing date for compiling items for its statement and the time the statement is received by the depositor; also known as a *deposit in transit.*
- **MICR** Magnetic ink character recognition, the script the bank uses to print the number of the depositor's account and the bank's number at the bottom of checks and deposit slips. A number written in this script can be read by electronic equipment used by banks in clearing checks.
- **Monetary denominations** Varieties of currency and coins, such as $5 bills, $1 bills, quarters, dimes, nickels, etc.
- **NSF check** A check drawn against an account in which there are *Not Sufficient Funds;* this check is returned by the depositor's bank to the drawer's bank because of nonpayment; also known as a *dishonored check.*
- **Outstanding checks** Checks which have been issued by the depositor and deducted on his/her records, but which have not reached the bank for payment and deduction by the time the bank issues its statement.
- **Petty Cash Fund** A cash fund used to make small immediate cash payments.
- **Petty cash payments record** A record indicating the amount of each petty cash voucher, and the accounts to which they are to be charged.
- **Petty cash voucher** A form stating who got what from the Petty Cash Fund, signed by (1) the person in charge of the fund, and (2) the person who received the cash.
- **Service charge** The fee the bank charges for handling checks, collections, and other items. It is in the form of a debit memorandum.
- **Signature card** The form a depositor signs to give the bank a sample of his/her signature. The bank uses it to verify the depositor's signature on checks, on cash items that he or she may endorse for deposit, and on other business papers that he or she may present to the bank.

Exercise 1 The Highline Hardware Company made the following bank reconciliation on April 30 of this year. Record the necessary entries in general journal form.

Bank Reconciliation		
Bank Statement Balance		$1,856.00
Add: Deposit of April 30		145.00
		$2,001.00
Deduct: Outstanding checks		
No. 191	$200.00	
No. 192	150.00	350.00
Adjusted Balance		$1,651.00
Book Balance of Cash		$1,380.00
Add: Proceeds of note collected		300.00
		$1,680.00
Deduct: NSF check of Thomas Bacon	$ 27.00	
Collection charge for note	2.00	29.00
Adjusted Balance		$1,651.00

Exercise 2 Pedro's Taco Shop deposits all receipts in the bank on the day received and makes all payments by check. On September 30, the Cash account showed a balance of $443 after all posting was completed. The bank statement received on September 30 had an ending balance of $301. Prepare a bank reconciliation, using the following information, and record the necessary entries in general journal form.

a The bank included with the September canceled checks a $2 debit memorandum for service charges.

b Outstanding checks, $194.

c The September 30 cash receipts, $316, were placed in the bank's night depository after banking hours on that date, and were not listed on the bank statement.

d Check no. 928, returned with the canceled checks, was correctly drawn for $31 in payment of the electric bill, and was paid by the bank on September 16, but it had been erroneously recorded in the check register and debited to the Utilities Expense account as though it were for $13.

Exercise 3 Nite and Day Diner calls you in as an accountant. Prepare a bank reconciliation for them, given the following information about their bank account for March, and record the necessary entries in general journal form.

a Balance of the Cash account in the general ledger, $1,408.83.

b Last balance shown on bank statement, $1,277.67.

c Service charge levied by bank appearing on debit memo, $4.16.

d Deposit put in night depository on last day of the month, not recorded on bank statement, $127.

Exercise 4 Pauline B. Biehler's bank account for May of this year indicates a balance of $915.30 on May 31. Her bank balance according to her check stubs on that date is $593. A comparison of the bank statement, canceled checks, and the memorandums with the check stubs reveals the following.

Prepare a bank reconciliation.

a Checks outstanding, $45.

b A deposit of $136 had been recorded twice in her check record.

c Biehler made a deposit of $416 on May 11, but forgot to record it in her check record.

d The bank deducted $2.70 for service charges; Biehler had not recorded it in her check record.

Exercise 5 Make entries in general journal form to record the following.

a Established a Petty Cash Fund, $80.

b Reimbursed the Petty Cash Fund for expenditures of $69: store supplies, $21; office supplies, $18; miscellaneous expense, $30.

Exercise 6 Make entries in general journal form to record the following.

a Established a Change Fund, $250.

b Record the cash sales for the day; the cash in the cash register is $862.

Exercise 7 The cash register tape for today indicates $961.16 as sales for the day. The cash count, including a $200 Change Fund, is $1,160.22. Make entries to record how much cash you will deposit in the bank today.

Exercise 8 Describe the nature of the entries that have been posted to the following accounts after the Change Fund was established.

Change Fund		Sales		Cash	
Bal. 200			946	944	
			998	999	
			1,069	1,066	

Cash Short and Over	
2	1
3	

Problems

Problem 13-1 The Tall Men's Fashion Shop deposits all receipts in the bank each evening and makes all payments by check. On November 30 its Cash in Bank account has a balance of $1,967.65. The bank statement of November 30 shows a balance of $1,920.25. The following information pertains to reconciling the bank statement.

a The reconciliation for October, the previous month, showed three checks outstanding on October 31: no. 1416 for $85, no. 1419 for $76.50, and no. 1420 for $126. Checks no. 1416 and 1420 were returned with the November bank statement; however, check no. 1419 was not returned.

b Checks no. 1499 for $39, no. 1516 for $21.60, no. 1517 for $101.50, and no. 1518 for $17 were written during November and have not been returned by the bank.

c A deposit of $410 was placed in the night depository on November 30 and did not appear on the bank statement.

d The canceled checks were compared with the entries in the check register, and it was observed that check no. 1487, for $78, was written correctly, payable to C. T. Hansen, the owner, for personal use, but was recorded in the check register as $87.

e A bank debit memo for service charges, $3.

f A bank credit memo for collection of a note signed by T. R. Pringle, $101, including $100 principal and $1 interest.

Instructions

1 Prepare a bank reconciliation.

2 Journalize the necessary entries in general journal form, assuming that the debit and credit memos have not been recorded.

Problem 13-2 On July 31 Powell's Gift Shop prepared its bank reconciliation, with three outstanding checks: no. 912 for $172, no. 918 for $76, and no. 919 for $146. The company deposits its receipts in the bank and makes all payments by check. The Paragon National Bank sent Powell's Gift Shop the following statement. (The debit memo for $49 is for an NSF check written by C. D. Carter. The debit memo for $2 is for a service charge.)

Paragon National Bank

Powell's Gift Shop
2164 N.E. Harding Ave.
Toledo, Ohio

Account no.: 167-616-218
Statement date: August 31, 19____

Checks and Other Debits		Deposits	Date		Balance
	Balance Brought Forward		Aug.	1	972 00
		326 00		2	1,298 00
172 00	76 00			4	1,050 00
146 00		412 00		5	1,316 00
206 00	139 00			7	971 00
200 00				8	771 00
621 00		437 00		9	587 00
		368 00		14	955 00
37 00	14 00			17	904 00
		419 00		18	1,323 00
183 00	350 00			23	790 00
		398 00		24	1,188 00
94 00		291 00		28	1,385 00
DM 49 00	DM 2 00			31	1,334 00

Powell's Gift Shop's partial cash receipts journal and check register are as shown at the top of the next page.

Powell's Gift Shop's Cash in Bank account in the general ledger appears directly below them.

Instructions

1 Prepare a bank reconciliation as of August 31.

2 Journalize the entries in general journal form, assuming that the debit memos have not been recorded.

Cash Receipts Journal			Page 5
		Cash in Bank	
Date		Debit	
19__			
Aug.	2	326 00	
	5	412 00	
	9	437 00	
	14	368 00	
	18	419 00	
	24	398 00	
	28	291 00	
	31	224 00	
	31	2,875 00	

Check Register			Page 9
		Ck.	Cash in Bank
Date		No.	Credit
19__			
Aug.	2	920	206 00
	3	921	139 00
	3	922	200 00
	6	923	621 00
	12	924	37 00
	13	925	14 00
	19	926	183 00
	19	927	350 00
	26	928	94 00
	27	929	119 00
	30	930	57 00
	30	931	186 00
	31		2,206 00

Cash in Bank						Account No. 111	
			Post.			Balance	
Date		Item	Ref.	Debit	Credit	Debit	Credit
19__							
July	31	Balance	✓			578 00	
Aug.	31		CR5	2,875 00		3,453 00	
	31		CkR9		2,206 00	1,247 00	

Problem 13-3 On March 1 of this year, Nolan Janitorial Supply Company established a Petty Cash Fund. The following petty cash transactions took place during the month.

Mar. 1	Cashed check no. 956 for $50 to establish a Petty Cash Fund, and put the $50 in a locked drawer in the office.
3	Bought postage stamps, $4, voucher no. 1 (Office Supplies).
4	Issued voucher no. 2 for telegram, $2 (Miscellaneous General Expense).
6	Issued voucher no. 3 for delivery charges on outgoing merchandise, $5.
9	B. W. Nolan withdrew $4.50 for personal use, voucher no. 4.
13	Bought postage stamps, $5, voucher no. 5.
19	Bought pens for office, $4.90, voucher no. 6.
23	Paid $3 for trash removal, voucher no. 7 (Miscellaneous General Expense).
28	Paid $5 for window cleaning service, voucher no. 8.
29	Paid $1.50 for telegram, voucher no. 9.
31	Issued and cashed check no. 1098 for $34.90 to reimburse Petty Cash Fund.

Instructions
1 Journalize the entry establishing the Petty Cash Fund in the cash payments journal.
2 Record the disbursements of petty cash in the petty cash payments record.
3 Journalize the summarizing entry to reimburse the Petty Cash Fund.

Problem 13-4 The Olson Beach Side Grocery made the following transactions during July involving its Change Fund, Cash Short and Over, and its cash sales.

July	1	Established a Change Fund, $300, check no. 986.
	7	Recorded cash sales for the week: cash register tape, $1,546; cash count $1,842.35.
	14	Recorded cash sales for the week: cash register tape, $1,214.10; cash count, $1,511.
	21	Recorded cash sales for the week: cash register tape, $1,482; cash count $1,783.25.
	31	Recorded cash sales for the remainder of the month: cash register tape, $1,892; cash count $2,188.50.

Instructions

1 Record the entry establishing the Change Fund in the cash payments journal.
2 Record the cash sales in the cash receipts journal. In making bank deposits, the firm holds back the amount of the Change Fund.
3 Post the appropriate entries to the Cash Short and Over ledger account. Where will the balance of this account appear in the income statement?

Problem 13-1A The Pink Daisy Fashion Shop deposits all receipts in the bank and makes all payments by check. On September 30 its Cash in Bank account has a balance of $3,073.60. The bank statement on September 30 shows a balance of $3,321.29. You are given the following information with which to reconcile the bank statement.

a The reconciliation for August, the previous month, showed three checks outstanding on August 31: no. 786 for $71.50, no. 789 for $117.60, and no. 790 for $49.43. Checks no. 786 and 789 were returned with the September bank statement; however, check no. 790 was not returned.
b A deposit of $398.36 was placed in the night depository on September 30 and did not appear on the bank statement.
c Checks no. 801 for $31, no. 803 for $18.40, no. 804 for $103, and no. 805 for $15.62 were written during September, but were not returned by the bank.
d A bank debit memo for service charges, $2.40.
e A bank credit memo for collection of a note signed by Franklin C. Hough, $404, including $400 principal and $4 interest.
f You compare the canceled checks with the entries in the check register, and find that check no. 797 for $69 was written correctly, payable to M. E. Francis, the owner, for her personal use. However, the check was recorded in the check register as $96.

Instructions

1 Prepare a bank reconciliation.
2 Journalize the necessary entries in general journal form, assuming that the debit and credit memos have not been recorded.

Problem 13-2A On June 30, Buchanan Auto Supply prepared its bank reconciliation with three outstanding checks: no. 1611 for $167, no. 1619 for $72.50, and no. 1620 for $137.20. The company, which deposits its receipts in the bank and makes all payments by check, receives the following statement from the Central National Bank. The debit memo for $37 is for an NSF check written by Thomas R. Keeler. The debit memo for $3.10 is for a service charge.

Central National Bank

Buchanan Auto Supply
8619 East Castle Blvd.
Chicago, Illinois 60611

Account no.: 761-142-786
Statement date: July 31, 19___

Checks and Other Debits		Deposits	Date		Balance
	Balance Brought Forward		July	1	1,163 16
72 50	167 00	491 50		3	1,415 16
137 20				5	1,277 96
236 25	159 89	415 72		6	1,297 54
120 00				8	1,177 54
429 60		439 16		9	1,187 10
		378 20		11	1,565 30
37 40	38 49			12	1,489 41
		291 76		15	1,781 17
182 71	368 70			17	1,229 76
96 87		142 90		18	1,275 79
DM 37 00				22	1,238 79
19 20				25	1,219 59
DM 3 10		368 93		28	1,585 42

A partial cash receipts journal and check register for Buchanan Auto Supply are as follows.

Cash Receipts Journal		Page 5	Check Register		Page 9
		Cash in Bank		Ck.	Cash in Bank
Date		Debit	Date	No.	Credit
19___			19___		
July 3		491 50	July 1	1621	236 25
6		415 72	2	1622	159 89
9		439 16	5	1623	429 60
12		378 20	5	1624	120 00
15		291 76	9	1625	38 49
18		142 90	9	1626	37 40
28		368 93	14	1627	182 71
30		165 69	15	1628	368 70
31		2,693 86	16	1629	96 87
			23	1630	19 20
			28	1631	110 00
			29	1632	71 19
			29	1633	163 20
			31		2,033 50

The Cash in Bank account in the general ledger appears at the top of the next page.

Instructions

1 Prepare a bank reconciliation as of July 31.

2 Journalize the entries in general journal form, assuming that the debit memos have not been recorded.

Cash in Bank							Account No. 111	
		Post.				Balance		
Date	Item	Ref.	Debit		Credit		Debit	Credit
19__								
June 30	Balance	✓					786 46	
July 31		CR5	2,693 86				3,480 32	
31		CkR9			2,033 50		1,446 82	

Problem 13-3A On April 1 of this year, the Alpine Ski Shop established a Petty Cash Fund, and the following petty cash transactions took place during the month.

Apr. 1 | Cashed check no. 1116 for $60 to establish a Petty Cash Fund, and put the $60 in a locked drawer in the office.
4 | Issued voucher no. 1 for telegram, $3 (Miscellaneous General Expense).
7 | Issued voucher no. 2 for typewriter ribbons, $4.90.
9 | Paid $4.50 for an advertisement in college basketball program, voucher no. 3.
16 | Bought postage stamps, $4, voucher no. 4 (Office Supplies).
20 | Paid $4.90 to have snow removed from sidewalk in front of store, voucher no. 5 (Miscellaneous General Expense).
25 | Issued voucher no. 6 for delivery charge on outgoing merchandise, $2.40.
28 | A. G. Coleman, the owner, withdrew $5 for personal use, voucher no. 7.
29 | Paid $1.60 for telegram, voucher no. 8.
30 | Paid Reliable Delivery Service $4.20 for delivery charges on outgoing merchandise, voucher no. 9.
30 | Issued and cashed check no. 1304 for $34.50 to reimburse Petty Cash Fund.

Instructions

1 Journalize the entry establishing the Petty Cash Fund in the cash payments journal.
2 Record the disbursements of petty cash in the petty cash payments record.
3 Journalize the summarizing entry to reimburse the Petty Cash Fund.

Problem 13-4A During May of this year, the Northside Cycle Shop has the following transactions involving its Change Fund, Cash Short and Over, and its cash sales.

May 1 | Established a Change Fund, $200, check no. 714.
6 | Recorded cash sales for the week: cash register tape, $1,291; cash count, $1,490.25.
13 | Recorded cash sales for the week: cash register tape, $1,424.30; cash count, $1,622.10.
20 | Recorded cash sales for the week: cash register tape, $1,378.25; cash count, $1,579.15.

| May 31 | Recorded cash sales for the week: cash register tape, $1,813.28; cash count, $2,009.74. |

Instructions
1 Record the entry establishing the Change Fund in the cash payments journal.
2 Record the cash sales in the cash receipts journal. (When Northside Cycle Shop makes deposits, it holds back the amount of the Change Fund.)
3 Post the appropriate entries to the Cash Short and Over ledger account. Where will the balance of this account appear in the income statement?

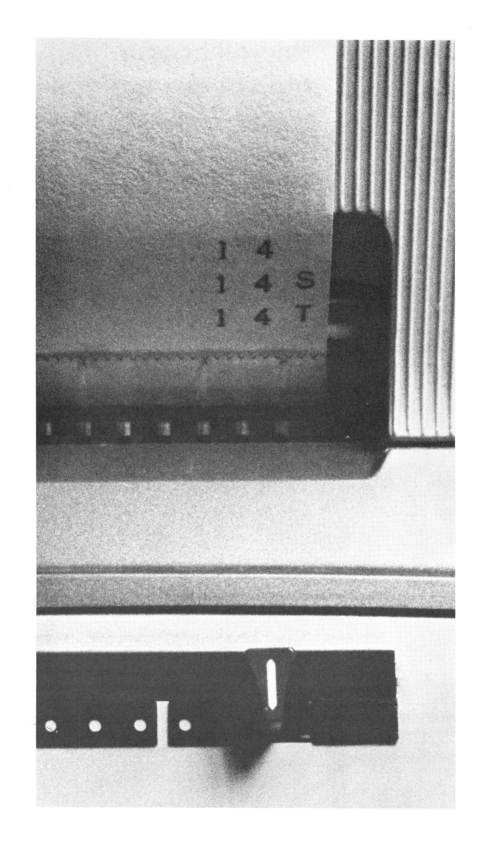

14 Payroll accounting: employee earnings and deductions

Said the employee collecting his paycheck: "Actually, I wouldn't mind Uncle Sam's tax bite—if he didn't come back for dessert." Anonymous

Introduction

Up to now, we've been recording employees' wages as a debit to Salaries or Wages Expense and a credit to Cash, and we've really been talking only about gross pay. We haven't said a word about the various deductions that we all know are taken out of our gross pay before we get to the net amount, or take-home pay. In this chapter we'll be dealing with types and amounts of deductions and how to enter them in payroll records, as well as journal entries for recording the payroll and paying the employees.

Objectives of payroll records and accounting

First we need to compute the total compensation for employees; for example, do they work on a wage or on a commission basis?

Next we must provide information needed for completing the various government reports—federal and state—that are required of all employers. Before the passage of the Social Security Act of 1936, there was no withholding tax, and paying employees was relatively simple. Now the law requires all business enterprises, both large and small, to withhold certain amounts from employees' pay for taxes, to make payments to government agencies by specified deadlines, and to submit reports on official forms. The governments impose penalties if the requirements are not met. So naturally employers are vitally concerned with payroll accounting, and anyone going into accounting, or involved with the management of any business, should be thoroughly acquainted with payroll accounting. To provide the necessary background, let's look at the laws affecting payroll accounting.

Employer/employee relationships

Payroll accounting is concerned only with employees and their compensations, withholdings, records, reports, and taxes. *Note:* There is a distinction between an employee and an independent contractor. An *employee* is one who is under the direction and control of the employer, such as a secretary, bookkeeper, sales clerk, etc. An *independent contractor,* on the other hand, is one who is engaged to do a definite job or service, and she or he may choose her/his own means of doing the work (*Examples:* an appliance repair person, a plumber, a CPA firm). Payments made to independent contractors are in the form of fees or charges, and they are billed in one lump sum; consequently they are not subject to any withholding or payroll taxes.

Laws affecting compensation of employees

Both federal and state laws require that the employer act as a collecting agent, deducting specified amounts from employees' gross earnings and sending the withholdings to the appropriate government agencies, along with reports substantiating the figures. In addition, there are certain payroll taxes to be paid by the employer, based on the total wages paid to employees.

Let's look at some of the more important laws that pertain to compensation of employees.

Federal income tax withholding

The withholding tax came into existence with the Current Tax Payment Act of 1943. The act requires not only that the employer withhold the tax and then pay it to the Internal Revenue Service, but also that employers keep records of the names and addresses of persons employed, their earnings and withholdings, and the amounts and dates of payment. The employer has to submit reports to the Internal Revenue Service on a quarterly basis (Form 941) and to the employee on an annual basis (W-2 form). With few exceptions, this requirement applies to employers of one or more persons. We'll discuss these reports and the related deposits in Chapter 15.

Federal Insurance Contributions Act (FICA)

This act, passed in 1935, provides for retirement pensions after a worker reaches age 62, disability benefits for any worker who becomes disabled (and for her or his dependents), and a health insurance program or Medicare after age 65. Both the employee and the employer have to pay FICA, or Social Security, taxes. The employer withholds FICA taxes from employees' wages and pays them to the Internal Revenue Service. The employer has to match the amount of FICA tax withheld from the employees' wages, and the employer's share is recorded under Payroll Tax Expense. We'll cover this in Chapter 15, as our concern here is with employees' deductions.

FICA tax rates apply to the gross earnings of an employee during the calendar year. After an employee has paid FICA tax on the maximum taxable earnings, the employer stops deducting FICA tax until the next calendar year begins. Congress has frequently changed the schedule of rates and taxable incomes, and undoubtedly will change it again in the future. The following table shows recent FICA tax rates.

Years	Tax on Employees, %	Tax on Employers, %	Maximum Taxable Income of Employees
1970	4.8	4.8	$ 7,800
1971	5.2	5.2	7,800
1972	5.85	5.85	9,000
1973	5.85	5.85	10,800
1974	5.85	5.85	13,200
1975	5.85	5.85	14,100
1976	5.85	5.85	15,300

The employer is required to keep records of the following information.
1 **Personal data on employee:** name, address, Social Security number, date of birth
2 **Data on wage payments:** dates and amounts of payments, and payroll periods
3 **Amount of taxable wages paid:** total amount earned so far during the year
4 **Amount of tax withheld from each employee's earnings**

Each quarter the employer has to submit reports to the Internal Revenue Service, recording the information on Form 941, the same form that is used to report the income tax withheld. The payment that the employer makes to the Internal Revenue Service consists of (1) the employee's share of the FICA tax, (2) the employer's matching portion of the FICA tax, and (3) the employee's income tax withheld. We'll talk about this in detail in Chapter 15.

Fair Labor Standards Act	The Fair Labor Standards Act, passed in 1938 and commonly known as the *Wages and Hours Law,* controls wages paid by employers engaged either directly or indirectly in interstate commerce. It establishes a minimum wage; in other words, it sets a floor under wages. It also establishes maximum hours a person may work; in other words, it sets a ceiling over hours. The minimum wage is $2.10 per hour ($2 for firms having a gross volume of business less than $200,000); this minimum is scheduled to increase. The maximum time to be worked per week is 40 hours. This means that a worker must be paid straight time for the first 40 hours, plus an overtime premium for hours worked in excess of 40. The overtime premium is at least half the regular rate, so that the rate for overtime work is usually expressed as *time-and-a-half.*

Over the years Congress has passed many amendments to the Fair Labor Standards Act, changes which have mainly involved increasing the minimum wage and extending the coverage to many groups of workers previously uncovered. The amendments of 1966 brought 8 million additional workers under the act, including farmhands, hospital orderlies, waiters and waitresses, and school janitors. For these newly covered workers, the minimum wage is increased on a sliding basis, until it gets up to the prevailing legal level for all workers.

Some businesses—such as hotels, motels, and restaurants—have maximum hours of 44 rather than 40 per week. Certain employees are also exempt: high-level administrative employees, the immediate family of a farmer, etc.

The Fair Labor Standards Act also includes child-labor restrictions: Children who are below a certain age cannot be hired to work in specified industries. Another amendment to the Fair Labor Standards Act is the Equal Pay Law of 1964, which says that an employer can't pay employees of one sex less than is paid to employees of the opposite sex for equal work on jobs that require equal skill, effort, and responsibility, and that are performed under similar conditions. There are certain exceptions to this, arising from differences based on a seniority system, a merit system, and a production system.

It's not just the federal government that has minimum-wage laws. Most states have them too. If an employee is covered by both federal and state regulations, then the higher rate prevails.

An employer is not required to submit specific reports about the following (but does have to keep records containing such information): personal data on employee, description of job, and earnings data (at straight time and at overtime).

Civil Rights Act of 1964	The Civil Rights Act forbids an employer from discriminating against anyone in hiring, firing, promoting, or imposing any other terms or conditions of employment on the basis of race, color, religion, sex, or national origin. Similar laws forbidding such discrimination have also been passed by more

than half the states, to apply where the federal government has no juris-
diction.

Employment Act of 1967

The Employment Act of 1967 forbids an employer to discriminate against
anyone on the basis of age. This law is intended generally to protect people
between 40 and 65. It is implied in this act, as well as in the Civil Rights
Act, that employers should keep detailed personnel and payroll records,
including employment applications, notations concerning their disposition,
job descriptions, copies of employment tests, seniority plans, merit systems,
etc.

Federal Unemployment Tax Act (FUTA)

The Federal Unemployment Tax Act is part of the original Social Security program, and like FICA is incorporated in the Internal Revenue Code.
The purpose of the act is to provide a pool of funds so that workers laid
off their jobs can collect enough benefits to live on. This tax is levied on
employers only, and they must pay these unemployment taxes to both the
federal and the state governments. The tax paid to the federal government
takes care of federal and state administrative expenses. The unemployment
taxes paid to the state government can be used as a deduction against the
federal unemployment tax. Beginning in 1972, for purposes of paying
unemployment taxes, a *qualified employer* is defined as one who employed
one or more persons for each of 20 different weeks within the calendar year
or the preceding year, or as one who had a payroll of $1,500 or more in
any quarter of the year.

Employers have to pay a federal unemployment tax of 3.2% on the first
$4,200 of wages paid to each employee during the calendar year. They may
deduct the amount they have paid in state unemployment taxes up to 2.7%
on the first $4,200 of wages paid to each employee during the calendar year.
When the employer is entitled to make the full deduction, then the effective
federal unemployment tax rate is .5% on the first $4,200 of wages paid
to each employee (3.2% − 2.7% = .5%). Reports must be submitted
annually, by January 31 of the year following the preceding calendar year.
We'll discuss these payments in Chapter 15.

State unemployment taxes

Each state is responsible for paying its own unemployment compensation
benefits. The revenue provided by the state unemployment tax is used
exclusively for this purpose.

However, there is considerable variation among the states. During recent
years, there has been a trend toward higher unemployment benefits; many
states have adopted an unemployment tax base of at least $4,200 and rates
of 2.7% or higher. They have also introduced amendments to take advantage
of the Federal Extended Benefits Program. The latter extends the payment
of unemployment benefits from 26 to 30 weeks beyond the normal period.

States require employers to file reports on a quarterly or 3-month basis, listing the names and amount of wages paid to each employee and a computation of the unemployment tax. As a substitute for the official state report form, many states permit employers to use Schedule A of Form 941, the Quarterly Report of Wages Taxable under FICA. Employers must pay the tax to the state at the time they submit the report.

Workmen's compensation laws

Workmen's compensation laws protect the employee and dependents against losses due to the employee's death or injury incurred on the job. Most states have laws requiring employers either to contribute to a state compensation insurance fund or to buy similar insurance from a private insurance company. The employer ordinarily pays the cost of the insurance premiums. The premium rates vary according to the degree of danger inherent in each job category. The employer has to keep records of job descriptions and classifications, as well as claims of insured persons.

State and city income taxes

Two-thirds of the states—besides requiring employers to deduct money from employees' earnings for federal income taxes—require employers to deduct money to pay state income taxes. A number of cities also require withholding for *city* income taxes. When these laws are in effect, the employer handles the reporting and payments in much the same manner as federal income taxes.

How employees get paid

Employees may be paid a salary or wages, depending on the type of work and the period of time covered. Money paid to a person for managerial or administrative services is usually called a salary, and the time period covered is generally a month or a year. Money paid for either skilled or unskilled labor is usually called wages, and the time period covered is hours or weeks. Wages may also be paid on a piecework basis. In practice, the words *salaries* and *wages* are somewhat interchangeable. A company may supplement an employee's salary or wage by commissions, bonuses, cost-of-living adjustments, and profit-sharing plans. As a rule, an employee is paid in the form of a check or cash. However, he or she may also be compensated in the form of merchandise, lodging, meals, or other property. When the compensation is in these forms, one has to determine the fair value of property or service given in payment for the employee's labor.

Calculating total earnings

When compensation is based on the passage of time, the accountant of course has to have a record of the number of hours worked by each employee. When there are only a few employees, this can be accomplished by means of a book record. When there are many employees, time clocks are the traditional method. Nowadays, for computer-operated time-keeping systems, employers use punched cards.

Wages

Let's take the case of Ronald R. Jones, who works for North Central Plumbing Supply. His regular rate of pay is $4 per hour. The company pays time-and-a-half for hours worked in excess of 40. In addition, it pays him double time for any work he does on Sundays and holidays. Jones's time card for the week looks something like this. He has a ½-hour lunch break during an 8½-hour day.

Time Card

Name: Jones, Ronald R.
Period: Nov. 1–7, 19___

Day	In	Out	Hours Worked Regular	Overtime
M	7:57	4:32	8	
T	7:56	4:37	8	
W	7:57	4:31	8	
T	8:00	6:32	8	2
F	8:00	5:33	8	1
S	7:59	1:02		5
S	7:55	12:04		4

Jones's gross wages are computed by one of two methods. The first method is as follows.

40 hours at straight time:	40 × $4 per hour =	$160
2 hours overtime on Thursday:	2 × $6 per hour =	12
1 hour overtime on Friday:	1 × $6 per hour =	6
5 hours overtime on Saturday:	5 × $6 per hour =	30
4 hours overtime on Sunday:	4 × $8 per hour =	32
Total gross wages		$240

The second method of calculating gross wages is often used when machine accounting is involved.

52 hours at straight time: 52 × $4 per hour = $208
Overtime premium
8 hours × $2 per hour premium = $16
4 hours × $4 per hour premium = $16

Total overtime premium	32
Total gross wages	$240

Salaries

Employees who are paid on a regular salary basis are often also entitled to premium pay for overtime. Thus you have to figure out their regular hourly rate of pay before you determine their overtime rate. For example, let's consider the case of Donna Slocum, who gets a salary of $860 per month. She is entitled to overtime pay for all hours worked in excess of 40 during a week at the rate of 1½ times her regular hourly rate. This past week she worked 44 hours, so we calculate her overtime pay as follows.

$860 per month $\times$ 12 months = $10,320 per year
$10,320 per year $\div$ 52 weeks = $198.46 per week
$198.46 per week $\div$ 40 hours = $4.9615 per regular hour

Earnings for 44 hours

40 hours at straight time:	40 $\times$ $4.9615	= $198.46
4 hours overtime:	4 $\times$ $7.44225 =	29.77
Total gross earnings		$228.23

Piece rate

Workers under the piece-rate system are paid at the rate of so much per unit of production. For example, Peter Ryan, an apple picker, gets paid $4.80 for picking a bin of apples. If he picks 6 bins during the day, his total earnings are 6 $\times$ $4.80 = $28.80.

Commissions and bonuses

Some salespersons are paid on a purely commission basis. However, a more common arrangement is a salary plus a commission or bonus. Assume that Rosie Perkins receives an annual salary of $9,600. Her employer agrees to pay her a 6% commission on all sales during the year in excess of $120,000. Her sales for the year total $140,000. Her bonus amounts to $20,000 $\times$ 6% = $1,200. Therefore her total earnings are $9,600 + $1,200 = $10,800.

Deductions from total earnings

Anyone who has ever earned a paycheck has had experience with the many types of deductions that account for the shrinkage. The most usual deductions are due to the following.

1 Federal income tax withholding
2 State income tax withholding
3 FICA tax (Social Security), employee's share
4 Purchase of United States savings bonds
5 Union dues
6 Hospital and life insurance premiums
7 Contributions to a charitable organization
8 Repayment of personal loans from the company credit union
9 Savings through the company credit union

Employees' federal income tax withholding

The amount of federal income tax withheld from an employee's wages depends on the amount of her or his total earnings and the number of exemptions claimed. Each exemption excludes $750 from the employee's taxable income for the year. An employee is entitled to one personal exemption, plus an additional exemption if he or she is over 65 or blind, and an exemption for each dependent. Each employee has to fill out, for the employer, an Employee's Withholding Allowance Certificate (Form W-4). See the illustration on page 360.

Employee's Withholding Allowance Certificate

The explanatory material below will help you determine your correct number of withholding allowances, and will assist you in completing the Form W–4 at the bottom of this page.

How Many Withholding Allowances May You Claim?

Please use the schedule below to determine the number of allowances you may claim for tax withholding purposes. In determining the number, keep in mind these points: If you are single and hold more than one job, you may not claim the same allowances with more than one employer at the same time; or if you are married and both you and your spouse are employed, you may not claim the same allowances with your employers at the same time. A nonresident alien, other than a resident of Canada, Mexico, or Puerto Rico, may claim only one personal allowance.

Figure Your Total Withholding Allowances Below

(a) Allowance for yourself—enter 1	1
(b) Allowance for your spouse—enter 1	1
(c) Allowance for your age—if 65 or over—enter 1	
(d) Allowance for your spouse's age—if 65 or over—enter 1	
(e) Allowance for blindness (yourself)—enter 1	
(f) Allowance for blindness (spouse's)—enter 1	
(g) Allowance(s) for dependent(s)—you are entitled to claim an allowance for each dependent you will be able to claim on your Federal income tax return. Do not include yourself or your spouse °	1
(h) Special withholding allowance—if you are single with only one employer, or married with only one employer and your spouse is not employed—enter 1°°	
(i) Allowance(s) for itemized deductions—if you do plan to itemize deductions on your income tax return, enter the number from the table on back°°	
(j) Total—add lines (a) through (i) above. Enter here and on line 1, Form W–4 below	3

* If you are in doubt as to whom you may claim as a dependent, see the instructions which came with your last Federal income tax return or call your local Internal Revenue Service office.
** This allowance is used solely for purposes of figuring your withholding tax, and cannot be claimed when you file your tax return.

See Table on Back if You Plan to Itemize Your Deductions

Completing Form W–4.—If you find that you are entitled to one or more allowances in addition to those which you are now claiming, increase your number of allowances by completing the form below and filing it with your employer. If the number of allowances you previously claimed decreases, you must file a new Form W–4 within 10 days. (Should you expect to owe more tax than will be withheld, you may use the same form to increase your withholding by claiming fewer or "0" allowances on line 1, or by asking for additional withholding on line 2, or both.)

▼ **Give the bottom part of this form to your employer; keep the upper part for your records and information** ▼

- Cut along this line -

Form **W-4** Department of the Treasury Internal Revenue Service	## Employee's Withholding Allowance Certificate (This certificate is for income tax withholding purposes only; it will remain in effect until you change it.)	
Type or print your full name Ronald R. Jones		Your social security number 543-24-1680
Home address (Number and street or rural route) 1620 West Seattle Way		Marital status ☐ Single ☒ Married (If married but legally separated, or spouse is a nonresident alien, check the single block.)
City or town, State and ZIP code Seattle, Washington 98116		

1 Total number of allowances you are claiming . . . . 　3

2 Additional amount, if any, you want deducted from each pay (if your employer agrees) . . . . $

I certify that to the best of my knowledge and belief, the number of withholding allowances claimed on this certificate does not exceed the number to which I am entitled.

Signature ▶ *Ronald R. Jones*　　　　　　　　Date ▶ *February 1*　, 19—

The employer retains this form, as authorization to withhold money for the employee's federal income tax.

For convenience, most employers use the Wage Bracket Withholding tables (available from the District Director of Internal Revenue) to determine the amount of federal tax to be withheld for each employee. These tables cover monthly, semimonthly, biweekly, weekly, and daily payroll periods, and are also subdivided on the basis of married and unmarried persons.

In order to determine the tax to be withheld from an employee's gross wages, first locate the wage bracket in the first two columns of the table. Next, find the column for the number of exemptions claimed, and read down this column until you get to the wage bracket line. On page 362 is shown a portion of the weekly federal income tax withholding table for married persons.

Assume that Ronald R. Jones, who claims three exemptions, had $240 gross wages for the week. His wage bracket is $240 to $250. Now, when we follow the three-exemption column, we see that the amount of income tax to be withheld from his wages is $28.40.

Many states that levy state income taxes also furnish employers with withholding tables. Other states use a fixed percentage of the federal income tax as the amount to be withheld for state taxes.

Employees' FICA tax withholding (Social Security)

The District Director of Internal Revenue also provides tables for FICA withholding in the booklet (Bulletin E) which includes the Wage Bracket Withholding tables for federal income tax. These tables cover the same time periods as the income tax tables. You merely follow the same procedure: Locate the wage bracket in the first two columns, and you'll see, on the same horizontal line, the amount of FICA tax to be withheld (see the illustration on page 363).

Let's get back to Ronald R. Jones, who had gross wages of $240 for the week ending November 7. Suppose that the total accumulated gross wages Jones earned prior to this payroll period were $7,834. His total gross wages including this payroll period are $8,074, which is well below the $15,300 assumed maximum taxable income. So we look at the table and see that the FICA tax withheld should be $14.04. Of course, if Jones's gross earnings prior to this payroll period had been greater than $15,300, then there would be no FICA tax deduction.

Payroll register

The payroll register is a form which summarizes the information about employees' wages and salaries for a given payroll period. In the illustration at the top of pages 364–365 we see a payroll register that was prepared to show the data for each employee on a separate line. This would be suitable for a firm with a small number of employees, such as North Central Plumbing Supply.

MARRIED Persons — WEEKLY Payroll Period

And the wages are—		\$0	1	2	3	4	5	6	7	8	9	10 or more
At least	But less than	\$0	1	2	3	4	5	6	7	8	9	10 or more

At least	But less than	0	1	2	3	4	5	6	7	8	9	10 or more
\$0	\$48	\$0	\$0	\$0	\$0	\$0	\$0	\$0	\$0	\$0	\$0	\$0
48	49	.10	0	0	0	0	0	0	0	0	0	0
49	50	.20	0	0	0	0	0	0	0	0	0	0
50	51	.40	0	0	0	0	0	0	0	0	0	0
51	52	.60	0	0	0	0	0	0	0	0	0	0
52	53	.80	0	0	0	0	0	0	0	0	0	0
53	54	.90	0	0	0	0	0	0	0	0	0	0
54	55	1.10	0	0	0	0	0	0	0	0	0	0
55	56	1.30	0	0	0	0	0	0	0	0	0	0
56	57	1.40	0	0	0	0	0	0	0	0	0	0
57	58	1.60	0	0	0	0	0	0	0	0	0	0
58	59	1.80	0	0	0	0	0	0	0	0	0	0
59	60	1.90	0	0	0	0	0	0	0	0	0	0
60	62	2.20	0	0	0	0	0	0	0	0	0	0
62	64	2.50	.10	0	0	0	0	0	0	0	0	0
64	66	2.90	.40	0	0	0	0	0	0	0	0	0
66	68	3.20	.80	0	0	0	0	0	0	0	0	0
68	70	3.60	1.10	0	0	0	0	0	0	0	0	0
70	72	3.90	1.40	0	0	0	0	0	0	0	0	0
72	74	4.20	1.80	0	0	0	0	0	0	0	0	0
74	76	4.60	2.10	0	0	0	0	0	0	0	0	0
76	78	4.90	2.50	0	0	0	0	0	0	0	0	0
78	80	5.30	2.80	.40	0	0	0	0	0	0	0	0
80	82	5.60	3.10	.70	0	0	0	0	0	0	0	0
82	84	5.90	3.50	1.00	0	0	0	0	0	0	0	0
84	86	6.30	3.80	1.40	0	0	0	0	0	0	0	0
86	88	6.60	4.20	1.70	0	0	0	0	0	0	0	0
88	90	7.00	4.50	2.10	0	0	0	0	0	0	0	0
90	92	7.30	4.80	2.40	0	0	0	0	0	0	0	0
92	94	7.60	5.20	2.70	.30	0	0	0	0	0	0	0
94	96	8.00	5.50	3.10	.60	0	0	0	0	0	0	0
96	98	8.30	5.90	3.40	1.00	0	0	0	0	0	0	0
98	100	8.70	6.20	3.80	1.30	0	0	0	0	0	0	0
100	105	9.40	6.80	4.30	1.90	0	0	0	0	0	0	0
105	110	10.40	7.70	5.20	2.70	.30	0	0	0	0	0	0
110	115	11.40	8.60	6.00	3.60	1.10	0	0	0	0	0	0
115	120	12.40	9.60	6.90	4.40	2.00	0	0	0	0	0	0
120	125	13.40	10.60	7.70	5.30	2.80	.40	0	0	0	0	0
125	130	14.40	11.60	8.70	6.10	3.70	1.20	0	0	0	0	0
130	135	15.40	12.60	9.70	7.00	4.50	2.10	0	0	0	0	0
135	140	16.40	13.60	10.70	7.80	5.40	2.90	.50	0	0	0	0
140	145	17.40	14.60	11.70	8.80	6.20	3.80	1.30	0	0	0	0
145	150	18.40	15.60	12.70	9.80	7.10	4.60	2.20	0	0	0	0
150	160	19.90	17.10	14.20	11.30	8.40	5.90	3.50	1.00	0	0	0
160	170	21.90	19.10	16.20	13.30	10.40	7.60	5.20	2.70	.30	0	0
170	180	23.90	21.10	18.20	15.30	12.40	9.50	6.90	4.40	2.00	0	0
180	190	25.60	23.10	20.20	17.30	14.40	11.50	8.60	6.10	3.70	1.20	0
190	200	27.30	24.80	22.20	19.30	16.40	13.50	10.60	7.80	5.40	2.90	.50
200	210	29.00	26.50	24.10	21.30	18.40	15.50	12.60	9.80	7.10	4.60	2.20
210	220	30.70	28.20	25.80	23.30	20.40	17.50	14.60	11.80	8.90	6.30	3.90
220	230	32.40	29.90	27.50	25.00	22.40	19.50	16.60	13.80	10.90	8.00	5.60
230	240	34.10	31.60	29.20	26.70	24.30	21.50	18.60	15.80	12.90	10.00	7.30
240	250	35.80	33.30	30.90	28.40	26.00	23.50	20.60	17.80	14.90	12.00	9.10
250	260	37.50	35.00	32.60	30.10	27.70	25.20	22.60	19.80	16.90	14.00	11.10
260	270	39.20	36.70	34.30	31.80	29.40	26.90	24.50	21.80	18.90	16.00	13.10
270	280	41.70	38.40	36.00	33.50	31.10	28.60	26.20	23.70	20.90	18.00	15.10
280	290	44.20	40.60	37.70	35.20	32.80	30.30	27.90	25.40	22.90	20.00	17.10
290	300	46.70	43.10	39.50	36.90	34.50	32.00	29.60	27.10	24.70	22.00	19.10
300	310	49.20	45.60	42.00	38.60	36.20	33.70	31.30	28.80	26.40	23.90	21.10
310	320	51.70	48.10	44.50	40.90	37.90	35.40	33.00	30.50	28.10	25.60	23.10

Social Security Employee Tax Table

5.85 percent employee tax deductions

Wages At least	But less than	Tax to be withheld	Wages At least	But less than	Tax to be withheld	Wages At least	But less than	Tax to be withheld	Wages At least	But less than	Tax to be withheld
$222.14	$222.31	$13.00	$233.25	$233.42	$13.65	$244.36	$244.53	$14.30	$255.48	$255.65	$14.95
222.31	222.48	13.01	233.42	233.59	13.66	244.53	244.71	14.31	255.65	255.82	14.96
222.48	222.65	13.02	233.59	233.77	13.67	244.71	244.88	14.32	255.82	255.99	14.97
222.65	222.83	13.03	233.77	233.94	13.68	244.88	245.05	14.33	255.99	256.16	14.98
222.83	223.00	13.04	233.94	234.11	13.69	245.05	245.22	14.34	256.16	256.33	14.99
223.00	223.17	13.05	234.11	234.28	13.70	245.22	245.39	14.35	256.33	256.50	15.00
223.17	223.34	13.06	234.28	234.45	13.71	245.39	245.56	14.36	256.50	256.67	15.01
223.34	223.51	13.07	234.45	234.62	13.72	245.56	245.73	14.37	256.67	256.84	15.02
223.51	223.68	13.08	234.62	234.79	13.73	245.73	245.90	14.38	256.84	257.01	15.03
223.68	223.85	13.09	234.79	234.96	13.74	245.90	246.07	14.39	257.01	257.18	15.04
223.85	224.02	13.10	234.96	235.13	13.75	246.07	246.24	14.40	257.18	257.36	15.05
224.02	224.19	13.11	235.13	235.30	13.76	246.24	246.42	14.41	257.36	257.53	15.06
224.19	224.36	13.12	235.30	235.48	13.77	246.42	246.59	14.42	257.53	257.70	15.07
224.36	224.53	13.13	235.48	235.65	13.78	246.59	246.76	14.43	257.70	257.87	15.08
224.53	224.71	13.14	235.65	235.82	13.79	246.76	246.93	14.44	257.87	258.04	15.09
224.71	224.88	13.15	235.82	235.99	13.80	246.93	247.10	14.45	258.04	258.21	15.10
224.88	225.05	13.16	235.99	236.16	13.81	247.10	247.27	14.46	258.21	258.38	15.11
225.05	225.22	13.17	236.16	236.33	13.82	247.27	247.44	14.47	258.38	258.55	15.12
225.22	225.39	13.18	236.33	236.50	13.83	247.44	247.61	14.48	258.55	258.72	15.13
225.39	225.56	13.19	236.50	236.67	13.84	247.61	247.78	14.49	258.72	258.89	15.14
225.56	225.73	13.20	236.67	236.84	13.85	247.78	247.95	14.50	258.89	259.06	15.15
225.73	225.90	13.21	236.84	237.01	13.86	247.95	248.12	14.51	259.06	259.24	15.16
225.90	226.07	13.22	237.01	237.18	13.87	248.12	248.30	14.52	259.24	259.41	15.17
226.07	226.24	13.23	237.18	237.36	13.88	248.30	248.47	14.53	259.41	259.58	15.18
226.24	226.42	13.24	237.36	237.53	13.89	248.47	248.64	14.54	259.58	259.75	15.19
226.42	226.59	13.25	237.53	237.70	13.90	248.64	248.81	14.55	259.75	259.92	15.20
226.59	226.76	13.26	237.70	237.87	13.91	248.81	248.98	14.56	259.92	260.09	15.21
226.76	226.93	13.27	237.87	238.04	13.92	248.98	249.15	14.57	260.09	260.26	15.22
226.93	227.10	13.28	238.04	238.21	13.93	249.15	249.32	14.58	260.26	260.43	15.23
227.10	227.27	13.29	238.21	238.38	13.94	249.32	249.49	14.59	260.43	260.60	15.24
227.27	227.44	13.30	238.38	238.55	13.95	249.49	249.66	14.60	260.60	260.77	15.25
227.44	227.61	13.31	238.55	238.72	13.96	249.66	249.83	14.61	260.77	260.95	15.26
227.61	227.78	13.32	238.72	238.89	13.97	249.83	250.00	14.62	260.95	261.12	15.27
227.78	227.95	13.33	238.89	239.06	13.98	250.00	250.18	14.63	261.12	261.29	15.28
227.95	228.12	13.34	239.06	239.24	13.99	250.18	250.35	14.64	261.29	261.46	15.29
228.12	228.30	13.35	239.24	239.41	14.00	250.35	250.52	14.65	261.46	261.63	15.30
228.30	228.47	13.36	239.41	239.58	14.01	250.52	250.69	14.66	261.63	261.80	15.31
228.47	228.64	13.37	239.58	239.75	14.02	250.69	250.86	14.67	261.80	261.97	15.32
228.64	228.81	13.38	239.75	239.92	14.03	250.86	251.03	14.68	261.97	262.14	15.33
228.81	228.98	13.39	239.92	240.09	(14.04)	251.03	251.20	14.69	262.14	262.31	15.34
228.98	229.15	13.40	240.09	240.26	14.05	251.20	251.37	14.70	262.31	262.48	15.35
229.15	229.32	13.41	240.26	240.43	14.06	251.37	251.54	14.71	262.48	262.65	15.36
229.32	229.49	13.42	240.43	240.60	14.07	251.54	251.71	14.72	262.65	262.83	15.37
229.49	229.66	13.43	240.60	240.77	14.08	251.71	251.89	14.73	262.83	263.00	15.38
229.66	229.83	13.44	240.77	240.95	14.09	251.89	252.06	14.74	263.00	263.17	15.39
229.83	230.00	13.45	240.95	241.12	14.10	252.06	252.23	14.75	263.17	263.34	15.40
230.00	230.18	13.46	241.12	241.29	14.11	252.23	252.40	14.76	263.34	263.51	15.41
230.18	230.35	13.47	241.29	241.46	14.12	252.40	252.57	14.77	263.51	263.68	15.42
230.35	230.52	13.48	241.46	241.63	14.13	252.57	252.74	14.78	263.68	263.85	15.43
230.52	230.69	13.49	241.63	241.80	14.14	252.74	252.91	14.79	263.85	264.02	15.44
230.69	230.86	13.50	241.80	241.97	14.15	252.91	253.08	14.80	264.02	264.19	15.45
230.86	231.03	13.51	241.97	242.14	14.16	253.08	253.25	14.81	264.19	264.36	15.46
231.03	231.20	13.52	242.14	242.31	14.17	253.25	253.42	14.82	264.36	264.53	15.47
231.20	231.37	13.53	242.31	242.48	14.18	253.42	253.59	14.83	264.53	264.71	15.48
231.37	231.54	13.54	242.48	242.65	14.19	253.59	253.77	14.84	264.71	264.88	15.49
231.54	231.71	13.55	242.65	242.83	14.20	253.77	253.94	14.85	264.88	265.05	15.50
231.71	231.89	13.56	242.83	243.00	14.21	253.94	254.11	14.86	265.05	265.22	15.51
231.89	232.06	13.57	243.00	243.17	14.22	254.11	254.28	14.87	265.22	265.39	15.52
232.06	232.23	13.58	243.17	243.34	14.23	254.28	254.45	14.88	265.39	265.56	15.53
232.23	232.40	13.59	243.34	243.51	14.24	254.45	254.62	14.89	265.56	265.73	15.54
232.40	232.57	13.60	243.51	243.68	14.25	254.62	254.79	14.90	265.73	265.90	15.55
232.57	232.74	13.61	243.68	243.85	14.26	254.79	254.96	14.91	265.90	266.07	15.56
232.74	232.91	13.62	243.85	244.02	14.27	254.96	255.13	14.92	266.07	266.24	15.57
232.91	233.08	13.63	244.02	244.19	14.28	255.13	255.30	14.93	266.24	266.42	15.58
233.08	233.25	13.64	244.19	244.36	14.29	255.30	255.48	14.94	266.42	266.59	15.59

Payroll Register
For week ending November 7, 19___

	Name	Total Hrs.	Earnings			Taxable Earnings		
			Regular	Overtime	Total	State Unempl.	Federal Unempl.	FICA
1	Anderson, Dennis	44	160 00	24 00	184 00			184 00
2	Bowlen, Ralph P.	40	140 00		140 00	30 00		140 00
3	Daniels, John N.	46	160 00	36 00	196 00			196 00
4	Drew, Nancy R.	40	110 00		110 00			110 00
5	Fennell, Roger D.	40	124 00		124 00			124 00
6	Harwood, Lance C.	40	360 00		360 00			
7	Jones, Ronald R.	52	160 00	80 00	240 00			240 00
8	Lyman, Mary C.	40	150 00		150 00			150 00
9	Miller, Robert M.	42	168 00	12 60	180 60			180 60
10	Olsen, Marvin C.	40	140 00		140 00	140 00	140 00	140 00
11	Stanfield, John D.	40	120 00		120 00	120 00	120 00	120 00
12	Tucker, Norman P.	40	245 00		245 00			20 00
			2,037 00	152 60	2,189 60	290 00	260 00	1,604 60

The columns marked Taxable Earnings refer to the amount of pay which is subject to taxation; the employer has to pay a tax on this amount. For example, North Central Plumbing Supply operates in the state of Washington, which has a tax rate of 3% on the first $4,800 paid to each employee during the calendar year. After a given employee's earnings top $4,800 in one year, the employer doesn't have to pay any more state unemployment tax on that employee's pay. A blank space indicates that the employee, during this calendar year, has already earned more than $4,800 (prior to this payroll period).

Now take Ralph P. Bowlen. His cumulative earnings prior to this payroll period were $4,770; as a result, only $30 of his current earnings are taxable for state unemployment. As we said before, under the Federal Unemployment Act, the first $4,200 of compensation paid to each employee during the calendar year is taxable. After the employee has earned $4,200, the employer doesn't have to pay any more federal unemployment tax. Look at Marvin C. Olsen and John D. Stanfield. Neither has earned $4,200 thus far during the year from North Central Plumbing Supply. The FICA-taxable earnings pertain to the employer's matching portion of FICA, based on the first $15,300 of earnings. The amounts in the FICA-taxable earnings column therefore indicate that these employees have not earned $15,300 so far during the year. But Norman P. Tucker has accumulated earnings of $15,280 prior to this pay period. Consequently, only $20 of his gross wages of $245 is taxable under FICA. Payroll taxes, as we shall see in Chapter 15, are determined by multiplying the taxable earnings by the tax rates.

The federal income tax withholding and the FICA (Social Security) deductions are required by law; the others are voluntary. One could set up special columns for any frequently used deductions. Here, Community Chest and Accounts Receivable are included as other deductions.

The Net Amount column represents the employee's take-home pay. The last

				Deductions				Payment		Expense Account Debited		
Federal Income Tax	FICA	U.S. Bonds	Union Dues	Hosp. Ins.	Other		Total	Net Amount	Ck. No.	Sales Sal. Exp.	Office Sal. Exp.	Warehouse Wages Exp.
22 70	10 76	6 00	3 00	6 00	CC	2 00	50 46	133 54	931	184 00		
21 80	8 19	8 00	3 00	7 00			47 99	92 01	932	140 00		
22 00	11 47	8 00	3 00	7 00	AR	30 00	81 47	114 53	933	196 00		
15 50	6 44	6 00		6 00			33 94	76 06	934		110 00	
12 70	7 25	6 00	3 00	6 00			34 95	89 05	935	124 00		
59 70		33 00		7 00	CC	2 00	101 70	258 30	936	360 00		
28 40	14 04	4 00	3 00	6 00	CC	2 00	57 44	182 56	937			240 00
17 90	8 78	10 00		6 00	CC	1 00	43 68	106 32	938		150 00	
16 50	10 57	9 00	3 00	7 00	CC	2 00	48 07	132 53	939	180 60		
15 90	8 19						24 09	115 91	940	140 00		
17 60	7 02						24 62	95 38	941	120 00		
28 50	1 17	18 00		7 00	CC	1 00	55 67	189 33	942		245 00	
279 20	93 88	108 00	18 00	65 00		40 00	604 08	1,585 52		1,444 60	505 00	240 00

columns are used for a distribution of the salaries or wages accounts to be debited. North Central Plumbing Supply now uses Sales Salaries Expense, Office Salaries Expense, and Warehouse Wages Expense. The sum of these three columns should equal the total earnings.

The payroll entry

Since the payroll register summarizes the payroll data for the period, it seems logical that it should be used as the basis for recording the payroll in the ledger accounts. However, it does not have the status of a journal; consequently, a journal entry is necessary. Here is the entry in general journal form.

19__					
Nov.	7	Sales Salary Expense		1,444 60	
		Office Salary Expense		505 00	
		Warehouse Wages Expense		240 00	
		Employees' Income Tax Payable			279 20
		FICA Tax Payable			93 88
		Employees' Bond Deductions Payable			108 00
		Employees' Union Dues Payable			18 00
		Employees' Hospitalization Insurance Payable			65 00
		Employees' Community Chest Deductions Payable			10 00
		Accounts Receivable, John N. Daniels			30 00
		Salaries Payable			1,585 52
		Payroll register page 68, for week ended Nov. 7			

Note that a firm records the total cost to the company for services of employees as debits to the salaries and wages expense accounts. To pay the employees, the firm now records the entry in the cash payments journal or check register.

Cash Payments Journal

Date	Ck. No.	Account Name	Post. Ref.	Sundry Accounts Debit	Sundry Accounts Credit	Cash Credit
19__ Nov.	7	822	Salaries Payable		1,585 52		1,585 52

An accountant could record the entire entry in the cash payments journal, as one can see that entries in the Salaries Payable account cancel each other out. The accountant would make out separate checks drawn on the regular bank account for each employee. The advantage of the general journal entry is that it provides the necessary detail, and it is useful when one check is drawn from the regular bank account for the entire payroll and then deposited in a separate payroll account. All the payroll checks are subsequently drawn on the payroll account. This simplifies the reconciliation of the regular bank account.

Paycheck

All the data needed to make out a payroll check are available in the payroll register. Here is the paycheck for Ronald R. Jones.

EMPLOYEE	TOTAL HOURS	O.T. HOURS	REG. PAY RATE	REG. PAY	O.T. PREM. PAY	GROSS PAY	INC. TAX	FICA TAX	SAVINGS BONDS	UNION DUES	HOSP. INS.	OTHER	TOTAL DED.	NET PAY
Ronald R. Jones	52	12	4.00	160.00	80.00	240.00	28.40	14.04	4.00	3.00	6.00	CC 2.00	57.44	182.56

VALLEY NATIONAL BANK 98-461 / 1252

1728 BIRCH STREET
SEATTLE, WASH. 98110

NORTH CENTRAL PLUMBING SUPPLY
1968 ARROW STREET N.W.
SEATTLE. WASHINGTON 98111   SEATTLE. WASHINGTON Nov. 7 19 ___ No. 937

PAY TO THE
ORDER OF ___ Ronald R. Jones _____ $ 182.56 ___

One hundred eighty-two and 56/100--------------------- DOLLARS

Robert C. Randall

⑆ 1252 ⑈ 0461 ⑈

Employee's individual earnings record

To comply with the government regulations described earlier, a firm has to keep current data on each employee's accumulated earnings, deductions, and net pay. For example, FICA taxes are deducted from the first $15,300 of earnings during the year. The source of this information is the payroll register, and the information is transferred to the employee's individual earnings record each payday. A portion of the earnings record for Ronald R. Jones is shown on pages 368–369.

Summary

Payroll accounting is concerned with the following:
- Computing compensation for employees
- Taking out required and voluntary deductions
- Paying employees
- Paying various government agencies
- Submitting required reports to government agencies
- Paying private agencies for employees' deductions for insurance, etc.

In this chapter, we have discussed important provisions of federal and state laws pertaining to employment. In earlier chapters, we showed the entry recording compensation of employees as a debit to Salaries or Wages Expense and a credit to Cash. We have now made the transition from this simplified entry to the complete entry, consisting of a debit to Salaries or Wages Expense, credits to the various deductions payable, and finally a credit to Cash for the amount of the employees' take-home pay.

First we record the information for the payroll period in the payroll register. Next, using the payroll register as the source of information, we record payroll entries in the general journal and the cash payments journal or check register.

To comply with the employment laws, any business firm should maintain a payroll register and an employee's individual earnings record.

Glossary

o **Civil Rights Act** An act which prohibits discrimination based on race, color, religion, sex, or national origin.
o **Current Tax Payment Act** Requires an employer to withhold employees' federal income tax as well as to pay and report the tax.
o **Employee** One who works for compensation in the service of an employer.
o **Employee's individual earnings record** A supplementary record showing personal payroll data and yearly cumulative earnings and deductions for each employee.
o **Employee's Withholding Exemption Certificate (Form W-4)** This form specifies the number of exemptions claimed by each employee and gives the employer the authority to withhold money for an employee's income taxes and FICA taxes.
o **Employment Act of 1967** This act prohibits discrimination based on age.

Employee's Individual Earnings Record

Name Jones, Ronald R.

Address 1620 West Seattle Way

Seattle, Washington 98116

Male   √   **Married**   √

Female   **Single**

No. of Exemptions 3

Line No.	Period Ended	Date Paid	Hours Worked Reg.	Hours Worked O.T.	Earnings Reg.		Earnings O.T.		Total		Accum. Earn.	
38	9/19	9/20	40		160	00			160	00	6,820	00
39	9/26	9/27	40		160	00			160	00	6,980	00
Third Quarter					1,920	00	——		1,920	00		
40	10/3	10/4	40		160	00			160	00	7,140	00
41	10/10	10/11	40	2	160	00	12	00	172	00	7,312	00
42	10/17	10/18	40	2	160	00	12	00	172	00	7,484	00
43	10/23	10/24	40	5	160	00	30	00	190	00	7,674	00
44	10/30	11/1	40	4	160	00			160	00	7,834	00
45	11/7	11/8	40	12	160	00	80	00	240	00	8,074	00
46	11/14	11/15	40	8	160	00	48	00	208	00	8,282	00
47	11/21	11/22	40	6	160	00	36	00	196	00	8,478	00
48	11/28	11/29	40	2	160	00	12	00	172	00	8,650	00
49	12/5	12/6	40	2	160	00	12	00	172	00	8,822	00
50	12/12	12/13	40		160	00			160	00	8,982	00
51	12/19	12/20	40		160	00			160	00	9,142	00
52	12/26	12/27	40		160	00			160	00	9,302	00
Fourth Quarter					2,080	00	242	00	2,322	00		
Yearly Totals					8,320	00	982	00	9,302	00		

Employee no. 5   Soc. Sec. No. 543-24-1680

Phone no. 663-2556   Date of birth 9/19/39

Notify in case of emergency Wife, Sarah

Pay rate $4.00   Per hour   √   Date employed 2/1

Equivalent   Per day _____   Date employment
hourly rate $4.00   terminated _____

                     Per week _____

                     Per month _____

Classification for workmen's compensation insurance Warehouse

		Deductions					Paid	
Income Tax	FICA	Bonds	Union Dues	Hosp. Ins.	Other	Total	Net Amt.	Ck. No.
17 90	9 36	4 00	3 00	6 00	CC 2 00	42 26	117 74	853
17 90	9 36	4 00	3 00	6 00	CC 2 00	42 26	117 74	865
261 90	112 32	52 00	39 00	78 00	26 00	569 22	1,350 78	
17 90	9 36	4 00	3 00	6 00	CC 2 00	42 26	117 74	877
21 10	10 06	4 00	3 00	6 00	CC 2 00	46 16	125 84	889
21 10	10 06	4 00	3 00	6 00	CC 2 00	46 16	125 84	901
24 30	11 12	4 00	3 00	6 00	CC 2 00	50 42	139 58	913
17 90	9 36	4 00	3 00	6 00	CC 2 00	42 26	117 74	925
28 40	14 04	4 00	3 00	6 00	CC 2 00	57 44	182 56	937
26 30	12 17	4 00	3 00	6 00	CC 2 00	53 47	154 53	949
24 30	11 47	4 00	3 00	6 00	CC 2 00	50 77	145 23	961
21 10	10 06	4 00	3 00	6 00	CC 2 00	46 16	125 84	973
21 10	10 06	4 00	3 00	6 00	CC 2 00	46 16	125 84	985
17 90	9 36	4 00	3 00	6 00	CC 2 00	42 26	117 74	997
17 90	9 36	4 00	3 00	6 00	CC 2 00	42 26	117 74	1009
17 90	9 36	4 00	3 00	6 00	CC 2 00	42 26	117 74	1021
277 20	135 84	52 00	39 00	78 00	26 00	608 04	1,713 96	
1,274 80	544 17	208 00	156 00	312 00	CC 104 00	2,598 97	6,703 03	

- **Fair Labor Standards Act (Wages and Hours Law)** An act which says that employers whose products are involved in interstate commerce must pay their employees a minimum wage specified by Congress, and must pay time-and-a-half to an employee for any hours worked in excess of 40 per week.
- **Federal Insurance Contributions Act (FICA)** This act currently decrees that an employee must pay 5.85% of the first $15,300 of compensation received during the calendar year as Social Security (FICA) tax; the employer must match this 5.85% contribution.
- **Federal Unemployment Tax Act (FUTA)** This tax is paid by employers only, and amounts to 0.5% of the first $4,200 of compensation paid each employee during the calendar year.
- **Payroll register** A supplementary record that summarizes information about employees' compensation for a particular payroll period.
- **State unemployment tax acts** These acts also specify taxes to be paid by employers only; rates and amounts of taxable incomes vary among the states. Many states levy at least 2.7% of the first $4,200 of earnings paid to each employee during the year.
- **Workmen's compensation laws** State laws guaranteeing employee benefits when the employee incurs an injury on the job.

Exercises

Exercise 1 From the illustration on page 362, determine the amount of federal income tax which an employer should withhold weekly for married employees with the following wages and exemptions.

	Total Weekly Wages	Number of Exemptions	Amount of Withholding
a	$107.80	1	
b	$259.45	5	
c	$311.19	6	

Exercise 2 From the illustration on page 363, determine the amount of Social Security tax an employer would have to withhold from employees with the following wages.

	Total Wages	Amount of Withholding
a	$244.60	
b	$224.71	
c	$243.90	

Exercise 3 Cyrus R. Peters works for the Far East Mechanical Corporation, which must abide by the Fair Labor Standards Act, in that it must pay its employees time-and-a-half for all hours worked per week in excess of 40. Peters's pay rate is $5.20 per hour. His wages are subject to federal income tax and FICA deductions only. He claims four income tax exemptions; Peters has a ½-hour lunch break during an 8½-hour day. His time card is as follows.

Time Card

Name: Peters, Cyrus R.
Period: March 5–11, 19___

Day	In	Out	Hours Worked Regular	Hours Worked Overtime
M	7:56	4:32		
T	7:52	5:04		
W	7:59	5:03		
T	8:00	4:34		
F	7:56	6:33		
S	8:00	12:01		
S				

Complete the following.

_____ hours at straight time × $5.20 per hour $ _____
_____ hours overtime × $7.80 per hour $ _____
Total gross wages $ _____
Federal income tax withholding (page 362) $ _____
FICA withholding (page 363) $ _____
Total withholding $ _____
Net pay $ _____

Exercise 4 Tony Mendozo, who works for Purity Dairy Products, worked 46 hours during the first week in March. His rate of pay is $4.80 per hour, and he receives time-and-a-half for all hours worked in excess of 40 per week. His wages are subject to the following deductions.
- Federal income tax (see page 362)
- FICA tax (see page 363)
- Industrial accident insurance of 1%
- Medical insurance, $7.60

He claims five exemptions for income tax purposes. Compute the following: regular wages, overtime wages, gross wages, and net pay.

Exercise 5 The following information was taken from the records of Hildebrand Fine Foods, Inc., a company which is subject to the Fair Labor Standards Act, for the first week of January.

Name	Hourly Rate	Hours Worked Reg.	Hours Worked O.T.	Total Earn.	Fed. Inc. Tax	FICA	Savings Bonds	Hosp. Ins.	Total	Net Pay
Aikens, A.	4 90	40	6				4 00	7 00		
Brown, B.	5 00	40	8				6 00	8 00		

Using the tables on pages 362 and 363, determine the amounts omitted. Aikens and Brown claim two exemptions each. In general journal form, record the payroll entry, debiting Wages Expense for the amount of the total earnings and crediting Cash for the net pay.

Exercise 6 Tanya Brock works for Nationwide Water Softeners, Inc., a company engaged in interstate commerce, which is subject to the provisions of the Fair Labor Standards Act. Nationwide has just adopted a 4-day, 40-hour work week so that its employees will spend less time and gasoline commuting and will have longer weekends.

Brock's pay rate is $5.70 per hour. During the first week of the change to the 4-day week, her working hours were as follows: Monday, 12 hours; Tuesday, 10 hours; Wednesday, 11½ hours; Thursday, 10½ hours. Compute the amount of her gross earnings for the week.

Exercise 7 In the following summary of columnar totals of a payroll register, determine the amounts that have been omitted.

Earnings

At regular rate	$6,975.79
At overtime rate	————
Total earnings	————
Deductions	
Income tax	1,038.50
FICA tax	406.72
Medical insurance	————
Union dues	200.00
Total deductions	1,870.22
Net amount paid	5,541.57
Accounts Debited	
Sales salaries	5,610.16
Office salaries	928.72
Warehouse salaries	————

Exercise 8 From Exercise 7, the total earnings are $7,411.79; warehouse salaries are $872.91, and the amount of the deduction for medical insurance is $225. In general journal form, complete the payroll entry, crediting Salaries Payable for the net amount paid.

Problems

Problem 14-1 Thomas T. Jenkins, an employee of Timely Products Company, worked 46 hours during the week of March 16 to 22. His rate of pay is $4.60 per hour, and he receives time-and-a-half for all work in excess of 40 hours per week. Jenkins is married and claims two exemptions on his W-4 form. His wages are subject to the following deductions.

- Federal income tax (use the table on page 362)
- FICA tax (use the table on page 363)
- Union dues, $1.80
- Medical insurance, $3.10

Instructions Compute the following: his regular pay, his overtime pay, his gross pay, and his net pay.

Problem 14-2 The Travelers' Rest Motel has the following payroll information for the week ended June 18.

Name	Daily Time M	T	W	T	F	S	S	Pay Rate	Federal Income Tax	Union Dues	Earnings at End of Previous Week
Albers, John	0	8	8	8	8	8	0	3 80	17 80	1 50	3,510 00
Conrad, Jean	8	8	8	8	8	0	0	2 60	15 00	———	2,392 00
Johnson, Donna	0	0	8	8	8	8	8	3 00	16 40	1 50	1,280 00
Mennen, Roy	0	4	8	8	8	8	8	2 40	15 70	———	1,686 00
Palmer, Ronald	8	8	8	8	8	4	0	3 50	21 30	1 50	3,430 00

The firm is subject to the Fair Labor Standards Act regarding minimum wages. However, being a motel, it is exempt from paying time-and-a-half for 44 hours of work or less. In other words, all hours are compensated at the regular rate. For each employee, taxable earnings for FICA are based on the first $15,300, and taxable earnings for unemployment insurance (state and federal) are based on the first $4,200.

Instructions

1 Complete the payroll register, using 5.85% of earnings for calculating FICA tax withholding.
2 Prepare a general journal entry to record the payroll.
3 Assume that the firm uses a special payroll bank account, and make the entry in the cash payments journal to record check no. 53.

Problem 14-3 The Arlington Products Company is subject to the Fair Labor Standards Act, and accordingly pays time-and-a-half for all hours worked in excess of 40 per week. The following information is available from the time cards and employee's individual earnings records for the pay period ended March 16.

Name	Clock Card No.	Daily Time M	T	W	T	F	S	S	Regular Rate	Income Tax Exemp.	Union Dues	Hospital Insurance	Earnings at End of Previous Week
Baker, Roger	76	8	8	8	10	8	0	0	5 20	2	3 00	3 60	1,720 00
Carl, Denise	77	8	8	8	8	8	0	0	5 70	2	3 00	3 60	1,210 00
Lindsay, Neal	78	8	8	8	8	8	4	4	5 00	4	3 00	4 50	2,170 00
Miller, Carla	79	8	8	9	9	8	6	0	5 10	3	3 00	4 00	2,230 00
Turner, Ted	80	8	8	8	8	8	0	0	6 00	4	3 00	4 50	2,320 00

For each employee, taxable earnings for FICA are based on the first $15,300, and taxable earnings for unemployment insurance (state and federal) are based on the first $4,200.

Instructions

1 Complete the payroll register, using the wage bracket income tax withholding table (page 362) and the FICA tax withholding table (page 363). Assume that all employees are married.
2 Prepare a general journal entry to record the payroll.
3 Assume that the firm uses a special payroll bank account; make the entry in the check register to record check no. 113 payable to the payroll bank account.

Problem 14-4 The Modern Trailer Supply Company is subject to the Fair

Labor Standards Act, and accordingly pays its employees time-and-a-half for all hours worked in excess of 40 per week. The following information is available from the time books and employee's individual earnings records for the pay period ended December 10.

Name	Pay Rate	Hours Worked	Federal Income Tax	Union Dues	Hospital Insurance	Earnings at End of Previous Week
Harmon, Peter	$5.20 per hour	44	22 00	2 00	3 00	8,600 00
Johnson, Patti	$250.00 per week	40	28 10	——	4 00	16,250 00
Mills, Norma	$230.00 per week	40	21 40	——	3 00	9,310 00
Peterson, Claude	$5.50 per hour	42	24 60	2 00	3 00	8,170 00

For each employee, taxable earnings for FICA are based on the first $15,300, and taxable earnings for unemployment insurance are based on the first $4,200 (state and federal).

Instructions

1 Complete the payroll register, using the FICA tax withholding table (page 363).

2 Prepare a general journal entry to record the payroll.

3 Record the payment of the employees, assuming that the company uses a cash payments journal, beginning with check no. 1781.

Problem 14-1A Jan R. Powell, an employee of Pacific Motor Freight, worked 47 hours during the week from February 15 to 21. Her rate of pay is $4.80 per hour, and she gets time-and-a-half for work in excess of 40 hours per week. She is married and claims three exemptions on her W-4 form, and her wages are subject to the following deductions.

● Federal income tax (use the table on page 362)
● FICA tax (use page 363)
● Union dues, $3.10
● Medical insurance, $5.25

Instructions Compute the following: her regular pay, overtime pay, gross pay, and net pay.

Problem 14-2A The Falcon Motor Lodge has the following payroll information for the week ended June 6.

Name	Daily Time							Pay Rate	Federal Income Tax	Union Dues	Earnings at End of Previous Week
	M	T	W	T	F	S	S				
Baker, Loren	8	0	0	8	10	8	8	3 80	19 10	1 70	3,960 00
Collier, Douglas	0	0	8	8	8	8	8	2 70	13 60	1 70	2,172 60
Edwards, Roberta	8	8	8	8	4	0	8	2 70	14 10	——	2,548 22
Stanski, Louise	0	4	8	8	8	8	8	4 00	19 50	1 70	3,980 10
Tolliver, Elwood	8	8	4	8	8	0	8	2 40	15 00	——	861 30

The firm is subject to the Fair Labor Standards Act regarding minimum wages. However, being a motel, it is exempt from paying time-and-a-half for 44 hours or less. In other words, all hours are compensated at the regular rate. For each employee, taxable earnings for FICA are based on the first $15,300, and taxable earnings for unemployment insurance (state and federal) are based on the first $4,200.

Instructions

1 Complete the payroll register, using 5.85% for calculating FICA tax withholding.

2 Prepare a general journal entry to record the payroll.

3 Assume that the firm uses a special payroll bank account; make the entry in the cash payments journal to record check no. 53.

Problem 14-3A The Florida Products Company is subject to the Fair Labor Standards Act and accordingly pays its employees time-and-a-half for all hours worked in excess of 40 per week. The following information is available from time cards and employee's individual earnings records for the pay period ended February 28.

Name	Clock Card No.	Daily Time M T W T F S S							Regular Rate	Income Tax Exemp.	Union Dues	Hospital Insurance	Earnings at End of Previous Week
Bannion, Carl	69	8	8	8	10	9	0	0	5 20	1	4 00	3 60	1,660 00
Degnan, Mary	70	8	8	8	8	8	5	0	5 20	3	4 00	5 00	1,730 00
Delaney, Roy	71	8	10	8	9	8	0	0	5 90	5	4 00	5 40	1,774 00
Jared, Harold	72	8	8	9	8	8	2	0	5 90	4	4 00	5 20	1,756 00
West, Clara	73	8	8	8	8	8	0	0	6 00	4	4 00	5 20	1,726 00

For each employee, taxable earnings for FICA are based on the first $15,300, and taxable earnings for unemployment insurance are based on the first $4,200 (state and federal).

Instructions

1 Complete the payroll register, using the wage-bracket income tax table (page 362) and the FICA tax withholding table (page 363). Assume that all employees are married.

2 Prepare a general journal entry to record the payroll.

3 Assume that the firm uses a special payroll bank account; make the entry in the check register to record check no. 113 payable to the payroll bank account.

Problem 14-4A The Nairn Refrigeration Company is subject to the Fair Labor Standards Act, and accordingly pays its employees time-and-a-half for all hours worked in excess of 40 per week. The following information is available from Nairn's time book and the employee's individual earnings records for the payroll period ending December 8.

Name	Pay Rate	Hours Worked	Federal Income Tax	Union Dues	Hospital Insurance	Earnings at End of Previous Week
Bergren, Willa	$5.10 per hour	46	24 30	4 00	4 50	9,332 00
Crocker, Carl	$260.00 per week	40	36 00	——	6 00	16,340 00
Gavin, John	$225.00 per week	40	23 40	——	4 50	8,330 00
Steiger, Henrietta	$4.90 per hour	48	29 20	4 00	4 50	9,966 00

For each employee, taxable earnings for FICA are based on the first $15,300, and taxable earnings for unemployment insurance are based on the first $4,200 (state and federal).

Instructions

1 Complete the payroll register, using the FICA tax withholding table (page 363).

2 Prepare a general journal entry to record the payroll.

3 Record the payment of the employees, assuming that the company uses a cash payments journal, beginning with check no. 3009.

15

Payroll accounting: employer's taxes, payments, and reports

In addition to his many sins against Christmas, Ebenezer Scrooge may be held accountable for a notable disservice to the profession of accountancy. By placing Bob Cratchit on a high stool, bent over a dusty ledger, with a long quill pen in his hand and a green eyeshade over his brow, Scrooge perpetuated a caricature of the accountant which persisted long after that miser's reconciliation with his fellowmen. Happily, this image has been dispelled. James M. Fremgen, *Accounting for Managerial Analysis*

After you have completed this chapter, you will be able to:
- Journalize entry to record payroll tax expense.
- Complete federal tax deposits and accompanying journal entries.
- Complete Employer's Quarterly Federal Tax Return, Form 941.
- Prepare wage and tax statements for employees, W-2 forms.
- Complete Transmittal of Income and Tax Statements, Form W-3.
- Prepare a quarterly report for state unemployment insurance and journalize related entry.
- Complete Employer's Annual Federal Unemployment Tax Return, Form 940.
- Calculate the premium for workmen's compensation insurance and journalize entry for payment in advance.
- Determine amount of adjustment for workmen's compensation insurance at end of year and record adjustment.
- Prepare a tax calendar for payments of employees' income and FICA taxes withheld and employer's payroll taxes.

Introduction

In Chapter 14 we talked about the computing and recording of payroll data such as gross pay, employees' income tax withheld, employees' FICA tax withheld, and various deductions requested by employees. Now we're going to get around to the payments of these withholdings, the taxes levied on the employer based on total payroll, and finally the official reports that you have to submit to government authorities.

Employer's identification number

As you know quite well, everyone who works has a Social Security number, a number which is a vital part of his or her federal income tax returns. For an employer, a counterpart to the Social Security number is the *employer identification number.* Each employer of one or more persons is required to have such a number, and it must be listed on all reports and payments of employees' federal income tax withholding and FICA taxes.

Now North Central Plumbing Supply (yes, we're back with *them* again!) is classified as a sole-proprietorship form of business. Since a sole proprietorship is not a separate legal entity, the tax account number must be listed in the name of the owner, Robert C. Randall. But if the company *were* incorporated, the tax number would be listed in the name of the corporation, since a corporation *is* a separate legal entity, and as such, maintains a separate legal existence; in other words, it may acquire, own, and dispose of property in its corporate name, and may also assume liabilities in its corporate name.

Form SS-4, the form used for filing an application for an employer identification number, is shown on page 380.

Employer's payroll taxes

An employer's payroll taxes are levied on the employer on the basis of the gross wages paid to the employees. Payroll taxes—like property taxes—are

FORM SS-4 (3-69)
PART 1
U.S. TREASURY DEPARTMENT—INTERNAL REVENUE SERVICE
APPLICATION FOR EMPLOYER IDENTIFICATION NUMBER

1. NAME (*TRUE name as distinguished from TRADE name.*)

Robert C. Randall

2. TRADE NAME, IF ANY (*Enter name under which business is operated, if different from item 1.*)

North Central Plumbing Supply

3. ADDRESS OF PRINCIPAL PLACE OF BUSINESS (*No. and Street, City, State, Zip Code*)

1968 Arrow St., N. W., Seattle, Wash. 98111

4. COUNTY OF BUSINESS LOCATION

King

5. ORGANIZATION Check Type

[X] Individual [ ] Partnership [ ] Corporation [ ] Other (*specify e.g. estate, trust, etc.*)
[ ] Governmental (See Instr. 5) [ ] Nonprofit Organization (See Instr. 5)

6. Ending Month of Accounting year

7. REASON FOR APPLYING (*If "other" specify such as "Corporate structure change," "Acquired by gift or trust," etc.*)

[X] Started new business [ ] Purchased going business [ ] Other

8. Date you acquired or started business (*Mo., day, year*)

Jan. 4, 19__

9. First date you paid or will pay wages (*Mo., day, year*)

Jan. 15, 19__

10. NATURE OF BUSINESS (*See Instructions*)

Wholesale plumbing

11. NUMBER OF EMPLOYEES IF "NONE" ENTER "0"

Non-agricultural	Agricultural
10	

12. If nature of business is MANUFACTURING, list in order of their importance the principal products manufactured and the estimated percentage of the total value of all products which each represents.

A   %

B   %   C   %

PLEASE LEAVE BLANK

R	DO	TA
FR		FRC

13. Do you operate more than one place of business? [ ] Yes [X] No
If "Yes," attach a list showing for each separate establishment:
a. Name and address.   b. Nature of business   c. Number of employees.

14. To whom do you sell most of your products or services?
[X] Business establishments [ ] General public [ ] Other (*Specify*)

PLEASE LEAVE BLANK →

Geo.	Ind.	Class	Size	Reas. for Appl.	Bus. Bir. Date

- -

FORM SS-4 (3-69)
PART 2
DO NOT DETACH ANY PART OF THIS FORM. SEND ALL COPIES TO INTERNAL REVENUE SERVICE

PLEASE LEAVE BLANK

NAME AND COMPLETE ADDRESS

1. NAME (*TRUE name as distinguished from TRADE name.*)

Robert C. Randall

2. TRADE NAME, IF ANY (*Enter name under which business is operated, if different from item 1.*)

North Central Plumbing Supply

3. ADDRESS OF PRINCIPAL PLACE OF BUSINESS (*No. and Street*)

1968 Arrow St., N. W.

(*City, State, Zip Code*)

Seattle, Wash. 98111

4. COUNTY OF BUSINESS LOCATION

King

5. ORGANIZATION Check Type

[X] Individual [ ] Partnership [ ] Corporation [ ] Other (*specify e.g. estate, trust, etc.*)
[ ] Governmental (See Instr. 5) [ ] Nonprofit Organization (See Instr. 5)

6. Ending Month of Accounting year

7. REASON FOR APPLYING (*If "other" specify such as "Corporate structure change," "Acquired by gift or trust," etc.*)

[X] Started new business [ ] Purchased going business [ ] Other

8. Date you acquired or started business (*Mo., day, year*)

Jan. 4, 19__

9. First date you paid or will pay wages (*Mo., day, year*)

Jan. 15, 19__

10. NATURE OF BUSINESS (*See Instructions*)

Wholesale plumbing

11. NUMBER OF EMPLOYEES IF "NONE" ENTER "0"

Non-agricultural	Agricultural
10	

12. Have you ever applied for an identification number for this or any other business? [X] No [ ] Yes
If "Yes," enter name and trade name (if any). Also enter the approximate date, city, and state where you first applied and previous number if known. →

DATE

Jan. 11, 19__

SIGNATURE

Robert C. Randall

TITLE

Owner

380   Employer's taxes, payments, and reports

an expense of doing business. North Central Plumbing Supply titles the account Payroll Tax Expense, and debits it for its matching of FICA taxes as well as for state and federal unemployment taxes. Consequently, the account looks like this.

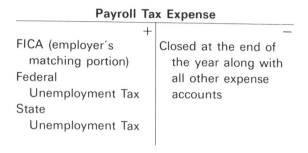

Payroll Tax Expense

+	−
FICA (employer's matching portion) Federal Unemployment Tax State Unemployment Tax	Closed at the end of the year along with all other expense accounts

If an accountant subdivides operating expenses on the income statement, she or he classifies Payroll Tax Expense as a general expense account.

Employer's matching portion of FICA tax

The FICA tax is imposed on both employer and employee. The firm's accountant deducts the employee's share from gross wages, and records it in the payroll entry under FICA Tax Payable, a liability account. He or she determines the employer's share by multiplying the same FICA tax rate (currently 5.85%) times the total FICA-taxable earnings [gross annual earnings (for the calendar year) for each employee up to $15,300]. The accountant gets the FICA-taxable earnings figure from the payroll register. In the following illustration we take another look at the Taxable Earnings columns from the payroll register for the week ended November 7, 19___, illustrated in Chapter 14 on pages 364–365.

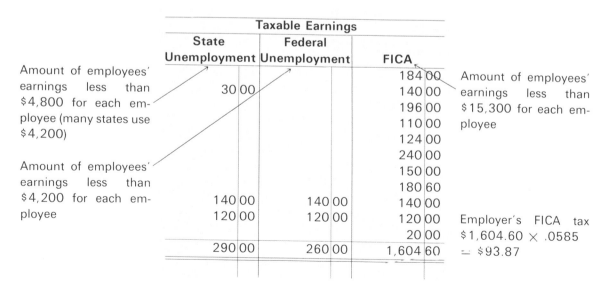

	Taxable Earnings		
	State Unemployment	Federal Unemployment	FICA
			184 00
	30 00		140 00
			196 00
			110 00
			124 00
			240 00
			150 00
			180 60
	140 00	140 00	140 00
	120 00	120 00	120 00
			20 00
	290 00	260 00	1,604 60

Amount of employees' earnings less than $4,800 for each employee (many states use $4,200)

Amount of employees' earnings less than $4,200 for each employee

Amount of employees' earnings less than $15,300 for each employee

Employer's FICA tax $1,604.60 × .0585 = $93.87

By T accounts, the entry to record the employer's portion of the FICA tax looks like this.

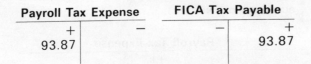

Payroll Tax Expense		FICA Tax Payable	
+	−	−	+
93.87			93.87

Note particularly that the FICA Tax Payable account is used for the tax liability of both the employer and the employee. This is logical because both FICA taxes are paid at the same time and the same place. There might be a discrepancy between the employer's and the employee's share of FICA taxes, due to the rounding-off process. The accountant calculates the employee's share by taking 5.85% of the taxable earnings of each worker, then adding these figures to find the total amount due for all employees. At the same time, she or he determines the employer's share by taking 5.85% of the taxable earnings of all the employees. The two figures may vary, but only by a few cents.

Employer's federal unemployment tax (FUTA)

The employer's federal unemployment tax is levied on the employer only. Congress may from time to time change the rate. But for now, let's assume that the present rate—.5% (.005) of the first $4,200 earned by each employee during the year (3.2% federal unemployment tax less 2.7% credit for amounts paid to the state as state unemployment tax)—applies. For the weekly payroll period for North Central Plumbing Supply, the tax liability is $1.30 ($260 of unemployment taxable earnings taken from the payroll register multiplied by .005). By T accounts, the entry is as follows.

Payroll Tax Expense	
+	−
260 × .005 = 1.30	

Federal Unemployment Tax Payable	
−	+
	260 × .005 = 1.30

Employer's state unemployment tax

This tax, like the federal unemployment tax, is paid by the employer only. The rate of state unemployment tax varies considerably among the states. During recent years, with the trend toward higher unemployment benefits, many states have adopted a base of at least $4,200 and rates of 2.7% or higher. However, let us assume here that North Central Plumbing Supply is subject to a rate of 3% of the first $4,800 of each employee's earnings. Accordingly, by T accounts, the state unemployment tax based on taxable earnings is as follows. As shown on page 381, $290 of earnings are subject to the state unemployment tax.

Payroll Tax Expense

+	−
$290 \times .03 = 8.70$	

State Unemployment Tax Payable

−	+
	$290 \times .03 = 8.70$

Journal entry for employer's payroll tax

In the foregoing, to make things clearer, figures for the three employer's payroll taxes have been presented separately. But now let's combine this information into one entry, which follows the regular payroll entry. North Central Plumbing Supply pays its employees weekly, so they also make their Payroll Tax Expense entry weekly.

Payroll Tax Expense	103 87	
FICA Tax Payable		93 87
Federal Unemployment Tax Payable		1 30
State Unemployment Tax Payable		8 70
To record employer's share of FICA tax and employer's federal and state unemployment taxes		

At this point let us restate in general journal form the entries that have been recorded, using the payroll register illustrated in Chapter 14 as the source of information. First, we record the payroll entry.

19__					
Nov.	7	Sales Salary Expense	1,444 60	
		Office Salary Expense	505 00	
		Warehouse Wages Expense	240 00	
		Employees' Income Tax Payable		279 20
		FICA Tax Payable		93 88
		Employees' Bond Deductions Payable		108 00
		Employees' Union Dues Payable		18 00
		Employees' Hospitalization Insurance Payable		65 00
		Employees' Community Chest Deductions Payable		10 00
		Accounts Receivable, John N. Daniels		30 00
		Salaries Payable		1,585 52
		Payroll register, page 68, for week ended Nov. 7		

Next, North Central Plumbing Supply, on the basis of the above entry, issues one check payable to a payroll bank account. To pay its employees, it will draw separate payroll checks on this payroll bank account.

Salaries Payable	1,585 52	
Cash		1,585 52
To record payment of employees (recorded in cash payments journal payable to payroll bank account)		

Finally, the entry to record the employer's payroll taxes is journalized.

Payroll Tax Expense	103 87	
FICA Tax Payable		93 87
Federal Unemployment Tax Payable		1 30
State Unemployment Tax Payable		8 70
To record employer's share of FICA tax and employer's federal and state unemployment taxes		

Reports and payments of FICA taxes and employees' income tax withholding

After an employer has paid the employees, he or she has to make payments in the form of federal tax deposits for (1) employees' income taxes withheld, (2) employees' FICA taxes withheld, and (3) the employer's share of FICA taxes. These deposits, putting the employers on a pay-as-you-go-basis, are made during the 3-month quarter. At the end of the quarter, the employer has to submit the Employer's Quarterly Federal Tax Return (Form 941) to the District Director of Internal Revenue, showing the amount of taxes due and listing the deposits.

For *large-sized* employers, if the combined total of undeposited employees' income taxes and FICA taxes levied on both employees and employer is greater than $2,000 for a *quarter-of-a-month period* (approximately 1 week), the employer has to make deposits within 3 banking days after the end of the period. These quarter-of-a-month periods end on the 7th, 15th, 22nd, and last day of any month. For example, assume an employer had $2,300 of undeposited taxes for a quarter-of-a-month period ending on Friday, September 7. Since the banks are closed on Saturday and Sunday, the employer would have to make the deposit by Wednesday, September 12.

For *medium-sized* employers, if the total undeposited income taxes and FICA taxes for any *month* is between $200 and $2,000, the employer has to make the deposit within 15 days after the end of the month.

But now suppose you're just a *small-sized* employer, and the total amount of your undeposited income taxes and FICA taxes at the end of the *quarter* is less than $200; you don't have to make a deposit until you submit your quarterly return, Form 941. Now remember that we're talking about a *quarter*. You keep records on the basis of a calendar year, with the first quarter ending March 31, the second quarter ending June 30, the third quarter ending September 30, and the fourth quarter ending December 31.

North Central Plumbing Supply, for the week ended November 7, had the following taxes due to the government.

Employees' federal income tax withheld	$279.20
Employees' FICA taxes withheld	93.88
Employer's FICA tax	93.87
Total	$466.95

For North Central, the monthly total of these combined taxes typically falls between $200 and $2,000. Consequently, they make their deposit monthly.

North Central's figures for the month of November are as follows.

Employees' federal income tax withheld	$1,142.60
Employees' FICA taxes withheld	371.16
Employer's FICA tax	371.16
Total	$1,884.92

North Central receives a federal tax deposit card (preprinted with the company's name and tax number) from the Internal Revenue Service. The accountant records the amount of the deposit and the name of the bank where the deposit is to be submitted (any authorized commercial bank or Federal Reserve bank). Commercial banks forward the deposits to the Federal Reserve banks, which are agents of the U.S. Treasury. The entry in general journal form on North Central's books looks like this.

19__				
Dec.	12	Employees' Federal Income Tax Payable	1,142 60	
		FICA Tax Payable	742 32	
		Cash		1,884 92
		To record payment of federal tax deposit (recorded in cash payments journal)		

Each deposit must be listed on Schedule B of the Employer's Quarterly

Federal Tax Return, Form 941. (This begins to sound pretty sticky, but when you actually get around to doing it, it isn't bad at all.)

Employer's Quarterly Federal Tax Return (Form 941)

The return must be filed by the end of the month following the end of the quarter. North Central's sources of information for its Employer's Quarterly Federal Tax Return are the payroll registers for the quarter and the employee's individual earnings records. After an employer has secured an identification number and has filed the first return, then, in the future, the Internal Revenue Service sends forms to her or him directly, with the employer's name, address, and identification number filled in. North Central Plumbing Supply's Form 941 for the fourth quarter is shown below and on page 387.

Before the accountant at North Central fills out Form 941, he or she has to make a list of the company's employees, showing their names, Social Security numbers, and amount of FICA-taxable wages paid to them during the quarter. The accountant gets this information from the employees' individual earnings records, lists the data on Form 941, and then determines the amount of the income tax withheld by looking in the Employees' Income Tax Payable ledger account. Note that during this quarter only 11 employees are listed on Form 941. Previously, one employee exceeded the maximum of FICA-taxable wages. Note also that the taxable wages are multiplied by 11.7%, which is the 5.85% contributed by employees plus the 5.85% matching share contributed by the employer. (Incidentally, the employer doesn't have to contribute a matching share of taxable tips.) Before completing the line that shows total deposits for the quarter, the accountant fills in Schedule B (below), indicating the amount and date of each deposit.

SCHEDULE B—RECORD OF FEDERAL TAX DEPOSITS

Deposit period ending:	A. Tax liability for period	B. Amount deposited	C. Date of deposit
Overpayment from previous quarter			
First month of quarter — 1st through 7th day			
8th through 15th day			
16th through 22d day			
23d through last day			
1 First month total . . . . ①	1,906.41	1,906.41	11/14
Second month of quarter — 1st through 7th day			
8th through 15th day			
16th through 22d day			
23d through last day			
2 Second month total . . . . ②	1,884.92	1,884.92	12/12
Third month of quarter — 1st through 7th day			
8th through 15th day			
16th through 22d day			
23d through last day			
3 Third month total . . . . ③	1,921.47	1,921.47	1/14
4 Total for quarter (total of items 1, 2, and 3)	5,712.80	5,712.80	
5 Final deposit made for quarter. (Enter zero if the final deposit made for the quarter is included in item 4.)		–0–	
6 Total deposits for quarter (total of items 4 and 5)—enter here and in item 20, page 1		5,712.80	

Form 941	**Employer's Quarterly**	
Department of the Treasury Internal Revenue Service	**Federal Tax Return**	

Schedule A—Quarterly Report of Wages Taxable under the Federal Insurance Contributions Act—FOR SOCIAL SECURITY

SSA Use Only

F ☐ 2 ☐ U ☐ E ☐
S ☐ 1 ☐ L ☐ T ☐
X ☐ 0 ☐ V ☐ A ☐

1. Total pages of this return including this page and any pages of Form 941a ▶	2. Total number of employees listed ▶	3. (First quarter only) Number of employees (except household) employed in the pay period including March 12th ▶
1	11	

4. EMPLOYEE'S SOCIAL SECURITY NUMBER	5. NAME OF EMPLOYEE (Please type or print)	6. TAXABLE FICA WAGES Paid to Employee in Quarter (Before deductions) Dollars Cents	7. TAXABLE TIPS REPORTED (See page 4) Dollars Cents
533 16 7285	Anderson, Dennis	2,282 00	
541 27 6982	Bowlen, Ralph P.	1,680 00	
539 87 1643	Daniels, John N.	2,322 60	
533 98 5379	Drew, Nancy R.	1,320 00	
526 71 8478	Fennell, Roger D.	1,586 80	
543 24 1680	Jones, Ronald R.	2,322 00	
533 62 1745	Lyman, Mary C.	1,800 00	
541 38 9394	Miller, Robert M.	2,248 20	
540 29 7162	Olsen, Marvin C.	1,670 00	
539 12 2796	Stanfield, John D.	1,430 00	
529 92 8131	Tucker, Norman P.	110 00	

If you need more space for listing employees, use Schedule A continuation sheets, Form 941a.
Totals for this page—Wage total in column 6 and tip total in column 7 ——▶ 18,771 60

8. TOTAL WAGES TAXABLE UNDER FICA PAID DURING QUARTER. $ 18,771.60 ◁
(Total of column 6 on this page and continuation sheets.) Enter here and in item 14 below.

9. TOTAL TAXABLE TIPS REPORTED UNDER FICA DURING QUARTER. $ None ◁
(Total of column 7 on this page and continuation sheets.) Enter here and in item 15 below. (If no tips reported, write "None.")

Employer's name, address, employer identification number, and calendar quarter. (If not correct, please change)

Name (as distinguished from trade name)
Robert C. Randall
Date quarter ended 12/31

▶ Trade name, if any
North Central Plumbing Supply
Employer Identification No. 64-7219618

Address and ZIP code
1968 Arrow St., N.W., Seattle, Wash. 98111
Entries must be made both above and below this line; if address different from previous return check here ☐

Name (as distinguished from trade name)
Robert C. Randall
Date quarter ended 12/31

▶ Trade name, if any
North Central Plumbing Supply
Employer Identification No. 64-7219618

Address and ZIP code
1968 Arrow St., N.W., Seattle, Wash. 98111

T	FP
FF	I
FD	TOT

10. Total Wages And Tips Subject To Withholding Plus Other Compensation . . . . ▶	18,771	60
11. Amount Of Income Tax Withheld From Wages, Tips, Annuities, etc. (See instructions) . . .	3,516	52
12. Adjustment For Preceding Quarters Of Calendar Year	-0-	
13. Adjusted Total Of Income Tax Withheld	3,516	52
14. Taxable FICA Wages Paid (Item 8) . . $ 18,771.60 multiplied by 11.7%=TAX	2,196	28
15. Taxable Tips Reported (Item 9) . . . $ -0- multiplied by 5.85%=TAX	-0-	
16. Total FICA Taxes (Item 14 plus Item 15) . . . . ▶	2,196	28
17. Adjustment (See instructions)	-0-	
18. Adjusted Total Of FICA Taxes . . . . ▶	2,196	28
19. Total Taxes (Item 13 plus Item 18) . . . . ▶	5,712	80
20. TOTAL DEPOSITS FOR QUARTER (INCLUDING FINAL DEPOSIT MADE FOR QUARTER) AND OVERPAYMENT FROM PREVIOUS QUARTER LISTED IN SCHEDULE B (See instructions on page 4)	5,712	80

Note: If undeposited taxes at the end of the quarter are $200 or more, the full amount must be deposited with an authorized commercial bank or a Federal Reserve bank. This deposit must be entered in Schedule B and included in item 20.

21. Undeposited Taxes Due (Item 19 Less Item 20—This Should Be Less Than $200). Pay To Internal Revenue Service And Enter Here . . . . ▶	-0-	

22. If Item 20 Is More Than Item 19, Enter Excess Here ▶ $ And Check If You Want It ☐ Applied To Next Return, Or ☐ Refunded.

23. If not liable for returns in the future write "FINAL" (See instructions) ▶ Date final wages paid ▶

Under penalties of perjury, I declare that I have examined this return, including accompanying schedules and statements, and to the best of my knowledge and belief it is true, correct and complete.

Date 1/31 Signature *Robert C. Randall* Title (Owner, etc) Owner

Withholding statements for employees (W-2 forms)

The employer has to furnish W-2 forms to employees on or before the January 31 following the close of the preceding year, or within 30 days after an employee leaves service. The source of the information on the W-2 form is the employee's individual earnings record. The record for Ronald R. Jones, presented in Chapter 14, will be our source for this example. The accountant fills out Form W-2 in quadruplicate and gives copies B and C to the employee.

For Official Use Only		Wage and Tax Statement 19	
North Central Plumbing Supply 1968 Arrow St., N. W. Seattle, WA 98111 64-7219618	◄ Type or print EMPLOYER'S name, address, ZIP code and Federal identifying number.	**Copy A For Internal Revenue Service Center** Employer's State identifying number	

21 ☐	Employee's social security number 543-24-1680	1 Federal income tax withheld $1,274.80	2 Wages, tips, and other compensation $9,302.00	3 FICA employee tax withheld $544.17	4 Total FICA wages $9,302.00
Name ►	Type or print Employee's name, address, and ZIP code below. (Name must aline with arrow) Ronald R. Jones 1620 West Seattle Way Seattle, WA 98116	5 Was employee covered by a qualified pension plan, etc.? No	6 °	7 °	
		8 State or local tax withheld	9 State or local wages	10 State or locality	
		11 State or local tax withheld	12 State or local wages	13 State or locality	
		° See instructions on back of Copy D			

Form **W-2**   Department of the Treasury—Internal Revenue Service

Employer's annual federal income tax reports

North Central sends copy A of each employee's W-2 form to the District Director of Internal Revenue on or before January 31. The accountant attaches these to Form W-3, the Transmittal of Income and Tax Statements, as shown here.

For Official Use Only			
Form **W-3** Department of the Treasury Internal Revenue Service	**Transmittal of Income and Tax Statements**	19	

Place an "X" in the proper box to identify type of document being transmitted

	PAYER'S identifying number	Enter number of documents	Form W-2 21	Form W-2P 22	Form 1099R 98
30 ☐	64-7219618	12	X		

	Type or print PAYER'S name, address, and ZIP code below (Name must aline with arrow).	All documents are: Place an "X" in the proper box.		All documents are: Place an "X" in the proper box.	
		Original	Corrected	With taxpayer identifying no.	Without taxpayer identifying no.
Name ►	North Central Plumbing Supply 1968 Arrow St., N. W. Seattle, Wash. 98111	X		X	

Magnetic tape or disk pack filers:
See the applicable Revenue Procedures
regarding transmittal of returns on magnetic tape or disk pack.

Under penalties of perjury, I declare that I have examined this return, including accompanying documents and to the best of my knowledge and belief, it is true, correct, and complete. In the case of documents without recipients' identifying numbers, I have complied with the requirements of the law by requesting such numbers from the recipients, but did not receive them.

Signature _Robert C. Randall_   Title _Owner_   Date _1/31_

To sum up: The employer must submit at the end of the calendar year, in one package, the following: (1) Employer's Quarterly Federal Tax Return for the fourth quarter, (2) copy A of all employees' W-2 forms, and (3) Form W-3. The employer keeps copy D of the W-2 forms.

Reports and payments of state unemployment insurance

Below and on page 390 is the return for state unemployment insurance for North Central Plumbing Supply for the first quarter, with the assumed state rate of 3% on the first $4,800 paid to each employee during the calendar year. The source of information for the wage report section is the employees' individual earnings records.

S.F. 5208 REV. 4-72

EMPLOYER'S TAX REPORT
PLEASE READ THE INSTRUCTIONS CAREFULLY ON THE REVERSE SIDE OF THE GREEN PRINT COPY.

STATE OF WASHINGTON
EMPLOYMENT SECURITY DEPARTMENT
P.O. BOX 367, OLYMPIA, WASHINGTON 98504

ORIGINAL
MAIL THIS COPY TO THE STATE OFFICE

ATTACH CHECK HERE

FEDERAL INDENT. NO.	TAX RATE	ANNUAL TAXABLE WAGE BASE EACH EMPLOYEE	CENTRAL OFFICE ONLY			NEW ACCOUNT	EMPLOYER NUMBER	
			INDUSTRIAL	AREA	CONT. SH.		ACCOUNT	BR
64-7219618	3.0%	$4,800				APPLIED FOR	462-718	
(ENTER IF NOT SHOWN)								

EMPLOYER'S NAME, ADDRESS.

Robert C. Randall
North Central Plumbing Supply
1968 Arrow St., N. W.
Seattle, Wash. 98111

▼ **FOR THE CALENDAR QUARTER ENDING** ▼

March 31, 19__

THIS REPORT DELINQUENT AFTER ONE MONTH
▲ FOLLOWING DATE SHOWN ABOVE ▲

	IN THE PAY PERIOD INCLUDING THE 12TH OF EACH MONTH OF THE QUARTER.	Jan.	Feb.	March	DO NOT USE THIS COLUMN
1. NUMBER OF COVERED WORKERS		1ST MONTH	2ND MONTH	3RD MONTH	
2. TOTAL WAGES (BEFORE DEDUCTIONS) PAID TO COVERED WORKERS DURING THIS QUARTER FOR EMPLOYMENT. INCLUDE OTHER REMUNERATION AND GRATUITIES SUCH AS VALUE OF MEALS, LODGING, ETC.		$	25,600	00	
3. DEDUCT WAGES - IN EXCESS OF THE INDIVIDUAL TAXABLE WAGE BASE (SHOWN IN THE SHADED BOX ABOVE.) SEE INSTRUCTIONS ON REVERSE SIDE.		$	-0-		
4. TAXABLE WAGES - (ITEM 2 MINUS ITEM 3)		$	25,600	00	
5. TAX DUE - MULTIPLY ITEM 4 BY TAX RATE (SHOWN IN TAX RATE BOX ABOVE)		$	768	00	
6. INTEREST - (1% PER MONTH OR 1/30TH OF 1% PER DAY ON OVERDUE TAX FROM DELINQUENCY DATE)		$	-0-		
7. ADJUSTMENTS - DO NOT ADJUST PAYROLL. SHOW PREVIOUS OVERPAYMENT OR UNDERPAYMENT EVIDENCED BY "STATEMENT OF ACCOUNT" ATTACHED.		$			
8. REMITTANCE - MAKE CHECKS PAYABLE TO: "EMPLOYMENT SECURITY DEPARTMENT"		$	768	00	

9. CHANGE IN BUSINESS - DATE OF CHANGE:_____

BUSINESS ACQUIRED BY:_____

NATURE OF CHANGE:

☐ SALE OR LEASE OF BUSINESS
☐ CEASED BUSINESS, NO SUCCESSOR
☐ CONTINUING, NO EMPLOYEES, CLOSE ACCOUNT
☐ CORPORATION FORMED
☐ CORPORATION DISSOLVED

☐ DECEASED PROPRIETOR OR PARTNER
☐ PARTNERSHIP FORMED
☐ PARTNERSHIP DISSOLVED
☐ CHANGE IN MEMBERS OF PARTNERSHIP
☐ OTHER CHANGES (ATTACH EXPLANATION)

NEW MAILING ADDRESS:_____
NEW BUSINESS ADDRESS:_____

10. I CERTIFY THAT THE INFORMATION CONTAINED IN THIS REPORT IS TRUE AND CORRECT; THAT THE WAGES REPORTED WERE PAID FOR EMPLOYMENT IN PAY PERIODS ENDING IN THE QUARTER INDICATED ABOVE; AND THAT NO PART OF THE TAX REPORTED WAS, OR IS TO BE DEDUCTED FROM WORKERS WAGES.

4/27	X _Robert C. Randall_	Owner
DATE SIGNED	SIGNATURE	TITLE

AUDIT SECTION	VALIDATION SPACE
TAX_____INT._____AUDITED BY_____	

EMPLOYER'S QUARTERLY REPORT OF EMPLOYEE'S WAGES

STATE OF WASHINGTON
EMPLOYMENT SECURITY DEPARTMENT
P.O. BOX 367. OLYMPIA. WASHINGTON 98504

ORIGINAL
MAIL THIS COPY TO
THE STATE OFFICE

FEDERAL IDENT. NO.	TAX RATE	WEEKS WORKED AMOUNT (ITEM 16)	CENTRAL OFFICE ONLY			NEW ACCOUNT		EMPLOYER NUMBER	
			INDUSTRIAL	AREA	CONT. SH.			ACCOUNT	BR
64-7219618 (ENTER IF NOT SHOWN)	3.0%	13				APPLIED FOR		462-718	

11.
EMPLOYER NAME, ADDRESS, AS SHOWN ON FORM S.F. 5208

Robert C. Randall
North Central Plumbing Supply
1968 Arrow St., N. W.
Seattle, Wash. 98111

12. FOR THE CALENDAR QUARTER ENDING

▼   ▼

March 31, 19__

IF MORE SPACE NEEDED FOR LISTING EMPLOYEES - USE CONTINUATION SHEETS S.F. 5208-A-I

16. NUMBER OF WEEKS EMPLOYEE EARNED THE AMOUNT (OR MORE) SHOWN IN THE SHADED WEEKS WORKED BOX (ABOVE LEFT).

LINE NO.	13. EMPLOYEE'S SOCIAL SECURITY ACCOUNT NUMBER PLEASE BE ACCURATE			14. EMPLOYEE'S LAST NAME, FIRST NAME AND INITIALS TYPEWRITE OR PRINT	15. TOTAL WASHINGTON WAGES PAID THIS QUARTER			DO NOT USE
					DOLLARS	CENTS		
1	533	16	7285	Anderson, Dennis	2,264	00	13	
2	541	27	6982	Bowlen, Ralph P.	1,680	00	13	
3	539	87	1643	Daniels, John N.	2,416	00	13	
4	533	98	5379	Drew, Nancy R.	1,320	00	13	
5	526	71	8478	Fennell, Roger D.	1,486	00	13	
6	518	79	9430	Harwood, Lance C.	3,872	00	13	
7	543	24	1680	Jones, Ronald R.	2,322	00	13	
8	533	62	1745	Lyman, Mary C.	1,800	00	13	
9	541	38	9394	Miller, Robert M.	2,252	00	13	
10	540	29	7162	Olsen, Marvin C.	1,684	00	13	
11	539	12	2796	Stanfield, John D.	1,440	00	13	
12	529	92	8131	Tucker, Norman P.	3,064	00	13	
13								
14								

ITEM 18. MUST AGREE WITH ITEM 2 OF "EMPLOYER'S TAX REPORT", S.F. 5208

17. TOTAL FOR THIS PAGE	NO. OF EMPLOYEES 12	25,600	00
18. TOTAL FOR THIS REPORT	NO. OF EMPLOYEES 12	25,600	00

19. TOTAL PAGES THIS REPORT

1

Various states differ with regard to both the rate and the taxable base for unemployment insurance. States often used to reward employers for maintaining stable employment by charging a rate of less than 2.7%, just as an automobile insurance company rewards safe drivers with lower premiums. However, this is no longer practiced extensively, as we have said, because of the trend toward increased unemployment compensation benefits. Most states these days impose a rate of *at least* 2.7%, levied on a base of at least $4,200. The state tax is usually due by the end of the month following the end of the calendar quarter; the due dates consequently coincide with the due dates of Form 941.

In general journal form, the entry is as follows.

19—				
Apr.	27	State Unemployment Tax Payable	768 00	
		Cash		768 00
		To record payment of state un-employment tax (recorded in cash payments journal)		

Reports and payments of federal unemployment insurance

Each employer who is subject to the Federal Unemployment Tax Act, as outlined in Chapter 14, must submit an Employer's Annual Federal Unemployment Tax Return, Form 940, not later than the January 31 following the close of the calendar year. This deadline may be extended until February 10, if the employer has made deposits paying the FUTA tax liability in full. The FUTA tax is calculated quarterly, during the month following the end of each calendar quarter. *If the accumulated tax liability is greater than $100, the tax is deposited in a commercial bank or Federal Reserve bank, accompanied by a preprinted federal tax deposit card,* like the form used to deposit employees' federal income tax withholding and FICA taxes. The due date for this deposit is the last day of the month following the end of the quarter, the same as the dates for the Employer's Quarterly Federal Tax Return and for state unemployment taxes.

The accountant computes the tax liability for the first quarter as follows.

Unemployment taxable earnings times FUTA tax rate (.5%)
$25,600 \times .005 = $128.00

The entry for the payment of the tax, in general journal form, is as follows.

Apr.	27	Federal Unemployment Tax		
		Payable	128 00	
		Cash		128 00
		To record payment of federal unemployment tax (recorded in cash payments journal)		

Unemployment-taxable earnings for the second quarter are $20,608, which means a tax liability of $103.04. Therefore the accountant makes a deposit. During the third quarter many employees passed the $4,200 mark for their total earnings for the calendar year, and the tax liability was accordingly reduced to $19.52.

North Central does not have to make a deposit following the third quarter, since the total accumulated liability is less than $100. The tax liability for the fourth quarter is $15.65. North Central can pay the unpaid tax liability of $35.17 ($19.52 + $15.65) when it files the Employer's Annual Federal Unemployment Tax Return (Form 940). Incidentally, if the employer's accumulated tax liability is less than $100, he or she doesn't have to make a deposit at all. Instead, he/she just files the tax when he/she files the annual federal unemployment tax return.

The annual return for North Central Plumbing Supply is as shown on the opposite page.

The employer should complete the quarterly state unemployment tax return for the last quarter of the year before he or she tries to prepare the Employer's Annual Federal Unemployment Tax Return, since the data from the state returns are the source of information for the federal Form 940.

Workmen's compensation insurance

As we said in Chapter 14, when we were describing the laws affecting employment, most states require employers to provide workmen's compensation insurance or industrial accident insurance, either through plans administered by the state or through private insurance companies authorized by the state. The employer usually has to pay all the premiums. The rate of the insurance premium varies with the amount of risk the job entails. Handling molten steel ingots is a lot more dangerous than typing reports. So it is very important that employees be classified properly according to the insurance premium classifications. For example, the rate for office work may be .15% of the payroll for office work, and the rate for industrial labor in heavy manufacturing may be 3.5% of the payroll for that category. These same figures may be expressed as $.15 per $100 of payroll and $3.50 per $100 of payroll.

Generally, the employer pays a premium in advance, based on his/her estimated payrolls for the year. After the year ends, the employer knows the exact amounts of the payrolls, so he/she can calculate the exact premium. At this time, depending on the difference between the estimated and the exact premium, the employer either pays an additional premium or gets a credit for overpayment.

At North Central Plumbing Supply, there are three types of work classifications: office work, sales work, and warehouse work. At the beginning of the year, their accountant computed the estimated annual premium, based on the predicted payrolls for the year, as follows.

Classification	Predicted payroll	Rate	Estimated premium
Office work	$25,000	.15%	$25,000 × .0015 = $ 37.50
Sales work	62,400	.5%	62,400 × .005 = 312.00
Warehouse work	9,000	1.8%	9,000 × .018 = 162.00
			Total estimated premium $511.50

Employer's Annual Federal Unemployment Tax Return

19

Name of State 1	State reporting number as shown on employer's State contribution returns 2	Taxable payroll (As defined in State act) 3	Experience rate period 4 From—	To—	Experience rate 5	Contributions had rate been 2.7% (col. 3 × 2.7%) 6	Contributions payable at experience rate (col. 3 × col. 5) 7	Additional credit (col. 6 minus col. 7) 8	Contributions actually paid to State 9
Wash.	462-718	57,400.00	1/1	12/31	3.0	1,549.80	1,722.00		1,722.00
	Totals ▶	57,400.00							1,722.00

10 Total tentative credit (Column 8 plus column 9) . . . . | 1,722 | 00

11 Total remuneration (including exempt remuneration) PAID during the calendar year for services of employees | 106,792 | 00

Exempt Remuneration	Approximate number of employees involved	Amount paid	
12 Exempt remuneration. (Explain each exemption shown, attaching additional sheet if necessary): _____			
13 Remuneration in excess of $4,200. (Enter only the excess over the first $4,200 paid to individual employees exclusive of exempt amounts entered on line 12)	12	53,550.00	

14 Total exempt remuneration . . . . | 53,550 | 00

15 Total taxable wages (line 11 less line 14) . . . . | 53,242 | 00

16 Gross Federal tax (3.2% of line 15) . . . . | 1,703 | 74

17 Enter 2.7% of the amount of wages shown on line 15 . . . . . | 1,437.53 |

18 Line 10 or line 17 whichever is smaller . . . . | 1,437.53 |

19 Net Federal tax (line 16 less line 18) . . . . | 266.21

Record of Federal Tax Deposits for Unemployment Tax (Form 508)

Quarter	Liability by period	Date of deposit	Amount of deposit
First	128.00	4/27	128.00
Second	103.04	7/12	103.04
Third	19.52		
Fourth	15.65		

20 Total Federal tax deposited . . . . | 231 | 04

21 Balance due (line 19 less line 20—this should not exceed $100). Pay to "Internal Revenue Service" . . ▶ | 35 | 17

22 If no longer in business at end of year, write **"FINAL"** here ▶

Under penalties of perjury, I declare that I have examined this return, including accompanying schedules and statements, and to the best of my knowledge and belief it is true, correct, and complete, and that no part of any payment made to a State unemployment fund, which is claimed as a credit on line 18 above, was or is to be deducted from the remuneration of employees.

Date ▶ 1/26   Signature ▶ *Robert C. Randall*   Title (Owner, etc.) ▶ Owner

T	
FF	
FD	
FP	
I	
T	

(If incorrect make any necessary change.) ▶

Name (as distinguished from trade name)
Robert C. Randall

Trade name, if any
North Central Plumbing Supply

Address and ZIP code
1968 Arrow St., N. W., Seattle, WA 98111

Calendar Year
19__

Employer Identification No.
64-7219618

16-■-1

Form **940**

Accordingly, as shown by T accounts, the accountant recorded the following entry.

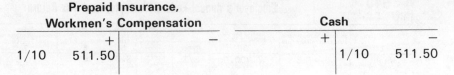

Prepaid Insurance, Workmen's Compensation				Cash	
+		−		+	−
1/10	511.50			1/10	511.50

Then, at the end of the calendar year, the accountant calculated the exact premium.

Classification	Exact payroll	Rate	Premium
Office work	$25,620	.15%	$25,620 × .0015 = $ 38.43
Sales work	63,000	.5%	63,000 × .005 = 315.00
Warehouse work	9,302	1.8%	9,302 × .018 = 167.44
			Total exact premium $520.87

Therefore, the amount of the unpaid premium is

Total exact premium	$520.87
Less total estimated premium paid	511.50
Additional premium owed	$ 9.37

Now the accountant makes an adjusting entry, similar to the usual adjusting entry for expired insurance; this entry appears on the work sheet. Also he or she makes an additional adjusting entry for the extra premium owed. By T accounts, the entries are as follows.

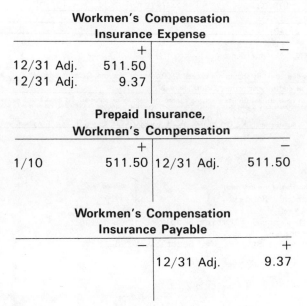

Workmen's Compensation Insurance Expense

+		−
12/31 Adj.	511.50	
12/31 Adj.	9.37	

Prepaid Insurance, Workmen's Compensation

+		−	
1/10	511.50	12/31 Adj.	511.50

Workmen's Compensation Insurance Payable

−		+
	12/31 Adj.	9.37

North Central Plumbing Supply will pay this amount of unpaid premium in January, together with the estimated premium for the next year.

Adjusting for accrued salaries and wages

Assume that $800 of salaries accrue for the time between the last payday and the end of the year. The adjusting entry is the same as introduced in Chapter 5.

Salary Expense	800 00	
Salaries Payable		800 00

Salaries Payable is a current liability account, and the employees' withholding taxes and deductions payable are also current liabilities. Actually, federal income taxes and FICA taxes levied on employees do not legally become effective until the employees are paid. Therefore, for the purpose of recording the adjusting entry, one should include the entire liability of the gross salaries and wages under Salaries Payable.

Adjusting entry for accrual of payroll taxes

As we have seen, the following taxes come under the Payroll Tax Expense account: the employer's share of the FICA tax, the state unemployment tax, and the federal unemployment tax. The employer becomes liable for these taxes only when the employees are actually paid, rather than at the time the liability to the employees is incurred. From the standpoint of legal liability, there should be no adjusting entry for Payroll Tax Expense. From the standpoint of the income statement, however, doing without this entry would mean that this accrued expense for payroll taxes would not be included; thus the expenses would be understated and the net income would be overstated, although by a rather inconsequential amount. In other words, the legal element is not consistent with good accounting practice, but we have to abide by the law.

Tax calendar

Now let's put it all together: North Central's combined monthly totals of employees' FICA taxes, employer's FICA tax, and employees' income tax withheld are usually greater than $200 and less than $2,000. So North Central's accountant, in order to keep up with the task of paying and reporting the various taxes, compiles a chronological list of the due dates. We are including only the payroll taxes here; however, sales taxes and property taxes should also be listed. When you think about the penalties for nonpayment of taxes by the due dates, this chronological list seems to be well worth the trouble.

Jan. 10	Pay estimated annual premium for workmen's compensation insurance. (This is an approximate date, as it varies among the states.)
31	Complete Employer's Quarterly Federal Tax Return, Form 941, for the fourth quarter, and pay employees' income tax withholding,

	employees' FICA tax withholding, and employer's FICA tax for wages paid during the month of December.
Jan. 31	Issue copies B and C of Wage and Tax Statement, W-2 forms, to employees.
31	Complete Transmittal of Income and Tax Statements, Form W-3, and attach copy A of W-2 forms for employees.
31	Pay federal unemployment tax liability for previous year and submit Form 940, Employer's Annual Federal Unemployment Tax Return.
31	Pay state unemployment tax liability for the previous quarter and submit state return, employer's tax report.
Feb. 15	Make federal tax deposit for employees' income tax withholding, employees' FICA tax withholding, and employer's FICA tax for wages paid during the month of January.
Mar. 15	Make federal tax deposit for employees' income tax withholding, employees' FICA tax withholding, and employer's FICA tax for wages paid during the month of February.
Apr. 30	Pay state unemployment tax liability for the previous quarter and submit state return, employer's tax report.
30	Complete Employer's Quarterly Federal Tax Return, Form 941, for the first quarter, and pay employees' income tax withholding, employees' FICA tax withholding, and employer's FICA tax for wages paid during the month of March.
30	Make federal tax deposit for federal unemployment tax liability if it exceeds $100.

Summary

The employer's taxes based on the payroll are as follows.

- FICA tax, 5.85% of taxable income (the first $15,300 for each employee)
- Federal unemployment tax, .5% of taxable income (the first $4,200 for each employee)
- State unemployment tax, which varies from state to state, approximately 2.7% of taxable income (approximately the first $4,200 for each employee)

After recording each payroll entry from the payroll register, the accountant makes the following entry to record the employer's payroll taxes.

Payroll Tax Expense	103 87	
FICA Tax Payable		93 87
Federal Unemployment Tax Payable		1 30
State Unemployment Tax Payable		8 70

Payment of the tax liabilities and sample journal entries are as follows.

1 Payment of the combined amounts of employees' income tax withheld, employees' FICA tax withheld, and employer's FICA tax falls into three brackets:

a If at the end of any quarter of a month (approximately 1 week) the cumulative amount of undeposited taxes so far for the calendar quarter (3 months) is $2,000 or more, deposit the taxes within 3 banking days after the end of the quarter-of-a-month period (7th, 15th, 22nd, and last day of month).

b If at the end of any month (except the last month of a quarter) the cumulative amount of undeposited taxes for the quarter is at least $200 but less than $2,000, deposit the taxes within 15 days after the end of the month.

c If at the end of a calendar quarter (3 months) the total amount of undeposited taxes is less than $200, no deposit is required, but make the payment at the time of submitting the Employer's Quarterly Federal Tax Return, Form 941.

19__				
Dec.	12	Employees' Federal Income Tax		
		Payable	1,142 60	
		FICA Tax Payable	742 32	
		Cash		1,884 92

2 Payment of state unemployment tax on a quarterly basis accompanied by the quarterly return.

19__				
Apr.	27	State Unemployment Tax Payable	768 00	
		Cash		768 00

3 Payment of federal unemployment tax. If the amount of the accumulated tax liability exceeds $100, then make a deposit, using the federal tax deposit form. Pay the remaining tax due by January 31 of the year following the close of the calendar year, using the Employer's Annual Federal Unemployment Tax Return, Form 940.

Apr.	27	Federal Unemployment Tax		
		Payable	128 00	
		Cash		128 00

4 Workmen's compensation insurance, based on a state plan or private insurance. At the beginning of the year, pay the premium in advance based on the estimated annual payroll. At the end of the year, when you know the actual payroll, adjust for the exact amount of the premium.

Glossary

o **Employer's identification number** The number assigned each employer by the Internal Revenue Service for use in the submission of reports and payments for FICA taxes and federal income tax withheld.

o **Federal unemployment tax** A tax levied on the employer only, amounting to .5% of the first $4,200 of total earnings paid to each employee during the calendar year. This tax is used to supplement state unemployment benefits.

- **Payroll tax expense** A general expense account used for recording the employer's matching portion of the FICA tax, the federal unemployment tax, and the state unemployment tax.
- **Quarter** A 3-month interval of the year, also referred to as a calendar quarter, as follows: first quarter, January, February, and March; second quarter, April, May, and June; third quarter, July, August, and September; fourth quarter, October, November, and December.
- **Quarter-of-a-month periods** These are periods representing due dates for tax deposits designated by the Internal Revenue Service as follows: from the 1st to the 7th of the month (inclusive), from the 8th to the 15th of the month (inclusive), from the 16th to the 22nd of the month (inclusive), and from the 23rd to the last day of the month (inclusive).
- **State unemployment tax** A tax levied on the employer only. Rates differ among the various states; however, they are generally 2.7% of the first $4,200 of total earnings paid to each employee during the calendar year, and are used to pay subsistence benefits to unemployed workers.
- **Workmen's compensation insurance** This insurance, usually paid for by the employer, provides benefits for employees injured on the job. The rates vary according to the degree of risk inherent in the job. The plans may be sponsored by states or by private firms. The employer pays the premium in advance at the beginning of the year, based on the estimated payroll, and rates are adjusted after the exact payroll is known.

Review of T account placement

The following sums up the placement of T accounts covered in Chapters 8 through 15 in relation to the Trial Balance Equation.

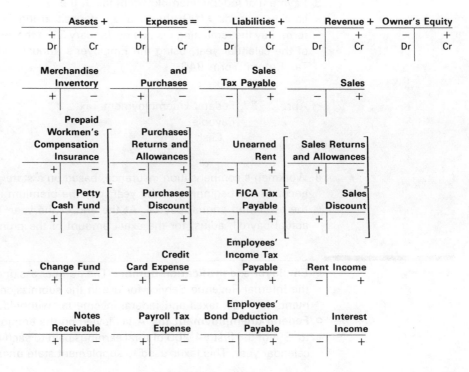

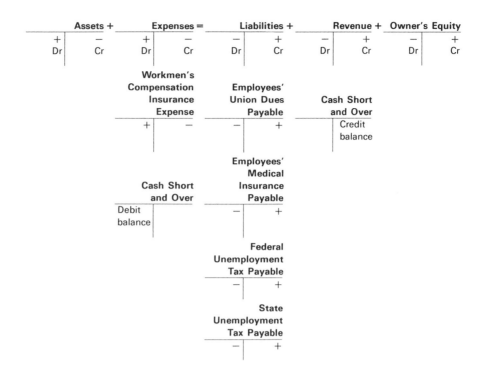

	Assets +		Expenses =		Liabilities +		Revenue +	Owner's Equity	
+	−	+	−	−	+	−	+	−	+
Dr	Cr	Dr	Cr	Dr	Cr	Dr	Cr	Dr	Cr

Workmen's Compensation Insurance Expense

+	−

Employees' Union Dues Payable

−	+

Cash Short and Over

	Credit balance

Employees' Medical Insurance Payable

−	+

Cash Short and Over

Debit balance	

Federal Unemployment Tax Payable

−	+

State Unemployment Tax Payable

−	+

Review of representative transactions

The following summarizes the recording of transactions covered in Chapters 8 through 15, along with a classification of the accounts involved.

Transaction	Accounts Involved	Class.	Increase or Decrease	Therefore debit or credit
Sold merchandise on account	Accounts Receivable	A	I	Dr
	Sales	R	I	Cr
Sold merchandise on account involving sales tax	Accounts Receivable	A	I	Dr
	Sales	R	I	Cr
	Sales Tax Payable	L	I	Cr
Issued credit memo to customer for merchandise returned	Sales Returns and Allowances	R	I	Dr
	Accounts Receivable	A	D	Cr
Summarizing entry for the total of sales invoices for sales on account for the month	Accounts Receivable	A	I	Dr
	Sales	R	I	Cr
Bought merchandise on account	Purchases	Purchases	I	Dr
	Accounts Payable	L	I	Cr
Received credit memo from supplier for merchandise returned	Accounts Payable	L	D	Dr
	Purchases Returns and Allowances	Purchases	I	Cr

Transaction	Accounts Involved	Class.	Increase or Decrease	Therefore debit or credit
Summarizing entry for the total of purchases of all types of goods on account	Purchases	Purchases	I	Dr
	Store Supplies	A	I	Dr
	Office Supplies	A	I	Dr
	Store Equipment	A	I	Dr
	Accounts Payable	L	I	Cr
Paid for transportation charges on incoming merchandise	Purchases	Purchases	I	Dr
	Cash	A	D	Cr
Sold merchandise, involving sales tax, for cash	Cash	A	I	Dr
	Sales	R	I	Cr
	Sales Tax Payable	L	I	Cr
Sold merchandise involving a sales tax and the customer used a bank charge card	Cash	A	I	Dr
	Credit Card Expense	E	I	Dr
	Sales	R	I	Cr
	Sales Tax Payable	L	I	Cr
Charge customer paid bill within the discount period	Cash	A	I	Dr
	Sales Discount	R	I	Dr
	Accounts Receivable	A	D	Cr
Paid invoice for the purchase of merchandise within the discount period	Accounts Payable	L	D	Dr
	Cash	A	D	Cr
	Purchases Discount	Purchases	I	Cr
First adjusting entry for merchandise inventory	Revenue and Expense Summary	OE	——	Dr
	Merchandise Inventory	A	D	Cr
Second adjusting entry for merchandise inventory	Merchandise Inventory	A	I	Dr
	Revenue and Expense Summary	OE	——	Cr
Adjusting entry for unearned revenue (Rent Income)	Rent Income	R	D	Dr
	Unearned Rent	L	I	Cr
Reversing entry for adjustment for accrued wages	Wages Payable	L	D	Dr
	Wages Expense	E	D	Cr
Reversing entry for adjustment for unearned revenue (Rent Income)	Unearned Rent	L	D	Dr
	Rent Income	R	I	Cr
Established a Petty Cash Fund	Petty Cash Fund	A	I	Dr
	Cash	A	D	Cr
Reimbursed Petty Cash Fund	Expenses or Assets or Drawing	E, A, OE	I	Dr
	Cash	A	D	Cr
Established a Change Fund	Change Fund	A	I	Dr
	Cash	A	D	Cr
Recorded cash sales (amount on cash register tape was larger than cash count)	Cash	A	I	Dr
	Cash Short and Over	E	I	Dr
	Sales	R	I	Cr

Transaction	Accounts Involved	Class.	Increase or Decrease	Therefore debit or credit
Recorded cash sales (amount on cash register tape was less than cash count)	Cash	A	I	Dr
	Sales	R	I	Cr
	Cash Short and Over	R	I	Cr
Recorded service charges on bank account	Miscellaneous General Expense	E	I	Dr
	Cash	A	D	Cr
Recorded NSF check received from customer	Accounts Receivable	A	I	Dr
	Cash	A	D	Cr
Recorded interest-bearing note receivable collected by our bank	Cash	A	I	Dr
	Notes Receivable	A	D	Cr
	Interest Income	R	I	Cr
Recorded the payroll entry from the payroll register	Sales Salary Expense	E	I	Dr
	Office Salary Expense	E	I	Dr
	FICA Tax Payable	L	I	Cr
	Employees' Income Tax Payable	L	I	Cr
	Employees' Bond Deduction Payable	L	I	Cr
	Employees' Union Dues Payable	L	I	Cr
	Salaries Payable	L	I	Cr
Issued check payable to payroll bank account	Salaries Payable	L	D	Dr
	Cash	A	D	Cr
Recorded employer's payroll taxes	Payroll Tax Expense	E	I	Dr
	FICA Tax Payable	L	I	Cr
	State Unemployment Tax Payable	L	I	Cr
	Federal Unemployment Tax Payable	L	I	Cr
Recorded deposit of FICA taxes and employees' income tax withheld	Employees' Income Tax Payable	L	D	Dr
	FICA Tax Payable	L	D	Dr
	Cash	A	D	Cr
Recorded deposit of federal unemployment tax	Federal Unemployment Tax Payable	L	D	Dr
	Cash	A	D	Cr
Paid state unemployment tax	State Unemployment Tax Payable	L	D	Dr
	Cash	A	D	Cr
Paid for workmen's compensation insurance in advance	Prepaid Workmen's Compensation Insurance	A	I	Dr
	Cash	A	D	Cr

Transaction	Accounts Involved	Class.	Increase or Decrease	Therefore debit or credit
Adjusting entry for workmen's compensation insurance, assuming an additional amount is owed	Workmen's Compensation Insurance Expense	E	I	Dr
	Prepaid Workmen's Compensation Insurance	A	D	Cr
	Workmen's Compensation Insurance Payable	L	I	Cr

Exercises

Exercise 1 Suppose that you are an accountant for a small business, and you get a premium notice for workmen's compensation insurance, stipulating the rates for the coming year. You have estimated that the year's premium will be as follows.

Classification	Estimated wages and salaries	Rate	Estimated premium	
Office work	$ 9,000	.10%		$ 9.00
Sales work	36,000	.78%		280.80
Warehouse work	9,000	1.80%		162.00
			Total estimated premium	$451.80

On January 27 the owner issued a check for $451.80. Record the entry in general journal form.

Exercise 2 Still with reference to Exercise 1, at the end of the year, the exact figures for the payroll are as follows.

Classification	Estimated wages and salaries	Rate	Estimated premium	
Office work	$ 9,000	.10%		$ 9.00
Sales work	37,800	.78%		294.84
Warehouse work	9,600	1.80%		172.80
			Total actual premium	$476.64
			Less estimated premium paid	451.80
			Balance of premium due	$ 24.84

Record the adjusting entries for the insurance expired as well as for the additional premium due.

Exercise 3 The payroll for the Sutro Company is as follows.

Gross earnings of employees	$100,000
Earnings subject to FICA tax	88,000
Earnings subject to federal unemployment tax	26,000
Earnings subject to state unemployment tax	26,000

Assuming that the payroll is subject to a FICA tax of 5.85% (.0585), a state unemployment tax of 2.7% (.027), and a federal unemployment tax of .5% (.005), give the entry in general journal form to record the payroll tax expense.

Exercise 4 The Mello Dairy had 100 employees throughout this year. The lowest-paid employee had gross earnings of $5,000. Assume that the Federal Unemployment Tax Act specifies a rate of 3.2% on the first $4,200 of gross earnings, and that the state unemployment tax is 2.7% of the same base. Mello Dairy, to conform to Form 940, is entitled to take credit against their federal tax by the amount paid to the state. (The effective federal unemployment tax is .5%.) Calculate (similar to Form 940) the following.

a The total unemployment tax for the year.
b The state unemployment tax for the year.
c The federal unemployment tax for the year.

Exercise 5 The earnings for the calendar year for the employees of Economy Shoe Repair are as follows.

Employee	Cumulative earnings
Bach, Ralph P.	$ 8,400.00
Lindahl, Doreen C.	16,400.00
Luhr, Alan D.	8,400.00
Weist, Terry D.	1,800.00
	$35,000.00

The employees had to pay FICA tax during the year at the rate of 5.85% on the first $15,300 of their earnings; the employer had to pay a matching FICA tax. Unemployment insurance rates were 2.7% for the state and .5% for the federal government on the first $4,200 of an employee's earnings.

a Determine the taxable earnings for FICA, state unemployment, and federal unemployment.
b Determine the amount of taxes paid by the employees.
c Determine the total amount of payroll taxes paid by the employer.

d What percentage of the employer's total payroll of $35,000 was represented by payroll taxes?

Exercise 6 The salary expense of the Dugdale Company this year was $150,000, of which $30,000 was not subject to FICA tax and $60,000 was not subject to state and federal unemployment taxes. Calculate Dugdale's payroll tax expense for the year, using the following rates: FICA, 5.85% of first $15,300; state unemployment, 3.0% of first $4,200; federal unemployment, .5% of first $4,200.

Exercise 7 On January 13, at the end of the second weekly pay period during the year, the totals of Piazza Transfer's payroll register showed that its driver employees had earned $2,200 and its office employees had earned $600. The employees were to have FICA taxes withheld at the rate of 5.85% of the first $15,300, plus $275 of federal income taxes, and $90 of union dues.

a Calculate the amount of FICA taxes to be withheld, and write the general journal entry to record the payroll.

b Write the general journal entry to record the employer's payroll taxes, assuming that the company has a merit rating that reduces its state unemployment tax rate to 2.5% of the first $4,200 paid each employee, and that the federal unemployment tax is .5% of the same base.

Exercise 8 The following information on earnings and deductions for the pay period ended December 14 is from J. C. Dillon and Company's payroll records.

Name	Gross Pay	Earnings to End of Previous Week
Fowler, Earl C.	190 00	2,500 00
Minski, Carl A.	320 00	16,000 00
Woods, Norma M.	200 00	10,000 00
Zimmer, Axel L.	210 00	10,500 00

Prepare a general journal entry to record the employer's payroll taxes. The FICA tax is 5.85% of the first $15,300 of earnings for each employee. The state unemployment tax rate is 3.0% of the first $4,200 of earnings of each employee, and the federal unemployment tax is .5% (.005) of the same base.

Problems

Problem 15-1 Gordon Johnson and Company had the following payroll for the week ended June 24.

Salaries		Deductions	
Sales salaries	$1,640.00	Income tax withheld	$230.00
Office salaries	280.00	FICA tax withheld	112.32
	$1,920.00	U.S. Savings Bonds	150.00
		Medical insurance	160.00

Assumed tax rates are:
- FICA tax, 5.85% (.0585) on the first $15,300 for each employee
- State unemployment tax, 2.7% (.027) on the first $4,200 for each employee
- Federal unemployment tax, .5% (.005) on the first $4,200 for each employee

Instructions Record the following entries in general journal form:

1 The payroll entry as of June 24
2 The entry to record the employer's payroll taxes as of June 24, assuming that the total payroll is subject to the FICA tax, and that $1,410 is subject to unemployment taxes
3 The payment of the employees as of June 27, assuming that Johnson and Company issues one check payable to a payroll bank account

Problem 15-2 The column totals of the payroll register of Cardozo and Son, for the week ended January 14 of this year, show that the sales employees have earned $1,700 and the office employees $300. Cardozo has deducted from the salaries of employees $336 for income taxes, $85 for medical insurance, $68 for union dues, and FICA tax at the rate of 5.85% (.0585) on the first $15,300 of their earnings.

Instructions Record the following entries in general journal form:

1 The payroll entry as of January 14
2 The entry to record the employer's payroll taxes as of January 14, assuming 2.7% (.027) of $4,200 for state unemployment insurance and .5% (.005) of $4,200 for federal unemployment insurance
3 The payment of the employees as of January 16, assuming that Cardozo issues one check payable to a payroll bank account

Problem 15-3 For the third quarter of the year, the Raymond Company, 3612 Milton Street, Cincinnati, Ohio 45230, received Form 941 from the Director of Internal Revenue. The identification number for the Raymond Company is 65-6715218. Their payroll for the quarter is as follows.

Name	Social Security Number	Total Earnings	Taxable Earnings Unempl. Ins.	Taxable Earnings FICA	FICA Withheld	Income Tax Withheld
Aikens, Thom	543-16-5990	2,280 00		2,280 00	133 38	306 00
Bower, Alma	562-17-2186	2,160 00		2,160 00	126 36	298 00
Phelps, Darien	540-13-9241	1,870 00	620 00	1,870 00	109 40	219 00
Smith, Noel	571-18-8702	1,960 00	280 00	1,960 00	114 66	231 00
Wake, Roger	541-09-7162	1,200 00	1,200 00	1,200 00	70 20	146 00
		9,470 00	2,100 00	9,470 00	554 00	1,200 00

The company has had five employees throughout the year. Assume that the FICA tax payable by the employees is 5.85% of the first $15,300 of their earnings and that the FICA tax payable by the employer is 5.85% of the first $15,300 paid to the employees. Mr. Thomas Raymond had submitted the following federal tax deposits and written the accompanying checks, as shown at the top of the next page.

On August 14, for the July payroll		On September 12, for the August payroll		On October 14, for the September payroll	
Employees' income tax withheld	$380.00	Employees' income tax withheld	$420.00	Employees' income tax withheld	$400.00
Employees' FICA tax withheld	176.00	Employees' FICA tax withheld	189.00	Employees' FICA tax withheld	189.00
Employer's FICA tax	176.00	Employer's FICA tax	189.00	Employer's FICA tax	188.99
	$732.00		$798.00		$777.99

Instructions

1 Complete Schedule B of Form 941.

2 Complete Schedule A of Form 941.

3 Complete the remainder of Form 941 dated October 27.

Problem 15-4 The Norton Company has the following balances in its general ledger as of March 1 of this year.

- FICA tax payable (liability for February), $220
- Employees' income tax payable (liability for February), $360
- Federal unemployment tax payable (liability for January and February), $16
- State unemployment tax payable (liability for January and February), $118
- Medical insurance payable (liability for January and February), $284

The company completed the following transactions involving the payroll during March and April.

Mar. 13	Issued check no. 1867, $580, payable to Citizens Bank and Trust, for monthly deposit of February FICA taxes and employees' federal income tax withheld.
31	Recorded the payroll entry in the general journal from the payroll register for March. The payroll register had the following column totals.

Total earnings		$2,400.00
Employees' income tax deductions	$360.00	
Employees' FICA tax deductions	140.40	
Medical insurance deduction	142.00	
Total deductions		642.40
Net pay		$1,757.60
Sales salaries		1,900.00
Office salaries		500.00

31	Recorded payroll taxes in the general journal. Employees' FICA tax is 5.85%, employer's is also 5.85%, state unemployment insurance is 2.7%, and federal unemployment insurance is .5%.
31	Issued check no. 2120, $1,757.60, payable to a payroll bank account.
Apr. 6	Issued check no. 2182, $426, payable to Fidelity Insurance Company in payment of employees' medical insurance for January, February, and March.

| Apr. 14 | Issued check no. 2231, $182.80, payable to the State Tax Commission, for state unemployment taxes for January, February, and March. The check was accompanied by the quarterly tax return. |
| 14 | Issued check no. 2270, $640.80, payable to Citizens Bank and Trust for monthly deposit of March FICA taxes and employees' federal income tax withheld. |

Instructions Record the transactions listed above in the general journal and the check register.

Problem 15-1A The Pieper Clinical Laboratory had the following payroll for the week ended June 15.

Salaries		Deductions	
Technicians' salaries	$1,860.00	Income tax withheld	$287.00
Office salaries	390.00	FICA tax withheld	131.63
	$2,250.00	U.S. Savings Bonds	160.00
		Medical insurance	180.00

Assumed tax rates are:
- FICA 5.85% (.0585) on the first $15,300 for each employee
- State unemployment tax 2.7% (.027) on the first $4,200 for each employee
- Federal unemployment tax .5% (.005) on the first $4,200 for each employee

Instructions Record the following entries in general journal form:
1 The payroll entry as of June 15
2 The entry to record the employer's payroll taxes as of June 15, assuming that the total payroll is subject to the FICA tax, and that $1,400 is subject to unemployment taxes
3 The payment of the employees as of June 18, assuming that Pieper Clinical Laboratory issued one check payable to a payroll bank account

Problem 15-2A The column totals of the payroll register of the Roosevelt Chair Company for the week ended January 28 of this year show that the sales employees have earned $1,920 and the office employees $360. Roosevelt has deducted from the salaries of employees $296 for income taxes, $90 for medical insurance, $72 for union dues, and FICA tax at the rate of 5.85% (.0585) on the first $15,300 of their earnings.

Instructions Record the following entries in general journal form:
1 The payroll entry as of January 28
2 The entry to record the payroll taxes as of January 28, assuming 2.7% (.027) for state unemployment insurance and .5% (.005) for federal unemployment insurance
3 The payment of the employees as of January 31, assuming that Roosevelt issues one check payable to a payroll bank account

Problem 15-3A The Sun Glow Products Company, of 2116 Latimer Boulevard, Phoenix, Arizona 85000, received Form 941 from the Director of

Internal Revenue. The identification number for Sun Glow Products Company is 75-8729114. Their payroll for the quarter is as follows.

Name	Social Security Number	Total Earnings	Taxable Earnings Unempl. Ins.	Taxable Earnings FICA	FICA Withheld	Income Tax Withheld
Aumell, Freda	539-27-6180	3,162 00		3,162 00	184 98	428 00
McCroskey, Mary	540-17-2298	2,384 00		2,384 00	139 46	316 00
Sierk, Henry	540-63-1979	1,916 00	840 00	1,916 00	112 09	253 00
Sikes, Hans	541-91-8603	2,170 00	320 00	2,170 00	126 95	294 00
Sisson, Donna	540-77-4862	1,476 00	1,476 00	1,476 00	86 34	199 00
		11,108 00	2,636 00	11,108 00	649 82	1,490 00

The company has had five employees throughout the year. Assume that the employees have paid a FICA tax of 5.85% on the first $15,300 of their earnings and that the employer has paid a similar percentage on their earnings. Fred Pelli, the owner, had submitted the following federal tax deposits and written the accompanying checks.

On August 12, for the July payroll		On September 13, for the August payroll		On October 12, for the September payroll	
Employees' income tax withheld	$471.00	Employees' income tax withheld	$494.00	Employees' income tax withheld	$525.00
Employees' FICA tax withheld	198.00	Employees' FICA tax withheld	212.00	Employees' FICA tax withheld	239.82
Employer's FICA tax	198.00	Employer's FICA tax	212.00	Employer's FICA tax	239.82
	$867.00		$918.00		$1,004.64

Instructions
1 Complete Schedule B of Form 941.
2 Complete Schedule A of Form 941.
3 Complete the remainder of Form 941 dated October 28.

Problem 15-4A The Sutton Auto Parts Company has the following balances in its general ledger as of March 1 of this year.
● FICA tax payable (liability for February), $310
● Employees' income tax payable (liability for February), $492
● Federal unemployment tax payable (liability for January and February), $16
● State unemployment tax payable (liability for January and February), $172
● Medical insurance payable (liability for January and February), $380

The company completed the following transactions involving the payroll during March and April.

Mar. 12	Issued check no. 2916, $802, payable to the Security Bank and Trust, for the monthly deposit of February FICA taxes and employees' federal income tax withheld.

Mar. 31	Recorded the payroll entry in the general journal from the payroll register for March. The payroll register had the following column totals.

Total earnings		$3,550.00
Employees' income tax deductions	$492.00	
Employees' FICA tax deductions	207.68	
Medical insurance deductions	190.00	
Total deductions		889.68
Net pay		$2,660.32
Sales salaries		3,000.00
Office salaries		550.00

31	Recorded payroll taxes in the general journal. Employees' FICA tax is 5.85%, employer's is also 5.85%, state unemployment insurance is 2.7%, and federal unemployment insurance is .5%.
31	Issued check no. 3183, $2,660.32, payable to a payroll bank account.
Apr. 14	Issued check no. 3219, $570, payable to Safety Insurance Company in payment of employees' medical insurance for January, February, and March.
14	Issued check no. 3699, $267.85, payable to the State Tax Commission, for state unemployment taxes for January, February, and March. The check was accompanied by the quarterly tax return.
14	Issued check no. 3715, $907.36, payable to the Security Bank and Trust for the monthly deposit of March FICA taxes and employees' federal income tax withheld.

Instructions Record the transactions listed above in the general journal and the check register.

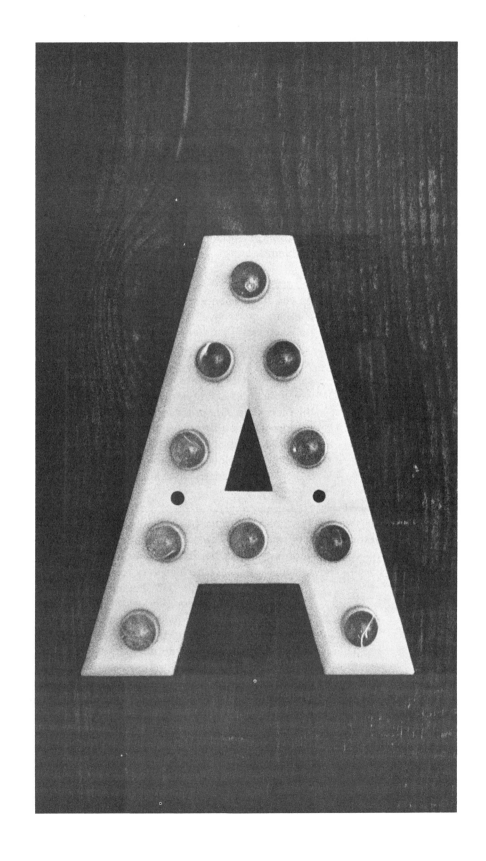

Appendix A
Data processing

Introduction

As you have been working your way through the problems of the previous chapters, you have learned to classify, record, and summarize business transactions—in other words, to *process* them. Business transactions, or the occurrence of business events, represent data. When you handle these data, you *process* them in order to formulate meaningful reports. Therefore, we can define *data processing* as the handling of facts concerning a business, which includes classifying, sorting, calculating, summarizing, and storing of the facts. The *data processing system* comprises the procedures, forms, and equipment used to process and report the data. When you think about it, you'll see that all along you've been engaged in data processing of the manual type. Now we're going to relate the manual method of data processing to the various mechanized methods.

Goal of a data processing system

The goal of a data processing system is to make available accurate, current information *when* it is needed, and as economically as possible. The information you get can be only as accurate as the facts you put into the system, and as accurate as the procedures you use in recording, processing, and reporting the facts. For example, suppose you're an accountant, and you record a charge for services rendered as $12.50 instead of $21.50. That incorrect fact you feed into the system will result in incorrect financial statements being reported out of the system. The machine can work with only the facts you put into it.

Any data processing system should be tailor-made for the business involved. The following principles should govern the choice of a data processing system.

1 The information should be produced as economically as possible, although the quickest method is not necessarily the most economical. The cost of operating the system should be compared with the benefits the system will yield to the company.

2 The internal control features should be good enough to safeguard the assets and ensure accuracy of the data.

3 The system should be flexible enough to accommodate increases in volume of data and changes in operating procedures.

Data processing methods

There are four methods of data processing: the *manual,* the *mechanical,* the *punched card,* and the *electronic.*

1 **Manual data processing method** This involves the recording and reporting of data by hand, using business forms such as journals and ledgers; information may also be stored in filing cabinets. The manual method is the one

Fig. A-1 Posting or book-keeping machine (photograph courtesy of Burroughs Corporation)

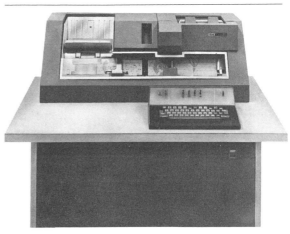

Fig. A-2 Key-operated card-punch machine (photograph courtesy of IBM)

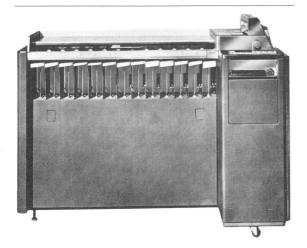

Fig. A-3 Card sorter (photograph courtesy of IBM)

that you have studied and used in working the problems at the end of each chapter. For small businesses, the advantages are that the method is quite flexible and that the cost of installation is minor.

2 Mechanical data processing method This includes the use of relatively simple office machines, such as typewriters, adding machines, cash registers, calculators, and posting machines (see Fig. A-1). The data processing system of small businesses usually comprises a *combination* of manual and mechanical methods. For small or medium-sized enterprises, the advantages are: (1) accuracy is greater than with manual methods alone; (2) recording speed is increased; and (3) records are neater and more readable.

3 Punched-card data processing method In this method, an operator records data by means of a machine that punches holes in cards (Fig. A-2). The

Fig. A-4 Reproducing punch machine (photograph courtesy of IBM)

Fig. A-5 Card collator (photograph courtesy of IBM)

Fig. A-6 Tabulator or accounting machine (photograph courtesy of IBM)

Fig. A-7 Basic units of an electronic computer data processing system (photograph courtesy of IBM)

operator takes the information directly from business documents, such as invoices, receipts, checks, etc. Other machines then process and sort the cards (Fig. A-3), and make printouts of the information. Equipment includes key-punch machines, sorters, reproducers, collators, and tabulators (Figs. A-4, A-5, and A-6). This method may be called semi-automatic, since human intervention is required both during and between the various states of processing. For medium-sized enterprises, the advantages are as follows: (1) data recorded on punched cards can be processed rapidly; (2) punched cards can be sorted into any order desired; and (3) business papers, records, and reports can be printed from punched cards.

4 **Electronic data processing method** The company which uses this system has operators who take data from business documents and record them on such input devices as punched cards, punched paper tape, magnetic tapes, and magnetic disks. The operator then feeds the input device into the computer, which performs all processing and printouts of the information (Fig. A-7). For large enterprises, the advantages are as follows: (1) these machines offer high-speed performance with a minimum amount of labor; (2) the machines have a large storage capacity; (3) stored data are readily available for reuse; (4) the machines are versatile enough to perform varied functions on demand; and (5) the machines have a logic capability so that they can make decisions during processing.

Information flowchart The various methods of processing information are diagramed as follows in an information flowchart.

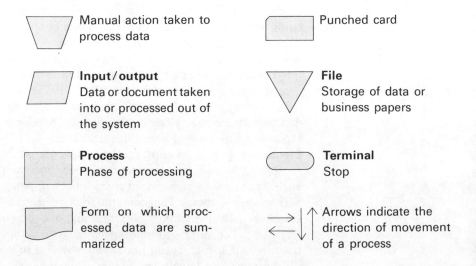

Data Processing Methods

Input
Raw data introduced into the system

Receipts
Checks
Employee time cards
Sales invoices
Purchases invoices
Other source documents

Direct

Direct

Punched cards

Punched cards
Punched paper tape
Magnetic tape
Magnetic disks

Manual
Handwritten journals
Handwritten ledgers

Mechanical
Bookkeeping machines
Adding machines

Punched-card
Punched-card machines

Electronic
Computers

Output

Updated accounts
Financial statements
Managerial reports

Symbolic flowcharts A symbolic flowchart uses symbols to show the sequence of steps required to complete all or a part of a data processing system. The following shows symbols commonly used in flowcharting.

Manual action taken to process data

Punched card

Input/output
Data or document taken into or processed out of the system

File
Storage of data or business papers

Process
Phase of processing

Terminal
Stop

Form on which processed data are summarized

Arrows indicate the direction of movement of a process

To enable you to compare the four methods of data processing from the point of view of the steps involved and the functions performed by the equipment, we now present a number of illustrations outlining the processing of familiar business transactions.

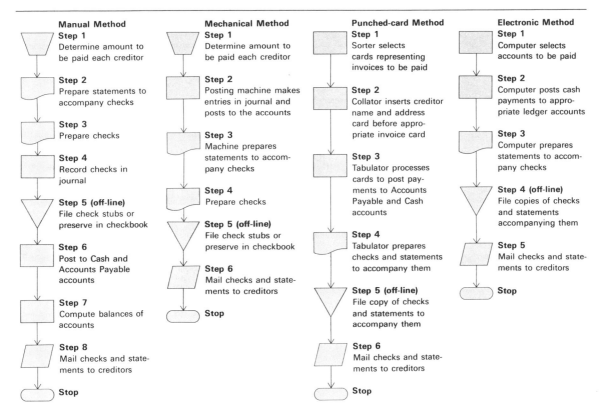

Manual Method

Step 1
Determine amount to
be paid each creditor

Step 2
Prepare statements to
accompany checks

Step 3
Prepare checks

Step 4
Record checks in
journal

Step 5 (off-line)
File check stubs or
preserve in checkbook

Step 6
Post to Cash and
Accounts Payable
accounts

Step 7
Compute balances of
accounts

Step 8
Mail checks and state-
ments to creditors

Stop

Mechanical Method

Step 1
Determine amount to
be paid each creditor

Step 2
Posting machine makes
entries in journal and
posts to the accounts

Step 3
Machine prepares
statements to accom-
pany checks

Step 4
Prepare checks

Step 5 (off-line)
File check stubs or
preserve in checkbook

Step 6
Mail checks and state-
ments to creditors

Stop

Punched-card Method

Step 1
Sorter selects
cards representing
invoices to be paid

Step 2
Collator inserts creditor
name and address
card before appro-
priate invoice card

Step 3
Tabulator processes
cards to post pay-
ments to Accounts
Payable and Cash
accounts

Step 4
Tabulator prepares
checks and statements
to accompany them

Step 5 (off-line)
File copy of checks
and statements to
accompany them

Step 6
Mail checks and state-
ments to creditors

Stop

Electronic Method

Step 1
Computer selects
accounts to be paid

Step 2
Computer posts cash
payments to appro-
priate ledger accounts

Step 3
Computer prepares
statements to accom-
pany checks

Step 4 (off-line)
File copies of checks
and statements
accompanying them

Step 5
Mail checks and state-
ments to creditors

Stop

**Recording, journalizing, and
posting cash paid to creditors on account (separate accounts are kept for each
creditor)**

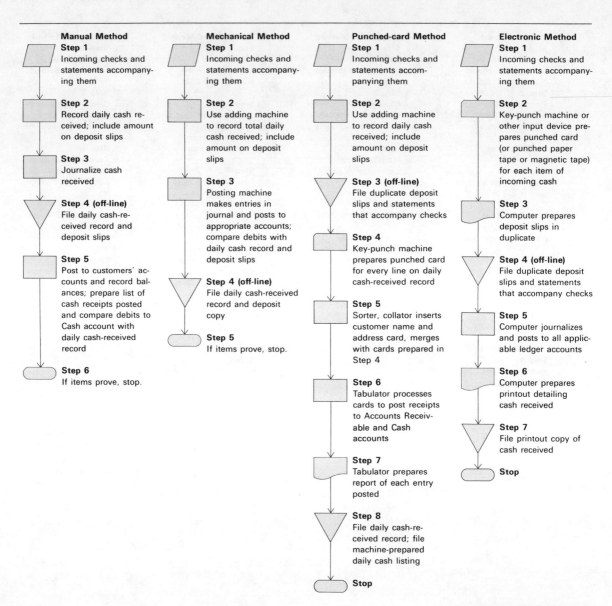

Manual Method
Step 1
Incoming checks and statements accompanying them

Step 2
Record daily cash received; include amount on deposit slips

Step 3
Journalize cash received

Step 4 (off-line)
File daily cash-received record and deposit slips

Step 5
Post to customers' accounts and record balances; prepare list of cash receipts posted and compare debits to Cash account with daily cash-received record

Step 6
If items prove, stop.

Mechanical Method
Step 1
Incoming checks and statements accompanying them

Step 2
Use adding machine to record total daily cash received; include amount on deposit slips

Step 3
Posting machine makes entries in journal and posts to appropriate accounts; compare debits with daily cash record and deposit slips

Step 4 (off-line)
File daily cash-received record and deposit copy

Step 5
If items prove, stop.

Punched-card Method
Step 1
Incoming checks and statements accompanying them

Step 2
Use adding machine to record daily cash received; include amount on deposit slips

Step 3 (off-line)
File duplicate deposit slips and statements that accompany checks

Step 4
Key-punch machine prepares punched card for every line on daily cash-received record

Step 5
Sorter, collator inserts customer name and address card, merges with cards prepared in Step 4

Step 6
Tabulator processes cards to post receipts to Accounts Receivable and Cash accounts

Step 7
Tabulator prepares report of each entry posted

Step 8
File daily cash-received record; file machine-prepared daily cash listing

Stop

Electronic Method
Step 1
Incoming checks and statements accompanying them

Step 2
Key-punch machine or other input device prepares punched card (or punched paper tape or magnetic tape) for each item of incoming cash

Step 3
Computer prepares deposit slips in duplicate

Step 4 (off-line)
File duplicate deposit slips and statements that accompany checks

Step 5
Computer journalizes and posts to all applicable ledger accounts

Step 6
Computer prepares printout detailing cash received

Step 7
File printout copy of cash received

Stop

Recording, journalizing, and posting cash received on account from charge customers (separate accounts are kept for each customer)

Manual Method

Step 1
Write out time cards listing employees' names and numbers; distribute to appropriate departments

Step 2
Compute time each employee worked

Step 3
Compute employees' earnings manually; record in payroll register

Step 4
Determine payroll deductions

Step 5
Compute net pay and prove payroll register

Step 6
Post payroll data to employees' earnings records; journalize and post payroll entry

Step 7
Write out employees' checks and check stubs or vouchers stating payroll data for employees

Step 8 (off-line)
File time cards

Step 9
Distribute checks to employees

Stop

Mechanical Method

Step 1
Typewriter prepares time cards listing employees' names and numbers; distribute to appropriate time clocks

Step 2
Calculator computes time each employee worked

Step 3
Posting machine computes earnings, deductions, and net pay

Step 4
Machine prepares checks and check stubs

Step 5
Machine posts employee earnings records

Step 6
Journalize and post payroll entry

Step 7 (off-line)
File time cards

Step 8
Distribute checks to employees

Stop

Punched-card Method

Step 1
Key-punch machine prints time cards listing employees' names and numbers; distribute to appropriate time clocks

Step 2
Key-punch punches data from time cards onto punched cards for each employee

Step 3
Verifier verifies punched cards for accuracy

Step 4
Sorter sorts punched time cards to individual employees

Step 5
Collator merges punched time cards with master employees' file

Step 6
Calculator computes total earnings, deductions, and net pay

Step 7
Tabulator records payroll register

Step 8
Tabulator prepares checks and vouchers to accompany checks

Step 9
Tabulator posts to employees' earnings records

Step 10
Sorter arranges master employees' file so that it can be used in the future

Step 11 (off-line)
File time cards and payroll register

Step 12
Distribute checks to employees

Stop

Electronic Method

Step 1
Key-punch machine prints time cards listing employees' names and numbers; distribute to appropriate time clocks

Step 2
Key-punch or other input device prepares punched cards (or tape or magnetic tape) to record data from time cards

Step 3
Computer calculates earnings; posts payroll data to ledger accounts and employees' earnings records

Step 4
Computer prepares payroll register, checks, and vouchers to accompany checks

Step 5 (off-line)
File time cards and payroll reports

Step 6
Distribute checks to employees

Stop

Preparing the weekly payroll and recording wages paid

The punched card as an input device

The *punched card* is a device that is used frequently today to feed information into machines. This is called an *input* device. Machines record data on standard-sized cards by punching holes in the cards. These holes constitute a language that all the machines of the tabulating system can understand, and thus it is easy to understand why a whole industry has grown up around them. An operator feeds these punched cards into machines, creating a steady flow of information and churning out records, invoices, paychecks, and tax information, as the illustrations on pages 417 to 419 demonstrate. These punched cards are used in conjunction with electronic computers. Data on magnetic tape or punched paper tape are often punched automatically onto cards too, just because the cards last longer and are easier to handle than magnetic or punched paper tape.

People also often use punched cards as *output* devices, to make statements of accounts and to record payroll checks.

Punched cards are so important that you'll find it worth your while to study the following illustration carefully.

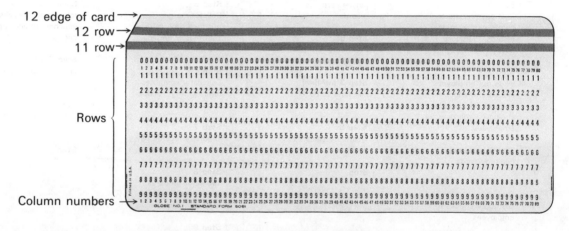

The small figures on the card just shown indicate that it has 80 columns, numbered from left to right. The large figures in the horizontal rows show that the card has 10 rows in each column, numbered from 0 to 9, inclusive, from top to bottom. In addition, as shown by the shaded rows, the blank space above the 0 row has room for two more rows, called the *11 row* and the *12 row.*

Recording numeric data in a punched card

The 0 through 9 rows record numbers. For example, if you punch the 6 row, this stands for the number 6. If you want to punch a two-digit number into the card, you must use two columns. For example, take the number 70: You punch the digit 7 in one column and the digit 0 in the *next* column. Look at columns 33 and 34 in the following illustration.

A group of columns—called a *field*—records a single item of information.

For example, on a card which records an employee's earnings and various deductions, five columns might be used to record the income tax deductions.

| 70 punched in columns 33 and 34 | 316 punched in columns 56 through 58 | 6904 punched in columns 72 through 75 |

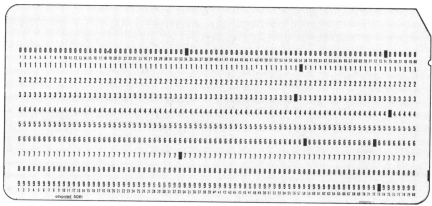

Recording alphabetic data on a punched card

When you punch letters on a card, you use the two additional rows, 11 and 12 (shaded areas on the card shown on page 420) as well as the 0 to 9 rows. In order to record a letter, you must punch *two* holes in the same column: One in row 0, or 11, or 12—called the *zone-punching area*—and one in rows 1 through 9, called the *digit-punching area* (see the figure below, which explains the alphabet).

| | Zone-punching area | D punched in column 48 | M punched in column 59 | W punched in column 70 |

12 row →
11 row →

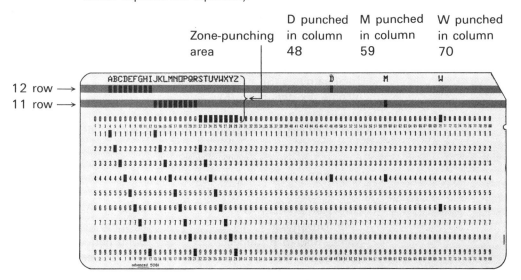

For example, you record the letter C by punches in the 12 row and the 3 row in the same column, and the letter A by punches in the 12 row and the 1 row in the same column, as you can see on the next page.

Name field

Department field

Planning the use of the punched card

After one decides what information is needed, the next step in using the punched card as an input device is to plan the arrangement of the information in the card. For example, a punched card that is to be used for an employee's earnings record ought to contain the following information. (The numbers in parentheses are the numbers of columns reserved for each field. For example, 18 columns will handle even a very long name.)

Employee number (2)
Date (6)
Employee's name (18)
Total hours (2)
Regular earnings (5)
Overtime earnings (5)
Total earnings (5)
Income tax deduction (5)

FICA tax deduction (5)
Hospital insurance deduction (4)
Bond deduction (5)
Union dues (4)
Community Chest deduction (4)
Total deductions (5)
Net pay (5)

One could also record other information, such as department or classification.

Sample payroll data for Ronald R. Jones are punched into the card shown on page 423. Details are as follows.

Employee number, 5
Date, November 7, 19___
Name, Ronald R. Jones
Total hours, 52
Regular earnings, $160.00
Overtime earnings, $80.00
Total earnings, $240.00
Income tax deduction, $28.40

FICA tax deduction, $14.00
Hospital insurance deduction, $6.00
Bond deduction, $4.00
Union dues, $3.00
Community Chest deduction, $6.00
Total deductions, $57.44
Net pay, $182.56.

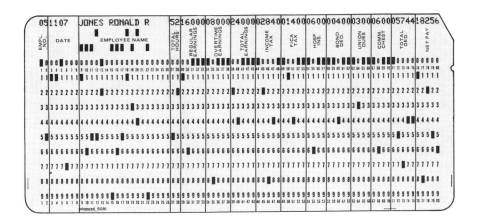

Magnetic tape as an input device

A business firm which keeps its books by the electronic computer method often uses magnetic tape as an input device. The main advantage of magnetic tape is its speed. The computer can read data recorded on magnetic tape faster than it can read punched cards or punched paper tape. In addition, a large amount of data can be placed on a small amount of tape. Data can be entered on magnetic tape directly by using a key-to-tape machine, having a keyboard similar to an electric typewriter. Magnetic tapes also have the advantage of being compact and thus readily stored.

Electronic computers

The electronic computer is the heart of an electronic data processing system. It consists of three basic components: the storage or memory unit, the arithmetic unit, and the control unit. The following diagram shows the functions performed by these units, as well as by input and output.

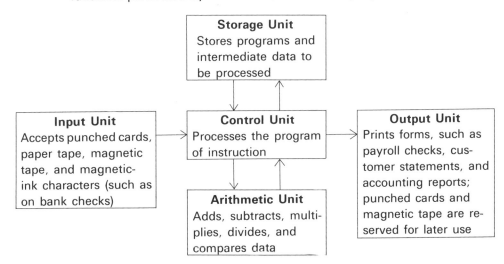

The *control unit* (see the diagram) directs the flow of data into, through, and out of the computer in accordance with a set of instructions called a *program.*

A program is a series of steps planned to carry out a certain process, such as the preparation of statements for customers. Each step in the program represents a command or instruction to the computer. The program is expressed in the form of codes and symbols, commonly called *machine language.* Two widely used languages are FORTRAN (FORmula TRANslation) and COBOL (COmmon Business Oriented Language).

Problems

Problem A-1 The Norfolk Distributing Company, which pays its employees weekly, has a card punched for each employee for each week. The company sends the punched cards to the Norfolk First National Bank, where the bank's computer completes the payroll register, compiles the employees' earnings records, and prints the paychecks.

Below we see the time card for Byron S. Thomas, one employee of the Norfolk Distributing Company. His payroll deductions are as follows: Income tax, $22.20, FICA, $11.47; hospitalization insurance, $4.50; bond deduction, $10.00; union dues, $7.00; and Community Chest, $1.25.

										HOURS	RATE	AMOUNT
NORFOLK DISTRIBUTING COMPANY			REGULAR							40	4.00	160.00
			OVERTIME							6	6.00	36.00
			TOTAL EARNINGS									196.00

Instructions Complete the payroll card in the Workbook, using a pencil to darken the spaces in which the computer would punch holes to record the necessary data. Print the interpretation of the code at the top edge of the card.

Problem A-2 Martinelli and Sons prepares punched cards giving the data for each weekly payroll. There are three punched cards in your Workbook for the weekly payroll period ending April 30, 1976.

Instructions In the space provided at the top of each card, write the data that are punched in the cards.

Problem A-3 The three cards used in Problem A-2, plus the additional six cards in the Workbook, are the weekly payroll cards of Martinelli and Sons for the payroll period ending April 30, 1976. The punched cards in the Workbook have the data recorded listed at the top of the cards, so that either a person or a machine may read the card.

Instructions

1 Remove from the Workbook and separate the cards, sorting them in alphabetical order according to the last name of each employee.
2 Manually record each card in the payroll register, total, and prove the columns. Omit the Taxable Earnings columns. Employees are paid by checks, beginning with check no. 917.
3 In general journal form, journalize the payroll entry, using the Wages Expense account, and crediting Cash for the net pay.

Problem A-4 The Rochester Office Supply Company uses punched cards in processing its accounting data. In this problem, process the cards manually, although these functions are normally performed by machines.

Instructions

1 Remove from the Workbook and separate the fifteen punched cards for the Rochester Office Supply Company; note that each is numbered in the upper right corner. The cards represent the following. Cards 1, 2, and 3 are customers' charge-account balances at June 30; cards 4, 5, and 6 are receipts on account from charge customers during July; cards 7 through 15 are sales made to customers on account during July.
2 Record the punched data at the top of cards 13, 14, and 15.
3 Sort the cards into numerical order according to customer order number.
4 Sort the cards for each customer according to dates, with the earliest date on top.
5 Prepare statements for the three customers, using the data recorded on the cards.
6 Resort cards 7 through 15 into numerical order by product number. For the purchasing department, prepare a report on the quantity of each product sold during July.
7 Resort cards 7 through 15 into numerical order according to salesperson number. For the purpose of determining sales commissions, prepare a report of sales by salespersons during July.

Index

A

Discount (cont.)
Cash   245
Purchase   230, 252
Sales   245
Trade   255–257, 258
Discrimination, laws forbidding   355–356
Dishonored check, defined   342
Double-entry accounting   9, 44–45 (illust.)
Defined   55
Dr   *see* Debit
Drawing   *see* Withdrawal
Drawing account   40

E

Earnings, taxable   364, 381
Earnings record   358–359 (illust.), 367
Defined   367
Economic unit   3
Defined   12
Electronic computers   423–424
Electronic data processing   415
Embezzlement, prevention of   254–255
Employee
Defined   367
Independent contractor distinguished from   353
Employee compensation   *see also* Wages
Calculation of   357
Types of   357
Employee's Withholding Allowance Certificate (Form W-4)   359, 360 (illust.)
Defined   367
Employer
Payroll taxes of   379–386
Unemployment taxes and   356–357
Employer's Annual Federal Unemployment Tax Return (Form 940)   391, 393 (illust.)
Employer's identification number   379
Defined   397
Employer's Quarterly Federal Tax Return (Form 941)   354, 357, 384, 386, 386–387 (illust.)
Employment Act of 1967   356
Defined   367
Endorsement   323–324, 324 (illust.)
Defined   342
Restrictive   324
Equal Pay Law   355
Equipment   299
Adjustments for depreciation of   101–102

Defined   55
Disadvantages of   75
Plus and minus signs for   39–40
Tax(es)   *see also* Income tax; Unemployment taxes
On employer   379–383
Sales   190–191, 202
Social Security   354, 361, 370, 381–386
Withholding   353–354, 359–361
Tax calendar   395–396
Temporary equity, defined   310
Temporary-equity accounts   130, 301
Defined   134
Time-and-a-half   355
Time card   357–358 (illust.)
Time clocks   357
Trade discount   255–257
Defined   258
Transaction   3, 7–10 (illust.)
Defined   12
Recording of   135, 399–402
Transit number   322
Transportation charges   227–228
Transposition error   54
Defined   55
Trial balance   37, 52–53, 52 (illust.)
Errors exposed by   53
Post-closing   132–133, 134
Trial Balance Equation   39
Defined   55
True balance   327
Two-column general journal   67

U-Z

Unearned revenue
Adjustment for   272–273
Defined   279
Unemployment taxes   356–357, 382–383
Defined   370, 397, 398
Report of   389–390 (illust.), 390–392
Wage Bracket Withholding tables   361, 362 (illust.)
Wages   357
Accrued   113, 395
Computation of   358
Laws affecting   353–357
Minimum   355
Wages and Hours Law   355
Defined   370
Wages expense, adjustments for   102–104

ABCDEFGHIJ–H–79876